The

of ⌐⌐⌐ ⌐⌐⌐⌐⌐,

The Sonic Swagger of Elvis Presley

A Critical History of the Early Recordings

GARY PARKER

McFarland & Company, Inc., Publishers
Jefferson, North Carolina

Library of Congress Cataloguing-in-Publication Data

Names: Parker, Gary R., 1950 July 12– author.
Title: The sonic swagger of Elvis Presley : a critical history
of the early recordings / Gary Parker.
Description: Jefferson, North Carolina : McFarland & Company,
Inc., Publishers, 2022. | Includes bibliographical references and index.
Identifiers: LCCN 2022014836 |
ISBN 9781476684314 (paperback : acid free paper) ∞
ISBN 9781476645148 (ebook)
Subjects: LCSH: Presley, Elvis, 1935–1977—Criticism and interpretation. |
Rock music—United States—To 1961—History and criticism. | Rock
music—United States—1961–1970—History and criticism. | Presley, Elvis,
1935–1977—Discography. | BISAC: MUSIC / Genres & Styles / Rock
Classification: LCC ML420.P96 P284 2022 | DDC 782.42166092—dc23/
eng/20220401
LC record available at https://lccn.loc.gov/2022014836

British Library cataloguing data are available

ISBN (print) 978-1-4766-8431-4
ISBN (ebook) 978-1-4766-4514-8

Front cover image © 2022 Shutterstock

Printed in the United States of America

*McFarland & Company, Inc., Publishers
Box 611, Jefferson, North Carolina 28640
www.mcfarlandpub.com*

To all that remain....
And to all that do not....
This book is lovingly dedicated.

Acknowledgments

Lots of folks to thank in this era of COVID, without whose generous assistance this book would not be possible:

To Carol Highsmith and the U.S. Library of Congress for images chronicling Elvis's early years.

A shout-out to Sue Conner and Hana Bennett for their invaluable assistance in all things art-related.

Gratitude extends to the good folks at the Tennessee State Library and Archives for their assistance in locating images of Memphis and Beale Street.

A tip of the Parker chapeau to friends of a musical bent who've helped guide me through the thickets of the sonic bramble; foremost among these are Gary St. Germain and James Holvay.

Heartfelt gratitude to those who knew and worked with Elvis Presley and were gracious enough to share their memories and perceptions with me, most prominently Ray Walker of the Jordanaires, Bob Moore, James Kirkland and others.

Deep appreciation to Julie Cornwell at E.W. Scripps and Kim Reis of *USA Today* for their help in unraveling copyright issues related to the *Memphis Press-Scimitar.*

Thanks to Dr. Gerald Chaudron, department head and associate professor at the University of Memphis libraries, for providing access to the university photographic archives.

And, of course, I am deeply indebted to those who preceded me, the music historians and keepers of the Presley flame, without whose yeoman-like efforts this book would be bereft: Ernst Jorgensen for dissecting and analyzing Presley's studio work, Peter Guralnick for his rightfully acclaimed set of Presley biographies, and Jerry Hopkins for his first-of-its-kind serious dive into all things Elvis.

A grateful nod, as always, to Dennis Hayes (wherever he is today) for the moment of inspiration nearly 30 years ago that changed everything.

And lastly, to my dear wife Kim for making me lucky beyond all expectation.

Table of Contents

Preface

I first became aware of Elvis Presley when I was six years old, a period when Presley was incandescent on stage and unbeatable on record. For a while, it seemed that everything Elvis did mattered. I'm not sure when that changed. Maybe on February 9, 1964.

In the years since his death in August of 1977, the rise-and-fall arc of Presley's musical and personal life has inspired hundreds of books, movies, documentaries, and commentaries, many purporting to sort out the contradictions that characterized his life and reveal "the true Elvis." And while I can't claim to have consumed all or even the majority of this material, in the years since I first glimpsed Presley on Ed Sullivan's Sunday night variety show, I've devoured more than my fair share. And what have I learned? That perspectives on Elvis Presley are as different as stars in the sky. Because, let's face it, Elvis was damned hard to pin down. Depending on whose characterization you accept, Presley exemplified, at varying points of his life, some or all of the following paradoxical traits: humble or grandly arrogant; devout or irreligious; brazen or blindly subservient; mannered or blatantly boorish; heartfelt or hypocritical; crazily generous or, maybe, just plain crazy.

Before proceeding, let me I confess that I undertook the writing of this book fueled by a certain hubris. Unlike previous historians and chroniclers, who, in my eyes, had failed at sorting out Presley's multiple sides, I, through diligent and exhaustive research, would sweep away the ambiguity and ambivalence that shrouded his life and, in the end, ferret out the real Elvis.

Well, that was then. Because, as I was soon to learn, hubris is often accompanied by a sobering jolt of reality. My deep dive into "all things Elvis" meant regular descents into a thicket of contrary and antithetical information—facts that didn't add up, accounts that varied dramatically, and reminiscences from friends and musicians that were hazy (understandable, given the passage of time) and even downright contradictory. And instead of resolving Presley's many perplexing paradoxes, my

1

research only unearthed more questions I found myself unable to answer. For example, was the "true Elvis" a balladeer with a subsidiary interest in rhythm and blues, or was it the other way around? Was Presley the bold musical innovator of the 1950s who single-handedly upended the music world or the seemingly cowed and timid figure who emerged from the army, poised for a fateful leap into, as someone once observed, "the oblivion of acceptability"? Was he the seemingly fearless rock 'n' roll rebel who, in the eyes of many, threatened the moral order of the 1950s, or the mama's boy who cried, "Everything I have is gone!" upon the death of his beloved mother? Was the "true Elvis" the observant soul who, throughout his life, turned to gospel music for moral sustenance, or was he the lothario who bragged crudely to his cadre of supplicants of his sexual conquests? I simply don't know. And what's more, I'm starting to think no one else does either. To wit, let's heed the words of Linda Thompson, Presley's longtime girlfriend, who, when asked who Elvis really was, replied: "He was a very dichotomous human being, very paradoxical. On the one hand, you know, he had this raucous image and he did have a raucous sense of humor, irreverent sense of humor. But he was very pious on another level and very puritanical" (CNN interview, 2007).

It seems clear that the distorting lens of history, not to mention the ambiguous perspective of Linda Thompson, has left us with a multiplicity of Elvises to sort through: Elvis the rebel and Elvis the observant; Elvis the anti-drug campaigner and Elvis the user; Elvis the musician and Elvis the poser; Elvis the legend and, for those who contend he still lives, Elvis the extant. The mystery of the multiple Elvises continues to intrigue me, and it's something I'll pursue further in subsequent pages. In the meantime, I'll leave it there and turn to the events that inspired me to write this book and what you'll encounter as you make your way through it.

By now, it's accepted lore that rock 'n' roll, or, as it was known in its earliest form, "rockabilly," was born in the late forties and early fifties of a mixed parentage of country and rhythm and blues, or, as it was referred to by radio station programmers in the 1950s, "race music." To Sam Phillips, the restless and creative force behind Sun Records, rockabilly had the potential to span the great divide that separated white audiences from the tough and gritty music that he loved.

To bring his dream to fruition, Phillips would turn to musicians who hailed from the worlds of country, rhythm and blues, and gospel and carried with them the legacies of Hank Snow, Junior Parker, and Fats Domino: Elvis Presley, Scotty Moore, and Bill Black, three men who would breathe life into a musical collective that, in years to come, would be recognized as the world's first rock 'n' roll band. Under the steady, guiding hand of Phillips, Elvis Presley, along with Moore and

Black, would generate thrilling and foundational recordings that sound as authentic and unmannered today as when they were recorded.

In the nearly 70 years since Elvis laid down such timeless tracks as "That's All Right," "Blue Moon of Kentucky," "Good Rockin' Tonight," and "Mystery Train," many of his groundbreaking achievements have been assimilated into the currents of popular music and emulated by others, significantly dimming their impact. Still, it's nonetheless critical to remember that between the years of 1954 and 1958, virtually nothing that Elvis did on stage—and little of what he put on record—had been seen or heard by anyone previously.

To be clear: Presley didn't invent rock 'n' roll and, to his credit, never proclaimed that he did. What he did, however, is carve out a space in popular music that didn't exist previously, one in which rhythm and blues was delivered to an audience that was mostly, if not completely, composed of white Americans and mostly, if not completely, unaware of its existence.

Like many who aspire to soar ever higher, Presley would come to a sad and well-chronicled end. It can certainly be argued that Elvis's great tragedy was in not understanding that he was a generational figure, one who would transcend the concerns of commerce and shifting public opinion and attain, like James Dean had before him and David Bowie, Madonna, and Michael Jackson would after him, legendary status. Instead of pursuing his art to the furthest creative corners in the years following his army stint, Presley, fearing the shifting attitudes of a fickle public, acquiesced to Tom Parker's plan of transforming him into an inoffensive figure of mass acceptance, a cynical calculation that Elvis swallowed whole. In the end, that center couldn't hold, and by the mid-sixties, Presley's career was in triage mode.

A musical resurrection in the closing years of the decade kindled hopes that Elvis had regained his artistic footing, but then, blocked by Parker and his own subservient nature from turning his dream of touring Europe into a reality, he lapsed into a soul-deadening, seemingly endless series of Las Vegas engagements that he continued, it seems, for no other reason than an inability to stop. And unlike artists capable of turning private turmoil into great art, Presley, increasingly addicted to drugs and seemingly with no more mountains to climb, simply gave up.

All of this is unfortunate, none of it unusual. The trauma that sudden wealth and outsized adulation can inflict on the human psyche has been chronicled time and again. Their impact on someone of extreme youth, who passes up opportunity after opportunity, as Presley so clearly did, to broaden and move into a true adulthood, is even more deleterious. Stir in unresolved issues related to the death of his mother— a relationship that never had the chance to graduate from one of dependency—along with clear indications of clinical depression, and the descent from grandeur to ruination is complete. The currents of life seem to ensure that no one, not even the Elvis Presleys of the world, get away clean. He slipped, he stumbled, he fell. But he also stormed, battled, and single-handedly elevated the unit cry of rock. It's simply indisputable that between the years of 1954 and 1958, Elvis Presley created a body of work that has proven itself imperishable.

Stop for a moment and imagine that in November 1955, Elvis Presley somehow vanishes, never to be heard from again. That's right, no "Hound Dog" or "Don't Be Cruel." No "My Baby Left Me," no "Jailhouse Rock." No "Mean Woman Blues" and (mercifully) no "My Way" or "You Gave Me a Mountain." Even if all that were true, Presley's primacy in the rock firmament would endure, based on just six timeless tracks he recorded before he reached 21 years of age: "That's All Right Mama," "Blue Moon of Kentucky," "Good Rockin' Tonight," "Mystery Train," "Baby Let's Play House," and "Milkcow Blues Boogie." The fact that he went on to produce extraordinary work for another three years serves as forceful evidence of his rightful place in music history.

In the pages of this book, you'll find a story of Elvis Presley, one I've tried to tell fairly. But be forewarned: I haven't attempted to tell the whole story. While you'll certainly encounter chapters that document Elvis in the years following 1960, the focus of this book is on Presley's early career. There are two reasons for this. First, it's my belief that Elvis's most cogent and lasting work was generated in the pre–army years of 1954 to 1958, and second, unless one is inclined to dig into Presley's private life and the accompanying controversies—and for the most part, I'm not—there's really not much to say regarding the years of 1960 through 1967, a period that Elvis dedicated to moviemaking.

A word also, regarding the judgments and opinions you'll encounter in the pages that follow. I have no doubt that some will find my perspectives on certain aspects of Presley's career, most pointedly, the years following his discharge from the U.S. Army, to be overly critical. Others, I'm sure, after consuming chapters addressing Elvis's early years, will accuse me of engaging in hagiography.

In the months I've spent preparing this book, I've poured over a copious amount of "Presleyana," books, articles, and documentaries that all purport to tell his story. Some fail to criticize Elvis. Others do nothing but. Somewhere between reverence and repudiation is where I discern truth. I hope you find that I've struck the right balance.

Gary Parker • Palm Springs, March 2022
Heu! Quod innocents debet pati.

1

A Mess of Blues

If you grew up very poor as Elvis and his family did, you quickly learned, and pretty much accepted, your status in life. You knew that you were different, that there were places that you were not welcome, crowds that you did not mix with, girls you did not approach.—Tupelo native Ron Brandon (Ron Brandon, elvisinfonet.com, 2011)

In the waning years of the Great Depression, Tupelo was experiencing something of a golden era. Located in the northeastern corner of Mississippi, the region was originally inhabited by the Chickasaw and the Choctaw, who, in the later years of the eighteenth century, watched the arrival of European and American settlers with alarm. The resulting conflict over land use was prolonged and bitter but was eased somewhat in 1801 when a treaty was signed, granting the new arrivals a right to till the land. After the draconian provisions of the Indian Removal Act were passed in 1830, the Chickasaw were forced to cede their land and resettle to Oklahoma, triggering an influx of white settlers and kicking off a land rush. By 1850, the most populated region of northeastern Mississippi was a settlement known as Harrisburg, but after the Mobile and Ohio Railroad laid tracks down a few miles away, residents, sensing opportunity, bolted and established a new settlement nearby. They named it Gum Pond after an ancient five-acre sinkhole bordered by a swamp and machete-dense vegetation.

It wasn't until the years following the Civil War that growth in the region increased sufficiently to warrant incorporation, and in 1870, Gum Pond became Tupelo, derived from the Chickasaw word *topala*, meaning "lodging place." In 1935, Tupelo became the first city in the Deep South to receive electricity from the Tennessee Valley Authority, and Franklin Roosevelt, eager to celebrate a New Deal triumph, personally flipped the switch that would finally bring hydroelectric power to rural regions of the American South. Though trumpeting itself as

"America's first TVA city," Tupelo also had the dubious distinction of being the last city to have a bank robbed by the notorious "Machine Gun" Kelly. Still, that didn't stop city fathers, eyeing empty tax coffers, from kicking off an ambitious campaign to lure the business and development that they viewed as critical to Tupelo's growth. By the mid-1930s, their gamble had paid off, and the city had assumed such luster that the 1938 New Deal *Works Progress Administration Guide* described Tupelo as "perhaps Mississippi's best example of what contemporary commentators call the New South" (*U.S. Works Progress Administration Guide*, 1938).

But when visitors crossed the Mobile and Ohio railroad tracks (in essence, the boundary line separating Tupelo from its poorer cousin to the east) they'd find themselves in a different world, one beset by poverty and inhabited by down-on-their-luck whites and sharecroppers. Residents of "Tupelo proper" referred to it with thinly veiled contempt as "East Tupelo," and in the 1930s it was a tough place to be born and an even rougher place to grow up. "East Tupelo had the reputation of being an extremely rough town," a local historian once noted. "Some citizens doubt that it was worse than other small towns, but others declare it to have been the roughest town in North Mississippi. The town had its red-light district called 'Goosehollow.' By 1940 the tiny community of East Tupelo was known to have at least nine bootleggers" (Dobbs, *A Brief History of East Tupelo, Mississippi*).

In fact, the railway tracks that separated the two municipalities comprised just one boundary line. There was a second, one that bifurcated East Tupelo and separated whites from blacks, but in truth it constituted a distinction without a difference. Because whichever side of the line you were unlucky enough to find yourself on, the struggles were pretty much the same: lives of hard luck and dashed hopes, twinned with a soul-deadening sense of "what's the use" that had become nothing less than a generational hand-me-down. It made them who they were: cynical, suspicious of strangers, insular.

None of which suggests that the poor unfortunates who, by birth or happenstance, found themselves on the wrong side of Tupelo's tracks were without at least some measure of solace. For, if the story of humankind teaches us anything, it's that there are truths that are known only to the poor. Because for the denizens of East Tupelo, and for the millions of poor everywhere, suffering often manifested itself in a fervid and life-long embrace of religion. For people who order their lives through faith, poverty was viewed as punishment for crimes they hadn't committed. If these same people found the truth of their lives too unpleasant, then, bolstered by faith, they would fashion their own truth—a deliverance, if you will. And by the time they'd left their churches on Sunday and made their way back to the colorless public housing that comprised their homes, certain truths would linger: there *was* a higher purpose to suffering; they *were* cursed by fate and injustice, and most importantly of all, *a better world awaited*, one where overdue rewards would be ladled out in steady and copious amounts for eternity.

Which, of course, brings us to the Presley family, who, if you're keeping track, check virtually all the boxes mentioned above. Gladys Smith was born on August 25, 1912, to a farming family of seven brothers and sisters who lived in Pontotoc County, Mississippi. After dropping out of high school, she divided her time between helping out on the family farm and toiling at a series of low-paying jobs. At the age of 20, following the death of her father, she landed a position at the Tupelo Garment Company in nearby Mill Town. Initially she rode a company bus to work, but she soon relocated to a small community just above the highway in East Tupelo. The job was demanding; she regularly worked 12-hour days, sometimes six days a week, operating a sewing machine. She toiled "by the piece," which meant that if she was productive, she might clear 13 dollars per week; if she wasn't, she risked being laid off. At some point, she was promoted to an inspector position, where it was her responsibility to count the buttons and buttonholes on each garment before it was packaged and distributed to local shops. But the work was grinding, and when she'd had enough, a brief search yielded a job at a local dressmaker, where she again ran a sewing machine. Despite her hardscrabble existence, friends remember Gladys as cheerful and upbeat and often said that she had never encountered a stranger, only a potential friend. Late period images of Gladys Presley reflect a puffy and stout figure, with raccoon circles framing her dark eyes, but in earlier years, she was not unattractive, with a svelte figure and a crown of raven hair.

Across town, Vernon Presley, alongside his father, would make his way to a neighboring farm each day at 6:00 a.m. where they would wrench out a living picking vegetables and hoeing cotton "on spec," meaning that compensation would be theirs only once the produce went to market. By the time he reached adulthood, Vernon, viewed by some local residents as borderline handsome, had become sullen and congenitally restless. During his twenties, he bounced from one menial job to another, never seeming to find his niche nor seeming to care. Years later, after he'd achieved success, a fan asked Elvis what his father did. He replied, "He doesn't do anything." Bones Howe, a music engineer and producer, who in later years would work with Elvis, understood these men well. "For me, having grown up in Florida, that was so vivid," Howe recalls, "because there's a lot of men in the South that grow up and don't do anything. Somehow, they're supported, they go fishing, they survive, there's a brother that gives them money or a wife—who knows how they do it? We see Vernon Presley as this distinguished looking guy with gray hair. But Vern Presley was a man who didn't do anything" (*Musician*, October 1992).

It's impossible to pinpoint precisely when Gladys Smith first encountered Vernon Presley. Some contend that she spied him on the street one day and introduced herself. Others suggest they met at a neighbor's house. Still others contend their initial meeting came during a tent revival that sprang up one day in a vacant lot in Tupelo. Whatever the truth, it would take Vernon's older brother Vester and Gladys's sister Clettes to finally link them together.

"Yeah," Vester Presley recalls, "I dated Gladys a few times and Vernon dated Clettes. Gladys didn't like my attitude much. I was too wild in those days. So, Gladys quit seeing me. Then, Vernon started dating Gladys and soon there was only one object of his affection, Gladys" (Dundy, *Elvis and Gladys*).

In early summer of 1933, Gladys and Vernon, in what appears to have been an impulsive act, were married in Pontotoc, Mississippi. Gladys, who was 21 at the time, stated on the marriage certificate that she was 19, perhaps embarrassed that Vernon—who added five years to his age, stating he was 22—was still a minor. To pay for the marriage license, they borrowed three dollars from friends, with whom they would live with for a short time, before moving in with Vernon's family. In the summer of 1934, Gladys learned she was pregnant and, sometime later, quit her job at the garment factory. As the weeks passed and her pregnancy became more difficult, Gladys told friends she was sure she was carrying twins. Vernon, who was working as a milk deliveryman at this point and desirous of building a modest home for his growing family, approached his boss for a loan. He offered an amount of $180, under the proviso that he would own the home and the Presleys would pay him rent. Once completed, the house would exemplify the type of cheap housing built by the thousands in the early years of the twentieth century. Commonly referred to as a "shotgun shack," the Presley home had a tiny front porch; two rooms heated by a small fireplace; and no indoor plumbing, just a well and a closeted toilet outside. The distance from the front door to the back was just 30 feet.

Following a prolonged and painful labor, Gladys, at 4:00 a.m. on January 8, 1935, delivered a stillborn baby. A half hour later, she would deliver a second, this one a healthy boy they named Elvis Aaron. (In a mix-up, likely due to a doctor's misunderstanding, the birth certificate

For the sum of $180, Vernon Presley secured this small Tupelo residence, commonly referred to as a "shotgun shack," just prior to his son's birth on January 8, 1935. The distance from the front to the back door was just 30 feet (photograph by Carol M. Highsmith, America Collection at the Library of Congress).

The tiny Presley bedroom where Vernon, Gladys, and Elvis were forced by necessity to share the same bed (photograph by Carol M. Highsmith, America Collection at the Library of Congress).

initially spelled "Elvis" as "Evis.") Because the family lacked money for a headstone, the stillborn child, named Jesse Garon after Vernon's father, was buried the following day in an unmarked grave at the Priceville Cemetery a few miles away. In the days following, Gladys suffered complications and was admitted to a local hospital, where tests revealed that she'd never again be able to conceive. The hospital bill of 15 dollars was paid by a county welfare agency.

Gladys's bond with her newborn was immediate and all-consuming. "Gladys thought he was the greatest thing that ever happened and she treated him that way," remembers a close friend. "She worshiped that child from the day he was borned to the day she died. She'd always keep him at home, or when she let him go play, she was always out seeing about him. And wherever she went, she always had Elvis with her. She wouldn't go nowheres without Elvis" (Hopkins, *Elvis, the Biography*). In later years, Elvis would comment on this period of his life, stating that Gladys hovered over him constantly and that, on the infrequent occasions when he did run off, Gladys would whip him, leaving him feeling unloved.

It's often been said that there's no nobility in poverty, but as undeniably tough as things were for the Presleys during this period, they nonetheless clung to something bordering on just that. A close friend of Gladys related a story of Elvis once finding a Coca Cola bottle and proudly bringing it home to his mother so that she might claim the two-cent deposit. When she learned that Elvis had taken it from a neighbor's porch, she spanked him and ordered him to return it. Years later, Vernon elaborated on the beliefs that bound the family together: "There were times we had nothing to eat but corn bread and water, but we always had compassion for people. Poor we were, I'll never deny that. But trash we weren't. We never had prejudice. We never put anybody down. Neither did Elvis" ("Elvis by His Father Vernon Presley," *Good Housekeeping*, January 1978).

From the moment he was born to the day of her death 23 years later, Gladys, as if determined to shelter her son from life itself, showered Elvis with constant babying, a style of child-rearing now referred to as "helicopter" parenting (describing those who "hover" over their children). Studies suggest that such overly protective behavior can lead to psychological issues, including depression and anxiety, for the child in later life and ultimately manifest a dependence on prescription medications. And though tongues wagged in East Tupelo that such fawning over Elvis "would ruin that child," most everyone in the Presley circle viewed Gladys's devotion to her son as perfectly normal.

In 1937, Gladys's uncle ascended to the role of sole preacher at East

Tupelo's Assembly of God Church, where the devout embraced, as had much of the South, the evangelical movement that swept the United States during the 1920s and 30s. Services were something akin to tent revivals where true believers would speak in tongues, pray fervently, and raise their voices in song. It was at one such gathering where the two-year-old Elvis made an early attempt at singing. "When Elvis was just a little fellow," Gladys Presley recalled later, "not more than two years old, he would slide down off my lap and run into the aisle and scramble up to the platform. There he would stand looking at the choir and trying to sing with them. He was too little to know the words, but he could carry the tune and he would watch their faces and try to do as they did" (*TV and Radio Mirror*, 1956). For the remainder of his life, Elvis remained devoted to spiritual music, a core component of the duality—or, if you prefer, hypocrisy—that would characterize his later years, when even during his most hedonistic period of womanizing and drug use, he nonetheless insisted on preparing for every recording session by warming up with gospel tunes.

When Elvis was two, the family was rocked when Vernon, along with his brother-in-law Travis, was charged with altering— revising the amount from four dollars to 40—and then cashing a check given to them by the Presley's landlord. Both men were found guilty and sentenced to a three-year term in Mississippi's maximum-security prison, commonly referred to as "Parchman Farm." On weekends, Gladys and Elvis would either board a Greyhound bus or prevail on friends or family to make the five-hour trip each way to visit Vernon.

Unable to make the 12-dollar monthly rent on their modest house during Vernon's incarceration, Gladys and Elvis were evicted. Now reliant on welfare and the kindness of in-laws for shelter, she and Elvis would spend months bouncing from one house to another, developments that would exact a toll on her once cheerful temperament. Once viewed by nearly everyone as friendly and upbeat, Vernon's absence transformed Gladys into someone commonly viewed by others as nervous and despondent. The situation was no less trying for her son; neighbors recall young Elvis sitting on the front porch, sobbing uncontrollably and crying out for his absent father. It was during this period that Elvis, plagued by nightmares and insomnia, would draw ever closer to his mother, whom he called "Satnin." To comfort him, Gladys would read the Bible and regale her son with stories of redemption and salvation. During such times, she would often lapse into baby talk, a practice that Elvis himself would perpetuate with the women in his life to the very end.

In February of 1939, Vernon's sentence was commuted and he was released from Parchman Farm after just eight months. Vernon's temperament, sullen and withdrawn at the best of times, was further calcified by a gnawing guilt that he'd shamed his family. When questioned about his father in later years, Elvis would say, "My daddy may seem hard, but you don't know what he'd been through" (cited by Presley friends Cliff Greaves and Charlie Hodge in separate interviews). Throughout Vernon's imprisonment, friends were forgiving, viewing his transgression as nothing more than a misstep in the life of an otherwise decent man. Still, the incident did nothing to lessen the burden of a family who, even without the stigma attached to Vernon's act—a topic that became verboten once Elvis achieved fame—had struggled to accept the reality of their daily lives.

"It was much more prevalent then than now," recalls Tupelo native Ron Brandon.

> If you grew up very poor as Elvis and his family did—and me and my family lived just a few miles down the road—you quickly learned, and pretty much accepted, your status in life. You knew that you were different, that there were places that you were not welcome, crowds that you did not mix with, girls you did not approach. It was hard to accept and naturally it was an obstacle that you wanted to overcome. When you read the stories of "hanging clothes on the line out back of Graceland, and chickens in the yard," just try to remember their background [interview with Ron Brandon, elvisinfo net.com, 2011].

"Lives of hard luck and dashed hopes." With eyes fixed warily on what lay ahead, the Presley family sits for this somber portrait, circa 1938 (Alamy. com).

Once reunited, the family moved to Pascagoula, Mississippi, on the Gulf Coast, where Vernon found work on a New Deal program to expand the local shipyards. When the work dried up a few months later, they returned to Tupelo, where they moved in with Vernon's brother, Vester. During this time, the jobs came and went. When there was sufficient money, the family would secure their own housing, only to return to Vester's when it dried up. Years later, Elvis would tally up the number of places they lived during this period, before finally settling on "at least seven." Things were undeniably tough, and while misfortune often serves to divide families, it seemed to only draw the Presleys closer. "Though we had friends and relatives, including my parents," Vernon was to state later, "the three of us formed our own private world" ("Elvis by His Father Vernon Presley," *Good Housekeeping*, January 1978). None of which is to suggest that the marriage of Gladys and Vernon was without strife. In subsequent years, family members would often speak of Gladys's volatility (a trait she would pass on to her son), her domination of Vernon, and of the vitriol that marked their disagreements, with more than one characterizing the relationship as "dysfunctional."

During this period, Elvis is remembered by those who knew the family as quiet and as something of a loner, "sweet and average," as one of his grade-school teachers described him. When not at school, he could be spotted playing by himself behind the family home or, at times, sitting on his front porch absorbed in comic books that filled his mind with visions of superheroes in capes (images that would linger and influence later sartorial choices). When Vernon invited him to go hunting with him one day, Elvis replied, "Daddy, I don't want to kill birds" ("Elvis by his Father Vernon," *Good Housekeeping*, January 1978). If the family had a few extra coins, Elvis would venture down to the local movie house, where he'd sit transfixed by the exploits of his favorite stars, Roy Rogers and Gene Autry.

In 1942, Vernon hooked on with a construction company 40 miles from Memphis, then following that, with a munitions plant, returning home on weekends only. When the war ended, relying on savings he'd accrued, Vernon made a down payment of 200 dollars on a one-room shack on Berry Street in East Tupelo, where all three members of the family were forced to sleep in the same bed. Years later, Vernon's second wife, Dee, would tell the *National Enquirer* that Elvis and his mother were intimate during this phase of their life, something that friends and relatives heatedly deny and for which no substantiation has ever emerged. It was also during this period of his life that Elvis, drawn by its power to sooth and inspire, increasingly turned to music for solace. The Presleys were regular attendees at the local Assembly of God church each Sunday, and friends recall Vernon, Gladys, and young Elvis joining in on the hymns, their voices robust enough to stand out from the large congregation. Elvis's growing fascination with music is perhaps best illustrated by an event that took place during his tenth year.

It happened during a morning prayer program at his grade school when Elvis spontaneously broke into song, in this case, "Old Shep," a Red Foley song about a boy and his dog. Liking what she'd heard, his teacher promptly marched Elvis to the school offices and ordered him to sing for the school principal, who was impressed enough to enter Elvis into a talent contest sponsored by local station WELO to be staged at the upcoming Mississippi-Alabama Fair and Dairy Show in downtown Tupelo. The event was something of a yearly big deal; schools were closed and buses would transport teachers, students, and residents to the event, where they would be admitted free of charge. In addition to carnival rides, the five-day event featured a livestock show and animal contests like mule-pulling and would showcase appearances by such Grand Ole Opry stars as Minnie Pearl and Pee Wee King. During the children's talent contest, 10-year-old Elvis, wearing bib overalls and glasses, took the stage and sang "Old Shep." "They entered me in a talent show," Elvis recalled later. "I wore glasses, no music and I won, I think it was fifth place in this state talent contest. I got a whipping the same day, my mother whipped me for something, I don't know, going on one of the rides. Destroyed my ego completely" (Burk, *Early Elvis: The Tupelo Years*).

In 1956, Gladys remarked on that day. "Elvis had no way to make music and the other kids wouldn't accompany him. He just climbed up on a chair so he could reach the microphone and he sang 'Old Shep'" (Burk, *Early Elvis: The Tupelo Years*).

For Elvis, a means to "make music" would come a year later when Gladys presented him with an inexpensive Gene Autry–model guitar for his birthday. He'd asked for a bicycle, but his mother, visualizing potential injury, shook her head. "Son," she said, "wouldn't you rather have the guitar? It would help you with your singing and everybody does enjoy hearing you sing" (*TV and Radio Mirror*, 1956). In the weeks following, Elvis picked up a few rudimentary chords from his uncle Vester, a devout country music fan, but it's likely that the bulk of his early training came from a 21-year-old church pastor named Frank Smith, who tells stories of Elvis bringing his guitar and a chord book to his house for lessons. With a few practice sessions under his belt, Elvis began a daily ritual of toting his guitar to school, where he serenaded schoolmates during recess. "He told us he was going to the Grand Ole Opry," a classmate recalls. "Not bragging, he just made the statement" (Dundy, *Elvis and Gladys*).

Elvis at 13, cast in bronze outside his Tupelo birthplace. "He told us he was going to the Grand Ole Opry," a classmate recalls. "Not bragging, he just made the statement" (photograph by Carol M. Highsmith, America Collection at the Library of Congress).

Shake Rag

In 1948, Elvis and his family found themselves on the move once again, this time taking a clapboard shack adjacent to an impoverished region east of the M&O railway tracks known as Shake Rag, a community that extended north to Main Street. How it came by its unique name remains in dispute to this day, but depending on your source, it was either because people would "shake their rags" (or clothing) fleeing local police or would wave kerchiefs to flag down passing trains.

In recent decades, thanks to its musical heritage and its location on what has become known as the Mississippi Blues Trail, Shake Rag has taken on a certain luster, but in the middle part of the twentieth century, it was, even by East Tupelo standards, a grim and grey place to live, chockablock with tumbledown shanties and home to the region's poorest black residents. As undeniably dismal as it was, Shake Rag would spring to life on weekends when the Pentecostal churches would overflow with parishioners in the grip of that "old time religion," singing at ear-splitting volumes, speaking in tongues and rolling in the aisles, all to the strains of pulsating music from the band of musicians positioned at the front. "You couldn't not hear it," recalls Elvis's cousin Billy Smith. "The walls were so thin, you could hear it outside" (Nash, *Elvis and the Memphis Mafia*). Further up the road were the juke joints and blues clubs where the less reverent would gather, and, if lucky, might find themselves entertained by such local legends as Willie C. Jones, "Tee-Toc," and Lonnie Williams.

Did Shake Rag's vibrant musical culture, as some have suggested, play a dominant role in shaping Elvis Presley's musical journey? Debatable. But was he influenced even marginally by the gospel music that wafted from local churches? Did the outsize antics of the devout in these very same churches instill an awareness that music, when combined with physicality, could inspire and energize? And did the soulful bluesmen who plunked and strummed in Shake Rag's bars and juke joints play at least some role in introducing rhythm and blues to the young boy? The answers are clearly, yes, yes, and yes.

In subsequent years, it's been suggested that Elvis, in search of new musical experiences, would tread the streets of Shake Rag after dark, soaking up the invigorating sounds that wafted from its bars. Some, including Tupelo resident Ron Brandon, remain skeptical of these claims.

"I sincerely doubt the stories of a white kid his age hanging around black neighborhoods at night," he says. "In the daytime maybe, but not at night. It simply was not safe and as protective as his mom was, she simply would not have allowed it."

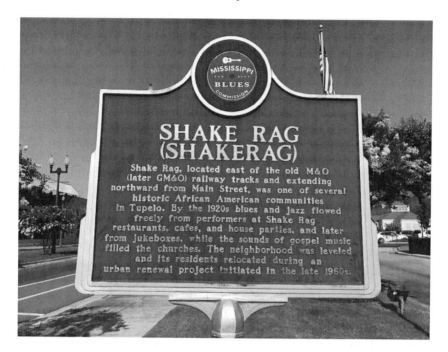

Decorative plaque along the Mississippi Blues Trail, commemorating the musical heritage of the Shake Rag area of Tupelo (photograph by Carol M. Highsmith, America Collection at the Library of Congress).

In the 1960s, Shake Rag was demolished to make way for a housing development. Today, a decorative plaque stands along the Mississippi Blues Trail to commemorate the legacy of the impoverished, but musically vibrant community. It reads:

SHAKE RAG (SHAKERAG)
This Mississippi Blues Commission historical marker along East Main Street in Tupelo marks the former location of a historical Jim Crow–era African-American neighborhood that was a fertile location for blues musicians, who had a great influence on a local boy named Elvis Presley.

Shake Rag, located east of the old M&O (later GM&O) railway tracks and extending northward from Main Street, was one of several historic African American communities in Tupelo. By the 1920s blues and jazz flowed freely from performers at Shake Rag restaurants, cafes, and house parties, and later from jukeboxes, while the sounds of gospel music filled the churches. The neighborhood was leveled and its residents relocated during an urban renewal project initiated in the late 1960s.

2

Memphis

In 1948, Vernon, who'd been driving a grocery truck, was canned, triggering yet another family move, this time a hundred miles northwest to Memphis, Tennessee, where they took up residence in a rooming house. By this point, Vernon's shiftlessness was becoming apparent even to his young son. Years later, Elvis was to remark of his father: "My Daddy's had a backache for thirty years. He wouldn't work if you put a gun to his head" (Nash, *Elvis and the Memphis Mafia*). Of the family fortunes when they arrived in Memphis, Elvis later stated: "We was broke, man. We packed all our belongings in boxes and put them in the trunk and on top of a 1939 Plymouth. Things had to be better" (Cosby, *Devil's Music, Holy Rollers and Hillbillies*). For a while, things were so bad that a return to Tupelo seemed inevitable, but Vernon ultimately landed a job at the United Paint Company, while Gladys found work in a drapery factory. While at the rooming house, the family shared one room and cooked their meals on a hotplate; the bathroom at the end of the hall was communal. As a home service advisor for the Memphis Housing Authority noted upon visiting the family: "Cook, eat and sleep in one room. Share bath. No privacy. Persons interviewed are Mrs. Presley and son. Nice boy. They seem very nice and deserving" (Memphis Housing Authority, Jane Richardson). Despite the hardship, Elvis, according to family and friends, remained upbeat. "He always knew he was going to do something," Vernon said later. "When we didn't have a dime, he used to sit on the doorstep and say, 'One of these days it'll be different'" (Johnson, *Elvis Presley Speaks!*).

In the fall of 1949, Elvis enrolled at Humes High, Memphis's predominantly white high school, where, despite his essentially reticent nature, he stood out by deviating from the "crew cut," an inexplicably popular male grooming style of the period where hair was shaved to the scalp except for a waxed hedgerow lining the front. Instead, Elvis piled his hair into a pompadour with a ducktail in the back, a look that he fussed over constantly using the comb in his back pocket. By his senior year, he augmented his look with a pair of thick sideburns that reached the bottom of his ears. At rare moments when money was less scarce, he'd shop at Lansky's on Beale Street, the clothing store that supplied the flashy stage threads worn by such celebrated musicians as Lionel Hampton, Duke Ellington, and B.B. King. Then, once adorned in Lansky fine-wear, Elvis would strut the Humes hallways in outfits—ruffled shirts, bolero jackets, and pants with a red stripe running down the side—that made him look, as some classmates joked, "like a movie usher." "I remember his first pink-and-black outfit," cousin Billy Smith recalls. "I thought, 'My God Almighty!' It was a complete switch for a white man to dress like that" (Nash, *Elvis and the Memphis Mafia*). In later years, Elvis would comment on his sartorial style of this period. "It was just something I wanted to do," he said. "I wasn't trying to be better than anybody else" (1972 interview).

Not surprisingly, such peacocking has a way of rubbing certain folks the wrong way, in this case, members of the Humes High football team. So, one day, wielding scissors, a few of Humes's finest tackled Elvis and dragged him into a bathroom. "That is a real story," classmate Red West recalls. "Elvis was always different. We had crew cuts, wore T-shirts and blue jeans, Elvis had the long duck-tail, the long sideburns and he wore the loud clothes and naturally he was a target for all the bullies. One day luckily I walked into the boys' bathroom at Humes high school and three guys were going to cut his hair just, you know, to make themselves look big or make them feel big or whatever and I intervened and stopped it" (*Hollywood Reporter*, July 19, 2017).

Incidents like these may account for the company Elvis kept during his high school years, which was predominantly female, and as acquaintances emphasize, certainly platonic—"pal-like," in their words. One exception was slight, dark-haired, raccoon-eyed George Klein, who saw qualities in Elvis others missed. Klein's closeness to Elvis even persisted after he was elected senior class president, a gesture that Presley never forgot. The friendship would endure; upon graduation, Klein would kick off a career as a disc jockey, and as Elvis ascended the musical ladder, he would unfailingly promote his career.

At some point during Elvis's freshman year at Humes, the Presley family qualified for a ground floor apartment at Lauderdale Courts, a federally subsidized housing project in the heart of Memphis where they paid a monthly rent of $35. "The Courts," as they were known, were viewed by many Memphians as a sad last stop, but for the Presleys they constituted a dramatic step up. For the first time, the family had two bedrooms, a sitting room, a kitchen, and their own bathroom. As long as the family never exceeded $2,500 in yearly income, their tenure at The

Courts was secure. Every day, Elvis walked the 10 blocks to school, often with Gladys at his side, a ritual that drew stares and withering comments from some of the Court inhabitants. "They treat him like he's two years old," one neighbor observed. Once in class, teachers found him pleasant and agreeable, with a warm and sunny personality, although one described Presley's English as "atrocious."

Beale Street

If Shake Rag provided the spark, then Memphis, with its swirling and vibrant musical currents, would fuel new and intriguing possibilities for young Elvis Presley. A mixed-race (over 40 percent of its residents were black) but still segregated city in the early 1950s, Memphis could boast of an aural heritage both raucous and reverent, and for music lovers in the early fifties, Memphis's Beale Street was the place to be. Not only an epicenter for the musically inclined, but for residents of eastern Arkansas, West Tennessee, and northern Mississippi, Beale

"A spirit, a symbol, a way of life." Beale Street, Memphis, circa 1954 (Alamy.com).

Street comprised a virtual northern gateway to the rich culture of the Mississippi Delta, "a meeting place for urban and rural styles," as someone once described it. Someone seeking musical nourishment on Beale Street in the early fifties would, depending on the day, pass clubs promoting appearances by such stalwarts as Muddy Waters, Bobby "Blue" Bland, and Albert King. In the words of local historian Nat D. Williams, "Come what may, there will always be a Beale Street, because Beale Street is a spirit ... a symbol ... a way of life.... Beale Street is a hope" (amromusic.com, June 2014).

In truth, Beale's music emporiums were but one component of Memphis's rich aural landscape; there was also radio. WDIA, which billed itself as "The Mother Station of the South," was the first radio station in the United States to be programmed exclusively by and for black people, and in 1954 it provided a steady diet of blues, R&B, and gospel for listeners in reach of its newly minted 50,000-watt signal. WDIA's roster of DJs included Rufus Thomas, who would have hits of his own in years to come with "Walking the Dog" and "Do the Funky Chicken," and, most notably, B.B. King, who, still under his given name of Riley King at this point, hosted a daily 15-minute show where he shilled for something called Pep-Ti-Kon, a bestselling concoction guaranteed to cure so-called "tired blood" (though its 12 percent alcohol content may have had something to do with its popularity). Each day, King would lean into his microphone and smoothly croon: "Pep-Ti-Kon, sure is good! You can get it anywhere in your neighborhood!"

As WDIA's signal faded after dark, those in search of a nighttime music fix would switch the dial to WHBQ, where, for six nights a week, Dewey Phillips, a jive-talking, uncorked well of energy, held court with his nightly *Red, Hot & Blue* radio show. In contrast to today's sterile and robotic radio formats, Phillips's daily sessions were wild, slapdash affairs, where "Daddy-O-Dewey" would veer madly from one musical genre to another ... some blues, then some pop, maybe some country and then who knows ... maybe a taste of gospel. It was all served up in a wiseass, hicker-than-thou backwoods staccato that prompted listeners to question if Phillips's energy was natural or perhaps chemically induced (which it was: Dewey's stimulants of choice during much of his life were amphetamines and corn liquor), especially during commercials where Phillips might promote a locally brewed beer as follows: "If you can't drink it, freeze it and eat it. If you can't do that, open up a cotton-picking rib and POUR it in" (memphismusicalhalloffame.com, 2009).

For those of a spiritual bent, Memphis offered the more observant but no less vibrant sounds that echoed from its houses of worship. A

"Daddy-O-Dewey" Phillips spinning the hits at WHBQ, 1955 (Alamy.com).

casual visitor to the city's Pentecostal and Baptist churches might find himself transfixed by the sight of parishioners seemingly in the grip of some otherworldly force, singing, dancing and rolling in the aisles. And if that weren't enough to slake the thirst of the most devout, there were the sacred music programs at the Ellis Auditorium on the corner of Poplar and Front, where gospel groups like Jake Hess and the Imperials, the Statesmen, or the Blackwood Brothers, who in 1951 had a national hit with "The Man Upstairs," would play to capacity audiences.

For a young Elvis Presley, Memphis represented nothing less than a sonic divide between musical worlds, one that he was more than willing to straddle. In later years, local musicians would speak of seeing Elvis at Beale Street blues clubs like the Paradise and Club Handy, snapping his fingers and bobbing his head in time to the music. And on Sunday nights, when the emphasis was more on singing than preaching, he could be spotted sitting alone at the East Trigg Baptist Church, drawn in by the enthusiastic vocalizing of the church choir. And if additional evidence were needed of Elvis's inherent musical eclecticism, he also embraced popular artists as diverse as Patti Page, opera crooner Mario Lanza, and Dean Martin during this period, though friend Lamar Fike later disputed Presley's affection for Dean Martin, saying "It was mostly obscure black guys" (Nash, *Elvis and the Memphis Mafia*).

During this period, Elvis started taking guitar lessons from 18-year-old Jesse Lee Denson, the only structured tutoring he would engage in throughout his life. The son of a local preacher, Denson also had a reputation around Memphis as a truant and juvenile delinquent. Initially reluctant to engage with the 16-year-old Elvis, Denson relented once pressed by his mother. "He showed up, he had a little itty-bitty Gene Autry–type guitar," Denson said later. "He really couldn't play, so I let him practice on mine" (Guralnick, *The Last Train to Memphis*). The sessions continued for a series of weeks, and each Saturday and Sunday, Elvis would return, learn a bit more, then go home and practice. Often, he'd strum his guitar in the stairwell of The Courts because he liked the echo effect, or, to the despair of complaining neighbors, in the family apartment or outside on the porch. Friends tell of walking past the Presley home, only to see Elvis on the front porch strumming his guitar and singing in a low voice, with Vernon and Gladys perched nearby. Some nights, cloaked in the nighttime darkness that seemed to imbue him with confidence, he'd play and sing for schoolmates who might stop by.

As time passed and his confidence grew, Elvis would occasionally play at school parties, but only after he'd moved to a far corner of the room—"way over yonder," as one friend recalled—and the lights were dimmed. During this period, music continued to play an increasingly central role in his life, and when he wasn't listening to such diverse artists as Hank Williams, Eddy Arnold, Teresa Brewer, Eddie Fisher, and Perry Como on the radio, he'd often visit the city's Overton Park, where full-scale concerts were often on the program. "I used to go there and listen to the concerts they had with the big orchestras," Elvis said later. "I watched the conductor, listened to the music for hours by myself. I was fascinated by the fact that these guys could play for hours, you know, and most of the time the conductor wouldn't even look at his sheet. I had records by Mario Lanza when I was seventeen, eighteen years old. I would listen to the Metropolitan Opera. I just loved music. Music, period" (1972 interview).

During this phase, Elvis's increasing self-confidence began to manifest itself in his personal style. In addition to the dress slacks he wore each day, Elvis began affecting a scarf, ascot-style, around his neck during his junior year—"as if he was a movie star," a classmate said. He also messed constantly with his hair, combing and re-combing it in a practiced fashion that invariably drew stares and muffled laughter. All of this contributed to his growing image among classmates as a "squirrel," and he continued to suffer abuse for his iconoclastic ways.

As a wood shop project, Elvis brought his guitar from home and over a period of days patched cracks in the fretboard and restored its finish before finally restringing it. Naturally, this drew the attention of his testosterone-infused schoolmates who crowded around him and asked him if he could play it. "Not really," Elvis replied, shaking his head. At that point, one of the boys grabbed Elvis from behind, locking his arms, saying that if he agreed to play something, they'd let him go. Once freed, Elvis reached for his guitar and expertly played an obscure Chet Atkins tune called "Under the Double Eagle," a performance a classmate said "blew [him] away." And though it's not clear when or where he picked it up, Elvis also began playing the piano during this period. A cousin recalls Elvis stopping by his house for a visit and, upon spotting an upright, sitting down and playing, something he had never seen him do before.

During his sophomore and junior years, Elvis worked after school, first as an usher at Loew's State Theatre, then at Precision Tool Company, a gig that was quickly truncated when the owners found out he was underage. Sometime during his senior year, he found work at a metal products plant, earning enough money to boost the Presleys' annual income over the Housing Authority limit and getting them booted out of The Courts.

In January of 1953, the family was on the move again, first to a rooming house near Humes High, then back to a rented room in a home just northeast of The Courts. In his senior year, Elvis's self-confidence had reached such a point that he decided to enter Humes High's annual minstrel show, where he played his guitar and sang a recent hit by Teresa Brewer. With his name misspelled as "Prestly" in the program and despite his terror at performing before his classmates, the appearance was a success. "I wasn't popular in school," he said later. "I wasn't dating anybody. I failed music—only thing I ever failed. And then they entered me in this talent show and I came out and did my first number, 'Till I Waltz with You,' by Teresa Brewer and when I came onstage I heard people kind of rumbling and whispering and so forth, 'cause nobody knew I even sang. It was amazing how popular I became after that" (1972 interview).

On the night of June 3, 1953, in a ceremony at Ellis Auditorium, Elvis, to the delight of Gladys and Vernon, received his diploma, the first member of the Presley family to graduate from high school. Years later, Elvis would marvel at the fact he'd successfully completed his studies. "Truthfully, I don't really know why they gave me a diploma," he would say. "I would just sit there in class and be looking out the window. I had no idea what the teacher was saying. I'd be thinking about Tony Curtis

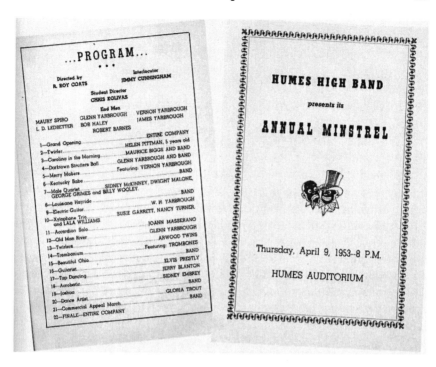

Humes High Minstrel Program, with Elvis billed as "Elvis Prestly," April 9, 1953 (Alamy.com).

and Marlon Brando and being a star and singing. I was just dreaming all the time" (Connolly, *Being Elvis*).

Dreams are aspirational and the formula for realizing them is always the same: Believe in yourself. Work hard. Never give up. It's the dreamer's refrain. But a dream as epic and extraordinary as Presley's— to sing and become famous, especially when cast in relief to the life that preceded it—seemed, to all but the most blindly optimistic, impossible.

3

The Memphis
Recording Service

Maybe it all began with Silas Payne, a man black and blinded by syphilis, who spun tales to the wide-eyed child of "molasses rivers and battercake trees." Or perhaps it was the midnight ride down Beale, past the glittering marquees of the blues clubs that stoked the young man's imagination and filled his head with animating notions of life, music, and freedom. Perhaps it doesn't matter. After all, stories of origin rarely boil down to a single moment. Unless, of course, you're talking about Sam Phillips and the origins of rock 'n' roll.

Born in Florence, Alabama, on January 5, 1923, to a family of 10, Samuel Cornelius Phillips spent many of his early years picking cotton on the family's farm. During these times, Sam worked shoulder to shoulder with black sharecroppers, and for the remainder of his life he would speak of their spiritual hymns and the traces they left on him. It was late one night in 1939 when Sam, along with his family, saw Beale Street for the first time and sensed the transfigurative power of music. "I just fell totally in love," he was to say later (*Daily Telegraph*, October 22, 2016). As time passed and music tightened its grip, Sam became something of a musician himself, taking up the sousaphone, the trombone, and the drums. In high school, he led a 72-piece marching band.

Gifted with an uncommon level of empathy, Sam soon began to harbor dreams of a law career to right what he viewed as societal wrongs. "When I was growing up, I wanted to be a criminal defense lawyer," he recalled, "because I saw so many people, especially black people, railroaded" (*Salon*, 2001). But the death of his father in 1941 forced Sam to abandon thoughts of a legal career and find work to support his family. After a series of dead-end jobs, including a stint in a funeral parlor, he landed a spot at Alabama radio station WLAY as an announcer. In years to come, Sam would repeatedly point to WLAY's progressive format and their dedication to playing music from both white and black musicians as a significant influence. It was while working at WLAY that Sam met his future wife, Becky, and in 1943, they married. It would be a union that would endure until Sam's death in 2003.

After a stop in Decatur, Alabama, Sam and Becky relocated in 1945 to Memphis, where he landed an afternoon gig playing country music at WREC radio. To his delight, he was also tasked with hosting something called the *Afternoon Tea Dance*, a weekend show that left him free to play rhythm and blues, music that was growing in popularity as the swing bands of the post-war era faded in popularity. It was during this period that Sam first began to nurture a dream of somehow breaking down the barriers that segregated American music, in essence, bringing black music to white audiences. In January of 1950, with seed money scraped together from WREC, Sam took the first step in making his dream come true when he launched the Memphis Recording Service in a storefront at 706 Union Avenue. Joining him in the fledgling enterprise was native Memphian Marion Keisker, a WREC colleague, who, as Sam's girl Friday, would manage the front office and handle the paperwork. Six years Sam's senior, Marion had hosted *Meet Kitty Kelly* at WREC, a talk show where she'd kibitz with visiting celebrities and run down the latest happenings in and around Memphis. Some around town believed that Marion was deeply in love with Sam Phillips, and there's no evidence to suggest otherwise, though their friendship would ultimately come to cross-purposes. At one point during this period, Marion was asked to describe Sam. He was, she said, "beautiful beyond belief, with a touch of real elegance" (Williamson, *Elvis Presley: A Southern Life*).

Transforming the building at 706 Union Avenue, formerly an auto repair shop, into the new Memphis Recording Service would prove arduous. For starters, Phillips replaced the structure's tin roof, then set about partitioning a section just inside the front door that would serve as a reception area. With that done, Sam spent days laboriously installing sound tiles to improve the acoustics in what would become the recording studio, only to be disappointed by the result. In the ensuing days, Phillips would pace the room step-by-step and clap his hands to map the reverb and echo quality of every area. This gave Phillips the information he needed to reconfigure the sound tiles to achieve the acoustic perfection he sought. From there, he outfitted the tiny control room and the studio with a Presto lathe recorder, a cluster of Altec speakers, a few RCA and Shure mics, and an aging RCA radio console. Then, feeling he was at last ready for business, he passed out business cards advertising his new recording service as ready to record "anything, anytime, anywhere."

The Memphis Recording Service may have been up and running, but any notions that Sam harbored of producing and recording hits had to wait. In the early months, Phillips barely made ends meet by recording weddings, funerals, and anyone walking through the door who wanted to hear what their recorded voice sounded like (at this point, home recorders were still a distant dream). Rates were $2.00 for a one-sided disc and $2.98 for two sides, with Sam operating the tape machine and Marion, broom in hand, sweeping up the leftover acetate shavings. As a hedge, both kept their jobs at WREC during the early going, with Sam putting in a full shift at the radio station before heading back to his studio in the afternoon. In addition to her reception duties, Marion was charged with helping to drum up business, and in the early months of operation, she managed to direct a number of WREC's commercial accounts to the new enterprise.

In June of 1950, Sam, still pursuing a dream of his own recording label, partnered with WHBQ nightly madman Dewey Phillips to kickstart Phillips Records, an enterprise that began on a shoestring while simultaneously billing itself as the "hottest thing in country." "Boogie in the Park," recorded in 1950 by Joe Hill Louis, was the company's inaugural release, but after selling just 400 copies, Phillips Records quietly folded.

In a move to drum up business for his Memphis Recording Service, Sam entered into an agreement with Chess and Modern Records in 1951 to record a number of Memphis-based artists on a strictly independent basis. Sam would run the sessions and, once completed, he would forward the master tapes to Chess or Modern, who would then produce and distribute the vinyl. During this phase, Sam brought the newly christened B.B. King into his studio where, between mid–1950 and June of 1951, such early classics as "Mistreated Woman," "Don't You Want a Man Like Me," and "B.B. Blues" were recorded. But without question, the most notable song to emerge from Sam's partnership with Chess Records was 1951's "Rocket 88," a track written by Ike Turner and credited to Jackie Brenston and his Delta Cats (Brenston being the saxophonist in Turner's band). Interestingly, an incident that took place during the "Rocket 88" recording session serves as an early illustration of the innovative and experimental approach that Sam Phillips would bring to producing and recording music.

It took place when Turner and his band, who were halfway to Memphis, stopped to fix a flat tire. But as they jacked up the car, an amplifier strapped to the car's roof crashed to the street. There was no visible damage, but once they were in the studio, it was clear that one of the amplifier's speaker cones was damaged, resulting in a distorted sound.

"That's that," a member of the band said dejectedly, but Sam, sensing an opportunity, grabbed a wad of paper, jammed it into the speaker cabinet and told the group's guitarist to play. The resulting sound resembled a saxophone, but not a saxophone anyone had ever heard. It was, in Sam's mind, *different*. It was soon clear that Sam's gambit had paid off; the growl from the damaged amp infused "Rocket 88" with a bite clearly essential to the song's appeal. "Instead of trying to hide that sound," Sam's son, Jerry Phillips, says today, "he brought it to the forefront" (*Popular Mechanics*, August 2016). Sometimes dubbed, however erroneously, as the "world's first true rock 'n' roll song" (there are simply too many contenders for this crown, but Wynonie Harris's 1948 cover of Roy Brown's "Good Rockin' Tonight" and Fats Domino's "The Fatman" from 1948 are worthy of consideration), "Rocket 88," fueled by its unique sound, made a steady climb to number one on the R&B charts, and the musical world quickly took notice of what was transpiring at the little shopfront on Union Avenue, as the following from the *Memphis Commercial Appeal* makes clear:

> [Sam Phillips] has agreements with two recording companies to locate and record hillbilly and race music. Race numbers are those tailored for the Negro trade. Sam auditions musicians with original songs. When he finds something he's sure will sell, he gets it on acetate and sends it to one of the companies. He doesn't charge the musicians anything. Sam may branch out one day, so he says if anyone wants to bring him a pop song, he'll be glad to look it over [*Memphis Commercial Appeal*, April 1951].

The experience of "Rocket 88" would signal a sea change in the life of Sam Phillips. Encouraged by the song's success and clinging to a dream of establishing his own studio, he quit his job at WREC and vowed that, from then on, he would record and sell his own records. In February of 1952, Sam severed his connections with Chess and Modern and renamed the Memphis Recording Service: it became Sun Records. "When I was leasing to other labels, they wanted me to compromise," he said. "They wanted a fuller blues sound than I did. They were selling excitement. I was recording the feel I found in the blues. I wanted to get that gut feel onto record" ("The Sun History," 706unionavenue.nl, 1997).

On March 27, 1952, Sun Records issued its first release, an instrumental by alto-saxophonist Johnny London titled "Drivin' Slow." Raw and echo-drenched, the track hasn't aged well, but supplies a tantalizing glimpse of what the record buying public could expect from Sun Records in years to come. In Sun's first year, Sam would record such soon-to-be prominent names as Howlin' Wolf (née Chester Davis), Junior Parker, and Rufus Thomas. Thomas's 1952 recording of "Bearcat" was concocted after Sam heard "Big Mama" Thornton's R&B hit

Magic contained within. Sun Records, 706 Union Avenue, Memphis (photograph by Carol M. Highsmith, America Collection at the Library of Congress).

"Hound Dog" and decided to record a response utilizing a male perspective while leaving the original song's structure largely intact. Phillips then rounded up a set of local musicians to record it and, with that done, rush released it. "Bearcat," a gritty R&B smoker that kicks off with the snarl of a feline and a contagious, though certainly familiar, groove, would be Sun's first genuine hit, but one that Sam would ultimately regret. Shortly following its release, the owner of Peacock Records, the outfit that released Thornton's original "Hound Dog," filed suit on behalf of Jerry Leiber and Mike Stoller, the songwriting duo who composed the song, charging Sam with copyright infringement. The court ultimately ruled against Phillips and, in addition to paying a royalty percentage to Peacock for every copy of "Bearcat" that Sun sold, Sam also had to absorb all legal fees associated with the case. As a result of the court's decision, the writing credits on "Bearcat" were changed to read "Leiber/Stoller."

With the court's decision putting a drain on Sun's already anemic revenues, Sam was forced to cut back. To keep costs down during this period, Phillips cut royalties to 3 percent from 5, a decision that, in another time and another place, might've resulted in open revolt from his roster of recording acts. In this case, it didn't. Sam's musicians knew not only that Phillips was a true appreciator rather than an appropriator of R&B but also that his love of their music was genuine and heartfelt. Besides, once things improved, he promised that the royalty rate would be returned to the former level, something none of them doubted.

With cash coffers nearly empty, Sam, desperate to uncover new performers, launched a talent search that extended even to the local prison. In 1953, Sun released "Just Walkin' in the Rain" by the Prisonaires, five cons who were currently passing their time at the state penitentiary in Nashville. For their recording session, the group was transported to Sun Studios in an armored vehicle under the watchful eye of armed guardsmen. While "Just Walkin' in the Rain" met with a measure of regional acceptance upon its release, the group proved to be just another one-hit wonder and quickly faded from memory. However, unlike the Prisonaires, the song itself would endure, and, three years later, "Just Walkin' in the Rain" would become a huge national hit for weepy balladeer Johnnie Ray.

Despite the regional popularity of the Prisonaires single, Sun's financial future remained bleak. Unless he found a way to expand the audience for his music, Sam knew that his fledgling studio's days were numbered. Throughout this period, Phillips continued to nurse his great dream of breaking down the wall that prevented white audiences from being exposed to the type of R&B he loved. "My aim was to try and record the blues and other music I liked and to prove whether I was right or wrong about this music," he said later.

> I knew, or I felt I knew, that there was a bigger audience for blues than just the black man of the mid–South. There were city markets to be reached and I knew that whites listened to blues surreptitiously. The base wasn't broad enough because of racial prejudice. It wasn't broad enough to get the amount of commercial play and general acceptance overall, not just in the South. Now these were basically good people, but conceptually they did not understand the kinship between black and white people in the South ["The Sun History," 706unionavenue.nl, 1997].

To understand how radical these notions were, it's instructive to remember the America of the early fifties. Tennessee, along with the rest of the southern United States, was still in the grip of a calcified racial animus. The Supreme Court's *Plessy v. Ferguson* ruling of 1896—which stated that as long as facilities provided to each race were equal, state and local governments were free to segregate—still held sway in America. A visitor to any Southern state in the early 1950s would likely encounter water fountains, public bathrooms, lunchroom counters and other common areas designated as either "white" or "colored." In its landmark *Brown v. Board of Education* decision in 1954, the Supreme Court overruled *Plessy v. Ferguson* and held that separate educational institutions and other public facilities were inherently unequal, ostensibly signaling the end of racial segregation. In truth, all it did was bring added force to a virulent, though less obvious form of racism that had sprung up in the South since Reconstruction, known as "Jim Crow." These were laws established in Southern states primarily to disenfranchise people of color and claw back any economic or social gains made by minorities in the wake of the Civil War.

All of this is being trotted forth to illustrate just what Sam Phillips was up against as he tried to break down resistance to his brand of blues-based music, an animus that extended even to station owners in the Memphis region. "You don't smell bad Sam," they would say when encountering Phillips around town. "Guess you didn't have session today" (*Rolling Stone*, February 13, 1986). The message was clear: Phillips was free to sign and record anyone he wanted, but they'd be damned if they'd play his stuff on their radio stations. Their charter was to play what white America wanted, and if record charts were any indication, what white America wanted was a solid diet of aural pablum from such hitmakers as Dean Martin, Patti Page, and Eddie Fisher. To Sam Phillips, a believer in the power and possibility of music, but also a man who harbored a seething resentment against discrimination, this was bullshit:

> I don't remember when—but I saw as a child—I thought to myself I suppose, that I should have been born black. Suppose that I would have been born a little more down on the economic ladder. I think I felt from the beginning the total inequality of man's inhumanity to his brother. And it didn't take its place with me of getting up in the pulpit and preaching. It took on the aspect with me that someday I would act on my feelings, I would show them on an individual, one-to-one basis ["Man Behind the Sun Sound," *Melody Maker*, 1957].

All of which presented Sam Phillips with a quandary. On the one hand, America's entrenched power structure and its antipathy toward black artists prevented him from broadening his audience and moving Sun toward profitability. But any thought of admitting defeat and cranking out bland pop was never an option; even if Phillips wanted to produce that type of music, he saw no point. In his own words, "There's only so many pieces in a pie" ("Man Behind the Sun Sound," *Melody Maker*, 1957).

It's impossible to pinpoint exactly when—likely during the early months of 1953—that Sam Phillips resolved to take a stand. If Sun Records was to survive, the calcified and regressive thinking that blocked him from expanding his audience had to be swept away. If not, he would go broke. He wasn't sure how—that would take planning and time—but the end result was never in doubt: before he was through, America's radio programmers would play his music on their stations. And if they didn't like it, well, they'd just have to eat it. As he was to say later, "I was shooting for the damn road that hadn't been plowed" ("Man Behind the Sun Sound," *Melody Maker*, 1957).

4

"Just play what you feel"

"What about the boy with the sideburns?"—Marion Keisker, 1954

Over a half-century later, there's still a debate about exactly who hit the record button on the Presto lathe recorder that summer day in 1953. Marion Keisker states firmly that she did: "The reason I taped Elvis was this: Over and over I remember Sam saying 'If I could find a white man who had the negro sound and the negro feel, I could make a billion dollars.' This is what I heard in Elvis ... what I guess they now call 'soul,' this negro sound. So I taped it" (Hopkins, *Elvis, the Biography*). Phillips, who shared a genuine bond with Marion and always spoke generously of her, demurs: "Well, I would love to say Marion did it. I wouldn't take anything away from Marion Keisker. I think she made the statement inadvertently. But it was simply me. That's all" (*Rolling Stone*, February 13, 1986).

In the days since his graduation from high school, Elvis Presley had spent his time bouncing between the Tennessee State Employment Office (where one interviewer noted on his report that Elvis's "flashily dressed 'playboy' type is denied by the fact he has worked hard for three summers") and numerous interviews for positions he didn't get. Finally, in July, he landed a job working as an assembler for a local machine shop. It was during this period that Marion Keisker first noticed the gaudily dressed young man who, day after day, paced back and forth outside Sun Studios' front door, as if trying to summon the nerve to enter.

On July 15, 1953, an article titled "Prison Singers May Find Fame with Record" appeared in the *Memphis Press-Scimitar* covering the Prisonaires and their unlikely recording career, a story that may have caught Elvis's attention. Whether it had or not, it's clear that, just days later, he again was perched outside Sun Studios, this time gripping a battered guitar. After likely taking a minute to ratchet up his nerve, he pushed his way through the front door and approached Marion Keisker, telling her he wanted to make a record. Various accounts over the years contend that Elvis entered Sun Studios that day to make a recording for his mother, though her birthday had already passed, while others suggest he just wanted to hear how he sounded.

As Elvis nervously shifted from foot to foot, Marion asked him what kind of singer he was. "'I sing all kinds," was his reply in this now famous exchange. Who did he sound like? "I don't sound like nobody" (*Rolling Stone*, February 13, 1986).

Given the seismic impact the two would have on American popular culture, it's tempting to characterize the initial meeting between Elvis and Sam Phillips as the momentous intersecting of two musical giants, but that's simply not the case. "There wasn't anything that striking about Elvis," Sam Phillips recounted later, "except his sideburns, which I kind of thought, well, you know, that's pretty cool, man. Ain't nobody else got them that long" (*Rolling Stone*, February 13, 1986).

After handing Marion $3.00 and pocketing two cents change, Elvis followed Sam, or Marion, depending on whom you believe, into the studio where, with the tape rolling, he completed versions of "My Happiness," a song performed by numerous artists, most prominently Ella Fitzgerald, in the late forties and "That's' When Your Heartaches Begin," a 1941 hit by the Ink Spots on which Elvis delivered an unintentionally hilarious spoken interlude. On both songs, Elvis accompanied himself on guitar, a sound that he'd later characterize as "somebody beating on a bucket lid" (1956 interview).

According to Sam, he waved Elvis into the control room when he was done and played him the completed tracks. It was at this point that Phillips noticed something about Elvis that he would never forget. "He tried not to show it," he was to say later, "but he felt so inferior. He reminded me of a black man in that way, his insecurity was so markedly like that of a black person" (Crouch, *Sun King*). As they listened to the playback, Sam sensed something in Elvis's voice—something he couldn't quite put his finger on—that stuck with him. If he found a song that suited him, he asked Elvis, would he be interested in recording again? After getting a stammered "Yes, sir" in reply, Sam led him back to the reception area, where he told Marion to write down Elvis's name and contact info, "just in case." Next to her scribbled notation, where she misspelled Elvis's surname as "Pressley," Marion added, "Good ballad singer. Hold."

In later years, Marion, notwithstanding her obvious affection for Sam, waxed bitter over the credit he received for discovering Elvis. After stating categorically that Phillips had misremembered the entire affair, she acidly stated that she hadn't seen the "great SCP [Sam Phillips]" recently and compared her experience at attempting (and failing) to get credit for discovering Elvis with "eating in a restaurant where the service is consistently poor and the food always unpalatable. If you keep going back, you forfeit the right to complain" (Moore and Dickerson, *That's Alright, Elvis*).

In late July, Elvis was laid off from his job at the machine shop and soon found himself back at the employment office, where he requested a job where he could "keep clean." In early fall, he was hired by a local tool manufacturer, where, for $1.55 per hour, he operated a drill press. On his days off, Elvis, still nursing dreams of a career in music, became a regular presence at Sun Studios, where he would make small talk and quiz Marion if she knew of a band in need of a singer. Sam would be there too, but popping in and out, seemingly too busy to spend much time with Elvis.

On January 4, Presley was back at Sun Studios, where he paid $8.25 for a second acetate and recorded a pair of mawkish tunes, "I'll Never Stand in Your Way" and "It Wouldn't Be the Same Without You," both featuring Elvis strumming an out-of-tune guitar. As lachrymose as the songs may be, Elvis's delivery was delicate and his voice appealing, suggesting that hours of singing in the hallways of The Courts and on Memphis front porches had paid off. In recent years, some biographers have characterized this session as a failure, suggesting that Presley's growing doubts about his chances of succeeding in music undermined his performance, but there's simply no evidence of that. In fact, Sam Phillips himself was later to grade the session as a success, his only concern being Elvis's overreliance on ballads. As he was to say later, he wanted something with a "little more tempo." Still, Sam remained interested; the kid, he felt, had something that was striving to reach him. It just hadn't ... yet.

In March of 1954, Elvis, hating the work and fed up with the razzing he was taking over his hair, quit the tool company. In mid–April, he landed a job driving a truck for Crown Electric; the job also came with an opportunity to train as an apprentice electrician, something that left Elvis conflicted. "I was in doubt as to whether I would ever make it, because you had to keep your mind right on what you're doing, you can't be the least bit absentminded or you're liable to blow somebody's house up. I didn't think I was the right type for it, but I was going to give it a try" (interview, 1956). The pay was 40 dollars a week, and it was understood that a portion of that would go to family expenses. As part of his duties, Elvis delivered supplies to industrial building sites around Memphis, which meant frequent trips past Sun Studios, something that didn't go unnoticed by Sam Phillips. "They sure are doing a hell of a lot of business around here," he thought to himself.

In April of 1954, Sam, still harboring a dream to bring R&B to white audiences and boost Sun's bottom line, saw something that surprised him. It was an article in *Billboard* magazine, titled "Teenagers Going for Music with a Beat," in which the magazine stated that society, or at least a youthful segment of it, was shifting towards R&B. "The teen-age tide has swept down the old barriers which kept rhythm and blues restricted at a segment of the population," it stated (*Billboard*, April 1954). As he devoured the article, Sam felt his hopes quicken, then just as quickly fade. Things were moving his way, of that he was sure. But he was also a realist. Rhythm and blues might be making inroads in places like New York or California, but this was the Deep South, where entrenched thinking still ruled radio playlists. "We were up a gum stump, so to speak," Sam said later. "The white disc jockeys wouldn't touch what they regarded as a negro's music, and the negro DJs didn't want anything to do with a record made by a white man." Still, change was inevitable, of that Phillips felt sure. But for it to take hold in Memphis, Sam knew he needed something—or maybe *someone*—to serve as a catalyst (www.elvis.com, June 28, 2008).

In the days and weeks following his January session, Elvis made repeated attempts at finding work as a singer. In late April, he secured and then failed an audition for the Songfellows, a local vocal quartet associated with the Blackwood gospel family. In May, resplendent in bolero jacket and pink shirt, he auditioned for a local band and was once again rejected. Years later, Elvis would dramatize this moment, suggesting that the band leader told him to "go back to driving a truck." True or not, the successive rejections left Elvis demoralized and gloomily weighing a future as an electrician.

By June, two months had elapsed since Sam Phillips had read the *Billboard* article suggesting that rhythm and blues was making inroads in white America. During that time, he'd weighed then swatted away as impractical numerous schemes for getting his music played on mainstream radio. But then, in early summer, something shifted in his mind. Maybe it was time, he thought, to wage his battle with a different cast. If the entrenched powers wouldn't play R&B, then maybe someone they deemed acceptable—in essence, an erstwhile Trojan horse—might induce them to. At that moment, Sam's mind flashed back to the kid who'd been hanging around lately, that kid with the sideburns. He possessed the fundamentals, of that Sam was sure. "He was the first one I had seen who had that potential," he said years later. "He had a different type of voice" (*Rolling Stone*, February 13, 1986). There was something else about the kid that Sam liked: he was *white*.

And so it was that on the afternoon of June 26, the phone rang in the Presley home. When Elvis answered, he heard the voice of Marion Keisker. Could he be at Sun Studios by 3:00 p.m. to record some additional material? In later years, Elvis would speak of that moment: "I was there before she hung up the phone" (interview, 1956). Once Elvis was in the studio, Sam, after a bit of small talk, sang the opening bars of "Without You," a song he thought might suit Elvis. To Sam's dismay, Elvis's performance of the tune was pallid and lackluster. Not giving up, Phillips asked Elvis to sing a bit of virtually every song he knew, hoping something might click with him. As Elvis ran through a series of wildly divergent songs, Sam realized for the first time that the boy's eclecticism was homegrown and that it stretched from pop to the pew. "I guess I must have sat there at least three hours," Elvis said later. "I sang everything I knew, pop stuff, spirituals, just a few words of anything I remembered" (Johnson, *Elvis Presley Speaks!*). Occasionally, Elvis glanced up at Sam in the control room in search of a smile, a nod, just any indication that Phillips liked what he heard, but none was forthcoming. Still, Sam continued to speak to Elvis in a measured tone, telling him to relax and just keep at it. And by all accounts, that's how the session ended, with Sam thanking Elvis and wishing him well, while giving no indication one way or the other of how he felt. Still, Elvis viewed the session as a hopeful sign. At the movies that night, Elvis leaned over to girlfriend Dixie Locke and whispered proudly that he'd been in a recording session earlier that day.

Scotty Moore

Winfield Scott Moore III was born on December 27, 1931, in Gadsden, Tennessee, 80 miles north of Memphis. He was the youngest of six in a musical family. "I have three brothers and I got the bug from them, I guess," Scotty recalls. "I remember my brother showed me one chord, just a good ol' long-handle A-chord, where you catch the A position with the little finger. I was maybe twelve by then, and I remember thinking, 'That's the most beautiful chord I've ever heard'" (Cronin, "The Sun King," *Country Guitar*, 1994).

His first guitar, a gift from his brother, was a Kalamazoo flattop acoustic. (Kalamazoo was a budget guitar line produced by Gibson between the years of 1933 and 1942.) "Two of my brothers were in the Navy," Scotty recalled later, "and the one next to me had bought a Gene Autry archtop, I think from Sears."

> It was a beautiful and shiny guitar and of course I didn't know anything
> about guitars and such then. And I had this little Kalamazoo which my

other brother had given me. So my other brother, Darrell, was fixing to be shipped off to the South Pacific and he says, "I don't want to take this beautiful guitar out there in the salt water. Let's trade guitars." And which foolish me, I did and I didn't know till years later that I got the wrong end of the deal. (Laughs) [Woods, *Vintage Guitar*, 1993].

Uninspired by school, Scotty dropped out at 14 and went to work on the family farm, a decision that paid dividends in one sense (providing enough money to buy a Gibson "jumbo," his first professional guitar), but also saddled him with a distaste for back-breaking labor. After a brief stint back at school, Scotty, at just 16, followed the lead of his brothers and joined the Navy. "I just had ants in my pants," he recalls. "I had tried farming and I thought 'I'm not digging this.' I didn't dig school. I think my brothers had something to do with it. I just wanted to do everything they did" (Moore and Dickerson, *That's Alright, Elvis*).

While in the service, Scotty, nurturing a growing love of music, fell in with a group of servicemen who would jam with him at the recreation hall or on the Navy vessel the *Valley Forge*. While playing at an off-base private party, Scotty met brunette, 18-year-old Mary Durkee; the two would soon marry. Once discharged from the Navy in 1952, Scotty and his wife returned to the Moore farm in Tennessee, but farm life and the family's strict religious beliefs didn't set well with Mary and they soon divorced. Sometime later, Scotty, while still dreaming of a life in music, started work at his brother's dry-cleaning business, cleaning and blocking hats. But weekends were mostly spent toting his newly purchased Fender Esquire guitar around Beale Street clubs in search of a gig or haunting record shops for new releases from his guitar heroes, Chet Atkins and Merle Travis.

As time passed and he honed his chops, Scotty snagged the occasional gig with local notables like Clyde Leoppard and his Snearly Ranch Boys, one of whom characterized Scotty as a "good straight country picker." During this period, the gigs came and went and the money Scotty earned during this period was, in his words, "paltry." As his confidence grew, Scotty decided to start a group of his own, but only with players he deemed sufficiently serious about making a living in music. So, in 1952, the Starlite Wranglers—a cowboy-hatted, revolving cast of honky-tonkers that at first played primarily on the weekends—was born. "We might end up with a trumpet, a steel guitar player, you know, any combination," Scotty said, "but everybody had to be able to play a little bit of what was currently the top pop tunes and country tunes, and be able to do some rhythm and blues. But above all, it had to be played where people could dance to it" (Woods, *Vintage Guitar*, 1993).

Sensing a future for the Wranglers, Scotty had a lawyer draw up a legal agreement, designating himself a manager and stipulating profit percentages for each member. When he wasn't toiling at his brother's dry-cleaning establishment, Scotty spent every waking moment promoting the Wranglers and attempting to expand their following. "I knew we had to get a radio show or a record out and get it played on the radio to get more publicity and better pay," he said later. "They might not like you any better, but you could say 'But we're on the radio' and ask for a little bit more" (Burke and Griffin, *The Blue Moon Boys*). Which is exactly what he said to Sam Phillips that first day at Sun Studios. "I met Sam when I was trying to get the group on record," Scotty recalls. "Sam was looking for talent, he was a very small operation at that time and we became friends" (1973 interview, Music City Recorders, Nashville).

Sam, a fount of unsuppressed passion and energy, and Scotty, a musical cousin and a good listener, clicked almost immediately. Over time, the two became so close they would meet almost daily at Taylor's, the little café next door to Sun Studios, where they'd sip coffee, talk music, and share goals. For Scotty, listening intently as Sam shared his dreamy yet disruptive notions about society and the musical changes he felt convinced were just around the corner, church was in session. "He knew there was a crossover coming," Scotty said later. "He foresaw that. I think that recording all those black artists had to give him an insight; he just didn't know where that insight would lead. Sam came from pretty much the same background as the rest of us, basically. We were just looking for something, we didn't know quite what it was. We would just sit there over coffee and say to each other 'What is it? What should we do? How can we do it?'" ("The Guitar That Changed the World," *Goldmine*, August 23, 1991).

During one meeting, Scotty raised the issue of his own group: Would Sam be interested in recording the Starlite Wranglers? As it turned out, he was, so a few days later, Scotty and his group were in the studio, laying down licks they hoped would win them a recording deal. "You sound good, pretty tight," Sam said after they ran through a few of their numbers. "Have you got any originals?" (Burke and Griffin, *The Blue Moon Boys*). Encouraged, Scotty, along with bandmate Doug Poindexter, quickly wrote "Now She Cares No More" and "My Kinda' Carrying On," both heavily country and miles away from the type of music Sun Studios would ultimately be known for. Still, Sam, finding the songs reasonably commercial, issued them as the A- and B-sides of a Sun release in May of 1954. "Well, he worked with us and he put it out on Sun," Scotty recalls. "Sam was great to experiment. He didn't have any money, we didn't have any money, but he was willing to try" (Woods, *Vintage Guitar*, 1993). But the record went nowhere, and Scotty and the

Wranglers, who'd undertaken the entire project on spec and received nothing in payment, soon resumed their routine of playing juke joints.

At this point, Elvis reappears in our story, and this is where things start to get a bit murky. According to Sam, in the weeks since he'd released "My Kind of Carryin' On," he'd been thinking more and more about Presley. The session back in January hadn't yielded much, but he saw potential and wasn't ready to give up. But Marion Keisker remembers it differently. According to her, she sensed something in Elvis and, for weeks, continually raised his name with Sam. Whatever the truth, by early July Sam had decided to give Elvis another shot, this time with an assist from Scotty, who yearned to escape a future of blocking hats for a living. In his version of how Elvis came into his life, Scotty points to an afternoon meeting at Taylor's. "This particular day," Scotty says, "it was about five in the afternoon—Marion was having coffee with us and Sam said 'Get his [Elvis's] name and phone number out of the file.' Then he turned to me and said 'Why don't you give him a call and get him to come over to your house and see what you think of him?'" (interview with Jerry Hopkins).

Phillips remembers it differently. "I called Scotty," Sam recalls. "He was working at his brother's dry-cleaning establishment between gigs with the Starlite Wranglers." Would Scotty be interested in playing on a Sun session with a local kid? When the answer came back affirmative, Sam posed another question. "I said 'Scotty, pick out who you think would be good to work with on the rhythm.' He picked out Bill Black" (1997 interview).

Bill Black

The oldest of 10 children, William Patton Black, Jr., was born in Memphis in 1926. Influenced by a father who played fiddle and banjo, Bill's first instrument was a rudimentary bass that he fashioned out of a cigar box and strings that were nailed to a board. A natural musician, Bill was playing guitar by age 10 and, while still in his teens, was picking up gigs in Memphis honky-tonks. In the last year of World War II, he was drafted into the army. While stationed at Fort Lee in Virginia, he met 15-year-old Evelyn Ercell, and following a brief courtship they were married the following year. Following his discharge, the couple returned to Memphis, where after bouncing around a bit, Bill landed steady work at the local Firestone tire plant. At night, Black, who by this time was playing upright bass, would haunt Beale Street clubs, seeking out the musically inclined for jam sessions and lobbying for paying gigs.

How Bill Black and Scotty Moore first encountered one another is unclear. In later years, Scotty suggested that it was at a jam session at a seen-better-days hangout an hour from Memphis called Shadow Lawn, but the fact that they became fast friends is not in doubt. In fact, the friendship grew so close that Scotty not only invited Bill to join the Starlite Wranglers, but also at one point moved into an apartment just doors down from Black.

During this phase, Bill played a Kay upright bass, the perfect instrument to complement his penchant for stage antics. How it started is subject to debate—some point to Bob Wills and his Texas Playboys—but beginning in the late 1940s, upright bass players, in addition to providing aural "ass" to their musical aggregations, were also expected to supply a measure of comic relief. Whoever gets the credit—or blame, depending on your perspective on this trend—it's clear that by the 1950s, the role of the "bassist as buffoon" was firmly cemented in the mind of music lovers. Affable and outgoing, Black was more than ready to assume this role for the Starlite Wranglers, and during this period he would often dress like a hayseed, straddle his bass like a horse, and leer madly at the audience through blackened-out front teeth. "Daddy loved to make people laugh," his son Louis said later. "He said 'We all got enough problems out here. Everybody's struggling trying to make a living. If I can give 'em a few moments of entertainment and maybe a little bit of humor that'll tickle 'em for a while, they can forget all their mess for a little bit'" (Burke and Griffin, *The Blue Moon Boys*).

On July 3, Scotty Moore, in response to Sam's urging, picked up the phone and rang the Presley home. After identifying himself as a "Sun Studios talent scout," he asked for Elvis. "He's at the movies," Gladys replied. Could he call Scotty back? A few minutes later, she was hastily scanning the rows at the downtown Suzore Theatre when she spotted her son. "Scotty Moore of Sun Records" was trying to reach him, she told him. Once back home, Elvis dialed Scotty, who asked Elvis if he'd be available for an audition the following day at his house. Not surprisingly, the answer was an enthusiastic "Yes."

The next day, Elvis, guitar in hand, knocked on the door of Scotty's apartment. "So Elvis came over," Scotty remembers, "and he had the pink shirt, pink pants with the typical ducktail hairstyle at the time, white shoes, which ... well he was a little ahead of his time for the way he was dressed which didn't bother me one way or the other 'cause I was interested in what he sounded like singing" (1973 interview, Music City Recorders, Nashville).

Once Elvis was inside, Scotty asked his wife to walk down to Bill Black's house and ask him to join them. A few minutes later, Bill arrived, and after a quick introduction, Scotty turned to Elvis and told him to "just play what you feel." While undoubtedly significant in the history of popular music, this meeting provided no hint of the rock 'n' roll rebel Presley would ultimately become. For the next few minutes, Elvis played nothing but ballads, each delivered at virtually the same tempo, each accompanied by his fluttering tenor and rudimentary guitar playing. Scotty's wife, initially curious about this young man in alien attire and greased-up hair, quickly grew bored with the non-stop balladry and slipped out the back door for a visit with Evelyn Black.

When Scotty signaled that he'd heard enough, he thanked Elvis and told him he'd "be in touch." Once he'd departed, Scotty turned to Bill. "What do you think?" "Well, ya know," Bill replied, "he didn't really impress me." Nonetheless, he did allow that "the cat sang pretty good." After Bill departed, Moore reached for the phone and dialed Sam Phillips. The kid didn't knock him out, Scotty told him, though he had good timing and a good voice. After thinking for a moment, Sam said, "Let's go into the studio and see what he sounds like on tape." Did Sam want a whole band to back Elvis up? "Nah," Phillips replied, "just you and Bill come over, just something for a little rhythm. No use making a big deal out of it" (Green, "Perhaps the First Rock & Roll Guitarist," *Guitar Player*, 1974).

Good Rockin' Tonight

"Men's stiff collars wilted by nine in the morning. Ladies bathed before noon, after their three o'clock naps, and by nightfall were like soft teacakes with frostings of sweat and sweet talcum. The day was twenty-four hours long, but it seemed longer."—Harper Lee, *To Kill a Mockingbird*

As innumerable chroniclers of Southern life have made clear, Memphis summers are not to be taken lightly. With average daily temperatures hovering at or near 100 degrees, no one who can avoid it dares to venture out after mid-morning. Clear days are bad enough, but when it rains and the humidity spikes, the moist air is converted into an airless and oppressive cupola that compels even the hardiest to seek shade. July 1, 1954, had dawned with clear, azure skies, but by mid-afternoon, storm clouds gathered and rain began to pelt Memphis streets, the moisture adding a stifling stagnation to air that felt dense enough to cut.

Inside 706 Union Avenue, there was no relief to be found. Wall-mounted air conditioners, increasingly prevalent during the 1950s, were nowhere in evidence; this was a recording studio, after all, and the incessant drone they generated would make recording sessions impossible. Anyway, Sun was being run at this point on nickels and dimes, and any thought of air-cooling devices more sophisticated than a few fans was ludicrous. In short, the working conditions at Sun Studios in the summer of 1954 were nothing short of brutal, and by late afternoon, the tie draped around Sam Phillips's neck hung loosely and his dress shirt was limp with sweat.

The Music—July 5–6, 1954—Sun Studios, Memphis

On July 5, Elvis arrived at Sun Studios at 7:00 p.m. for his first non-self-financed recording session. After some quick hellos, the session, essentially a continuation of the audition of the day before, began with Elvis, Scotty, and Bill working on "Harbor Lights," a Bing Crosby hit from 1950 that was likely selected because it was the only song that all three knew all the way through. Plaintive, dirge-like, and with a middle-eight burdened by a whistling passage from Elvis, "Harbor Lights" was nowhere close to what Sam was looking for.

The next song they attempted was "I Love You Because," a ballad that had been a recent country hit for Ernest Tubb. As Presley worked his way through the song, Sam struggled to hide his agitation. To Phillips, Elvis's approach was all wrong. He was focusing too much on ballads, and, most critically, he was imitating not originating. First it was Crosby, now he was trying to sound like Ernest Tubb. Sam's approach to record making might best be summed up by "Harmonica Frank" Floyd, a blues musician who worked with Phillips in 1951. "Old Sam had one thing to tell me," Floyd recalled. "Said it over and over. 'Gimme something different. Gimme something unique'" (Marcus, *Mystery Train*).

Phillips, who'd been impatiently drumming his fingers in the control room, finally rose from his chair and approached the three musicians in the studio. "I told Elvis, Scotty and Bill, 'We want to look for things that we can do in a medium-to-real-up tempo. We've got to approach this thing to try to get the attention of younger people and I knew that tempo had a lot to do with that, rather than just a great lyric and beautiful melody'" ("The Man Who Invented Rock & Roll," *Rolling Stone*, 1998).

With his words falling upon deaf ears, the session ground on, with seemingly endless attempts at nailing down something fresh falling flat. Finally, frustrated and dismayed, Sam saw no point in continuing. It was late, he announced from the control room. They all had to be at work the next day. Maybe they'd try it again the next night. Or, the unspoken implication was, maybe they wouldn't.

At that moment, Elvis, realizing that another Bing Crosby or Earnest Tubb cover might send Sam screaming from the building, decided that *it was here* that he would make his stand. Or perhaps, he'd just run out of fucks to give. Whatever the explanation, he reached for his guitar.

"Elvis picks up the guitar and starts just bangin' on it," Scotty recalls, "and starts singing 'That's All Right' [a blues track first performed by Arthur 'Big Boy' Crudup], just a tension release, you know, doing something to break the monotony. And Bill picked up his bass and started slapping the strings, and I started trying to get in somewhere with what was going on" (*The Elvis Presley Story*, Watermark Inc., Radio Documentary, 1971).

"The door to the control room was open," Sam recalled later.

The mics were on, Scotty was in the process of packing up his guitar, I think Bill had already thrown his old bass down—he didn't even have a cover for it—and the session was, to all intents and purposes, over. Then Elvis struck up on just his rhythm guitar, "That's All Right, Mama" and I mean he got my attention immediately. That was what I was looking for! There was no question in my mind. I didn't give a damn what the song was. That was the sound, the feel, even the tempo. I think we moved the tempo around, but we didn't do much to that song, man. We did a couple, three, maybe four takes on it, and we had something that we had been looking for months ["The Man Who Invented Rock & Roll," *Rolling Stone*, 1998].

In the decades since, *that moment*—the second that Elvis launched into "That's All Right"—has been characterized as either one of the most monumental cultural events of the twentieth century or, in the words of Frank Sinatra, the birth of "a music sung, played and written for the most part by cretinous goons." For Sam Phillips, it was the sound of the wall that separated black music and white audiences about to crumble.

Critically important to the appeal of "That's All Right" is the innovative fretwork of Scotty Moore. "On the lead, I was thinking about horns, like a horn riff," he recalls.

I was a fan of Merle Travis—I'd never seen him, but I'd heard the records. I sat at home and listened to how him and Chet [Atkins] did the thumb and finger stuff—I could tell it was the thumb they were using. Up until then I'd been playing straight pick, so when we did "That's All Right," I started doing it that way. But it needed more rhythm. I must have had the thumb pick in my pocket from when I was playing at home, so I started doing the finger thing and putting these little stab notes in [Cronin, *Country Guitar*, 1994].

For the next two nights, Sam, Elvis, Scotty, and Bill were once again back in the studio, this time for Elvis's first "official" Sun session (he'd clearly passed his audition the day before). But any hope that the magic of Monday night might be rekindled was quickly dashed. Nothing seemed to jell, and repeated attempts to lock down an acceptable take of the one song they focused on—the Rodgers and Hart standard "Blue Moon" that had been a 1949 hit for Billy Eckstine—failed. Still, the session was beneficial, providing Elvis, Scotty, and Bill with an invaluable opportunity to get better acquainted, personally and musically.

Late Wednesday night, Sam reached for his phone and dialed Dewey Phillips at WHBQ. Dewey—someone Rufus Thomas once described as "a man who just happens to be white"—was on a roll at this point, effortlessly able to tap into the teenage gestalt via his nightly *Red, Hot & Blue* radio show. For disc jockeys in the 1950s, it was all about hits and discovering and playing them before anyone else. For most DJs, this meant regular meetings with record company reps and listening as they pitched their latest product in hopes of striking auditory gold. But schmoozing with promo men held little fascination for Dewey Phillips. Seeing no value in wasting time with middlemen, Phillips would approach distributors on his own, badgering them for new releases by hot artists. When that approach didn't produce results, there was always Sam Phillips, with whom Dewey had forged a close friendship. Interestingly, Marion Keisker, unlike Sam, viewed Dewey Phillips with contempt and tried to avoid ever being in the same room with him.

Over the past two years, Sam and Dewey had forged an arrangement. If Sam found an artist he was enthused about, he'd cut an acetate and hand it off to Dewey, who, trusting in Sam's instincts, would usually play it on his show. Depending on the level of enthusiasm from Dewey's listeners, Sam would either sign the artist or send them on their way. So when Dewey answered the phone Wednesday night and heard the excitement in Sam's voice, he wasted no time in telling Sam he'd stop by Sun Studios later that night.

Sometime after midnight, Sam, with Dewey at his side and a six-pack of Falstaff beer in front of them, hit the play button on the Lathe recorder in the Sun Studios control room. Depending on the year, Sam Phillips's memory of how Dewey reacted to "That's All Right" varies; in one account, Dewey's response was akin to a sonic gut punch. "Goddam, man," Sam recalls Dewey yelling once the song was done. "I got to have it!" At other times, Sam remembers Dewey sitting wordlessly—"reticent," in his words—as the song played over and over, only to have Dewey ring him early the next morning saying he couldn't get "That's All Right" out of his head. What is clear, however, is that Dewey wanted a dub; "That's All Right" would be featured on his *Red, Hot & Blue* show that night.

The next day, Sam cut two acetates and dropped them off at WHBQ's front office, then rang Elvis with the news that his song would premiere on Dewey's program in just hours. But instead of being thrilled at the news, Elvis reacted with alarm. And when "That's All Right" hit the airwaves later that night, he was at the movies. "I thought people would laugh at me," he said later. "Some did. Some are still laughing, I guess" (*Saturday Evening Post*, 1965).

"Get yasself a wheelbarrow load of mad hogs," Dewey screamed as he cued up the acetate, "and run 'em through the front door and tell 'em Phillips sentcha! This is Red Hot and Blue comin' atcha from the Hotel Chisca. And now we got somethin' new! Good people, this is Elvis Presley!" And with that, a Presley record was played over the public airwaves for the first time. (elviscommercialappeal.com, 2012).

By the time the last notes of "That's All Right" faded, the phone lines in the WHBQ control room were afire. For Dewey Phillips—and for DJs everywhere—listener feedback was essential, providing the surest sign you were doing something right or, conversely, a sobering message you'd missed your mark. But for the next 10 minutes, every call that Dewey received had the same request: "Play it again!" Phillips, needing no encouragement and spouting "Daddy-O-Dewey has the hits!" proceeded to spin "That's All Right" seven more times without interruption.

In Memphis, you were either in or you were out. Dewey Phillips was "in," which meant that his show was must-listen radio no matter where you were, even a sock hop at the Holy Rosary Catholic Church. "Sometime during the evening, a couple went out to the parking lot," Memphis resident Billie Chiles recalls, "and turned their car radio on. They came running downstairs yelling, 'Come up here quick! You ain't going to believe what Dewey Phillips is playing on the radio!'" (Burk, *Early Elvis: The Humes Years*).

At home, crouched before the radio, Gladys Presley sat in stunned disbelief. "Hearing them say his name over the radio just before they put on that record. That shook me," she said later (Dundy, *Elvis and Gladys*). As she and Vernon gabbed excitedly, the phone rang. It was Dewey Phillips, looking for Elvis. When Gladys explained that he was at the movies, Dewey, in a motor-mouth cadence, told Gladys to get her "cotton-picking son down to the WHBQ studios now!" After pulling up at Memphis's Suzore Theatre, Vernon and Gladys quickly prowled row after row until they spotted Elvis and relayed the message.

Minutes later, fidgety and jigging his legs, Elvis was seated next to Phillips in the WHBQ control room. After telling Dewey that he'd never been interviewed before, Phillips replied, "Just don't say nothing dirty." "He sat down," Dewey recalls, "and I said I'd let him know when we were ready to start. I asked him where he went to high school, and he said 'Humes.' I wanted to get that out, because a lot of people listening had thought he was colored. Finally, I said, 'All right Elvis, thank you very much.' 'Aren't you going to interview me?' he asked. 'I already have,' I said. 'That mike's been open the whole time.' He broke out in a cold sweat" (*Esquire*, "A Hound Dog to the Manor Born," February 1968).

When his shift ended, Dewey rang his wife. What did she think? "I told him I loved it," Dot Phillips recalled later. "He went on to say he believed Elvis had a hit. Dewey cherished that moment with Elvis. He would tell it time and time again" ("Memories of Elvis Shared by a Close Friend," *Trenton Herald Gazette*, 1978).

For years to come, Elvis would speak of Thursday, July 8, 1954, as a turning point, one that signaled a stunning and seismic shift in his fortunes. For Sam Phillips, who sat in the Sun control room sipping a beer as it all unfolded, the events of the evening were an affirmation of what he'd felt all along: that with the right singer and the right song, he could bring his brand of R&B to an entirely new audience. And if he needed further convincing (he didn't), he'd have it the following day when advance orders for "That's All Right" flooded the Sun offices. The evidence was everywhere: Sam Phillips had a hit.

It's what he didn't have that troubled him.

6

"That's a pop song, nearly about"

When he arrived at Sun Studios on Friday, Sam Phillips had to confront two challenges, both triggered by the outsized public response to "That's All Right" the night before. First, he had to get Elvis, Scotty, and Bill officially signed to Sun Records. Secondly, with orders pouring in for actual vinyl that radio stations could play, he had to rush all three back to the studio to fashion a flip side to "That's All Right." A lack of studio documentation makes it difficult to pinpoint precisely when these sessions started; Scotty Moore later stated that the group spent "three-or-four nights" woodshedding, tossing out songs and ideas in the hope that something might click. If that's true, then, counting backwards, it's likely that the initial session began on Friday, July 9.

The Music—July 9, 1954—Sun Studios, Memphis

Once in the studio, Elvis, along with Scotty and Bill, struggled at first to fashion a flip side to "That's All Right." "If you listen to some of the very first recordings you can tell we were just experimenting," Scotty Moore said later. "Sam was listening to Elvis' voice; we were doing the best we could with two instruments" (Woods, *Vintage Guitar*, November 1992). Then, as it sometimes does, the mood in the studio shifted and Bill Black suddenly broke into a cartoonish falsetto and began frenetically slapping the strings of his bass. "Bill started whacking his bass on both sides with his hands and singing 'Blue Moon of Kentucky,' an old Bill Monroe song, which was originally in waltz time," Scotty Moore says. "Elvis knew the words and he started singing along up-tempo with Bill" (Wingate, "The Guitar Man," *Music Mart*, 2005). Poking his head out of the control room, Sam Phillips was delighted. "Hell, that's different," he said. "That's a pop song, nearly about"

(*The Complete Sun Sessions*, RCA, 1987). That was all the encouragement Elvis, Scotty, and Bill needed. Sensing that they'd hit pay dirt, they ran the song again, working out their parts before devising the combustible opening so key to the tune's appeal.

The completed studio master is propelled by Elvis's vocal and guitar and bolstered by Black's dynamic slap bass attack that creates the illusion of percussion, a technique he developed by loosening the top string of his bass while generating rhythm on the instrument's second and third strings. "Blue Moon of Kentucky" jumps from the speakers at a breakneck pace, and the song's instrumental breaks showcase three musicians in nothing less than an epic groove. It wasn't quite rock and it wasn't R&B. It wasn't even country. In fact, Bill Monroe, upon hearing Elvis's version of "Blue Moon of Kentucky," said he "hated it." What it was, in fact, was the stirring of a cross-cultural music form that, for lack of a better word, would soon be known as rockabilly.

"Blue Moon of Kentucky" is also notable as the first track to showcase Sam Phillips's use of echo. In 1954, Phillips acquired two state-of-the-art Ampex 350 recorders and immediately began tinkering with their features. At some point, he found himself wondering what would happen if he ran a recorded signal from the first recorder through the second Ampex machine. The result intrigued him. The physical distance between the machines produced an audible delay, resulting in an echo that Sam dubbed "slapback," an effect that, in days to come, would become a crucial component of the Sun Studios sound.

In truth, Sam Phillips's inventiveness didn't end there. In the months leading up to the recording of "That's All Right" and "Blue Moon of Kentucky," Sam, in a quixotic quest to make his records sound like no one else's, started fiddling around with sound levels, in this case messing with how voices and musical backing interacted. "If you go way back and listen to those old records like Bing Crosby, the singer will be way out in front of the music, even if it's a huge orchestra," Scotty Moore remembers. "Well, that was the first thing that hit me when Sam recorded Elvis, because there wasn't a bunch of us and he made Elvis' voice like another instrument. He put the voice closer to the music, and that hadn't really been done before, not to my knowledge" (Wingate, "The Guitar Man," *Music Mart*, 2005).

Today, producer and former Sun Studios engineer Curry Weber agrees. "He felt that the rhythm section needed to be enhanced ... so he would push the microphones closer in onto the instruments," Weber states. "That was so unorthodox at the time, but the station owners really loved the way the broadcast sounded on the radio" (Weber, *Popular Mechanics*, August 16, 2014).

As both Moore and Weber make clear, bringing Elvis's voice closer to the music was critical to the appeal of Presley's early work. Today, some 70 years on, someone listening to "Blue Moon of Kentucky" and "That's All Right" might still marvel that all that noise came from just three musicians. All of which makes the reaction of early promoters understandable: upon hearing Elvis's early recordings and fully expecting a four- or five-piece band to walk in the door, they would register shock when just Elvis, Scotty, and Bill sashayed in.

It's also important to note that, for Elvis, "That's All Right" would kneecap a potential future as full-time balladeer and refashion it into something fresh and vital; with "That's All Right," Presley's essence is revealed, and over the next four years, he would, in seemingly effortless succession, release some of the most influential and powerful songs in music history and, not incidentally, sing them better than anyone ever could. Of course, nobody gets away clean, and, in future years, wealth and indulgence would cloud his vision and the lessons of July 1954 would be forgotten. But for now, the *juju* had been summoned and his future was ablaze with potential.

On July 19, Sun Records rush released "That's All Right" and "Blue Moon of Kentucky" to radio stations throughout the south, with the label crediting the tune to "Elvis Presley with Scotty and Bill." In the years since, "That's All Right" has achieved near mythic stature in the history of popular music, viewed by many as nothing less than rock's "big bang," a seismic event that kickstarted a musical and cultural revolution. To bolster that perspective, one just needs to examine the lives of such foundational figures as Sam Phillips, Scotty Moore, and Dewey Phillips who literally spent the remaining decades of their lives recounting where they were and what they were doing when the song sprang into existence.

Some pundits have even gone so far as to suggest that on the night of July 5, 1954, with "That's All Right," Elvis Presley single-handedly invented an entirely new musical form. "It is vital to remember," Greil Marcus stated in his dated but still venerated essay "Elvis Presliad," that "Elvis was the first young Southern white to sing rock 'n' roll, *something he copied from no one but made up on the spot* [emphasis mine]" (Marcus, *Mystery Train–Images of America in Rock 'N' Roll Music*). As even as late as 2004, one national publication—*Rolling Stone*—followed suit, stating in no uncertain terms in an article titled "Truck Driver Invents Rock" that Presley had invented the genre (*Rolling Stone*, June 24, 2004).

Scotty Moore himself, whom you figure should know, once described "That's All Right" as "raw" and "completely different" from anything that preceded it.

Early Sun Records promotion, trumpeting the success of Elvis, Scotty, and Bill's first single.

All of this, of course, is hooey. Even a cursory listen to the post-war output of artists like Junior Parker, John Lee Hooker and others makes it clear that what has come to be known as rock 'n' roll was in fact being played in road houses and juke joints throughout the South at least a decade prior to 1954. Further, Marcus's claim that Presley was the first young Southern white to sing rock 'n' roll is also demonstrably false, with Carl Perkins serving as a prime example of his errancy. Perkins, as a member of the Perkins Brothers, gigged in Tennessee juke palaces and taverns as early as 1946, playing a hybrid of country and blues, in essence, an early version of the musical form that in future years would be dubbed rockabilly. When rock pioneer Gene Vincent was asked if "That's All Right" and "Blue Moon of Kentucky" were examples of a completely new sound, he demurred, saying that "a lot of people were doing it before that, especially Carl Perkins" (Venhecke, *Race with the Devil*), a fact that Scotty Moore himself finally acknowledged in 1992: "I mean, it was a fluke that it all happened," Moore said, "because that kind of music was being played all through the Southeast—Louisiana, Arkansas, Mississippi, Tennessee" (*Guitarist*, November 1992).

"That's All Right" may have been "raw" when compared to the cheese that preceded it that July 5 night ("Harbor Lights" and "I Love You Because"), but in truth, it simply cannot compete with the grit and stripped-down authenticity of Arthur Crudup's original, which sounds like it was recorded in a Tennessee shotgun shack on a whiskey-soaked midnight. Additionally, Scotty's earlier "completely different" claim is shot down by even a cursory examination of pre–1954 R&B. 1947's "You Got to Run Me Down" by Jazz Gillum, 1948's "Boogie Chillin" by John Lee Hooker, and 1950's "The Fat Man" by Fats Domino are just three of many songs that summon the tempo and feel that imbues "That's All Right" with its swing.

Elvis, to his credit, would never claim he'd invented anything and regularly dismissed suggestions that he had. "The colored folks been singing it and playing it just like I'm doin' now, man, for more years than I know," he said in 1956. "They played it like that in the shanties and in their juke joints and nobody paid it no mind 'til I goosed it up. I got it from them" ("Elvis Presley Is a Worried Man," *Charlotte Observer*, June 27, 1956).

What *was* different about "That's All Right" and what Sam Phillips, Elvis, Scotty, and Bill can fully take credit for is, first, redefining the musical genre that would come to be known as "rock 'n' roll" as guitar-based and not horn- and keyboard-centric (as exemplified by such pioneers as "Big Joe" Turner and Fats Domino) and secondly, migrating R&B away from large aggregations so common at the time to three- or four-piece combos, and in so doing, create the world's first rock 'n' roll band: Elvis Presley, Scotty Moore, and Bill Black.

All of which brings us back to Sam Phillips and his oft-stated dream of desegregating American music. After hearing Elvis kick into "That's All Right" on July 5, he may have said, "Hell, that's different," but he knew better. From an early age, Sam had cut his teeth on, schooled himself in, and, by 1954, arguably knew more about R&B than any white man in the Deep South ever had. What was different, and what, in the end, would enable Sam to fulfill his dream of expanding the audience for his music, boils down to one man: Elvis Presley. In the coming months, Presley would tap into something primal, an undercurrent of youthful rebellion that, once unleashed, would take on the strapped-down cultural values of the 1950s and, in so doing, transform himself into a national figure of youthful insurrection. All of this enabled Presley, through intuition, not design, to kick down walls of resistance that Sam Phillips had only flailed at. But all that was for another day, because now, Sam had found what he'd been looking for. As he was to state countless times in the coming decades, "I knew he had the fundamentals of what I wanted" (*Rolling Stone*, February 13, 1986). And what Sam Phillips wanted, what he'd always wanted, was a white boy who could sing the blues. And now he had it.

Given the enthusiastic public response to "That's All Right" and "Blue Moon of Kentucky," Sam found himself on the receiving end of enthusiastic requests from Memphis DJs for copies of the new songs. Prominent among these was Bob Neal, host of *High Noon Roundup* on WMPS, and, curiously, "Sleepy-Eyed John" Estes at WHHM, who in the past had been critical of Sam Phillips and music that came from Sun Studios. Sleepy-Eyed John's sudden enthusiasm initially perplexed Sam, until he realized that Estes, who fancied himself as a businessman extraordinaire, had designs on managing Elvis. In an attempt to head him off, Sam convinced Scotty to act as Elvis's manager.

"It was really just a ploy to tell you the truth," Scotty Moore said later.

> When the radio station got to playing the first record pretty heavy, several people around Memphis started calling Elvis wanting to book him, manage him, or do this or that. He didn't know what to tell them or how to deal with it. We were talking about it one day and Sam said, "Well, I'll tell you what Elvis. Do a management contract and that way you can tell people that you're already under contract. Then you won't be lying or anything. Just do it for a year and that will give us time to look around and find somebody we all like" [Wood, *Vintage Guitar*, 1993].

And so it was that on Monday, July 12, Scotty Moore, who'd known Elvis Presley for a total of eight days, signed a managerial contract that stated:

"Whereas, W.S. Moore, III, is a band leader and a booking agent, and Elvis Presley, a minor age 19 years, is a singer of reputation and renown, and possesses bright promises of large success, it is the desire of both parties to enter into this personal management contract for the best interests of both parties."

In addition to naming Scotty as manager, it also allowed Moore to "take over the complete management and professional affairs of Elvis Presley, book him professionally for all appearances" and "promote him, generally in his professional endeavours." In exchange for these services, Scotty would receive "ten percent of all earnings from engagements, appearances and bookings made by him." At the same time, Elvis, Scotty, and Bill agreed to divvy up all future proceeds at a 50–25–25 split, an agreement that was sealed with nothing more than handshakes and one that would later haunt both Moore and Black. Later that day, Scotty, contract in hand, met with Elvis and Gladys and Vernon Presley to get their signatures. At this point, Elvis was still a minor and needed a parent's signature to make the agreement legally binding.

With the ink still drying on the contract, Scotty quickly arranged

Elvis and the Blue Moon Boys in this early promotional shot. Left to right: Scotty Moore, Elvis Presley, and Bill Black (*Memphis Press-Scimitar*).

for Elvis, Bill, and himself to perform publicly for the first time the following weekend as special guests of the Starlite Wranglers at the Bon Air Club on the outskirts of town. On Saturday, July 17, the three, with Scotty and Bill now calling themselves "The Blue Moon Boys" in homage to their most recently recorded tune, stepped onstage to an audience Sam Phillips would later describe as "pure redneck" and played the only two songs they knew. The reaction was mild, and when it was over, Elvis was despondent, convinced, despite assurances from Sam, that he'd bombed.

In coming days, the trio would once again support the Wranglers, only to discover that Wrangler vocalist Doug Poindexter openly resented sharing the stage with the flashy kid in the crazy clothes. As time passed, his disdain would extend to Moore and Black, who, though still members of the Wranglers, were now steadily moonlighting with Elvis. Though, in Scotty's words, there wasn't "fallout," Elvis and the Blue Moon Boys would soon split from the Wranglers for good. Years later, Doug Poindexter commented on the dustup. "At the time, the record business was in a funny state," he recalled, "and I wasn't sure that I wanted to go with it. Scotty and Bill had the chance to go to Shreveport with Elvis and they wanted to go ahead with it, but I stayed in Memphis. Sam forgot about me and I guess it was for the best. There was no way of knowing that success was coming to Presley. Frankly, I thought the boy would starve to death" (Escott and Hawkins, *Sun Records: The Brief History of the Legendary Label*). Poindexter, who would leave the music business for good in late 1954, would ultimately go to work for Continental Baking Company, the outfit responsible for such staples of the American diet as Twinkies and Wonder Bread. He died in 2004, characterized by fellow Sun recording artist Barbara Pittman as one of the bitterest men she'd ever known.

In the days following, the trio, in need of a setlist, kicked off a series of rehearsals in a room above the dry cleaners where Scotty worked. In addition to "That's All Right" and "Blue Moon of Kentucky," songs that would ultimately make the group's repertoire included "Tweedlee Dee," a song originally done by LaVern Baker in 1954; "Money Honey," a Drifters hit from 1953; and "Fool, Fool, Fool" by the doo-wop group the Clovers. During this period, Elvis was mentored by both Scotty and Bill on how to behave in front of a crowd and on the ways of show business in general. In the end, all three would take divergent roads, but for now, and for the ensuing two years, they would live like brothers.

As they fleshed out their setlist, Elvis and the Blue Moon Boys picked up gigs in Memphis area juke joints and roadhouses including Sleepy-Eyed John's Eagle's Nest. Initially, they played only during intermissions, but as their following grew, they were quickly elevated to top billing. "I had to bring him on and then I had to follow him," recalls Jack Clement, who fronted the Eagle's Nest house band. "When he came on, just the three of them, with Scotty on electric guitar and Bill slapping that bass, it was magic" (Moore and Dickerson, *That's Alright, Elvis*).

7

We're Gonna Move

Encouraged by the initial response, Sam and Marion sent copies of "That's All Right" and "Blue Moon of Kentucky" to radio stations and distributors in surrounding states in an effort to boost sales. It was also around this time that Sam became aware of an upcoming show at Memphis's Overton Park outdoor amphitheater that was scheduled for July 30. Billed as a "hillbilly hoedown" and promoted by WMPS's Bob Neal, the show would feature, as the ads touted, "the sensational radio-recording star Slim Whitman." Several days after the record was released, as Bob Neal recalls, "Sam Phillips called me and said 'Hey, you got a show coming up, why don't you put Elvis on?' I had a concert at the Overton Park Shell, an outdoor thing. [Elvis] was quite nervous. He told me 'Oh, Mr. Neal, I'm scared to death.' But when the time came, he hopped right out there and hit 'em head on. He stole the show" (*Country Music*, December 1977).

On Wednesday, July 28, Marion Keisker, with designs on getting Elvis featured in a local newspaper, took him to the offices of the *Memphis Press-Scimitar* at 495 Union Avenue for an interview with Edwin Howard, the son of the paper's publisher.

"I'll never forget," Howard said later of his first meeting with Elvis, "he looked like the wrath of God. Pimples all over his face, Ducktail hair. Had a funny-looking thin bow tie on. He was very hard to interview. About all I could get out of him was yes and no" (Burk, *Elvis, A 30-Year Chronicle*). The article itself, titled "In a Spin," ran the following day and stated that "That's All Right" might become "the biggest hit that Sun ever pressed."

On a sticky July 30 evening, Elvis and the Blue Moon Boys arrived at Overton Park to play the first of two scheduled sets. Elvis, jumpy at the best of times, was nearly overcome by anxiety and, according to Sam Phillips, was so beset by stage fright he appeared "pitiful." This was a hillbilly show in front of a hillbilly audience; he'd flopped the last time he faced a redneck crowd at the Bon Air. What if he failed again? After doing his best to reassure him—"they're going to love you" were Sam's exact words—Presley made his way backstage. By the time Bob Neal signaled that it was time for Elvis, Scotty, and Bill to take the stage, Elvis's nervous system was in open revolt and only by applying a death grip to his guitar was he able to camouflage his trembling hands. Once onstage, he took a moment to steady himself. Then, after edging up to the microphone, he raked his pick against the strings of his guitar.

"Well, that's all right mama, that's all right for you...."

As he lurched into the song's opening lines, Elvis, now on the balls of his feet, began jigging his right leg in time with the music. As he did, a murmur rose from the crowd, a sound that, seconds later, grew into screams. "I was on a show as an extra added single," Elvis would recall later.

> A big jamboree at an outdoor theater, outdoor auditorium. I came out on stage and I was scared stiff. It was my first big appearance in front of an audience and I came out and was doing a fast tune, one of my first records. And everyone was hollering and I didn't know what they were hollering at. Everybody was screaming and everything. And I came offstage and my manager told me they were hollering because I was wiggling my leg. And I was unaware of it. And so I went out for an encore and I kind of did a little more and the more I did, the wilder they went.

In hindsight, it's impossible to overstate the significance of the Overton Park appearance to the career of Elvis Presley. Presley wasn't the first to bring black rhythms and feeling into popular music, nor even the first white singer to do so. What made Elvis different to the crowd that day at Overton Park, and would make him a figure of controversy to nationwide audiences in the months to come, was not just that he "sounded black," but, as has been noted by others, that he did something previously unseen by country music audiences: he shook his ass, and that, to country and hillbilly singers alike, was considered low class and something no respecting white boy should ever do. "The country artists basically always just stood around and played," says Wanda Jackson. "And they didn't move. They didn't do any gyrations, let's call it that. And he did" (*Goldmine*, December 25, 2011).

In years to come, U2's Bono would say of Elvis and Bob Dylan: "Elvis freed the body and Dylan freed the mind." But as history shows, the performance at Overton Park that day would not just free Presley's body, but his mind too. Suddenly, the withdrawn country boy, once so timid he had to be coaxed to play his guitar in front of others, would find himself physically liberated, his shyness swept aside as he experienced the once-in-a-lifetime thrill of playing before his first enthusiastic crowd. And once he saw the effect his performance had on his audience, his mind immediately went to work on making it happen again. In his words, "I kind of did a little more and the more I did, the wilder they went" (interview with Paul Wilder, August 5, 1956).

In early August, taking note of local record sales, the record industry "bible," *Billboard* magazine, published a review of "That's All Right" and "Blue Moon of Kentucky": "Presley is a potent new chanter who can sock over a tune for either country or the r&b markets. On this new disk, he comes through with a solid performance on an r&b type tune and then on the flip side, does another fine job with a country ditty. A strong new talent" (*Billboard*, August 7, 1954).

In the weeks following the Overton performance, Sam Phillips was on the road, meeting with distributors, DJs and record store owners to pitch his new product. The reaction, depending on the day and the location, would range from enthusiasm to outright derision. At KOSE in Osceola, Arkansas, a local DJ, after hearing "That's All Right" for the first time, looked at Sam through widened eyes. "That's not pop, it's not r&b, it's not country. What is it?" In Tupelo, record spinner Bobby Ritter had much

the same response: "I was kind of perplexed by it." Still, he agreed to play it, and within days it became the station's most requested song. To the other extreme, there was the reaction of Ernest Bowen of Tupelo's WELO, who told Sam Phillips in no uncertain terms that his new record was "a piece of crap." Instead of being offended, Sam diplomatically explained that things were changing, that new sounds were finding their way onto country charts, and asked Bowen to at least give the song a chance. "So we did," Bowen recalls, "and from there

ELVIS PRESLEY EXCLUSIVE SUN RECORDING ARTIST

Elvis's first publicity photograph, 1954 (*Memphis Press-Scimitar*).

on, the music began to change and changed rapidly after that. Younger people started listening to radio instead of putting a nickel into the jukebox. I look back on it and that's where it began to turn" (*Cowboy Songs*, Number 41, June 1955).

Bowen may have needed convincing, but to the record-buying public, "That's All Right" and "Blue Moon of Kentucky" were anything but "pieces of crap." By the third week of August, *Billboard*'s regional country and western chart showed both songs entering the top five. Interestingly, while "That's All Right" was listed by Sun as the A-side, jukebox operators, DJs, and retailers favored the flip side, and "Blue Moon of Kentucky," at least for the initial months after its release, outdid "That's All Right" in popularity. Before it faded, the single would sell in excess of 20,000 copies, an extraordinary success for an independent regional label. And not surprisingly, the press took notice, as this article from the *Memphis Press-Scimitar* makes clear:

> Elvis Presley can be forgiven for going round and round in more ways than one these days. A 19-year-old Humes High graduate, he has just signed a recording contract with Sun Record Co. of Memphis and already has a disk out that promised to the biggest hit that Sun ever pressed. "The odd thing about it," says Marion Keisker of the Sun office, "is that both sides seem to be equally popular on popular, folk and race record programs. This boy has something that seems to appeal to everybody. We've just gotten the sample record out to the disk jockeys and distributors in other cities, but we got big orders yesterday from Dallas and Atlanta" [*Memphis Press-Scimitar*, July 14, 1954].

In an effort to trade on the record's success, Sam reached out to Jim Denny, manager of the Grand Ole Opry, in hopes of snagging an appearance for Elvis at the venerated country music event. Had Denny heard "That's All Right"? He'd heard it, he told Sam, but hadn't liked it. Still, he didn't rule out an appearance for Elvis on the Opry, if "he could fit him in."

The Music—August, September 1954—Sun Studios

On August 19, Elvis, Scotty, and Bill were back in the studio to take another stab at the Rodgers and Hart standard "Blue Moon," a song previously recorded by a myriad of artists. In its original form, "Blue Moon" is a lament that, in its final stanza, is transformed into a message of salvation. Elvis, however, recast it as a chronicle of unrequited love, skipping the bridge and the final redemptive verses and replacing them with a spectral falsetto. The song's hypnotic feel was largely due to Scotty

Moore who, in an early example of string "tapping," muted the fifth and sixth strings of his guitar, generating a "clip-clop" effect. Before they were through, Elvis, Scotty, and Bill attempted take after take of "Blue Moon," until Sam, unsure of what they had, called a halt to the session. Phillips, in fact, was so doubtful of the song's potential that the track would never be released by Sun and would only reach the public two years later when RCA, scavenging for anything Elvis-related, released "Blue Moon" as a single. The song entered the *Billboard* Hot 100 at number 89 in 1956 and never climbed higher than number 55. In years to come, "Blue Moon" would take on something akin to legendary status primarily due to Elvis's haunting vocal enhanced by Sam's slapback echo, guitar work from Scotty Moore that sounds as if he's playing from a distance of miles, and an atmospheric melancholia that would lead the *Los Angeles Times* to remark on the song's "primal beauty" and declare it in 2011 to be Presley's best ballad ("Presley's Blue Moon: His Best Ballad?" *Los Angeles Times*, August 18, 2011).

Even when not recording, Elvis continued to frequent the Sun offices to pass the time with Marion and simply check up on how his record was doing. Marion's perspectives on Elvis at this point are revealing. "My total image of Elvis was as a child," she recalls. "His attitude toward people was the equivalent of tipping your hat as you walk down the street—'Good evening ma'am, good evening sir'—but not showing off. He was like a mirror in a way, whatever you were looking for, you were going to find in him. It was not in him to lie or say anything malicious. He had all the intricacy of the very simple" (Guralnick, *Last Train to Memphis*).

September 10 found Elvis, Scotty, and Bill back in the studio, where existing studio logs indicate that six songs were recorded: "Tomorrow Night," "Satisfied," "I'll Never Let You Go (Little Darlin')," "I Don't Care If the Sun Don't Shine," "Just Because," and "Good Rockin' Tonight."

Of the six tracks laid down during this session, one, "Good Rockin' Tonight," would attain mythic status in the years following its release. Written and recorded in 1947 by Roy Brown, "Good Rockin' Tonight" was covered a year later by bluesman Wynonie Harris. The Brown version is the tamer of the two, horn-heavy with a barrelhouse piano that imbues the track with a New Orleans vibe. In its rhythmic structure and emphasis on the backbeat, Harris's version more closely echoes qualities that, in future years, would be associated with rock 'n' roll.

Blessed with an infectious swagger and imbued with a joyous demand that you simply open up your ears, Presley's "Good Rockin' Tonight" stands to the present day as one of early rock's most seminal works. Essential to the song's appeal are the enormous contributions of

Scotty Moore, who used both pick and fingers on his Gibson ES-295 to generate the song's warm rhythmic textures while the percussive bass lines of Bill Black provide the track with its irresistible swing. Most critically, "Good Rockin' Tonight" supplies unbeatable testimony that, when provided with the right material, Elvis Presley, Scotty Moore, and Bill Black could attain musical transcendence and, in so doing, create music that could appeal equally to both white and black audiences.

On October 4, Sun Records released "Good Rockin' Tonight" and "I Don't Care If the Sun Don't Shine" to the Memphis area as Elvis's second single, with a more extended release planned for six weeks later. The delay was due to the continued popularity of "That's All Right," which was still selling well. Initial reaction was positive; in its review *Billboard* magazine said that the single "could easily break loose," a statement that would prove prescient. In its first week, "Good Rockin' Tonight" sold in excess of 4,000 copies.

In late September, the Grand Ole Opry's Jim Denny contacted Sam Phillips with good news: Elvis, Scotty, and Bill had been cleared to perform one song, in essence an audition, during Hank Snow's upcoming appearance. On the morning of October 2, Elvis, Scotty, Bill, and Sam shoehorned themselves into Sam's 1951 Cadillac (Bill's bass was strapped to the roof) for the 200-mile trek to Nashville. Anticipation and excitement were at a fever pitch; after all, this was *The Opry*,

Elvis's second single for Sun Records, "Good Rockin' Tonight" and "I Don't Care If the Sun Don't Shine," sold more than 4,000 copies in its initial week (*Memphis Press-Scimitar*).

hallowed ground where country music greats had trod the boards. But as they so often do, dreams and reality would quickly clash, because once they were inside the Opry's home base, Nashville's Ryman Auditorium, all four were stunned at what they saw. Instead of the glittering palace they'd imagined, they encountered a cramped stage, dilapidated pews, and a building that cried out for a fresh coat of paint. Elvis thought back to those long-ago Saturday nights when he and Gladys and Vernon would sit in a semicircle in front of the family radio listening to Roy Acuff and Red Foley and how he'd fantasize of someday playing there too. The Opry had been his grandest dream, but there was nothing grand about this. To make matters worse, Jim Denny approached them and, after sizing them up, said he was being cheated. He'd been promised the full group that played on "That's All Right," he said. Where was the rest of the band?

Minutes before he took the stage, Elvis warily approached Bill Monroe. Word around country music circles was that Monroe hated what Elvis had done to his "Blue Moon of Kentucky" and was out for blood. But to Elvis's surprise, Monroe was pleasant, even going so far as to tell him that he was thinking of cutting another version of the song that would more closely echo Elvis's version. "He came into the dressing room where I was at," Monroe said later. "He apologized for the way that he changed 'Blue Moon of Kentucky.' I told him 'Well, if it gives you your start, that's all right with me'" (*Elvis Presley, A Boy from Tupelo*, RCA Records, 2017).

When Elvis and the Blue Moon Boys finally took the stage in a jammed auditorium at 10:15 p.m., Elvis was playing his new Martin D-18, which he'd purchased just a week earlier for $175. In testimony to his growing self-confidence, a metal plate affixed just below the instrument's F-hole spelled out "Elvis Presley." Jim Denny had promised the group no more than one song, and figuring that it was best suited for the Opry's audience, Elvis and the band played "Blue Moon of Kentucky." The response was polite at best, and, depending on which account you believe, Jim Denny's response upon Elvis leaving the stage was either "The boy's not bad," or "Go back to driving a truck." Whatever the truth, Elvis rated the whole experience as a failure.

"The Opry crowd was polite," Scotty Moore recalls.

They didn't boo, hiss or anything. They didn't jump up and down in their seats, but they didn't do that for anybody. But Elvis was disappointed. It was a big thing to be on the Grand Ole Opry stage. That was a week or two before we did the Louisiana Hayride, and I remember Bill [Black] and I saying, "What are we gonna do now? This is it, as high as you can go." We just went out and did our regular thing. I guess "Blue Moon of Kentucky" was

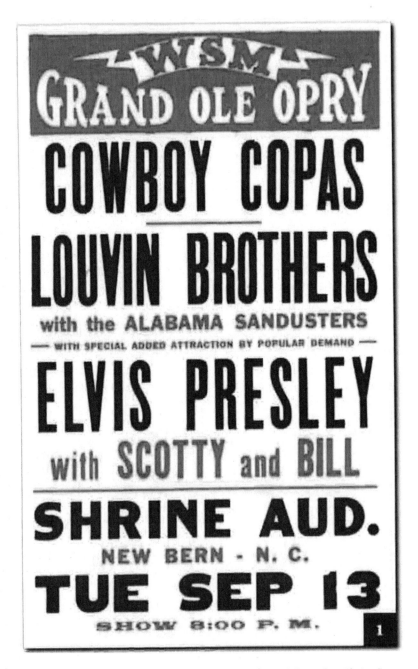

"They didn't boo or hiss or anything." Promotional flyer for Elvis, Scotty, and Bill's first appearance at the fabled Grand Ole Opry, September 13, 1954 (*Memphis Press-Scimitar*).

what got him on at the Opry, 'cause it was a country song. I think a lot of it was that the crowds at the Opry weren't from here in town and the records hadn't gotten out further. Only a handful of people on that given night had heard it. But he went over big at the Louisiana Hayride [Cronin, *Country Guitar*, 1994].

The Louisiana Hayride may not have matched the Grand Ole Opry in prestige and influence, but because of its central role in launching the careers of such country stalwarts as Hank Williams, Kitty Wells, Faron Young, and others, it was known as "The Cradle of the Stars." Broadcast over 50,000-watt KWKH each Saturday night from the 4,000-seat Shreveport Municipal Auditorium, the Hayride at its peak was so popular it was networked to 28 states and was carried overseas via U.S. Armed Forces radio. In the days following Elvis's appearance at the Opry, Sam Phillips had contacted Pappy Covington, talent scout for the Hayride, in hopes of landing an upcoming spot for Presley. After taking Sam's call, Covington approached Horace Logan, the Hayride's director and pistol-packing emcee. Logan had heard "That's All Right" on local station KCIJ and expressed hesitation. Presley, Logan averred, was black. "Nope," Covington replied, before informing Logan that Elvis had just recently shared a stage with Slim Whitman. Slim Whitman? That was good enough for Covington.

Two weeks later, Elvis, Scotty, Bill, and Sam were on the road again, this time headed for Shreveport, a seven-hour drive from Memphis. Perched in the back seat, Elvis and Sam were talking music. "You remember Clyde McPhatter?" Phillips recalled years later.

Elvis thought Clyde McPhatter had one of the greatest voices in the world. We were going somewhere, down to the Louisiana Hayride or Nashville, and we were singing in the car. Well, Bill Black couldn't carry a tune in a bucket and Scotty was worse. So Elvis and I were the only good singers in the car. But we were talking about Clyde McPhatter and he said "You know, if I had a voice like that, man, I'd never want for another thing." But Elvis knew he had talent. I think he just had a little trouble gaining confidence.

According to Phillips, Elvis harbored other dreams in addition to idolizing McPhatter. "He loved to sing and always wanted to play guitar real good," Sam recalls. "Of course, he never did learn to play guitar that good. And he wanted to play piano like Jerry Lee Lewis. Oh, he loved Jerry Lee's playing, thought it was unbelievable" (Dawson, *Country Music*, December 1977).

Once in Shreveport, they checked into the downtown Captain Shreve Hotel; then Elvis and the band paid a courtesy call on a local DJ who helped break "That's All Right" in Louisiana. Elvis, resplendent in black pants and a pink shirt, told the DJ how grateful he was, but the record-spinner's wife, who was also present, was clearly unimpressed. "That boy," she said to her husband after Elvis was out of earshot, "needs to wash his neck" (*Cradle of the Stars*, PBS 1984).

A day or two before Elvis and the Blue Moon Boys were scheduled at the Hayride, a local area drummer stopped by Pappy Covington's office to pass the time. While he was there, he asked him to play the new record by someone named "Elvis Presley" from Memphis. As the Hayride house drummer, Dominic Joseph (D.J.) Fontana knew he'd be providing percussion for the young singer the following Saturday. After listening to "That's All Right," "Blue Moon of Kentucky," and "Good Rockin' Tonight" (newly released in the Shreveport area), Fontana eased back in his chair. "That's good," he said. "How many musicians they got? Five? Six?" When the reply came back "three," he was floored (*Country Music*, December 1977).

"D.J. was working at the Louisiana Hayride and working clubs in and around Shreveport with all the Hayride acts and we met him when we went down there," Scotty Moore recalled. "The best I can remember, he played with somebody else on the show and we heard and liked him and asked if he would like to play with us the next time. And he did. He would speed up or slow down just like we would and we said, 'Boy, this is great'" (Woods, *Vintage Guitar*, November 1992).

Just before they assumed the Hayride stage on Saturday, Elvis, Scotty, and Bill met briefly with Fontana to go over the two songs they would play that night. Interestingly, Fontana would keep time behind a stage curtain, unseen by the audience; at this point, drummers had yet to be embraced by country music fans.

"They came in as guest artists," Fontana recalls.

> He was invited to the Hayride because his first record was going good. I had heard the record, but at that time I didn't really understand what they were doing. I had done it all, worked club dates playing pop things, combos, cocktail music, then when I went to work for the Hayride, I was learning the country end of it. But I heard the slapping bass, the echo and everything and I thought what kind of record is that? When they asked me if I'd help that first night, I said "Sure, that's what I'm here for. But I don't really know what you guys are doing. I'll just kinda stay out of the way until I get the feel of it." That slapping bass kind of took the place of the drums and Scotty had the echoplex guitar and it was popping back. And then Elvis was playing rhythm. So I did it that first night and somehow or another, it fell together [*Country Music*, December 1977].

When Elvis bounded on the stage that night, he was greeted by announcer Frank Page.

"Elvis, how are you this evening?"

"Just fine," replied Elvis, who was decked out in a white suit, black shirt, and bow tie, with two-tone shoes. "How are you sir?"

"You all geared up with your band?"

"I'm all geared up!" said Elvis. "I'd like to say how happy we are to be out here. It's a real honor for us to have ... get a chance to appear on the Louisiana Hayride. And we're going to do a song for you.... You got anything else to say sir?"

"No, I'm ready."

"We're gonna do a song for you we got on the Sun record. It goes something like this" (*Elvis, The Beginning Years, 1954–1956*, RCA, 1983).

With D.J. knocking out the beat behind the curtain, Elvis and the band played both sides of their first single. In subsequent years, primitive recordings have surfaced of this performance and show the band performing well, although Bill Black's bass is virtually indistinguishable, as is Elvis's rhythm guitar when he ventures away from his microphone during instrumental breaks.

According to those present, including Elvis himself, the audience reaction was tepid. "He jumped around too much on the stage during his first show," singer Merle Kilgore recalled, "and the crowd was stunned. They didn't know what to think. He really just overdid it and he was all upset. He said 'Man, I really screwed up'" (interview with Leon Beck, 1958).

Comments such as these suggest that Elvis bombed in his first appearance at the Hayride. But available recordings of the event simply don't support that. While the audience certainly reacts to Elvis's stage movements, the impression seems to be one of surprise and delight, not disapproval. Additionally, Elvis is greeted with warm applause at the conclusion of both "That's All Right" and "Blue Moon of Kentucky."

However mixed the perspective might be regarding Presley's first set, there was virtually unanimous agreement on his second. "I'd never seen anything like it before," singer Jimmy C. Newman recalls. "Here comes this guy, I guess you could call him an amateur, rings of dirt on his neck, but he had it all right from the start. He didn't work into it, he just knew what he was going to do. We'd just stand in the wings and shake our heads. 'It can't be, it can't last, it's got to be a fad'" (Guralnick, *Last Train to Memphis*).

So rapturous was the reception, Pappy Covington extended an offer to Elvis, Scotty, and Bill to become Hayride regulars, an unimagined stroke of good fortune that they could scarcely believe. For the next year, they would be paid union scale, Elvis at $18 per show and Scotty and Bill $12 each for 52 consecutive weeks. To seal the deal, both Gladys and Vernon were required to sign the Hayride contract on Elvis's behalf.

For Elvis and Scotty, the contract meant that both could soon quit their jobs and be full-time musicians. Vernon Presley, upon learning of Elvis's plan, became troubled, telling his son, "You should make up your mind either about being an electrician or playing a guitar. I never saw a guitar player that was worth a damn" (1972 interview).

Days later, the *Memphis Press-Scimitar*, in an article titled "Elvis Presley Clicks," reported on Presley's latest triumph:

> Elvis Presley, Memphis' swift-rising young hillbilly singing star, is now a regular member of the Louisiana Hayride Show. The Hayride specializes in picking promising young rural rhythm talent—and it took just one guest appearance last Saturday for the young Memphian to become a regular [*Memphis Press-Scimitar*, October 20, 1954].

Four days earlier, *Billboard* magazine reported that "Bob Neal of WMPS was planning a fall tour with Elvis Presley." Neal, a local DJ, was an early supporter of Elvis and, despite having no experience in artist management, had nonetheless approached Sam Phillips weeks earlier about taking control of Elvis's career. Scotty Moore was Elvis's manager, Sam replied, but if Neal wanted to schedule some bookings, that would be fine. Hearing of this, Scotty, instead of feeling slighted, flashed a grin. He'd become Elvis's manager merely to keep fast-talking Memphis hucksters at bay. He'd never sought the spotlight and wanted nothing more than to be a working musician. If Bob Neal could help out with bookings, he welcomed it.

Sam's verbal agreement with Neal may have reduced pressure on Scotty, but it would ultimately prove to be a harbinger of ill fortune for both him and Bill Black. At this point, Scotty and Bill's sole agreement with Sam Phillips was a verbal one, for a 50–25–25 split that covered only live appearances and nothing for recording work. In essence, they were independent contractors who served at the whim of their employers—Sam Phillips at first and, in future years, Elvis himself—in an arrangement that completely disregarded the critical role both played in crafting a sound that was sweeping the South. Scotty Moore himself states that Elvis was cognizant of the unfairness of this setup. Presley, Scotty said, told him in the fall of 1954 that recording royalties should be split the same way as live performances, 50–25–25. Scotty demurred, suggesting that Elvis would at some future date find that arrangement unfair. Still, convinced that Presley was sincere, Scotty put forth a compromise. What if he and Bill got one-quarter of 1 percent, meaning that Elvis's cut from record profits would be reduced from 3 percent to 2.5. Would that be fair? "Fine," replied Elvis. However, nothing was ever committed to paper, an omission that, in years to come, would torment both Scotty and Bill.

With the go-ahead from Sam and no objections from Scotty, Bob Neal, relying on connections in the music industry, managed to land gigs for Elvis, Scotty, and Bill for November and December in small towns throughout Mississippi and Arkansas. It was also during this period that Neal, in an effort to expand his contacts, reached out to a Tennessee promoter best known for recently managing country star Eddy Arnold.

8

Andreas Cornelis van Kuijk

The man who gained renown in entertainment circles as Tom Parker, manager of Elvis Presley, was actually born Andreas Cornelis van Kuijk on June 26, 1909, in the Netherlands, the seventh of 11 children. For decades, it was believed that Parker was born in West Virginia and, after being orphaned at the age of 11, was raised by an uncle who ran something called "The Great Parker Pony Service." In the years following Presley's death in August of 1977, this was revealed to be hokum, a product of Parker's attempt at self-reinvention.

The facts show that, as a teenager, van Kuijk worked as a carnival barker in his hometown of Breda in the Netherlands. Following a move to Rotterdam, where he found work toiling on boats, van Kuijk jumped ship at age 18, determined to reach New York. In later years, it has been theorized that van Kuijk's motivation for escaping his home country was to avoid possible charges related to a homicide in Breda, in which he was deemed "a person of interest." During his early months in the New York area, van Kuijk found work with a "tent Chautauqua," a form of early twentieth-century entertainment that showcased lectures by prominent figures in politics and theology, interspersed with musical performances. Some Chautauqua speakers preached a prosperity theology that linked faith with material wealth, while others would hold forth on such diverse topics as prison reform and relations between the sexes.

Following a brief return to the Netherlands, at age 20 van Kuijk returned to the U.S. to stay; trading on his experiences in Breda, he secured employment with a carnival. Deciding to enlist in the U.S. Army, van Kuijk, in an effort to disguise his immigration status, adopted the name of "Tom Parker." Following a two-year stint at Fort Shafter in Hawaii, Parker decided to re-enlist, a decision he quickly came to regret, as shortly thereafter, he went AWOL. He was quickly captured, charged, and convicted of desertion. As punishment, he was committed to solitary confinement, a sentence that manifested in Parker a psychosis so severe it necessitated a lengthy stay in a mental hospital. Once released, he was dismissed from the service.

With his army stint behind him, Parker found work with Royal American Shows, a traveling carnival based primarily in Florida. "Royal American was the granddaddy of all the traveling caravans," close friend Oscar Davis recalls. "It was headquartered in Tampa. He [Parker] handled the food" (Hopkins, *The Life and Times of Colonel Tom Parker*). It was during this phase that Parker, always on the lookout for a soft touch, honed his skills at snookering rubes. Years later, Parker would brag about a gimmick he used when, as a chiseler-in-training, he ran a hot dog concession on the carnival runway. The buns he used were a foot long, but the wieners were just half that. Why give customers a complete dog, he figured, when you could just have a hunk of wiener sticking out of each end of the bun? He'd then fill out the middle section with cheap condiments and *voila*. If anyone complained—and they did—he'd point to a piece of wiener sitting in the sawdust below (which he'd earlier placed there himself) and tell the customer, "You dropped your meat, boy. Now move along."

In later years, as Parker perfected his skills at clipping rubes, he referred to himself as a "snowman" and actively recruited members into a farcical "Snowman's League," a loose fraternity of like-minded scam artists forever in search of new and better ways of separating yokels from their money. Among the league by-laws were the following:

> "Any of our members have to be good enough snowers so they can make up their own snow stories without calling on any of the top snowers."
>
> "One rule you must always abide by: one never snows anyone for other than to do good."
>
> "Never take advantage of anyone that you have been able to snow under and allow other snowers to snow you from time to time, even if you know you are being snowed."

As Parker told a reporter years later, "There's no one who can shovel it like me" (Hopkins, *The Life and Times of Colonel Tom Parker*).

By 1938, Parker, his skills as a bullshit artist fully honed, worked his way into the music industry as a promoter and soon made the acquaintance of singer and songwriter Gene Austin. For the ensuing months, Parker, trading on his experience as a carny, successfully promoted shows in and around Florida, but when Austin decided to relocate to Nashville, the partnership ended and Parker took a job with the Florida Humane Society. It was also during this time that undocumented immigrants were offered a chance by the U.S. government to become citizens, if, in return, they agreed to fight during World War II. After weighing this offer, Parker ultimately passed, fearing that his shady past might be exposed.

While promoting the Humane Society in Florida, Parker crossed paths with a number of country music figures, including Eddy Arnold, Roy Acuff, and Minnie Pearl. After convincing them of his promotional acumen, Parker arranged a tie-in between a few local businesses and the performers. "We went down there and he tied in with some chain, like Kroger," Pearl recalls, "and it was smart promotion because it filled the house several times" (Hopkins, *The Life and Times of Colonel Tom Parker*). Growing bored with mere promotion and eying the big money involved in artist management, Parker, heeding a suggestion from Acuff, headed to Nashville. "I presume I was the first one to invite Tom to Nashville," Acuff recalled later. "I suggested he come to Nashville and meet the boys" (*Rolling Stone*, September 22, 1977).

By 1945, Eddy Arnold was impressed enough with Parker to name him his personal manager. "'Earthy,' I guess a lot of people might describe him," Arnold said later, "uneducated maybe. A lot of times people think they're dealing with a rube. 'Oh, I can take him,' they decide. They don't take him. He's ahead of 'em before they even sit down across a table ... he fools 'em. They think, because his English might be faulty (he might say a word wrong here and there), 'Oh, I'll handle him.' They walk right into his web" (Arnold, *It's a Long Way from Chester County*). On the rare day when Arnold was ill and couldn't perform, Parker—a former employee of the Humane Society, if you recall—would trot out his alternate act, "Colonel Parker's Dancing Chickens." He'd place chickens on a red-hot plate and charge customers to watch the birds "dance" to avoid burning their feet.

How did "Tom Parker" become "Colonel" Tom Parker? Well, in addition to managing Arnold, Parker also helped promote a former country singer named Jimmie Davis in his successful campaign for governor of Louisiana. Once in office, Davis bestowed the honorary title of "Colonel" on Parker, a sobriquet he would utilize to great effect for the remainder of his life.

By 1952, Parker was devoting more and more of his time promoting country star Hank Snow, a development that Arnold watched with dismay. By 1953, he'd had enough and fired Parker. For the next two years, Parker devoted himself to Snow's career, and the two men eventually became partners in what became known as "Jamboree Attractions," an outfit with a mission statement of promoting up-and-coming country artists.

9

Got a Lot o' Livin' to Do

In the days following his Hayride success, Elvis was back in Memphis, occupying something resembling a *terra incognita*. No longer simply "Elvis," he was now viewed by virtually everyone as a bona fide celebrity. "Good Rockin' Tonight" had climbed to number three on the Memphis singles charts, an event that was detailed in the latest issue of *Billboard* magazine, which praised him as a "sock new singer." Coverage in the local papers was also commonplace at this point, with stories providing breathless accounts of Presley's blossoming career. While naturally thrilled by his sudden good fortune, Elvis was nonetheless thrown by the strange way people now acted when in his presence. The casual back and forth that previously characterized interactions with friends and former schoolmates was now replaced with an awkwardness that left him uneasy. Even girlfriend Dixie Locke was acting oddly, telling him that she no longer felt part of what he was doing, that he'd somehow "moved on."

All of this served to make a sudden visit to Humes High a few days later so comforting. It was late fall and Elvis was tooling around town in his Lincoln coupe when he spied the high school football team preparing to leave for a game. Spotting Red West, the schoolmate who had rescued him that day in the boys' bathroom, Elvis pulled over to say hello. Relieved at the natural way Red greeted him, Elvis mentioned that he was scheduled to play a show in a couple of days and invited Red to join him. Things went well, and in the days to come West would become a constant companion.

If Elvis's sudden notoriety in Memphis left him uneasy, Shreveport, where he would perform for the next 12 months as part of the Louisiana Hayride, was another matter entirely. Here, he was not only seven hours from home, but, metaphorically, a lifetime away from the watchful eye of Gladys and the constraining cocoon she'd woven around him. Holed up at the Al-Ida motel with Scotty and Bill, Elvis ate when he wanted, slept when he felt like it and just generally reacted as any young man would when experiencing his first taste of freedom. In this case, "free-dom" meant hanging out at Murrell's Café on Market Street, picking through the R&B releases at Stan's Records, or hanging out and playing practical jokes with Scotty and Bill. Not incidentally, it also meant having his pick of the myriad young girls now lining up to throw themselves at him. The nightly calls to his mother continued, where he'd play the part of the dutiful and observant son, a role that he would hone and play to perfection until her death four years later. But when the calls ended and he flung his motel door open to find a bevy of teenage girls clamoring for his attention, the liberated Elvis would appear, ready to sample all the delights that Shreveport had to offer. For Presley, it was the fulfillment of a vision he'd harbored since daydreaming of stardom back in Humes High. For struggling musicians everywhere, it was a life that could scarcely be imagined.

   When not playing the Hayride, Elvis, Scotty, and Bill toured the South, playing one-nighters in honky-tonks and juke joints. "The first one wasn't a nation-wide thing," Scotty Moore recalled. "It was more

Elvis signing the agreement designating Bob Neal as his manager, December 1954. Left to right: Sam Phillips, Elvis, Bob Neal (*Memphis Press-Scimitar*).

in the Southwest, Mississippi, Arkansas, Texas. We started doing some shows, and it was rough, it was wild. It wasn't an overnight success, by any means. But even in those early days the crowds were just as ecstatic as now, but not as large" (Green, "Perhaps the First Rock & Roll Guitarist," *Guitar Player*, 1974).

In December of 1954, the *Memphis Press-Scimitar*, in an article titled "Neal is Manager for Young Star," reported that Elvis Presley had concluded a deal with local disc jockey Bob Neal to manage him. "Presley, who appears each Saturday night on the Louisiana Hayride in Shreveport," the paper reported, "said increasing demands for appearances made a manager necessary and he preferred a Memphian for the job." The affiliation was announced simultaneously with release of Presley's latest records, "Milkcow Blues Boogie" and "You're a Heartbreaker" (*Memphis Press-Scimitar*, December 29, 1954). Again, because Elvis was still underage, the contract also contained the signatures of Gladys and Vernon Presley. The agreement, which officially took effect on January 1, 1955, stipulated that Neal would book dates on an exclusive basis and that he would also leverage his contacts with the Louisiana Hayride network to set up engagements for Elvis in regions as far-flung as West Texas and New Mexico. Now, in his role as Elvis's official representative, Neal approached Tom Parker with a proposal that the two, in conjunction with Parker's Jamboree Attractions, work together to promote Elvis to regions outside the Deep South. Only moderately interested, Parker assigned his assistant Tom Diskin to evaluate Presley's potential, which to Diskin meant listening to Elvis's records, attending a couple of shows, and then reporting back to Parker on what he'd learned. In the end, Diskin told Parker to "forget it." Presley, he said, was nothing more than a hillbilly entertainer and not a good fit for Jamboree Attractions.

The Music—November, December 1954— Sun Studios, Memphis

Between appearances at the Hayride and their small regional tours, Elvis, Scotty, and Bill returned to Sun Studios (most likely in late November, the exact date is uncertain) to record "Milkcow Blues Boogie," a follow-up to "Good Rockin' Tonight." Originally known simply as "Milkcow Blues," the song was written by Kokomo Arnold in the mid–1930s and became a hit for Bob Wills and his Texas Playboys in the mid–1940s. It was Sam Phillips's idea to amend the title. "There was no boogie in it," Sam said later. "Who would take an old broken-down hillbilly song called 'Milkcow Blues' and attempt to foist in on the public? We did" (*Elvis Presley, A Boy from Tupelo*, RCA Records, 2017).

Presley's version begins as slow burner, until, seemingly unable to restrain himself, Elvis signals for a halt. "Hold it, fellas," he intones, "that don't move me! Let's get real, real, gone for a change," at which point, Elvis, Scotty, and Bill kick into a slightly unhinged but full-throttle assault on Bob Wills's cornpone version of 1946. The song's false start concerned Sam Phillips—jukebox operators, after all, frowned on records with spoken intros—but the end result was so infectious, everyone agreed that the record had to be released "as is."

A true high-water mark, "Milkcow Blues Boogie" stands today as a stunning musical artifact and provides solid testimony to what Elvis, Scotty, and Bill were capable of producing. Standout bass work from Black propels the song, and a hiccuping delivery from Elvis, including an exhortation to "Let's milk it!" prior to Scotty's solo, contributes to the tune's epic groove. Years later, when asked to comment on his guitar playing during this period, Scotty waxed modest:

> I hated most of the stuff I was doing, 'cause I was trying to play something I wasn't schooled in. It was a challenge playing the thumb-and-finger stuff and trying to play fills; I was stretched to the limit. For the most part, if someone asks me to go back and play it note for note, I can't do it. We were just jamming, but I would always try to find something that would accent the singer of the song. We were experimenting. Make more noise, that was the whole thing. That was one reason we were always in open keys; it was easier to get rhythm using the open strings. Some of those riffs may have

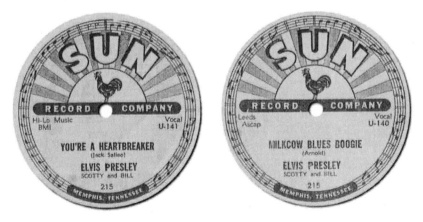

"**Hold it fellas ... that don't move me! Let's get real, real gone for a change.**"
Sun's release of "Milkcow Blues Boogie" and "You're a Heartbreaker" in December of 1954 established one cogent and inescapable musical truth: *It was on* (*Memphis Press-Scimitar*).

come, like, after ten takes, when I was just burnt out with it. Finally, you just get so frustrated and mad, and it was just "Dammit, take *that one!*" [Cronin, *Country Guitar*, 1994].

Also recorded this day was a slice of straight-up, country pop written by Tennessee theater manager and part-time songwriter Jack Sallee, who just happened to be at Sun Studios one day cutting some promos. When Sam mentioned he was looking for new material, he went home and, a couple of days later, returned with "You're a Heartbreaker."

On December 28, "Milkcow Blues Boogie" and "You're a Heartbreaker" were released as Elvis's newest single. In a 1997 *Washington Post* essay extolling "Milkcow Blues Boogie," Dave Nicholson states: "Something is happening when Elvis interrupts the slow blues intro to Kokomo Arnold's 'Milkcow Blues Boogie'—'Hold it fellas. That don't move me. Let's get real, real gone, for a change'—and if you don't get it, then you just might be the Mr. Jones Bob Dylan sang about a decade or so later" (Nicholson, "The King and Us," *Washington Post*, August 17, 1997). "Milkcow Blues" extended Elvis, Scotty, and Bill's string of extraordinary singles and, along with "That's All Right" and "Good Rockin' Tonight," established one cogent and inescapable musical truth: *It was on.*

10

Playing for Keeps

On January 1, 1955, the day Bob Neal's contract took effect, Elvis, Scotty, and Bill were packing for a weeklong tour of Mississippi, Arkansas, and Texas, including a stop in San Angelo, where he would be billed as "Alvis Presley." Throughout this period, the trio caravanned relentlessly throughout the South, playing everything from high school gyms and roadhouses to flatbed trucks in parking lots, where they were usually outfitted with nothing more than a vocal microphone and a public address system. In Lubbock, Elvis was greeted backstage by Waylon Jennings, an employee of radio station KLLL in the process of developing a friendship with Buddy Holly. Jennings later recalled Elvis telling him that his next record would be "Tweedle Dee," an R&B track then on the charts by LaVern Baker. While in Lubbock, Elvis, Scotty, and Bill made a stop at WDAV, where they performed "Shake, Rattle and Roll" and a 12-bar blues, "Fool, Fool, Fool." Of all existing recordings of Presley's earliest live performances, these, aurally speaking, remain among the best, with Elvis's rhythm guitar and Bill Black's bass prominent throughout.

By the early months of 1955, Elvis, thanks to his series of hit singles, was starting to attract media attention outside the immediate Memphis area, as the following article in the *Morristown Gazette Mail* illustrates:

> A teen-age court ward used a ball bat to bludgeon the 15-year-old daughter of a family that gave him a home. He said he and the pretty girl had argued over Elvis Presley. Carol Taylor was in very critical condition at Sequoia Hospital [*Morristown Gazette Mail*, January 24, 1955].

In early January, Elvis and the Blue Moon Boys were back at the Louisiana Hayride, where they performed "Money Honey," "Blue Moon of Kentucky," "I Don't Care If the Sun Don't Shine," and "That's All Right." Despite an ill-advised addition of a honky-tonk piano to their sound, the audience response was electric. Watching from backstage

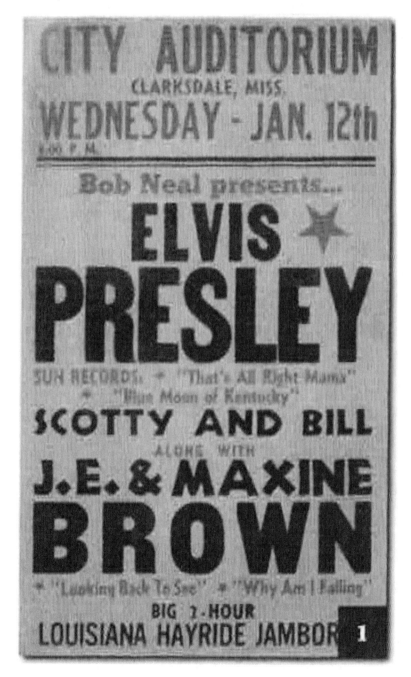

Promotional flyer advertising Elvis's appearance for the Louisiana Hayride in January of 1955.

was Tom Parker, who, despite the critical response to Presley from his assistant, was on hand to size up Elvis for himself.

After completing his set, Elvis and Parker were introduced. "I promote a lot of shows, Elvis," the Colonel told Presley. "I'm going to try to set you up on some of those shows so I can see exactly what you do. Would you like that?" Elvis certainly would. Following the meeting, it was clear to Bob Neal that Parker was impressed with Elvis and serious about securing future bookings for him (*Elvis Presley, A Boy from Tupelo*, RCA Records, 2017).

Just over a week later, Elvis, Scotty, and Bill were at the Community Center in Sheffield, Alabama, to play a show. It was a gig that all three viewed as an important step forward. "The feeling was that you hadn't made it until you had played the Sheffield Community Center," Sam Phillips recalled. "Today, that's hard to believe, but that's how it was" (*Elvis Presley, A Boy from Tupelo*, RCA Records, 2017).

The Music—February 1955—Sun Studios, Memphis

In early February, Sam urged Elvis, Scotty, and Bill to take a break from touring and return to Sun Studios to record new material. For this session, they completed three new tracks: a cover of Ray Charles's "I Got a Woman," Charles Singleton and Rose Marie McCoy's "Trying to Get to You," and Arthur Gunter's "Baby Let's Play House." These songs, for the first time, were credited to "Elvis Presley and the Blue Moon Boys." In Scotty's words, "we thought of ourselves as a group" (Green, "Perhaps the First Rock & Roll Guitarist," *Guitar Player*, 1974).

And what a group they were. The first song they worked on, "Baby Let's Play House," is arguably the finest recording that Elvis Presley, Scotty Moore, and Bill Black ever produced. Blatantly suggestive and musically searing, "Baby Let's Play House" features a pair of heavily echoed, paint-peeling solos from Scotty on his Gibson ES-295, dynamic bass and percussive support from Bill Black, and a boot-in-the-balls vocal performance from Presley that's so outrageous he struggles to sustain it to the song's conclusion. In the years since its release, "Baby Let's Play House" has assumed its rightful place among rock's most seminal and influential recordings. In 1966 John Lennon would appropriate the line "I'd rather see you dead little girl than to be with another man" for the Beatles tune "Run for Your Life," and in 1977 Led Zeppelin's Jimmy Page would tell an interviewer, "The record that made me want to play guitar was 'Baby Let's Play House.' There was just so much vitality and energy coming out of it" (*Ultimate Guitar*, 1977).

Without question, much of the "vitality and energy" that Page spoke of could be credited to the man perched behind the console in Sun's small control room, Sam Phillips. Years later, Scotty Moore would comment on what it was like to record for Sun during this period. "You didn't have the baffling and separation then; everybody would get as close together as they could," Moore recalled. "Back then musicians played off each other. They didn't play loud; they played where they could hear each other in the studio, and that natural leakage—as I learned later when I got into engineering—actually helped to blend the tonal quality" (*Guitarist*, 1992).

The other two songs recorded during this session—Ray Charles's R&B workout "I Got a Woman" and "Trying to Get to You," Elvis's version of a song that was a regional hit for a little-known Washington-based doo-wop group called the Eagles—were never released by Sun and, amazingly, were lost by RCA when they took possession of Sun's master recordings. As a result, Presley was forced to re-record them late in 1955 and early in 1956.

With the recording session behind them, Elvis, Scotty, and Bill continued their breakneck touring of the South. Life on the road for rock's first touring band bears virtually no resemblance to the great tours of today, in which caravans of 18-wheelers shuttle electronics, lighting, stage setups, instruments, and hundreds of technicians from venue to venue. For Elvis and the Blue Moon Boys, getting to the next gig was no more complicated than stowing guitars and Scotty's amp in the trunk and lashing Bill's bass to the roof of their car.

"Even in the early days before *Heartbreak Hotel*, we'd often play gigs that were maybe 400 miles apart," Scotty said later.

> We'd finish up one thing one night and then have to jump in the car, and we'd barely make it to the next one the next night. So we never heard what the people thought about us. Every time we'd play somewhere, there would be somebody there that lived in another part of the country, so the word would get around real quick. It didn't spread as fast then as it would today, because the media wasn't as big as it is now [Wingate, "The Guitar Man," *Music Mart*, 2005].

In later years, Moore would speak of one of the less appealing aspects of life on the road, the lack of variety in the group's setlist. In the beginning, they played what hits they had and then would stir in some current R&B hits to flesh out their set. All three grew sick of regurgitating the same tunes every night, and it was only after they'd been in the studio and laid down a sufficient amount of new music that their setlist would expand and ease the tedium.

On Sunday, February 6, in an engagement where he was fifth billed

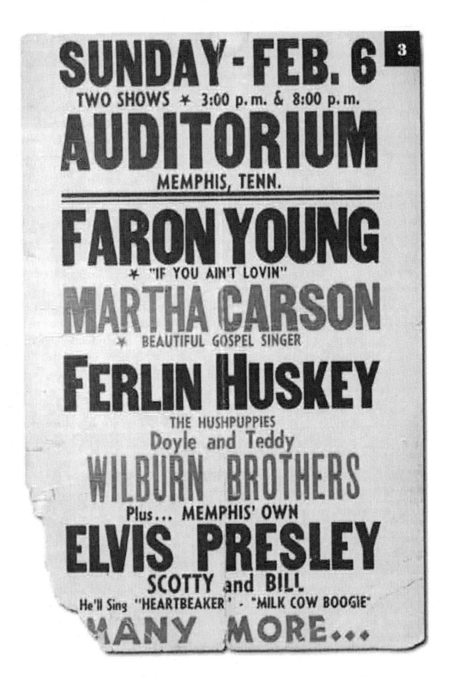

Elvis, Scotty, and Bill were back in Memphis for two shows in early 1955, as this promotional flyer shows.

behind Faron Young, Martha Carson, Ferlin Husky, and the Wilburn Brothers, Elvis played two shows at Memphis's Ellis Auditorium. To commemorate the occasion, the local paper devoted a four-column spread to Elvis, saying "A white man's voice singing negro rhythms with a rural flavour has changed life overnight for Elvis Presley" (*Memphis Press-Scimitar*, February 5, 1955).

As Elvis, Scotty, and Bill launched into their set, a restaurant across the street from the Ellis Auditorium was the site of a first ever meeting between Sam Phillips and Tom Parker. Also present were Bob Neal and Parker's assistant, Tom Diskin. If subsequent accounts are to be believed, things didn't go well. Sam, with his bullshit alarm forever on high alert for hustlers and chiselers, took an immediate dislike to the bulldozer-blunt Parker, who began by characterizing Sun Records as a "small-time" outfit that was completely ill equipped to further Elvis's career. To make matters worse, Parker, without consulting either Sam or Bob Neal in advance, let it slip that he'd made an overture to RCA records about purchasing Elvis's contract. Still, despite the enmity, no bridges were burned between the two men; the Colonel needed Elvis, and Sam, burning through cash at a bonfire pace, needed money to keep his small label afloat. The meeting concluded with a bright moment, with Parker telling everyone that he'd secured a prime spot for Elvis on Hank Snow's upcoming tour.

In late February, Elvis, Scotty, and Bill were in Cleveland for their first appearance outside the Deep South. While there, Elvis met the nationally syndicated DJ Bill Randle of WERE radio. "He was extremely shy," Randle recalls. "Talked about Pat Boone and Bill Haley as idols and called me 'Mr. Randle.' Very gentlemanly and interesting, he knew a lot about the music and the people and the personalities in Memphis and it was very exciting" (van Gestel and Rijff, *Elvis Presley, Memphis Lonesome*). In fact, Randle was so impressed with Elvis and the Blue Moon Boys that he promised to recommend them to a friend who produced the nationwide *Arthur Godfrey's Talent Scouts*, a 1950s precursor to later shows like *America's Got Talent* and *American Idol*.

On March 13, Elvis, billed as "the Be-Bop Western Star of the Louisiana Hayride," played a show at the Fair Park Coliseum in Lubbock, a booking arranged through Parker's Jamboree Attractions. Interestingly, one of the supporting acts was "Buddy and Bob," a country and western duo that featured a young Buddy Holly. It was during this tour that Bill Black, in an effort to pick up some extra cash, began selling pictures of Elvis to fans before and after shows for 25 cents apiece. To Bill's delight, sales were brisk. During an unedited interview with Elvis in the summer of 1955, Black can be heard in the background, pitching his product: "Here I have a brand, spankin' new pose of Elvis for a picture. And they'll be sellin' the same ol' price of only a quarter. And I'll have about four or five million of them. I'll have plenty of 'em, before the show, during the intermission, after the show. The fact is, I may sell them out there all night long!" (interview with Elvis Presley, Texarkana, August, 1955).

Departing Lubbock, Elvis, Scotty, and Bill hooked up with the Hank Snow tour where they were billed third, behind Snow and hillbilly comic the Duke of Paducah. A few days later, they found themselves in Odessa, Texas, where, before a crowd of over 4,000, they shared the bill with a weak-chinned and bespectacled young man with an operatic voice. "I couldn't overemphasize how shocking he looked and seemed to me that night," Roy Orbison said later of first seeing Elvis. "He told jokes that weren't funny, and his diction was real coarse like a truck driver's. There was pandemonium in the audience because the girls took a shine to him and the guys were getting a little jealous. His energy was incredible, his instinct was just amazing. I just didn't know what to make of it. There was just no reference point in the culture to compare it [to]. In a concert hall, he would be mocked, but here, he was magnificent" (elvis-history-blog.com, August 2014).

"No reference point" also serves as an apt description of the radical transformation that overcame Presley as he took the stage. Night after night, the shy kid who impressed everyone with his politeness and manners morphed into someone who prowled the stage with abandon, with the psychic energy of a repressed id seemingly unleashed. "First thing," remembers Orbison, "he came out and spat on the stage. In fact, he spat out a piece of gum." Such behavior, of course, might rub some—the tour's ostensible star, the genteel and courtly Hank Snow, for instance—the wrong way. Increasingly angered by Elvis's antics, Snow at one point dismissed Presley as a "young punk." Later, some would suggest that Snow's resentment of Elvis was related to envy over Presley's uncanny ability to read his audiences. The subdued reception to his first Louisiana Hayride performance had left a deep impression. Elvis now understood that every audience was different and that what worked with one might fail with another. "I see people all different ages and things," he once said. "If I do something good, they let me know it. If I don't, they let me know that too. It's a give and take proposition, in that they give me back the inspiration. I work absolutely to them. They bring it out of me, the inspiration. The ham" (interview, 1972).

Watching Elvis's rapid maturation as a performer with interest was Tom Parker. The Colonel knew nothing about music—an ignorance he would blithely carry to his grave—but he knew something about show business. Night after night, he'd watch as Elvis upstaged Snow, then marvel at the throng of teenage girls who invariably gathered outside the stage door. It was "in the air," he thought, that intangible quality that anointed stars and sidelined also-rans; he'd seen it with Snow, Eddy Arnold and others. But this was different; it was bigger, crazier. The kid had a future, of that he was sure, but not with little Sun Records. Sam Phillips's limited resources, Parker knew, would make it impossible to interest promoters beyond Sun's distribution range in booking the young singer. Getting him away from Sun would be easy; Phillips, to his mind, was a small-time operator, more concerned with art than with commerce. Besides, Sun was teetering on the verge of bankruptcy and, without an infusion of funds, was certain to go under. No, Sam Phillips wasn't the problem. The real test would be winning over Elvis and his parents. Hell, the kid even called home to his mother every night, speaking, it seemed to him, in a language all their own. Bluster and B.S. had carried him this far, but winning over Vernon and Gladys Presley, Parker knew, required a different approach, one based on honesty and sincerity. And faking those, he knew, would be easy.

The Music—March 1955—Sun Studios, Memphis

In March, Elvis and the Blue Moon Boys were back in the studio and, for the first time, would record with a drummer, Memphis teenager Jimmie Lott, who first came to Sam's attention a year earlier when his high school band made a pair of recordings at Sun.

In this, their second session in less than a month, Elvis, Scotty, and Bill would lay down two tracks. The first was written by Stan Kesler, a steel guitarist who, drawn by the sounds emanating from the little studio on Union Avenue, had started hanging around the Sun offices in hopes of catching Sam's eye. Ultimately he did, and Sam began using Kesler in the fall of 1954 as an occasional session man. Once he learned that Phillips was looking for material for Elvis, Kesler came up with "I'm Left, You're Right, She's Gone," a composition that Elvis would record twice during this session, once as a slow ballad that lacked punch and again as a more traditional up-tempo pop record, this time with Lott on drums. During this session, the group also took a stab at Webb Pierce's "How Do You Think I Feel," a Latin-flavored tune that was ultimately abandoned, though in the fall of '56 Presley would rework the song in a session for RCA.

Ten days later, Elvis, Scotty, Bill, and Bob Neal were on a plane to New York, where, thanks to Bill Randle's recommendation, they'd landed an audition for *Arthur Godfrey's Talent Scouts*. Neither Elvis nor Bill had ever flown before, and it was a first trip for everyone to New York. The sights and sounds of the Big Apple initially enthralled them, but once in Godfrey's studio, their spirits fell when they were treated dismissively by Godfrey's staff. Following the audition, the show's producer, clearly unimpressed, mentioned that he might be in touch. A day later, a representative from the show contacted Randle, informing him that Elvis "wasn't ready for the big time."

Any lingering disappointment over the New York trip, however, was soon shunted aside by the demands of touring, and by the spring of 1955, the gigs were virtually non-stop. A typical setlist during this phase might consist of "That's All Right," "Blue Moon of Kentucky," "Good Rockin' Tonight," "I Got a Woman," "Trying to Get to You," "Milkcow Blues," "Tweedle Dee" and maybe a Chuck Berry song that had recently made the charts. The band's stage setup was primitive, with just two microphones, one for Elvis and another for Bill's bass, with Scotty's amp on a chair behind him. A lack of on-stage monitors meant that none of them could hear themselves, and, night after night, the band competed with an ever-increasing volume of screams emanating from the audience. In later years, D.J. Fontana would speak of Elvis's almost uncanny ability to stay on track despite the backward conditions. "Elvis would never miss, even though he couldn't hear. I never saw him break meter. He always came right back in there. How he didn't get lost is beyond me" (Moore and Dickerson, *That's Alright, Elvis*). In later years, Elvis would speak fondly of this period. "It was always exciting," he said. "We slept in the back of the car and we'd do a show and get off-stage and get in the car and drive to the next town and sometimes get there in time to wash up and do the show" (1972 interview).

Bob Luman, who himself would go on to a successful career in music, recalls the moment when, as a high school boy, he first saw Elvis. "So the cat comes out, wearing red pants and a green coat with pink shirt and socks and he had this sneer on his face and stood behind the mike for five minutes, I'll bet, before he made a move. Then he hit his guitar a lick and he broke two strings. Hell, I'd been playing ten years and I hadn't broken a *total* of two strings." At that point, girls began to scream and Luman felt a chill run up his back. "That's the last time," Luman states, "that I tried to sing like Webb Pierce or Lefty Frizzel" (Guralnick and Jorgensen, *Elvis Day by Day*).

On April 25, Sun released "Baby Let's Play House" and "I'm Left, You're Right, She's Gone" as Elvis's fourth single. In its review, *Cash Box* found "Baby Let's Play House" to be "a real different, fast-paced piece on which Presley sparkles," while judging the flip side as "intriguing and forceful with a solid beat." Throughout the spring and summer, both tracks competed for airplay, but by August, "Baby Let's Play House" had gained the most. By year's end, it would end up as the 22nd most popular song on *Cash Box*'s top country chart (*Cash Box*, May 1955).

In May, Elvis, Scotty, and Bill, along with Hank Snow, hooked up with Parker's Jamboree Attractions for a tour of Louisiana, Florida, Alabama, Virginia, and North Carolina. This tour, on which Elvis received "Extra Added Attraction" billing, also featured the Carter Sisters, Slim Whitman, and Faron Young. To ease Hank Snow's concerns over being upstaged, Elvis appeared in the show's first half, just prior to the intermission. By now, riots were not uncommon, and in Jacksonville, Florida, Elvis triggered one, telling an audience of more than 14,000 at the conclusion of his set, "Girls, I'll see you backstage." In a flash, females by the hundreds descended on Presley's dressing room, where they tore at his clothes before finally being dispersed by security.

Watching all this with interest was Tom Parker. Hell-bent on tightening his grip on Elvis, Parker dashed off a note to Bob Neal in May, suggesting that henceforth, he (Parker) should "carry the ball" in all matters related to booking and promotion, a suggestion that would, in essence, make him Presley's de facto manager. Instead of being offended, Bob assented. At heart, Neal was a realist. He knew that Parker and his Jamboree Attractions were more capable than he was of taking Elvis's career to the next level. Neal also had business interests in Memphis that he was loath to be away from. "I had a contract with Elvis," Neal stated later, "and when, through part of my efforts, Parker got interested, we had a partnership agreement. You see, I was doing quite well with my radio program in Memphis. We had a record store, a large family and I didn't really ... well, I felt that Elvis was going to be very big and I didn't want to get into the picture of being gone from town all the time. So, I preferred to stay there and more or less turn everything over to the Colonel" (Rockville International, 1973).

After three shows in Texas, Elvis, Scotty, and Bill returned home to Memphis in early July for a two-week vacation. It was during this period that Elvis's steady girlfriend, Dixie Locke, noticed that something had changed since she last saw him. Where he was once satisfied doing things with just the two of them, now he wanted—in truth, needed—lots of people around him, as if the high he experienced from touring could only be sustained by coupling himself to a newly constructed cabal of courtiers. In just weeks, the two would split, but until that fateful day, Dixie would rarely spend another moment alone with Elvis. All of which made Presley's ever-present jealousy all the stranger to her. He was clearly pulling away, but when he was on tour, she'd nonetheless receive calls where Elvis would pester her with questions about what she'd been doing and whom she'd been seeing. He had no reason to worry: most nights, she was at the Presleys' house, where she and Gladys would shuck peas and speak hopefully of a time when she and Elvis would marry and raise a family.

While in Memphis on vacation, Elvis repeatedly spoke to Gladys and Vernon in glowing terms regarding Tom Parker and what a great job he'd done promoting the recent tour. In truth, both were unmoved by his enthusiasm. Parker might be okay, they told Elvis, but he had a commitment to a man they both liked, Bob Neal, and he should honor it. Besides, Parker's recent barrage of phone calls and his promises of what he could do for Elvis had been annoying. "Elvis was talking about [what] a great man he had met, how smart he was and all of that," Vernon said later. "Gladys and I warned him that we really didn't know anything about this man and anyway, he had an agreement with Bob Neal" ("Elvis, by His Father Vernon Presley," *Good Housekeeping*, January 1978). Elvis may have had stars in his eyes, but he was, first and foremost, the dutiful son. He was fully committed to both Neal and Sun Records he told them, news that he quickly relayed to Bob. When Neal informed Parker of this fact, the Colonel, completely unruffled, called RCA producer Steve Sholes minutes later, telling him that Elvis was on the cusp of exploding nationally and that RCA should make an immediate bid to purchase his contract from Sam Phillips.

11

Sneaking Around
Through Music

With his vacation—a period during which *Cash Box* announced that he was voted the number-one "Up and Coming Male Vocalist" by U.S. country music disc jockeys—drawing to an end, Elvis was back at Sun Studios in mid–July to craft a follow-up to "Baby Let's Play House." As he had in March, Sam Phillips brought in a percussionist for this session; in this case, he recruited local musician Johnny Bernero to play drums.

The Music—July 11, 1955—Sun Studios, Memphis

Back in February, Elvis, along with Scotty and Bill, had tried and failed to nail down an acceptable version of "Trying to Get to You." In July, with Bernero's percussion adding some needed muscle, they succeeded. Potent and powerful, "Trying to Get to You" would, in the years ahead, endure as one of Presley's personal favorites, showing up in his 1968 comeback special and as a staple of his tour setlist. In the song's lyrics, Elvis, with a celestial assist, makes his way back to his one true love, transforming "Trying to Get to You" into something of a *noir* classic while supplying prima facie evidence of the emotionally compelling music Presley was capable of producing in the mid-fifties. A close examination of this track reveals the lack of an acoustic rhythm guitar, suggesting that it was Elvis playing the keyboard heard on the recording.

As impressive as the final version of "Trying to Get to You" is, it's the second song recorded this day that confers legendary status to this session. "Mystery Train," a hit for Junior Parker and the Blue Flames, was originally recorded by Sam Phillips and released by Sun in 1953. For his version, Elvis overlaid the lyric and melody of the Parker original atop the tempo and feel of the song's B-side (Parker's "Love My Baby") to come up with this extraordinary recording. *Rolling Stone* magazine ranks

"Mystery Train" as the 77th greatest track of all time and calls it "one of Presley's most haunting songs." Sam Phillips would later pronounce "Mystery Train" as his greatest achievement, saying, "I'm sorry, but it was a fucking masterpiece!" (Guralnick, *The Last Train to Memphis*).

"Mystery Train" is also notable as the first track to feature two new additions to Scotty Moore's sonic arsenal. In the days prior to the session, Scotty traded his Gibson ES 295 for a Gibson L5, preferring the L5's tone and action. It was also during this period that he first utilized his new EchoSonic amplifier. "Sam Phillips used the slapback tape delay on 'That's All Right' and 'Blue Moon' and others," Scotty recalls.

> He had two tape machines—he'd cut it straight and transfer it to get the slapback. I remember thinking, "If we get a job somewhere, how am I gonna get that sound onstage?" It was about that time I heard Chet Atkins get that effect. With us, the echo effect was on the whole record, but here came Chet and it was just on the guitar. So I just checked up on it and found out he used a custom-made amp with a tape loop built in, made by a guy named Ray Butts up in Cairo, Illinois. So I got in touch with him and ordered the amp. It's called the EchoSonic. He wouldn't sell it on time, so the music store in Memphis bought it and put it in payments for me. It was like $498, which was heavy duty back then. Mine was the third one ever made. The first record I ever cut with that amp was "Mystery Train" [Cronin, "The Sun King," *Country Guitar*, 1994].

The third song recorded this day, "I Forgot to Remember to Forget," has an interesting history, having been issued by both Sun and RCA during 1955. The track was originally released by Sun on August 20, with "Mystery Train" as the B-side. When RCA purchased Elvis's contract on November 21, 1955, they took ownership of all Sun's master recordings as part of the deal. As a result, RCA re-released the song in December with a much wider distribution. Ultimately, the track reached the number-one position on *Billboard*'s C&W Best Sellers in Stores chart and number two on the *Cash Box* Country Singles chart in March of 1956. The flip side, "Mystery Train," peaked at number 11 on the national *Billboard* country chart.

On July 20, Elvis, Scotty, and Bill resumed touring for Parker's Jamboree Attractions, with shows in Missouri, Arkansas, Texas, and Florida, where they would share billing with actor/comedian Andy Griffith, who'd recently been a hit in "No Time for Sergeants" on the *U.S. Steel Hour* TV program. In Jacksonville, a riot broke out when fans crashed through security lines and mobbed Elvis, ripping off his shirt and coat before security finally rescued him. Back home in Memphis, word of the melee reached Gladys and, fearful for Elvis's safety, she made the first of many attempts to reach Bob Neal to express her concern. While all this transpired, Neal, hungering for a permanent return to Memphis, was doing his best to convince Elvis that his future lay with Tom Parker.

For the early months of 1955, Elvis, Scotty, and Bill had kicked around the notion of adding a drummer to their act. All three had responded positively to having a percussionist in the studio, and with a drummer supporting them on stage, they might be heard over the screams that were now commonplace wherever they played. Initially, Elvis balked at adding a full-time member to the band, saying he didn't think they could afford it. After a bit of back and forth, Scotty and Bill told Elvis that if he'd hire D.J. Fontana, whom they all liked, as a salaried employee, they'd split the cost of his $100 per week salary, a proposal that Elvis deemed acceptable. So on August 8, 1955, in Tyler, Texas, D.J. Fontana played his first gig as a permanent, albeit salaried, member of Elvis and the Blue Moon Boys.

With the addition of drummer D.J. Fontana, the world's first true rock 'n' roll band was now a quartet, establishing for a generation of musicians to come the configuration template of two guitars, bass, and drums. Left to right: Scotty Moore, Bill Black, D.J. Fontana (*Memphis Press-Scimitar*).

It was also during this period that Elvis would meet a performer whom he clearly admired. "I had lived in Texas," Pat Boone recalls, "and I had seen his name on some country jukeboxes and I wondered how in the world a hillbilly could be the next big thing, especially with a name like Elvis Presley."

> So I was curious and sure enough, at the high school auditorium where we did this thing, he came backstage and already he had a little entourage. Now nobody in Cleveland had ever heard of him, so the fact that he had an entourage struck me as funny. I went, over-dressed in my button-down collar and thin tie and white buck shoes, and introduced myself. He mumbled something I couldn't understand, leaned back against the wall with his head down and never looked me in the eye. So I said "Boy, Bill Randle thinks you're really going to be big" and he said "Mmm, mrrrbllde...," sort of a country twang mumble. I just couldn't tell what he was saying. He had his shirt collar turned up and his hair was real greasy, and it was, well, he was always looking down you know, like he couldn't look up. I thought to myself, what's the matter with this guy? [*Rolling Stone*, April 1990].

Boone wasn't the only one to find Presley odd, at least according to Carl Perkins. "People would laugh at his sideburns and his pink coat and call him sissy," he recalls. "He had a pretty hard road to go. In some areas, motorcycle gangs would come to the shows. They would come to get Elvis, but he never worried about it. He went right out and did his thing and before the show was over, they were standing in line to get his autograph too" (*Rolling Stone*, September 22, 1977).

As the Presley caravan rolled on through the South, Tom Parker continued his outreach to Vernon and Gladys Presley, stating repeatedly that he had "a very good deal pending" that would please them both. By August 3, he was poised to make his move. First he persuaded Gladys and Vernon to attend a meeting in Little Rock, where Presley was performing; it would include himself, Tom Diskin, Bob Neal, and, of course, Elvis. Then, during the course of the meeting, Parker would suggest that he, with enthusiastic support from Neal, be named "special advisor" to Elvis. Parker sensed that Vernon was coming around; recent promises of future riches had softened his resistance. Nonetheless, Gladys remained skeptical. The riot in Jacksonville had clearly unnerved her, and because it took place during one of Parker's tours, she doubted his ability to take care of her boy. Anyway, she liked and trusted Bob Neal and saw no reason for Elvis to make a switch.

"Elvis mentioned on more than one occasion when some of us were sitting around, that his mother didn't really trust Colonel Parker and didn't like him," Presley family friend Arlene Cogan said later. "Vernon would tell us that when Colonel Parker would come to the house and get

Elvis locked up for a meeting, that he couldn't even talk to his own son until Parker left" (Begley, elvisinfonet.com, 2009).

The meeting ended in a stalemate. After Gladys expressed concerns over what happened in Jacksonville, Parker apologized for the security lapse and promised that nothing like that would ever happen again. He then added that if Elvis signed a contract with him he wouldn't have to play these "little dates" and could move into more prestigious gigs where security would be more robust. With Gladys still hesitant, Parker decided on a strategic withdrawal, telling everyone that nothing needed to be signed that day. Elvis, while expressing support for his mother, was nonetheless convinced that his future lay with Tom Parker and his Jamboree Attractions.

In the following days, Elvis resumed touring, playing dates in Arkansas. Then, on August 5, he made a triumphal return to Memphis's Overton Park, where, on a bill that included Johnny Cash and Sonny James, he played to an audience of more than 4,000. Among the crowd was Marion Keisker, who hadn't seen Elvis perform since his Opry appearance a year earlier. To her surprise, the reserved mother of a young son found herself screaming along with everyone else. Also in the crowd that day was country western guitarist Chet Atkins. "I couldn't get over the eye shadow he was wearing," Atkins said later. "It was like seeing a couple of guys kissin' in Key West" (Cosby, *Devil's Music, Holy Rollers and Hillbillies*).

Following a brief cooling off period after the failure of the Arkansas meeting, Parker began to cannonade Gladys and Vernon with phone calls and telegrams urging them to reconsider. To bolster his case, the Colonel prevailed upon Hank Snow, an artist the Presleys revered, to make regular calls to Gladys and Vernon on his behalf. Apparently Snow's ministrations did the trick, because on August 15 the principals gathered once again, and this time all three Presleys signed an agreement naming Parker as special advisor to Elvis for a period of one year with an option for another two, with Bob Neal, ostensibly, remaining as Elvis's manager. Taking all this in with a burgeoning sense of foreboding was Scotty Moore.

"He just kept encroaching and then when he got Elvis, he knew he had a product," Moore recalls. "And I'll give the old feller credit where credit was due: He'd spend $100 to beat you out of one buck just to prove he could do it" (*Washington Post*, August 10, 1997).

Newly empowered, Parker quickly set to work undercutting two men who'd played a critical role in the rise of Elvis Presley: Scotty Moore and Bill Black. Just days after becoming Presley's special advisor, Bob Neal, acting on Parker's instructions, informed Scotty and Bill that their verbal agreement of a 50–25–25 split with Elvis was no longer tenable. Elvis was the star, Neal explained, and crowds were flocking to see him, not them. Neal then laid it out: henceforth, they'd be paid a salary of $200 per week when working and $100 when they weren't. And when touring, both men would pay their own expenses. Scotty and Bill were stunned. They'd considered Elvis a friend, someone who would honor his agreements, which was why they'd never insisted on a written contract. Now, what began as a partnership based on friendship and trust had devolved into nothing more than a business arrangement. "I remember there was quite a bit of unhappiness at this at that time," Neal said later. "That they would quit and so on. But they stayed" (Hopkins, *Elvis, the Biography*). Neal would later contend that the idea for the pay cuts had originated from a conversation with Elvis and his parents, but the timing and Parker's lifelong contempt for musicians, which he expressed in both verbal and non-verbal ways until the day he died, makes it clear that the decision was his. In the years ahead, Scotty would repeatedly point to this day as the moment his relationship with Elvis began a downward spiral.

As it turns out, Parker's campaign to screw Scotty and Bill was just getting started. Later that month, the Colonel cornered Bob Neal and suggested that he approach Elvis with a proposition: if Presley agreed to dump Scotty and Bill, Parker would arrange for Hank Snow's group to back him for future tours. At this, Neal balked and refused to even raise the issue with Elvis. But Parker still wasn't done. For weeks he'd watched with annoyance as Bill Black sold 8×10 photos of Elvis before and after each show. Bill didn't make much from it, maybe a dime in profit per picture, but it came in handy. But to Parker, a dime was a dime, and soon the word came down: henceforth, any concession work would be handled by Parker himself. If Bill wanted to assist, fine, but at a reduced profit rate. Insulted and angry, Black said no.

In October, Elvis was back on tour with Hank Snow for a series of shows that attracted coverage in local newspapers, including this from Oklahoma:

> Elvis Presley, a twenty-year old fireball from the Louisiana Hayride, will be an added starter today when Bill Haley, Hank Snow and many other top-notchers put on two western music hoe-downs at Municipal Auditorium. It's hard to pick out an individual standout from the array of stars scheduled for the appearance, but Presley might be the one the teen set will be watching most closely. His combination of country music and bop has captured the fancy of the young set in a way few stars have managed and his extreme youth and good looks add to his popularity [*The Oklahoman*, October 16, 1955].

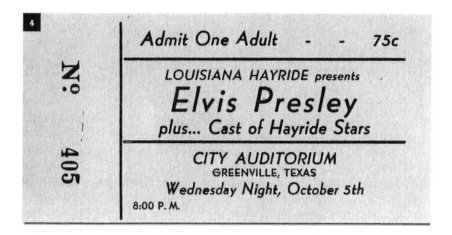

Ticket stub for Presley's October 5, 1955, appearance in Greenville, Texas, for yet another Louisiana Hayride performance.

There was also this from Austin, Texas:

The nationally famous Louisiana Hayride will roll into the Skyline Club Thursday night with a full-load of hillbilly music and performers as its cargo. Heading the show will be Elvis Presley, young western music sensation whose distinctive brand of vocalizing has made him probably the hottest hillbilly attraction of the day. Labeled the "king of western bop" by his fans, Presley has become widely popular for his knack of combing hillbilly music with modern "rock 'n' roll" fare, a unique blend in evidence on such Presley hit records as "That's All Right," "Blue Moon of Kentucky" and "Good Rockin' Tonight" [*The Austin American*, October 6, 1955].

A similar perspective from Paris, Texas:

Presley, "the king of western bop" as many of his fans call him, is a twenty-year old youngster who has set the field of country music to talking with his unusual combination of folk music spiced with a "rock 'n' roll" beat. His Sun records are in demand by folk music fans coast-to-coast. A natural sense of rhythm along with a unique voice benefited from his childhood surroundings in which country music and negro blues were every day to him [*Paris News*, October 3, 1955].

The Music—November 1955—Sun Studios, Memphis

In November, Elvis, Scotty, and Bill, this time with drummer Johnny Bernero, were back in the studio to come up with a B-side for "Trying to Get to You." "When It Rains, It Really Pours" was a blues track that Sam was clearly enthusiastic about, but, by all accounts, the atmosphere at this session was glum, likely due to recent moves by Parker. Throughout the session, Scotty struggled to find his groove, and even the usually upbeat Bill was sullen and withdrawn. Ultimately, attempts at nailing down an acceptable recording would fail, as Johnny Bernero makes clear. "We were recording a good while," Bernero recalls. "Elvis went into the control room and talked to Sam a good half-hour. He came out and told me 'Johnny, we're not going to be able to finish this session.' Still, he paid me the fifty dollars" (Jorgensen, *Elvis Presley, A Life in Music*).

Elvis and Sam may have spent 30 minutes in the control room discussing *something*, but it wasn't "When It Rains, It Really Pours." In the weeks prior to this session, Tom Parker had continued his machinations, turning every trick he knew to get Elvis away from Sun Records and signed to a major label. His preference was RCA; both Hank Snow and Eddy Arnold recorded for the label, and producer Steve Sholes, who was a friend, had handled A&R duties for both. But even as he pushed RCA, Parker courted other labels, spinning tales of just how big a star Elvis would be, in an obvious attempt to trigger a bidding war. Given the fact that Elvis was still contracted to Sun Records, Parker's involvement in all of this might appear unseemly. But the Colonel, forever in search of a weakness he could exploit, knew that Sam Phillips was in a bind. Record promotion was revenue draining and time consuming and kept Sam away from his real love, discovering new artists and recording. Manufacturing had also exacted a huge toll on Sun's bottom line, in essence forcing Sam to pay in advance for records that might not sell. None of this was news to Parker, and he was acutely aware that in the waning months of 1955, Sun's thin resources were stretched nearly to the breaking point.

Whether by birth or circumstance, Sam Phillips was a dreamer, a member in good standing among the world's true fantasists. But he was also a realist. With no intention of ever being a one-artist producer, Sam, even as Elvis prospered, had worked earnestly to build a stable of promising new artists, including Carl Perkins, Jerry Lee Lewis, and Johnny Cash, performers he desperately wanted to promote, if only he had the resources. There was another wrinkle to all this. For years, Sam had wanted his own Memphis radio station, one for which he and he alone would determine who and what was played. But all this took money, something currently in very short supply. By January of 1955, things had become so tough Sam composed the following missive to his brother:

I have told you repeatedly that Sun liabilities are three times the assets and I have been making every effort possible to keep out of bankruptcy. Anyone less interested in saving face would have given it up long ago, but I intend to pay every dollar the company owes—including you—even while I know there is no possible way to ever get out with a dollar [Escott and Hawkins, *Good Rockin' Tonight*].

Things finally came to head in early fall when Sam called Parker to complain of stories he'd heard from distributors that the Colonel was working behind his back. Parker, feigning surprise and protesting his innocence, nonetheless decided to approach the issue head-on. Was he interested in selling Elvis's contract? "Well, I just might be," came the reply. When prompted for a price tag, Sam said he'd mull it over and call him back. Minutes later, the phone rang in Parker's office. The price, Sam said, was $35,000, plus an additional $5,000 to cover what he owed Elvis in back royalties. Sam knew that no artist had ever been sold at such a price and expected the Colonel to recoil, but, to his surprise, Parker didn't blink.

On Saturday, October 29, a meeting was held at the Memphis Holiday Inn with Phillips, Parker, and Tom Diskin in attendance. After prompting Sam to repeat his asking price for Elvis, Parker, in an attempt to haggle, balked, saying he wasn't sure he could raise that much. After a bit of negotiation, Sam and the Colonel settled on an option deal, under which Parker would pay Sam $5,000 within two weeks, with a balance of $30,000 to be paid by December 1. If he failed, the $5,000 would be non-refundable and the option would not be extended.

At this point, Parker was still playing record label against record label, trumpeting Elvis's potential and reminding all that both *Billboard* and *Cash Box* had named Elvis as country music's most promising new talent. On November 15, the word came down: RCA, fearing they would lose Elvis to a competitor if they didn't act, agreed to purchase Elvis's contract from Sam at his asking price of $35,000. So, on November 21, a group that included Sam, Tom Parker, Tom Diskin, Jamboree partner Hank Snow, and a couple of RCA distributors gathered at 706 Union Avenue to sign contracts that would officially make Elvis Presley RCA's newest recording artist. As a condition of the deal, Sun agreed to hand over all tapes and immediately stop distribution and sales of anything Elvis recorded for Sun by December 31.

For his part, Elvis would realize a 5 percent royalty per recording (a 2 percent increase) and, additionally, would receive a percentage of any songs he recorded by the RCA-affiliated Hill and Range music publishing group, an outfit founded in 1945 by Julian Aberbach, later joined by his brother Jean. Under this practice, a composer who wanted his song to be recorded by Elvis first had to agree to surrender one third of his potential royalties, which were paid by the record company to the song publisher. Once received by the publisher, the royalties would ordinarily be split 50–50 with the composer (or composers), but under the Hill and Range setup, one-third was carved out to be paid to Elvis personally. The result? The songwriter received 33 and ⅓ percent in royalty instead of the industry standard 50 percent. At the height of its success in the mid–1950s, Hill and Range was responsible for as many as two-thirds of all songs recorded in Nashville, and for years to come Elvis would insist on recording H&R songs almost exclusively, a decision that, in future years, would prove disastrous.

On November 22, the *Memphis Press-Scimitar* trumpeted the sale of Elvis to RCA on its front page:

> Elvis Presley, 20, Memphis recording star and entertainer who zoomed into the bigtime and the big money almost overnight, has been released from his contract with Sun Record Co. of Memphis. Phillips and RCA offices did not reveal terms but said the money involved is probably the highest ever paid for a contract release for a country-western recording artist. "I feel Elvis is one of the most talented youngsters today," Phillips said, "and by releasing his contract to RCA Victor, we will give him the opportunity of entering the largest organization of its kind in the world, so his talents can be given the fullest opportunity" [*Memphis Press-Scimitar*, November 22, 1955].

It's interesting to note that the *Press-Scimitar*'s article makes no mention of some truly momentous news that occurred at this same time. Tom Parker, with an assist from RCA, had connected with Jack Philbin, the producer of CBS-TV's *Stage Show*, hoping to arrange a national television appearance for Elvis, his first. The program, something of a ratings also-ran against the more popular *Perry Como Show*, was hosted by bandleaders Tommy and Jimmy Dorsey. Ultimately an agreement was reached under which Elvis would make his nationwide TV debut in January, news omitted from the *Press-Scimitar* article likely due to the fact that final details for the appearance were still being ironed out between Parker, the Dorsey brothers, and Philbin.

The sale of Elvis Presley to RCA would provide Sun Records with a desperately needed financial lifeline, one that would serve as critical fuel for the emergence of new Sun artists. And while there's no denying that Sam Phillips lost Elvis to a man he despised, a man to whom Elvis would demonstrate an almost canine fealty until the day he died, Sam could nonetheless look back on what he'd accomplished with pride. Over the past year, he'd staked a rebel flag in the heart of mainstream America and showered it with sounds that rattled with energy and intensity. And in so doing, he'd not only changed music, he'd changed the country. None of it was easy—he hadn't expected it to be. But it was his vision and it was not to be fucked with. In the waning years of his life, he would reflect on the struggle and what had been accomplished:

> I had to keep my nose clean. They could have said "This goddam rebel down here is gonna' turn his back on us. Why should we give this nigger loving sonofabitch a break?" But I had the ability to be patient. I wasn't looking for no tall stump to preach from. And I sensed in [Elvis] the same kind of empathy. I don't think he was aware of my motivation for doing what I was trying to do, not consciously anyway, but intuitively, he felt it. The lack of prejudice on the part of Elvis Presley had to be one of the biggest things that ever could have happened to us. It was almost subversive, sneaking around through the music, but we hit things a little bit, don't you think? I went into this no-man's land and I knocked the shit out of the color line [Guralnick, *Last Train to Memphis*].

12

RCA

When Elvis arrived at RCA's Nashville recording studios in January for his first session with a major label, he had no way of knowing that he was already being second-guessed. In recent days, recording industry scuttlebutt was that Carl Perkins, with his recently recorded "Blue Suede Shoes," was about to break nationwide, reports that triggered fear among RCA executives that they'd signed the wrong Sun artist. A quote in the November issue of *Billboard* magazine did little to soothe their concerns. "Anyone who buys Elvis Presley," the article stated in no uncertain terms, "will get stuck." Was RCA stuck? They simply didn't know. But whatever the reality, they weren't about to take any chances. Which meant that when it came to recording Elvis, they would retreat to proven methods and attempt to duplicate the unique sound of Elvis's Sun hits (*Billboard*, November 1955).

In truth, Steve Sholes and RCA's engineers simply had no idea how Sam Phillips created what was increasingly being referred to around the recording industry as the "Sun Sound." In the days leading up to the session, Sholes had called Phillips and asked him to share his recording secrets, but Sam, pleasantly but firmly, refused. After days of tinkering, the closest that Sholes and RCA could come to replicating Sam's slapback soundscape was by staging a microphone at one end of a hallway and a speaker at the other end, then routing the sound back to the studio.

"The first record we did for RCA, it was literally a long hallway," Scotty Moore recalls.

> Sam had been using tape echo, or slapback, and whether he was doing it on purpose or not, he also treated Elvis' voice like another instrument. The voice was real close to the rest of the music and most times back then, in country and pop, the vocal was always way out in front; even on RCA the voice was out more than we were used to. But in "Heartbreak Hotel," which was a real deep echo, they had a speaker set up at one end of this long hallway and a microphone at the other end, and a sign on the door saying

RCA VICTOR RECORD BULLETIN

BIGGEST C&W RECORD NEWS OF THE YEAR!

In Elvis Presley we've acquired the most dynamic and sought-after new artist in country music today, one who's topped the "most promising" category in every trade and consumer poll held during 1955!

Promotion is being spearheaded with disc jockey records to the entire Pop and C&W "A" lists, an initial coverage of more than 4,000 destinations!

Page ads will appear this week in Billboard and Cash Box, reprints about 10 days later. The issues will carry full publicity on Presley's joining the label.

It's imperative that you follow up this all-market approach to every station receiving Pop or Country service. Use the trade articles to sell your dealers and one stops across the board!

The tunes: I FORGOT TO REMEMBER TO FORGET and MYSTERY TRAIN. The number: 20/47-6357. The name: ELVIS PRESLEY, one that will be your guarantee of sensational plus-sales in the months to come!

955-489
11/28/55

John Y. Burgess, Jr., Manager
Sales and Promotion
Single Record Department

RCA record industry bulletin, announcing their purchase of Elvis's contract from Sun Records, November 28, 1955.

"DON'T OPEN THE DOOR WHEN THE RED LIGHT IS ON." Room echo back then was virtually unheard of in recording, although they used it in motion pictures for sound effects [*Guitarist*, 1992].

"The only thing I remember is that they were trying to get that echo sound," D.J. Fontana recalls. "They'd run some mikes down the hallways. They wanted to have the same sound that he had with Sam, but they never did get it" (interview with D.J. Fontana, elvis.com.au, January 1, 2016).

Prior to the session, Steve Sholes had sent Elvis a list of 10 possible songs and asked him to select the five he favored. Around the same time, Sholes tapped guitarist Chet Atkins to serve as session manager, which meant he'd oversee all scheduling and book the necessary musicians and technicians. For vocal support, Elvis specifically requested the Jordanaires, the quartet he'd seen perform at numerous gospel programs in and around Memphis. In addition to Scotty, Bill, and D.J. (the move to RCA would signal an end to their being known as "The Blue Moon Boys"), the session would also include Floyd Cramer on piano.

To Elvis's disappointment, he would be greeted by just a single Jordanaire, Gordon Stoker, when he arrived for work. The remaining vocal support, Atkins informed Elvis, would fall to members of the Speer Family, a gospel group recently signed by RCA. Stoker, already annoyed at Chet for not including the rest of his group, was also struck by his cavalier attitude toward Presley. "He didn't think Elvis would be around long," Stoker said later. "He said 'You know, we've signed this kid from Memphis, but, you know, he's a passing fad'" (Moore and Dickerson, *That's Alright, Elvis*).

Years later, Atkins would remark on his first meeting with Elvis. "I set the session for the afternoon, and he came in with pink trousers with blue stripes and he was real nice. He'd 'yes sir' and 'no sir' you to death. He was very respectful, a little too much" (*Rolling Stone*, September 22, 1977).

Respectful, maybe, but according to Stoker, Presley nonetheless never forgave Atkins for forcing members of the Speer family onto his recordings. "Well, as soon as he got to the session, Elvis said to me, 'Where are the other Jordanaires?' I said, 'Well, Chet didn't want me to use 'em.' You know, after that, he never liked Chet. He called him a sneaky son of a bitch" (Burke and Griffin, *The Blue Moon Boys*).

The Music—January 10–11, 1956— RCA Studios, Nashville

With the studio jury-rigged for echo, Elvis's initial RCA session kicked off at 2:00 p.m. on January 11. As the crow flies, Memphis was just over 200 miles from Nashville, but the distance between Sam Phillips's and RCA's recording methods could be measured in light years. Elvis, Scotty, and Bill had grown accustomed to Sun's casual approach to recording. If something didn't click, Sam would merely pop his head outside the control room and say something like, "Guys, let's try another one." Now, all three had to acclimate themselves to Nashville's more structured approach with a recording engineer calling out numbers for each take.

The first song they attempted was "I Got a Woman," the Ray Charles R&B classic from 1954. For his part, Elvis seemed relaxed, appearing not to notice that, for the first time, he'd hear the echo effect live in the studio. (At Sun, the slapback was applied only when the track was completed.) Because "I Got a Woman" had been a staple of his live act for nearly a year, things went smoothly, and, within an hour, Elvis completed a studio master.

Next up was "Heartbreak Hotel," a song co-written by Mae Axton and Tommy Durden. Axton, an employee of Tom Parker, was also the mother of songwriter-guitarist Hoyt Axton. Inspiration for the song came from a newspaper article about a man who committed suicide and left a note saying, "I walk the lonely street." Echo-drenched and moody, with instrumental breaks that evoke a 2:00 a.m. melancholy, "Heartbreak Hotel," along with "Baby Let's Play House" and "Mystery Train," would inspire countless young males in future years to make tracks to the nearest pawn shop for their first guitar. Rock figures ranging from John Lennon to Tom Petty to Paul McCartney have sung the praises of this swampy and atmospheric song. "When I heard it, it was the end for me.... I remember rushing home with the record," said Lennon (Norman, *John Lennon—The Life*). "It could have been the national anthem," raved Petty, "It rocks and when the piano comes in, it starts to roll in this really sensual way. The track is very spooky and very empty" (Zollo, *Conversations with Tom Petty*). "It's an amazing song," agreed McCartney. "His phrasing, his use of echo, it's all so beautiful. It's the way he sings it, too. As if he's singing it from the depths of hell. It's a perfect example of a singer being in command of the song" (*Rolling Stone*, August 2015). Critical to the song's appeal is Floyd Cramer, whose keyboard stylings imbue the track with a sense of descending gloom. It's interesting to note that in performing the song live, Presley never once attempted to sustain the recorded version's murky feel, instead using the song's instrumental breaks to incite his heavily female audience with energetic stage antics.

Following take 7, everyone sensed that something extraordinary had been achieved. Even Chet Atkins, who'd been so dismissive of Elvis prior to the session, found himself overwhelmed by what he was witnessing and, during a break, called his wife, telling her to get to the studio immediately. "I told her she'd never see anything like this again, it was so damn exciting" (Arena Television, *Tales of Rock & Roll—Heartbreak Hotel*, 1991).

At 5:00 p.m. everyone broke for dinner and then at 7:00 p.m.

reconvened to start work on "Money Honey," a 1953 hit for the Drifters. Ultimately, they'd make seven attempts at perfecting the tune, but only by splicing takes 5 and 6 were they able to complete a satisfactory master.

At 4:00 p.m. the following day they were back at it, this time to work on "I'm Counting on You," a ballad by songwriter Don Robertson, who, before he was through, would contribute 14 songs to the Presley songbook. Early takes of this tune border on perfection, but Elvis, feeling he could do better, decided to push on. It would require 17 attempts before he was satisfied. From there, they went to work on "I Was the One," a doo-wop flavored ballad composed by Aaron Schroeder, Bill Peppers, Claude Demetrius, and Hal Blair, which they wrapped up after just seven tries. Elvis was particularly proud of his work on this track and, at his urging, "I Was the One" would ultimately end up as the flip side to "Heartbreak Hotel."

Years later, Steve Sholes would comment on his initial session with Elvis. "When we first started recording," he recalled, "the way he held his guitar was pretty close to where his mouth was and we were trying to record him vocally at the same time because we didn't do tracking in those days."

> The guitar was so loud you couldn't hear his voice. We moved the mike around and so forth and we finally ended up using a ukulele pick, a felt pick. He played the guitar so hard that every two or three takes he would break a string. And even after we got the ukulele pick, he was still breaking strings. I remember one take we were doing, he dropped the ukulele pick in the middle of a take, but he kept on banging the thing with his fingers. Jesus, when we got done with the take, his fingers were bleeding, so I said to him "Why didn't you quit?" "Oh," he said, "it was going so good, I didn't want to break it up" [Hopkins, *Elvis, the Biography*].

With Elvis's first RCA session completed, Steve Sholes, with acetates of the five completed songs under his arm, flew to New York to play them for company executives. Their reaction stunned him; it wasn't that they simply disliked the songs he'd recorded, they hated them. They didn't sound like his Sun records, they said. Why? After conferring among themselves, they told Sholes to immediately drag Elvis back into the studio and try again. "Not possible," Sholes replied. First of all, he'd spent two full days laying down what to his mind were five good tracks and had no intention of not releasing them. Besides, Elvis, Scotty, Bill, and D.J. were currently touring and unavailable. Elvis would be back in New York at month's end to appear on the Dorsey brothers' *Stage Show*, his first nationwide television appearance. Wouldn't it make sense to schedule another session then? Reluctantly, they agreed. But in the meantime, Sholes had his marching orders: figure out what had gone wrong.

13

Promised Land

After a return to Shreveport for what would be their final Louisiana Hayride appearance, Elvis played a series of one-nighters in Texas. Then, with their appearance on the Dorsey brothers' *Stage Show* program looming, Elvis, Scotty, Bill, and D.J. arrived in New York on Wednesday, January 25 to begin rehearsals. To Tom Parker, Elvis and the Dorseys were a perfect match. Elvis needed national TV exposure, and their *Stage Show*, a perennial also-ran in the Nielsen ratings, needed a shot in the arm.

When Parker was initially contacted by *Stage Show* producers Jack Philbin and Tino Barzie weeks earlier regarding Elvis, both men, before extending a contract, wanted to know what he looked like. When handed a picture of Elvis, Philbin and Barzie registered surprise, with Philbin declaring that Elvis was a "guitar playing Marlon Brando!" "I started looking around for new acts—like some country-and-western people," Tino Barzie recalls. "Somebody turned me on to an act handled by Tom Parker. I asked, 'What's his name?' 'It's Elvis Presley.' I said, 'Elvis? What kind of name is that?' I tracked Presley down in New Orleans [where he was headlining The Louisiana Hayride] and spoke to Tom Parker. I told him we'd like to use Elvis on several shows. He was thrilled to death. I booked Elvis for the following Saturday. I bought him for four shows for a total of five thousand dollars" (Levinson, *Tommy Dorsey: Livin' in a Big Way*). The contract that Elvis and Tom Parker signed also contained an option for two additional appearances.

When he arrived for rehearsals at New York's Nola Studios, Elvis was at his most respectful and humble, actions that nonetheless failed to impress comedian Jackie Gleason, who was on hand that day. "I don't like this guy," the rotund comedian told Dorsey. The bandleader disagreed, saying "I like his kisser" before adding "Don't worry about him." If Gleason had doubts about Elvis, Dorsey's band members were even more caustic. "During our rehearsal with him, some guys fell off the bandstand laughing at Elvis," recalled one Dorsey musician. "It was so shocking to all of us, we couldn't believe it." "We didn't like him because he looked dirty," said another, "and he needed a haircut. We thought he never bathed." Still, Dorsey held fast. "You see that guy Elvis Presley—he's going to be one of the biggest names in show business in a short time" (Levinson, *Tommy Dorsey: Livin' in a Big Way*).

At 8:00 p.m. on January 28, *Stage Show* aired on CBS. In what must certainly stand as one of the new medium's starkest contrasts, the program opened with an unintentionally hilarious segment of mincing showgirls mock-playing vibraphones, trailed by a pair of acrobatic dancers, who, if still extant, are likely nursing spinal cord issues. Once the amusement subsided, New York disc jockey Bill Randall made his way to the microphone to introduce Elvis. "We think tonight that he's going to make television history for you," he said. At that point, Elvis, in a white tie, black shirt, and speckled coat, entered, nodded to Scotty, and then, eschewing the use of a pick, launched into Big Joe Turner's "Shake, Rattle and Roll." Following Scotty's solo break—during which an arm-waving, gum-chewing Bill Black egged Elvis on with "Go, Go, Go!"—Elvis switched gears and tore into another Turner song, "Flip, Flop and Fly." Then, after a bow and a wave, it was over, with the audience, in one attendee's words, exhibiting a mixture of "amusement and shock." For a 21-year-old in his first appearance before a national audience, Elvis delivered a stunningly assured performance, suggesting that the past year's breakneck string of one-nighters had paid dividends in the way of confidence.

A day or two later, *Memphis Press-Scimitar* reporter Bob Johnson rendered the following impression of Elvis's *Stage Show* appearance:

> Presley puts intensity into his songs. Over-emotional? Yes. But he projects. He "sells." Elvis has arrived.... But you can't throw that much into something without it telling. It'll wear him out. It will exhaust him emotionally and physically. He's twenty now [actually twenty-one]. If he's wise, he'll slow down a little and live another twenty years [Johnson, *Elvis Presley Speaks!*].

Following Elvis's appearance, the show's staff was inundated with complaints from viewers stunned that the respected Dorsey brothers would allow someone like Presley on their program. But for the Dorseys, ratings were king, and when the numbers came in, they felt vindicated; Elvis had just delivered the program's highest-ever rating. Peter Levinson, in his biography of Tommy Dorsey, wrote that "Elvis Presley *was* rock 'n' roll," a musical form "which was suddenly embraced by the emerging generation as its own music. Its sound shattered the complacency of the 1950s and broke the ground for the antiestablishment culture coming in the following decades. The combination of saxophones and brass no longer carried the melody; guitars took their place" (Levinson, *Tommy Dorsey: Livin' in a Big Way*, Da Capo Press, 2009).

"We did the first show with Tommy and Jimmy Dorsey," Scotty Moore remembered, "and with that, coupled with the first record we did on RCA, 'Heartbreak Hotel,' it was just like an atomic bomb going off! Nobody even had time to think after that. A phenomenon, really! And even being as close to it as I was. It's still hard for me to realize it. I think I'm still getting shock waves out of it" (Green, "Perhaps the First Rock & Roll Guitarist," *Guitar Player*, 1974).

The Music—January 30–31, February 3, 1956— RCA Studios, New York

While the controversy over Elvis's *Stage Show* appearance continued to rage, Elvis and the band convened at RCA studios in New York on Monday, January 30, for his second RCA session. Once again, to Elvis's annoyance, the Jordanaires weren't present and, instead of Floyd Cramer, keyboard duties would be handled by RCA session player Shorty Long.

In addition to being Presley's first New York recording session, January 30 also signaled another first: from this day forward, virtually every Presley session would kick off with Elvis picking his way through a stack of Hill and Range demos compiled by H&R representative Fred Bienstock to select songs to record. One by one, the demos would be fed from the control room into the studio. If Elvis liked it and wanted to hear it again, he'd point to the top of his head, saying, in essence, "play it from the top." If he wasn't interested, he'd make a slashing motion across his throat. Once a song was settled on, it then became a group affair, with Elvis working out the arrangement with Scotty, Bill, and D.J.

Interestingly, the first track they attempted was "Blue Suede Shoes," a track recently recorded by Carl Perkins for Sun Studios. As a rule, Elvis would resist recording a song that was presently associated with another performer. "He would never do a song while it was in the charts for another artist," Jordanaires bass singer Ray Walker recalls. "He said 'That's stealin' and I'm not gonna do it'" (author interview with Ray Walker, September 18, 2020). But Steve Sholes, feeling the heat from his higher-ups that Presley's work thus far hadn't matched the authenticity of his Sun sides, was pressing Elvis to cover the tune. Elvis acceded, but on two conditions: that Sholes first get an OK from Sam Phillips and that the track not be released as a single. Before he was through, Elvis would make multiple tries at perfecting his version of "Blue Suede Shoes," before finally giving up after 10 attempts. Take 10 was "good enough" he told Sholes; besides, Elvis felt there was no way he could improve on Carl Perkins's original.

From there, Elvis and the group started work on Arthur Crudup's "My Baby Left Me," a track that, by the time they were done, would rightfully assume its place among Presley's finest recordings. Kicking off with a venomous flourish by D.J., a dizzying descending bass line from Bill that triggers stabbing fills from Scotty, "My Baby Left Me" is the sound of the world's first rock 'n' roll band at full-throttle. Ignited by a deliciously slurred invocation from Elvis to "play the blues boys," the song's bridge is nothing short of revelatory, with sizzling offbeat ride-tom work from D.J., gutbucket fills from Scotty, and sizzling support from Bill's slap bass. It may have been the product of an RCA session, but "My Baby Left Me" rings with all the clarity and authenticity of Presley's most compelling Sun Studios sides.

The next three songs, "One-Sided Love Affair," "So Glad You're Mine," and "I'm Gonna Sit Right Down and Cry (Over You)," are grievously burdened by the presence of pianist Shorty Long, who seems hell-bent on bringing a western-saloon ambiance to all three tracks. The intro to "One-Sided Love Affair" is typical of Long's contributions to this session and is so incongruous and ill considered it's simply stunning that Presley, who by this time was clearly in charge of his recording sessions, retained it.

On January 31, the second day of recording, a young reporter named Fred Danzig, who supplied wire copy for numerous U.S. radio stations, was on hand to interview Elvis. His first impression of music's hottest performer was not dissimilar to that of other reporters of the time. Upon entering the studio, he encountered "a tall, lean young man standing in the hallway waiting for us." His shirt, he recalled later, was "the likes of which I have never seen before. It was a ribbon shirt, light lavender in color. Elvis said it cost $70. I also noted that his blue alligator loafers were scuffed and worn-down at the heels. He had on a gray sports jacket and dark gray slacks. His fingernails were chewed down to where there was no biting room left." Overall, Danzig found Elvis to be fascinating "just for that face alone," he said. "If you saw him on the street, you'd say, 'Wow, look at that guy.'"

During a break in recording, Elvis joined Danzig in the control room to conduct the interview. Elvis, Danzig noted, "wasn't the most articulate kid in the world," but did have a surprisingly deep knowledge of the blues. "I was surprised to hear him talk about the black performers down there [Memphis] and how he tried to carry on their music," he noted (Danzig, *The Day No One Wanted Elvis*, manuscript copy, January 1956).

On February 3, Elvis, Scotty, Bill, and D.J. returned to the studio to record their versions of Lloyd Price's "Lawdy Miss Clawdy" and "Shake, Rattle and Roll," the 12-bar blues shouter that Bill Haley & His Comets pushed to the top of the charts in the summer of 1954. Steve Sholes considered neither song to be worthy of a single release, but envisioned them as candidates for a future Presley album. During the recording of "Shake, Rattle and Roll," Sholes expressed concern over a line in the song—"You're wearing those dresses and the sun comes shining through"—that he found objectionable, but turned a blind eye to the truly lascivious verse that follows: "I'm like a one-eyed cat, peeping in a seafood store." Once Scotty, Bill, and D.J. completed the instrumental track, Elvis overdubbed his vocals, and take 12 was slated as the master.

With recording completed, Elvis was scheduled to appear at a press reception above Times Square the following day. It's this affair, perhaps more than any other, that made something clear: in 1955, you may have needed to explain why you were a Presley fan, but by 1956, you had to explain why you weren't. The press reception, which was held in a room with public access, quickly escalated into a near-riot when Elvis was swarmed by passersby who realized what was going on. Instead of fleeing, Presley held his ground and calmed the gathering, and, for the first time in his career, was subsequently rewarded with positive press coverage. Three days later, Elvis was back with the Dorsey brothers for a second appearance on *Stage Show*. In contrast to his first performance before a shell-shocked audience, this time Elvis was greeted with full-throated female screams when he kicked into "Tutti Frutti," which he concluded with convulsive upper body movements that suggested he'd just been riddled with sniper fire. In the days following the telecast, Steve Sholes composed a note to Tom Parker, praising Elvis for his behavior at the press reception and his appearance on the Dorsey show. "I thought Elvis did even better Saturday night than he did on the previous week's show," Sholes said. Then turning to the press reception, Sholes continued: "At the press party he mingled with all the guests and made a very good impression there. As a result, he is very hot material here in New York and with any luck at all, I think we all should do extremely well" (*Elvis, The Complete Fifties Masters*, RCA, June 1992).

Elvis, Scotty, Bill, and D.J. spent the following week touring Virginia and North Carolina, before returning to New York on February 11 for a third *Stage Show* appearance where Elvis shared billing with comedian Jackie Mills and singer Ella Fitzgerald. More than any other, it's this appearance that established that U.S. teenagers are now fully in the grip of an escalating Presley-mania. Unlike his first two *Stage Show* performances, the screams were virtually non-stop, clearly energizing a supremely confident Presley. Scotty seemed to lose his way during his "Blue Suede Shoes" solo, but no one seemed to notice or mind, and the response to "Heartbreak Hotel" was nothing short of kinetic, especially when Elvis, with Bill waving his arms skyward to egg him on, slide-stepped toward Scotty during the song's instrumental breaks.

Sheet music from early 1956, reflecting Elvis's new association with the Hill and Range song publishing company.

It's interesting to note that despite the outsized success of his *Stage Show* appearances, any mention of Elvis in U.S. newspapers at this point remained relatively rare, and what little there was was mainly related to advertisements for upcoming performances. However, in what appears to be the first review by a major newspaper, the *Winston-Salem Journal* served up their appraisal of Presley's appearance in North Carolina in February of 1956:

> A most remarkable young man named Elvis Presley came to town yesterday and rocked the staid old Carolina Theater to its very dignified roots. Mr. Presley must be seen if he is to be believed—and even then, he seems somewhat unbelievable. He plays ("beats" would be a better word) the guitar. He sings (almost any other word would be better there). But, somehow, he wows 'em [*Winston-Salem Journal,* February 17, 1956].

After taking note of the new music form sweeping the country, the paper continued.

> Mr. Presley is a part of the new musical phenomenon called "Rock 'n Roll." He slouches; he mugs; he bumps and grinds. He brings to the stage one of the most monumental conceits seen in these parts in many a day. But he produces, which makes the conceit all right. Singing such 20th century classics as "Blue Suede Shoes" and "Tutti Frutti," he sent a matinee houseful of teen-agers and other music-lovers into an orgy of hand-clapping, foot-stamping and tonsil-straining screaming. It is extremely doubtful that the Carolina Theater has ever seen a more enthusiastic audience. The frenzy, the hysteria, the wild and wonderful shrieks of sheer joy.... These were reserved for the remarkable young man with the long hair, the pearly teeth, the stylish slouch, the incredible conceit: Elvis Presley [*Winston-Salem Journal,* February 17, 1956].

In numerous interviews conducted well after the fact, both Scotty Moore and D.J. Fontana would often remark on Elvis's seemingly endless supply of energy during this period. Usually exhausted by the conclusion of a show, both men desired nothing more than a quick bite before heading off to bed. For Elvis the reaction was altogether different, and D.J. and Scotty recount numerous instances of marching Elvis up and down the street outside of their hotel to burn off sufficient energy to enable him to sleep. For decades, it's been assumed that Presley's energy during his pre–army years was purely natural and that any exposure to stimulants didn't take place until he was turned on to pep pills while stationed in Germany. However, in recent years evidence has surfaced that Elvis was actually artificially fueled as early as 1956 and was likely turned on to uppers by Dewey Phillips, who himself was a fierce devotee of "better living through chemistry."

Additional evidence of possible pre–army drug experimentation comes from Scotty Moore himself. While Scotty was touring Florida with an Elvis-themed nostalgia show called *All the King's Men* in the 1990s, he was approached by a former member of the Jacksonville police department who reminded Scotty of a day in 1956 when Elvis was rushed to the hospital to have his stomach pumped, suggesting he'd ingested something toxic. Additionally, any suggestion that Elvis had no connection with controlled substances prior to his army services is refuted by home movies that have surfaced in recent years, including one from 1957 in which Elvis is clearly shown sharing a marijuana joint with a friend.

14

Steppin' Out of Line

In multiple ways, the spring of 1956 can be seen as the most significant period of Elvis Presley's career. In March, Elvis's last connection with Bob Neal was severed when Neal and Tom Parker signed an agreement designating Parker as the "sole and exclusive Advisor, Personal Representative and Manager in any and all fields of public and private entertainment" of Elvis Presley. It's also in the early months of 1956 that Elvis would make his first significant impact on America's national record charts: in March, "Heartbreak Hotel" climbed to number 14 in the *Billboard* Hot 100 chart, the first time that a Presley record cracked the top 20, before making a steady climb to the number-one position. That same month, his debut album, the eponymously titled *Elvis Presley*—a stylistic gumbo consisting of seven tracks from the January Nashville sessions and five previously unreleased Sun sides—was released. In their March 14 review of the album, *Billboard* magazine stated:

> This young singer from the south is the latest performer to cash in on frenetic high-jinks. In this collection Presley works through a repertory that's a blend of hillbilly and rock 'n' roll, ranging from such contemporary classics as "Tutti Frutti" to the Rodgers & Hart oldie, "Blue Moon," in which an echo effect and some falsetto piping almost succeeds in making the song unrecognizable [*Billboard*, March 14, 1956].

Shortly following its release, the album rose to the top of the LP charts, where it reigned for 10 weeks, and became the first RCA album to sell more than 300,000 copies on its initial release.

Throughout March, Elvis and the band maintained their steady schedule of touring, with stops in Memphis on March 9, then on to Atlanta, Charleston, Columbia, Augusta, Lexington, and Richmond before winding up in Washington, D.C., on the March 23. Virtually every show that Elvis performed during this period contained a level of fireworks, but his appearance in Lexington is particularly noteworthy and was typical of the response that Presley encountered throughout this tour, as Lexington's *Dispatch* reported:

> A whirlwind blew into Lexington last night. The whirlwind is Elvis Presley, 21-year-old singing sensation of the nation who has become what many experts describe as the "biggest drawing power in the entertainment world." Elvis slouched his shoulders, wiggled them, spread his legs, wiggled them, and the sighs and cries grew even louder. When he talked, it was louder cries. When he strummed his guitar, the noise got louder and when he sang bedlam broke loose. Using all types of intricate motions as he delivered his songs, many of them top-selling RCA Victor hits, Elvis showed his audience what has gained him fame as the new "bobby-soxers" favorite of the nation [*Lexington Dispatch*, March 22, 1956].

In a press conference following the performance, Elvis thanked his fans, spoke of his parents, and then blurted out, against the express instructions of Tom Parker, news of an upcoming screen test for producer Hal Wallis and Paramount Pictures for a role in *The Rainmaker*,

Elvis, Scotty, Bill, and D.J. at full throttle in this performance shot from 1956. Left to right: Scotty Moore, Elvis Presley, and Bill Black, with D.J. Fontana obscured (Alamy.com).

a film to star Burt Lancaster and Katharine Hepburn. On March 25, following yet another appearance on *Stage Show*, Elvis was in Hollywood for his screen test. Meanwhile Scotty, Bill, and D.J. headed back to Memphis after first making a detour to Dover, Delaware, to visit Carl Perkins, who, along with two of his brothers, was hospitalized following a serious auto accident on March 21.

Elvis's screen test turned into a three-day affair, during which producer Hal Wallis and film technicians would weigh his suitability for the big screen. To Elvis's amusement, his first assignment required him to mime to his recording of "Blue Suede Shoes" in front of cameras while strumming a stringless prop guitar.

"The transformation was incredible," recalls screenwriter Allan Weiss, who was on hand to witness the test.

> Electricity bounced off the walls of the soundstage. One felt it as an awesome thing—like an earthquake in progress, only without the implicit threat. Watching this insecure country boy, who apologized when he asked for a rehearsal as though he had done something wrong, turn into absolute dynamite when he stepped into the bright lights and started lip-synching the words of his familiar hit. He believed in it and he made you believe it no matter how "sophisticated" your musical tastes were [Peary, *Close Ups: The Movie Star Book*].

The second phase of the screen test consisted of Elvis acting out two scenes from *The Rainmaker*, in which Elvis would play Burt Lancaster's younger brother. When the tests were completed, Hal Wallis announced that he was satisfied, though there were rumblings around the Paramount lot that throwing an untested Presley in with heavyweights like Katharine Hepburn and Lancaster was courting disaster. Wallis, who was aware of the scuttlebutt, didn't waver and in the end signed Elvis to a seven-year, three-picture deal.

On April 3, Elvis was in Southern California for his first appearance on the *Milton Berle Show*, to be televised from the deck of the USS *Hancock*, an aircraft carrier docked at a naval station in San Diego. In contrast to *Stage Show*, the Berle show constituted a giant leap forward for Elvis. At this point, Berle was a major star, referred to in media circles as "Mr. Television," primarily due to his embrace of the fledgling medium in its earliest and most primitive days. During rehearsals, D.J. Fontana was thrilled to encounter a personal hero, drummer Buddy Rich, who was on hand as a member of the Harry James Orchestra. But instead of greeting Fontana pleasantly, Rich was brusque, and when Elvis and the band kicked into "Blue Suede Shoes" during rehearsals, Rich was heard to audibly say to James, "This is the worst."

For this performance, Elvis played to an audience composed primarily of sailors who were perched on the ship's deck while a stiff wind blew in from the sea. Dressed head to toe in black with a scarf hanging loosely around his neck, Elvis, after being introduced by Berle as "America's newest singing sensation," started off with "Blue Suede Shoes." Sonically, the performance lacked in virtually every respect. Elvis's rhythm guitar completely evaporated the minute he moved away from his microphone, and Bill Black's bass, barely perceptible at the best of times, simply couldn't hold its own against the open-air elements. None of this however, was sufficient to tame Black's enthusiasm. During instrumental breaks, he once again straddled his bass like a horse, waving his arms wildly and urging Elvis to "Go, Go Go!" Despite the obstacles presented by the elements, the performance was received wildly by the gathered audience. One observer, however, was not happy. Following the show, Tom Parker, with Elvis, Scotty, and D.J. looking on, launched into a broadside against Black. "Play your instrument," he told Black, cut out the "showboating," and stop upstaging "my boy." Humiliated, Black turned to Elvis, seeking support. None was forthcoming. Black would do as he was told going forward, but the resentment over this latest subjugation would fester and ultimately trigger a breaking point.

With the Berle show behind him, Elvis played a pair of shows in San Diego over successive days to more than 11,000 frenetic fans. It was the beginning of a 15-city tour, during which Presley, incredibly, was supported by a comedian, a group of acrobats, and a xylophone player, Parker's laughable and typically tone-deaf notion of what Elvis's teenage audience wanted. In spite of this, Presleymania continued unabated, and while shows in earlier months may have been conducted in theaters and clubs, for this tour, auditoriums and coliseums became the norm, which, from a performance standpoint, left Elvis, Scotty, Bill, and D.J. uneasy. With just Scotty's lone amp, Bill's acoustic bass, and a mic for Elvis over the venue's public address system, being heard over the screams that now characterized Presley concerts was difficult enough. But now, with a move into larger venues, what hope did they have of being heard at all?

"The crowds would get so loud sometimes," Scotty later recalled, "that that was all you heard. It was literally just like being under water." At times, the cacophony would reach such a level that the only way Scotty, Bill, or D.J. could stay on track was by watching Elvis. "I've said this many times over the years," Moore continues, "but I really do think we were the only band ever that was literally directed by the singer's rear end, because we would take cues from Elvis' movements when we

Elvis performing "Heartbreak Hotel" for the TV cameras in 1956. Shortly following this performance, Tom Parker instructed Bill Black to cut out the showboating and stop upstaging "his boy." Left to right: Scotty Moore, Elvis Presley, Bill Black (Alamy.com).

couldn't hear what he was singing" ("Interview with Scotty Moore," *Courthouse News*, June 29, 2016).

"We had to do the best with what we had," D.J. Fontana told *Rolling Stone* magazine in 1977 (*Rolling Stone*, September 22, 1977). Audible or not, songs performed on this tour included "Baby Let's Play House"; "Heartbreak Hotel," which Elvis regularly introduced as "Heartburn Motel"; "Long Tall Sally"; "I Was the One"; "I Got a Woman"; "Only You"; "Blue Suede Shoes"; "Money Honey"; and "Tutti Frutti."

As his fame grew to ever-greater heights, Elvis, during this period, began taking incoming fire from the press on an almost daily basis. Any notion of rock 'n' roll being treated seriously or seen as an art form was still over a decade away, and critics in the mid-fifties still viewed the music, if they deigned to consider it music at all, as an affront to good taste. The following *Rocky Mountain News* review of Elvis's April 8 show in Denver, titled "Rage Over Elvis Presley Is a Bit Sickening," serves as a typical example what was being said during this period: "There's a new rage of the age—Elvis Presley. As far as I'm concerned, I hope this rage passes into oblivion as quickly as it has sprung up. It's a toss-up of which was worse, Elvis or his fans. I'd say the edge goes to Elvis" (*Rocky Mountain News*, April 10, 1956).

Following an appearance in Amarillo on April 13, Elvis, Scotty, Bill, and D.J. chartered a plane to take them to Nashville for a quick two-day recording session. The plane ride was tortuous: the pilot immediately lost his way, necessitating an unplanned stop in El Dorado, Arkansas, to refuel. Once they were finally back in the air, an engine cut out because someone had forgotten to switch the plane over to the full fuel tank. The experience left Elvis and the band shaken, with Elvis vowing upon reaching Nashville that he'd never fly again.

The Music—April 14, 1956—RCA Studios, Nashville

The near calamity of the plane flight, an early—9:00 a.m.—start time, and Elvis's disappointment at learning, yet again, that just a single Jordanaire, Gordon Stoker, was present likely contributed to the failure of this session. To make matters worse, everything was delayed by the presence of a *Life* magazine photographer and a representative from RCA who were on hand to conduct an interview and present Elvis with his first gold record for "Heartbreak Hotel." By the time the session finally wrapped, it had taken three hours and a total of 17 takes just to arrive at a single acceptable song, "I Want You, I Need You, I Love You." From Elvis's perspective, the only positive that came out of the entire experience was Chet Atkins's assurance that, for all future recording sessions, a full complement of Jordanaires would be present.

Meanwhile, back in Hollywood, Steve Sholes was feeling the heat. RCA, with plans to release a second Presley LP by the fall, was pressuring Sholes for new material. But aside from "I Want You, I Need You, I Love You," which ultimately would be left off the album anyway, he had nothing. In a letter to Tom Parker, Sholes complained that the Nashville session had been "a hassle" and made it clear he needed more material from Elvis. To further complicate matters, Sholes now suspected that Chet Atkins, the man he'd personally selected to handle the Nashville sessions, wasn't a good fit for Elvis, a performer that Atkins had openly derided.

In the days following the abortive Nashville session, Elvis and the band resumed their tour and in ensuing days would play gigs in San Antonio, Corpus Christi, Waco, Tulsa, Oklahoma City, Fort Worth, and Houston. On Sunday, April 15, Elvis was in his dressing room in San Antonio sipping on a soft drink and fielding questions from the press. Was he mobbed wherever he went these days? "If I say yes, it would be bragging," he replied. "If I said no, it would be lying." Would he sing in the movies? "I'm not," he replied, "I mean as far as I know, 'cause I took strictly an acting test and I wouldn't care too much about singing in the movies" (*San Antonio Express*, April 16, 1956).

Growing weary of the questions, Elvis, still trailed by reporters, made his way to a pipe organ situated just outside of his dressing room. "These things fascinate me," he remarked, and then played what one reporter described as "passable renditions" of "Silent Night," "Harbor Lights," and several other tunes. The next day, the *San Antonio Express* had this to say about his performance:

> You couldn't hear Elvis in the front row. Uproar exploded each time he looked as though he might open his mouth. A flash of white teeth from Elvis, a loose hipped slur of dance steps, a Brando-like gaze from soulful blue eyes, and the floor vibrated with 6,000 stamping feet, whistles shattered the air. Cries of "Look this way, Elvis" and "Here, over here!" drowned Elvis out [*San Antonio Express*, April 16, 1956].

Too Hot to Handle

Although it's impossible to pinpoint exactly when, it was likely during this period that news stories linking Elvis with juvenile delinquency first began to surface. Fueled by movies like *The Wild One* and *The Blackboard Jungle* and an increasing proliferation of articles in national publications decrying an increase in youth crime, fears of juvenile delinquency were gripping 1950s America. Adding fuel to the fire were condemnations by leading religious figures, who characterized rock 'n' roll as the "devil's music" and a breeding ground for hooliganism. None of this, of course, went unnoticed by the entertainment world, as this April 1956 article in *Variety* makes clear:

> Rock 'n' roll—the most explosive show biz phenomenon of the decade—may be getting too hot to handle. While its money-making potential has made it all but irresistible, its Svengali grip on the teenagers has produced a staggering wave of juvenile violence and mayhem. Rock 'n' roll is now literal box office dynamite—not only a matter of profit, but a matter for police. On the police blotters, rock 'n' roll has been writing an unprecedented record. In one locale rock 'n' roll shows, or disk hops where such tunes have been played, have touched off every type of juvenile delinquency [*Variety*, April, 11, 1956].

Anyone with a fourth-grade education can easily spot the logical fallacy of this article, but for Corpus Christi building manager Tom Davis, it had the ring of truth. With Elvis scheduled to play in his city on April 16, it was too late for Davis to cancel the show, but in the days following Elvis's sold-out performance, Davis told the *Corpus Christi Caller* that Presley and rock 'n' roll were contributing factors to juvenile delinquency and in the future, similar shows would be banned in Corpus Christi (*Corpus Christi Caller*, April 18, 1956). A number of local officials, including the chief of police, protested, but once news of Davis's edict hit the wire services, city managers around the country, fearing a take-over of their cities by music-crazed teenagers, began passing ordinances against rock 'n' roll shows. Virtually overnight, Elvis was transformed into a symbol of everything that was wrong with America's youth, and his reputation as a fomenter of youthful lawlessness would trail him like a shadow he couldn't shake for the better part of two years and would be a stigma that only a two-year hitch in Uncle Sam's army would dissipate.

No one was more concerned by the increasingly negative press coverage Elvis was attracting than Tom Parker. In the 1950s, newspapers were America's primary source of information, wielding an influence and power over public opinion scarcely imaginable in today's digitized and internet-dominated world. With columns by personalities like Walter Winchell and Ed Sullivan syndicated on a daily basis to thousands of newspapers from coast to coast, a single uncomplimentary review could threaten livelihoods and endanger careers. With that in mind, Parker, in what can only be viewed in hindsight as a ludicrous move, decided that it was time to expose Elvis to a more adult audience, in this case Las Vegas, where any chance of chaos and disruption would be, at best, minimal. How could anyone charge Elvis with fueling juvenile delinquency, Parker reasoned, if no juveniles were present?

And so it was that on April 24, Elvis, Scotty, Bill, and D.J. pulled into the Sagebrush State to kick off a two-week engagement at Las Vegas's New Frontier Hotel. For this appearance, Parker had billed Elvis as the "Atomic Powered Singer," apparently feeling that associating Elvis with ground zero at a nearby Nevada nuclear testing sight was somehow a plus. For the duration of this appearance, Elvis would share the bill with Freddy Martin and his orchestra, comedian Shecky Greene, and a group of showgirls collectively known as "the Venus Starlets."

Despite Parker's promotional efforts, the Las Vegas engagement would prove star-crossed from the first night. Instead of teenage adulation, Elvis faced an audience of predominantly older people, who, while certainly curious about this musical upstart, were anything but rapturous. Every performer confronts moments like these at some point during their career, but only the most seasoned know how to handle it.

Young and untested, the "Atomic Powered Singer" did the only thing he knew to do: try harder, as if sheer application of will could win the blasé crowd over. It didn't.

"I don't think the people there were ready for Elvis," D.J. Fontana would later say of the experience. "We tried everything we knew. Usually Elvis could get them on his side. It didn't work that time" (elvis-history-blog.com, April 2016). For his part, Bill Black used humor to explain the entire affair. "For the first time in months," he said later, "we could hear ourselves when we played out of tune. After the show, our nerves were pretty frayed and we would get together in pairs and talk about whoever wasn't around to defend himself" ("Elvis Presley, The New Singing Rage," *Tiger*, 1956). The reaction to Elvis was so tepid that on the engagement's second night, he was demoted, and Shecky Greene would close the show from then on.

Las Vegas audiences may have been cool to Elvis, but their response was positively rapturous in comparison to press coverage of the entire affair, including this from the *Las Vegas Star*: "For the teenagers, the long, tall Memphis lad is a whiz, but for the average Vegas spender or show-goer, a bore. His musical sound with a combo of three is uncouth, matching to a great extent the lyric content of his nonsensical songs" (*Las Vegas Star*, April 28th, 1956).

No less disdainful was the respected *Newsweek*, which, in a May 14 article titled "Hillbilly on a Pedestal," pithily characterized Elvis's presence at the New Frontier as a "jug of corn liquor at a champagne party" (*Newsweek*, May 14, 1956).

By this point, Elvis was mostly inured to bad press. But a bored and disdainful audience was something else entirely, and the experience shook him deeply. In need of something to distract him from his first professional failure, he didn't have far to look. With its glittering lights, gaudy showrooms, and its "town that never sleeps" ethos, Las Vegas was love at first sight for Elvis. Following his nightly performances at the New Frontier, he'd do the town, taking in shows, hanging out with fellow musicians, and hustling showgirls. And in one case, he even engaged in a bit of creative appropriation.

It took place at the Sahara Lounge, where Elvis, along with Scotty, Bill, and D.J. were on hand to see the musical-comic aggregation, Freddy Bell and the Bellboys. At some point, Bell launched into a comedic sendup of Jerry Leiber and Mike Stoller's "Hound Dog." Elvis, who had the original version by "Big Mama" Thornton in his personal record collection, recognized the tune immediately. "They played that song, and since we only did one or two shows, we went by every night to listen to them," D.J. Fontana recalls. "They were playing the arrangement we finally put on record. We went to New York and Elvis said, 'Do you guys remember how that group did that record?' It was a real good show tune. That's actually where we got the idea" (*Modern Drummer*, May 1985).

"When we heard them perform that night, we thought the song would be a good one for us to do as comic relief when we were on stage," Scotty Moore said of the tune. "We loved the way they did it. They had a piano player [Russ Conti] who stood up and played—and the way he did his legs they looked like rubber bands bending back and forth. Jerry Leiber and Mike Stoller wrote the song for 'Big Mama' Thornton, but Freddie and The Bell Boys had a different set of lyrics. Elvis got his lyrics from those guys. He knew the original lyrics but he didn't use them" (Moore, and Dickerson, *Scotty and Elvis: Aboard the Mystery Train*).

The New Frontier engagement may have been a bust, but no matter. Vegas was now in Presley's blood, and once back in Memphis, he would talk endlessly of the town to anyone who'd listen and vowed to return as soon as possible. Of course, at this point, Elvis could scarcely envision the critical role Vegas would play in his future, serving first as the site of a creative rebirth, then, finally, as a soul-sapping grave from which he'd be unable to extricate himself.

Back home, Elvis was at last able to spend his first nights in a house he'd recently purchased for his family in an upscale area of Memphis. The respite was short lived; on Saturday, he was back on tour, with stops scheduled in Minnesota, Wisconsin, Arkansas, Missouri, Kansas, Nebraska, and Iowa. On May 15, he was back in Memphis for a one-nighter, where he told the local newspaper, "More than anything else, I want the folks back home to think right of me. Just because I managed to do a little something, I don't want anyone back home to think I got the big head" (*Memphis Commercial Appeal*, May 13, 1956).

On June 5, Elvis returned to Hollywood for his second and final appearance on *The Milton Berle* show, where he would share the bill with comedian Arnold Stang and actress Debra Paget. The show opened with Elvis engaging in a skit and a bit of tomfoolery with Berle, before moving to a stage, where, with Scotty, Bill, and D.J. poised behind him, he would kick into "Hound Dog."

In the weeks and months leading up to his second Berle appearance, Elvis was increasingly being accused of engaging during his performances in salacious and suggestive movements that some suggested were designed to incite a sexual response in his female following. When confronted with these charges, Presley invariably pushed back, stating repeatedly that any movements were unplanned and instinctive and nothing more than natural responses to his music. But with "Hound Dog" on the Milton Berle show of June 5, Elvis threw all of that into a cocked hat. Whether it was the gyrations he unleashed at the end of each verse or the frenetic dance steps that carried the band into the instrumental break, Presley was clearly out to see what he could get away with. The performance was so incendiary the usually sure-handed Scotty Moore, clearly thrown by what he was witnessing, fumbled his way through his solo. Throughout Elvis's frenetic performance, one can sense the palpable frustration of the newly reined-in Bill Black, who'd like nothing more than to straddle his bass and elevate the madness. Then, with the song approaching its conclusion, Presley upped the ante, launching into a half-time coda and a series of stripper moves that drew

Elvis in rehearsal for his second appearance on the Milton Berle show, June 5, 1955. Left to right: Elvis Presley, Scotty Moore, D.J. Fontana (Alamy. com)

gasps from the audience and were so blatant and over-the-top that Elvis himself struggled to keep a straight face.

Following the performance, Berle, whistling through his fingers, bolted onto the stage screaming "How 'bout my boy?" prompting the audience, still not sure what they've just witnessed, to applaud. For Middle America, the performance was an outrage, one that made it clear that Presley had no interest in playing by the same rules as everyone else. But for the young, Elvis's performance, along with his hair, clothes, attitude, and bravura, were components of a crucial strangeness that was, as it would be for the Beatles seven years hence, essential to his appeal. However, for the pundits and tastemakers who filled newspapers columns with their insights, critiques, and witticisms, the performance was viewed somewhat less charitably, as this nugget from the *New York Daily News* makes clear:

> Popular music has reached its lowest depths in the "grunt and groin" antics of one Elvis Presley. The TV audience had a noxious sampling of it on the Milton Berle show. Elvis, who rotates his pelvis, was appalling musically. Also, he gave an exhibition that was suggestive and vulgar, tinged with the kind of animalism that should be confined to dives and bordellos. No wonder there have been so many reports of teen-age riots and other outbursts in towns and cities where Elvis has made personal appearances [*New York Daily News*, Wednesday, April 7, 1956].

The *New York Herald Tribune* was even less impressed:

> The last appearance of this unspeakably untalented and vulgar young entertainer brought forth such a storm of complaints both from press and public that I imagine any entertainer would hesitate to try him again on television. But, as I say, where do you go from Elvis, short of open obscenity which is against the law? Popular music has been in a tailspin for years now and I have hopes that with Presley it has touched bottom and will just have to start getting better [*New York Herald Tribune*, April 9, 1956].

The *New York Journal-American,* while stopping short of accusing Elvis of obscenity, did suggest that Elvis's stage moves were akin to an "aborigines mating dance," before finally concluding that "he can't sing a lick" (*New York Journal-American*, Wednesday, April 7, 1956).

In what can only be viewed as piling on, the *Pittsburgh Sun-Telegraph*, in the weeks ahead, would print an article containing the opinions of prominent celebrities on Elvis and rock 'n' roll. Among those published were these comments from composer Meredith Wilson: "Rock & Roll," the composer of *The Music Man* stated bluntly, "is the music of idiots" (*Pittsburgh Sun-Telegraph*, August 11, 1956).

All of which brings us to Steve Allen, the talented actor, comedian, musician, and host of a primetime NBC variety show. Allen had seen Elvis's initial appearance on *Stage Show* and, sensing a ratings bonanza, had signed him to appear on his Sunday night program. Formerly the host of NBC's *Tonight Show*, Allen had moved to Sunday night expressly to challenge CBS's *Ed Sullivan Show* for rating primacy. But now, in the wake of Presley's performance on the Berle show, Allen was under pressure from both the public and wary sponsors to cancel his appearance. While seeming to take complaints regarding Elvis seriously, Allen simply had no intention of cutting him loose; television was about ratings, and right now the American public wanted to see the kid for themselves and figure out what all the fuss was about. Still, Allen was savvy enough to know that, unless he said or did something to assuage the bluenoses, neighborhood PTAs, and religious leaders who were out for Elvis's head, he risked a boycott by nervous program sponsors.

In an attempt to quell the controversy, Allen, in the days preceding his broadcast, composed an open letter to Presley critics that appeared in newspapers across the country. "The anti–Presley arguments I've been hearing seem a bit illogical," he stated. "You see, he has made many TV appearances before the Berle show, all without arousing any hue or cry, so there can be no firm basis for keeping him off TV altogether." But then, to avoid appearing overly sympathetic to Elvis, he shifted direction: "The heart of the matter is that he thoughtlessly indulged in certain dance movements on his last TV appearance which a number of people thought objectionable." From there, Allen, presumed to speak for Elvis. "He knows he made a mistake with the Milton Berle business and I think he's smart enough not to do it again." The entertainer then concluded by assuring TV viewers that they will not be "offended by Elvis on any program over which I have control. We'll show you a new side of the boy."

Among those who rallied to Elvis's defense during this period was his Berle co-star, Debra Paget. "Although I usually don't form an opinion of a person until I have met him," she explained, "frankly I looked forward to my first meeting with Elvis Presley with mixed emotions. I'd heard and read a lot about this new young singing sensation from Tennessee—and most of it was not complimentary." But, the actress said, she'd been quickly won over by Elvis's sensitivity. "At first I'd been under the impression that he was quite indifferent to the attacks made on him for the way he sings, dresses, wears his sideburns, and all the other comments. But he isn't. Not that he'd admit the fact easily to a stranger.... I could tell he was deeply hurt when his performances were criticized, or when he was threatened with being banned from certain cities" (*TV and Movie Screen*, April 1957).

As the controversy continued to rage, Elvis was back on tour, with shows in San Diego, Los Angeles, Phoenix, Tucson, Atlanta, and a stop in Charlotte, North Carolina, where a reporter caught up with him in a restaurant and asked him if he'd submit to an interview. "Sure, I'll talk," Elvis replied. "Sit down. Most of you guys, though, be writin' bad things about me, man." Noticing a girl in the next booth staring at him, Elvis smiled. "Hi ya, baby," he said. What about the Berle show, the reporter wanted to know. Is what he did obscene? "Did you see the show?" Elvis asked. "This Debra Paget is on the same show. She wore a tight thing with feathers on the behind where they wiggle most. And I never saw anything like it. Sex? Man, she bumped and pooshed out all over the place. I'm like Little Boy Blue. And who do they say is obscene? Me!"

At that moment, a waitress brought Elvis some coffee. As she poured it, he fingered the lace on her outfit. "Aren't you the one?" he says to her. When asked how long rock 'n' roll would last, Elvis shook his head. "When it's gone, I'll switch to something else. I like to sing ballads the way Eddie Fisher does and the way Perry Como does. But the way I'm singing now is what makes the money. Would you change if you was me?" ("Elvis Presley is a Worried Man," *Charlotte Observer*, June 27, 1956).

On July 1, Elvis rode the train from Richmond, where he'd performed the night before, to New York's Pennsylvania Station, where he then hopped a cab to the Hudson Theatre, where rehearsals for the Allen show were taking place. After quick run-through of his first number, "I Want You, I Need You, I Love You," Allen, to prepare Elvis for his appearance later that night, rolled out a marble stand on which was perched a basset hound, to whom Elvis, outfitted in tie and tails, would croon "Hound Dog." It was all part of Allen's plan to showcase a "new Elvis Presley" to America. In subsequent years, much has been written and said regarding the supposed humiliation Elvis experienced over all this, but when he was queued by the stage manager later that night, he hit his mark, did what he was told, and sang to the dog.

Steve Allen was clearly hoping for a ratings coup, and he got it. The program's ratings were sensational, with Allen's program besting the more popular *Ed Sullivan Show* by almost six points. However, if Allen's "new Elvis" was intended to placate critics, the ploy flopped. "Insofar as this corner is concerned," the *New York Times* opined, "the young man has lost none of his indescribable monotony as a singer." The *New York Journal-American* was no less critical, saying that "Elvis Presley was a cowed kid on Steve Allen's opus last night.... NBC's promise to de-gyrate the controversial hip-swingin' singer was kept. It proved Presley's excitement is not his voice but his erotic presentation. Once his gears were shifted into a picture suitable for a Sunday evening, it was plain he couldn't sing or act a lick" (*New York Times, New York Journal-American,* July 2, 1956).

In recent years, the chin-strokers who populate the ranks of rock intelligentsia have expressed outrage at Steve Allen and the way he presented Presley. By shoehorning Elvis into evening wear and forcing him to croon to a canine, the feeling goes, he'd somehow emasculated rock's first pure rebel. No less a personage than producer and Bruce Springsteen manager Jon Landau said of the performance, "As a child, I was deeply offended. There was something wrong there. Elvis," he continued, "why are you letting them do that to you?" Taking it even further, rock critic Dave Marsh posited that Allen deliberately set out to undermine an entire swath of American life. "Steve Allen, he was out to humiliate an entire culture he would have called hillbillies. It was all a smear" (*Elvis the Searcher,* HBO, April 2018). In later years, even Priscilla Presley would weigh in on the whole affair. "It was humiliating," she said. "After that, he didn't like Steve Allen at all."

All of this suggests that Elvis was nothing more than a bumpkin swimming in deep water surrounded by Hollywood sharks, condemned to a humiliation he was helpless to prevent. And all of this, of course, is ridiculous. Just four years hence, fresh from the army and wielding a power unmatched by anyone in the history of show business (as Tom Petty noted of Presley during this period, "I've often wondered if there'd ever been a twenty-one year old with that sort of power that could mobilize millions with a wave of his hand"), Elvis would willingly participate in the humiliating *Welcome Home Elvis* show with Frank Sinatra, a program containing segments so cringeworthy they make the Allen show seem dignified by comparison (*Los Angeles Times,* April 13, 2018).

Elvis's descent into post–army movie and musical mediocrity is indisputable. The only question, as Marsh poses above, is why Elvis allowed it. In recent years, a number of explanations have been trotted forth, ranging from the trauma of his mother's death, an ill-advised allegiance to Tom Parker, or a U.S. Army stretch for which he was congenitally ill-suited. That's a debate I'll avoid for the moment. But one thing is certain: any suggestion that Elvis, following the Allen humiliation, would in the years ahead—a period in which his influence and power were unrivaled—forcefully stand his ground against future debasement and humiliation is specious at best. Or has everyone forgotten "Do the Clam"?

While backstage at the Allen show, Elvis received a phone call from someone who once pledged to have nothing to do with him. "Ed [Sullivan] called Elvis backstage," Steve Allen recalls, "and offered him $50,000 to make, I don't know, three or four appearances on Ed's show. Our top then was what the top price throughout television was, $7,500 a week, and I wasn't interested in paying anyone any more than that. So, by this bold stroke, Ed simply took Elvis away from us" (HBO, *Elvis the Searcher*, April 2018). In the end, Elvis, after conferring with Parker, agreed to a total of three appearances on the Sullivan show, with the first scheduled for September 9.

Later that same night, Elvis was interviewed on the *Hy Gardner Calling* television program. Gardner was a highly influential entertainment reporter and syndicated columnist for the *New York Herald Tribune*. The *New York Times* once described Gardner's writing as "an art form," but as an interviewer he was dreadful, posing such inane questions as "What do you think about most of the time?"—queries that Elvis fielded with a thinly-veiled contempt. The ultimate square, Gardner toggled between posing as a bold defender of the moral order and as an obsequious worm. Perhaps in response to the Allen humiliation earlier that evening, Elvis dropped the aura of politeness that usually characterized his dealings with the press and actually stood his ground, telling Gardner that he failed to see how any music form could contribute to juvenile delinquency. When Gardner, turning scold, asked Elvis if he's "learned anything" from the criticism leveled against him, Presley fired back, "No I haven't," to which Gardner snidely responded, "Oh, you haven't huh?" In subsequent years, it's been suggested that Elvis's sleepy-eyed and truculent performance on this program was calculated to evoke his idol, James Dean. Whether that's true or whether Presley was simply too tired to maintain the carefully cultivated image of a polite Southern boy, it makes no difference. Because if parents tuning into the show were seeking reassurance that the idol their children were currently rallying behind was, in fact, harmless, he had none to offer.

15

First in Line

At 2:00 p.m. the following day, Elvis was back at RCA's New York recording studios, where, following an extraordinary 71 takes, he would emerge with three completed tracks. Of the three, one would show up on a subsequent extended play 45, another would comprise the B-side to his next single, and a third would be embraced by half the country as anthemic and condemned as subversive by the other half.

The Music—July 2, 1956—RCA Studios, New York

Surviving outtakes make it abundantly clear that it was the 21-year-old Elvis Presley, not ostensible producer Steve Sholes, who controlled this session. Even when Sholes pronounced a take satisfactory, Elvis, if not happy, overruled him and insisted on doing it again. And if one of the musicians made a mistake, forcing a new attempt, Elvis remained nonplussed. "In his own reserved manner," journalist Alfred Wertheimer wrote, "he kept control, he made himself responsible. When somebody else made a mistake, he sang off-key. The offender picked up the cue. He never criticized anyone, never got mad at anybody but himself. He'd just say, 'Okay, fellas, I goofed'" (Wertheimer, *Elvis '56: In the Beginning*).

They began the session with "Hound Dog," a song that Elvis had vowed to record after seeing Freddie Bellman's performance of the tune during his visit to Las Vegas. Studio logs for this session show that they made upwards of 31 attempts at arriving at a studio master, but in truth, that number likely includes false starts and versions that broke down after just a few bars. "I've seen it written, 'they did seventy takes on this,' but a lot of these might be the count-off between every start," Scotty Moore said later. "And back then they would slate each false start" (*Guitarist*, November 1992).

In the days following its release, "Hound Dog" would comprise nothing less than a frontal assault on the Comos, Martins, Sinatras and other purveyors of 1950s "easy listening," signaling that the old rules of engagement no longer held sway. Even today, more than 60 years later, it's still possible to sense the bewilderment and outrage of mainstream artists, who, upon hearing "Hound Dog," had to realize that the ground was shifting beneath their feet. Outright contempt for the song extended not just from the musical community—where one respected critic opined, "For sheer repulsiveness coupled with the monotony of incoherence, 'Hound Dog' hits a new low in my experience" ("Race," *Melody Maker*, October 10, 1956)—to Middle America and even into the halls of government, where one congressman was quoted as saying, " Elvis Presley's 'Hound Dog' music is certainly most distasteful to me, and violative of all that I know to be in good taste" (Denisoff and Romanowski, *Risky Business: Rock in Film*). For these folks, and countless others, "Hound Dog" wasn't just musical and cultural heresy, but irrefutable evidence of a decline in western civilization.

The studio master of "Hound Dog" shows Messrs. Presley, Moore, Black, and Fontana stripped down for fighting. When questioned about his savage soloing on this track, Scotty Moore replied, "To me, it was an angry song. People used to ask me if I was mad at someone. I'd say 'Yeah, I was.' It was a rough, grunting song and that's what I tried to portray" (Moore and Dickerson, *That's Alright, Elvis*). "Hound Dog" would not only serve to galvanize a generation of teenagers, but in the years ahead would take on something akin to an afterlife. In 2011, *Rolling Stone* magazine ranked "Hound Dog" as number 19 in its "500 Greatest Songs of All Time" list. It also remains one of the best-selling singles of all time, with more than ten million copies sold (*Rolling Stone*, April 7, 2011).

As an aside, it's interesting to note that, on a train trip back home to Memphis following this session, Elvis was spied playing a dub of "Hound Dog" on a cheap record player. Asked why he relied on such an inexpensive device to evaluate his latest song, he replied, "Because that's how the kids will hear it" (*Musician*, October 1992).

"Don't Be Cruel," seen as a potential B-side for "Hound Dog," was next up. It was written by Otis Blackwell, who before he was through would also compose such early rock standards as "All Shook Up" and "Great Balls of Fire." For "Don't Be Cruel," Blackwell reluctantly agreed to give up a portion of his publishing rights, the shady arrangement set up by Tom Parker in which composers were arm-twisted to forsake a cut of their publishing in order to have their songs recorded by Presley. This practice—in essence, an artistic shakedown—was tolerated by songwriters in the fifties due to Elvis's hit-making prowess. As Presley's popularity faded in the following decade, the policy, incomprehensibly, endured, driving songwriters to other artists and saddling Elvis with musical dreck that would nearly destroy his career.

The completed version of "Don't Be Cruel" is masterful, with essential contributions from both Bill Black and Presley, who provided the track's unique percussive effect by keeping time on the backside of his guitar case. Interestingly, Scotty Moore's participation was minimal on this track.

"For 'Don't Be Cruel,' I turned my E string down to a low D," Moore recalls. "I played the intro and then I played a chord at the end, but that was all I did on it. One thing you realize now is that the songs and the music and the excitement is still there in those records" (Wingate, "The Guitar Man," *Music Mart*, 2005).

During this session, Elvis also completed a master recording of "Any Way You Want Me," a ballad ultimately released in September of 1957 on an extended play 45. The session of July 2 is also notable as the first time that all four Jordanaires, to Elvis's great relief, were present.

With recording behind him, Elvis returned by train to Memphis, where, on July 4, he performed at Russwood Park before a wildly enthusiastic hometown audience. In an obvious reference to his appearance on the Steve Allen show, Elvis told the audience, "Those people in New York are not going to change me none. I'm gonna' show you what the real Elvis is like tonight." The following day, Presley began the first extended vacation he's had since reaching national fame, with much of it spent with Memphis steady June Juanico.

In subsequent years, June would speak of a private moment she shared with Presley she found intriguing. Seated outside with Elvis one night, he softly told her to relax her mind and body until she was so at ease, she felt as if she could float. If you did it often enough, he said, someday you'd reach the moon and the stars. Surprised at his words, June asked him how long he'd been doing this. "Since I was a little boy," he replied. "I learned a long time ago not to talk about it. People think you're crazy when you talk about things they don't understand" (Guralnick, *Last Train to Memphis*). It was while Elvis was on vacation that Ed Sullivan made it official, announcing to the press that Elvis, someone that he had publicly disdained, had signed to make three appearances on his Sunday night variety show, for which he would be paid $50,000.

On the heels of that announcement, there was another, this one from Hollywood producer Hal Wallis, who informed the press that he'd waived his right to produce Elvis's first movie, ostensibly due to a failure to come up with a satisfactory script, but more likely due to an escalating series of exasperating demands from Tom Parker. Instead, Presley's first movie would be Paramount's *The Reno Brothers*, a Civil War–era drama in which he'd star with Richard Egan and Debra Paget. It would start filming on August 22. In an interview with *Parade* magazine, Elvis spoke of his goals for the picture. "I've made a study of Marlon Brando," he said. "I've made a study of poor Jimmy Dean. I've made a study of myself and I know why girls, at least the young 'uns, go for us. We're sullen, we're broodin', we're something of a menace. I don't understand it exactly, but that's what the girls like in men. I don't know anything about Hollywood, but I know you can't be sexy if you smile. You can't be a rebel if you grin" (*Parade*, September 30, 1956).

On August 3, Elvis, Scotty, Bill, and D.J. launched a 10-day tour of Florida, and the *Miami Herald* was on hand to review opening night:

> Elvis Presley, a big shouldered kid in a pink coat and long black pants, staggered onto the stage at the Olympia Theater Friday like a drunken Brando. And the mob, which stretched way up into the darkness of the theater, stood up and shrieked. It vibrated the air, piercing everything like a trillion tiny knives in the dimness. "Oh, go man, go!" one girl in shorts screamed, her frantic hands at her black hair, eyes stunned and face contorted. And how they screamed. Presley jogged around the mike and opened his mouth and the mob drowned the sound away. He loosened his white tie and licked his lips and tried again, but the jam of teenage girls wouldn't let his voice go. "Nothing like it since Sinatra started," one cop said. "I don't see how these kids can get so excited" [*Miami Herald*, August 4, 1956].

The cross-town *Miami News* reviewed the tour's second show and, judging from the following comments, they were not amused:

> For the second day, Elvis Presley, the vaudeville Valentino, rocked along his bumpy road to success here today after his fanatical followers engaged in a small-scale street riot. Young girls (many less than teen-age), not a few youths and even a number of elderly deserters from Liberace's ranks witnessed their "lover boy," as they call him, do the most obscene burlesque dance this reporter has seen in more than twenty years of getting around. From the theater wings, it was possible to see that the 21-year-old Presley's ribald routine is not of the emotions, as he's been telling the press around the country—his pelvic performance is clearly contrived. Also, far from fervor of the uncontrolled type are his other million-dollar stage mannerisms—the slack-jawed gibberish, the glassy gape of a hypnotized hillbilly, the unmannered gesture of wiping the nose, the staggering and shaking as if he had a bad fit [*Miami News*, August 4, 1956].

In addition to drawing the ire of the local news media, by late 1956, Elvis found himself squarely in the crosshairs of the national press, as this piece from *Look* magazine illustrates:

> Elvis Presley's fame is a legend of the "American Dream" of success that is overshadowed by a nightmare of bad taste. Here are some of the "Dream" elements: Elvis never took a lesson on his guitar, cannot read music. He paid

$4 to make his first record and a twister of a reaction began: he was a smash hit on the hillbilly circuit by 1955, without strong promotion. It seems certain that his 1956 income will top $500,000. He does not smoke or drink and night clubs bore him. But Presley is mostly a nightmare. On stage, his gyrations, his nose wiping, his leers are vulgar. When asked about the sex element in his act, he answers without blinking his big brown eyes: "Ah don't see anything wrong with it. Ah just act the way Ah feel." But Elvis will also grin and say "Without mah left leg, Ah'd be dead." Old friends, like the Memphis Press-Scimitar's Bob Johnson, advise him to clean up his "dances." Elvis listens and then goes out and does the same, very old things. His naïve intransigence threatens his future. Presley has taken the rock 'n' roll craze to new sales heights. He has also dragged "big beat" music to new lows in taste [*Look*, August 7, 1956].

By this time, even normally mild-mannered Canadians couldn't resist piling on, as this snippet from Saskatchewan's *Leader-Post* demonstrates: "I've never seen a male 'hoochie-koochie' dancer before," said Dan Cameron, the paper's music critic.

It seems to me extraordinarily distasteful in a man. An excessive development of rhythm seems to be the basic element of his music. Rhythm was developed centuries ago by all primitive peoples. The Australian aborigines, the most backward people on Earth, also have developed a form of music with rhythm, but little melodic content. The lack of control and exhibitionism of Elvis Presley is to my mind, a barbaric influence [*The Leader-Post*, Regina, Saskatchewan, November 17, 1956].

As troubling as these articles may have been to Elvis, it would be an August 8 story in the *Tampa Bay Times* that would really sting. Titled "Elvis is Draft Bait," the story revealed that Presley had recently registered with the draft board in Memphis. In the article, Elvis mentioned that he hadn't heard from the board since he'd registered and said, "I hope I never do." When asked whom he'd vote for in the upcoming election, Elvis said, "I haven't thought too much about it, but I guess I'll vote for Eisenhower or anyone who'll stop the draft" (*Tampa Bay Times*, August 8, 1956). Interestingly, when questioned about his political leanings less than a month later, Elvis had apparently veered left, saying to a reporter, "I'm strictly for Stevenson. I don't dig the intellectual bit, but I'm telling you man, he knows the most" (*New York Herald Tribune*, August 18, 1956).

The Music—August 24, September 4–5, October 1, 1956—Fox Studios, Hollywood

On August 22, principal photography for *The Reno Brothers* began at 20th Century–Fox studios in Hollywood. During breaks in filming,

Elvis found himself on a movie lot soundstage where he'd record the four songs he was scheduled to sing in the film. Elvis, assuming that Scotty, Bill, and D.J. would provide the instrumental backing, had brought his bandmates with him from Memphis; however, a Fox musical director deemed them, to a mixture of annoyance and amusement from Scotty and Bill, who'd cut their teeth on country music, "not hillbilly enough," and the sessions proceeded with studio musicians.

The four songs recorded during these sessions are "We're Gonna Move," "Let Me," "Poor Boy," and a reworking of the standard "Aura Lee," a song that was outfitted with new lyrics and retitled "Love Me Tender." Because the film was set in the years just following the Civil War, all four songs were performed on acoustic instruments. Elvis received co-writing credit on each, yet another Tom Parker scheme that in years hence would sully Elvis's reputation among the musical community. In subsequent years, some biographers have asserted that Presley himself found the practice dishonest, going so far as to quote him as saying, "I've never written a song in my life. It's all a big hoax. I get one third of the credit for recording it. It makes me look smarter than I am." In his highly regarded *Last Train to Memphis*, author Peter Guralnick contends that Elvis said this "on a number of public occasions" but fails to provide substantiation. For my part, I've been unable to unearth solid evidence that he ever did (Guralnick, *Last Train to Memphis*).

Of the film's four pedestrian tracks, "We're Gonna Move" is arguably the best, with a charming strummed guitar-backing and appealing two-part harmony. However, the song's inherent appeal is undermined by the laughable way it's presented in the film, with an 1870s Elvis, surrounded by a flock of "jus' simple folks," gyrating fifties-style across a front porch. The studio master of "We're Gonna Move" is a splice of takes 4 and 9, with vocals, handclaps, and finger-snapping overdubbed separately.

The subtlety of the film's title track is clearly targeted at softening Presley's image with Middle America. Credited to Vera Matson, the song's lyrics were actually composed by her husband, *Love Me Tender*'s musical director Ken Darby, who made the following observation of Presley after encountering him in the studio: "He adjusted the music and the lyrics to his own particular presentation," Darby recalls. "Elvis has the most terrific ear of anyone I have ever met. He does not read music, but he does not need to. All I had to do was play the song for him once, and he made it his own! He has perfect judgment of what is right for him. He exercised that judgment when he chose 'Love Me Tender' as his theme song" (Bloginroll.blogspot.com, 2016).

"Love Me Tender" was released as a single by RCA in September with "Any Way You Want Me" as the B-side, and by the first week of November, it claimed the number-one slot on both the *Billboard* and *Cash Box* singles charts. In early September, in a move to capitalize on what most everyone viewed as a sure hit, *The Reno Brothers* was retitled *Love Me Tender.*

The two remaining tracks, "Poor Boy" and "Let Me," are undistinguished, added to the film purely to capitalize on Elvis's current popularity. "Poor Boy" was recorded on August 24, with an additional verse completed on September 4. "Let Me" was initially laid down as a purely instrumental track on September 4, with Elvis applying his vocals a day later.

The Music—September 1–3, 1956— Radio Recorders, Hollywood

During a break in the filming of *Love Me Tender,* Elvis, Scotty, Bill, and D.J. gathered at Radio Recorders over Labor Day weekend for three days of non-soundtrack recording. This session came at the insistence of both Colonel Parker and Steve Sholes, who had a goal of generating enough material to cobble together an album and a new single to be released in the always-critical fourth quarter of 1956.

Joining this session as a sound engineer was 23-year-old Bones Howe, who, in future years, would establish himself as a successful record producer. In later years, he spoke of his memories of working with Elvis and his band.

"I first did some work with Elvis in September of 1956 in Hollywood at Radio Recorders," Howe recalls.

Elvis drove out from Tennessee in a stretch Cadillac with drummer D.J. Fontana and guitarist Scotty Moore, with all their gear in the back seat. Elvis and the guys stayed in Hollywood at the Roosevelt Hotel or the Plaza and later, the Knickerbocker. As an engineer and having played, I knew the rhythm section was piano, bass and drums. So the other guys beside Elvis were important too. A good rhythm section is three guys joined at the hip. Elvis would come in with Hill & Range music publishers and he would record only their songs at Studio B. They would show up with a box of acetate dubs and my job on those sessions, aside from running the tape machines, was that I had a turntable there which was hooked up to a playback system. I would take these dubs outs, one at a time, and put them on a turntable and play it outside to him. The guys would learn the song off the demo. Elvis ran the session and Steve Sholes ran the clock [Kubernik, *Turn Up the Radio!*].

The sessions of early September would be among Presley's most productive, and by the time they wrapped up on September 3, 13 studio masters were in the can.

The first track of the September 1 session was another Stan Kesler ballad, "Playing for Keeps," which featured Elvis on piano and prominent vocal support from the Jordanaires. Interestingly, during this session, just as during the session for "Hound Dog," Elvis's tendencies toward perfection were on display. Before he was through, he'd make 18 attempts at perfecting an acceptable studio master of "Playing for Keeps." In the end, he still found each attempt lacking in one way or another, and the completed studio master is a tape splice of takes 7 and 18.

The next song was a Jerry Leiber and Mike Stoller ballad titled "Love Me." Heavily echoed, with sparse instrumentation and call-and-response vocal support from the Jordanaires, "Love Me" works on just about every level and endures to the present day as one of Presley's most effective fifties ballads. In his otherwise impressive chronicle of Presley's recorded work, *Elvis Presley, A Life in Music*, Ernest Jorgenson contends that Leiber and Stoller once characterized "Love Me" as one of the worst songs they'd ever written; however, in a 2006 interview, Mike Stoller directly contradicts that, calling "Love Me" a "favorite old song of ours." No less a personage than Led Zeppelin's Robert Plant agrees, citing "Love Me" as a personal and inspirational favorite. He recounts an amusing story related to the song and a mid–1970s meeting between Led Zeppelin and Presley (Jorgensen, *Elvis Presley, A Life in Music*). "At that meeting," Plant recalls, "Jimmy Page joked with Elvis that we never sound-checked—but if we did, all I wanted to do was sing Elvis songs.

> Elvis thought that was funny and asked me, "Which songs do you sing?" I told him I liked the ones with all the moods, like that great country song "Love Me." So when we were leaving, after a most illuminating and funny ninety minutes with the guy, I was walking down the corridor. He swung 'round the door frame, looking quite pleased with himself, and started singing that song: "Treat me like a fool..." I turned around and did Elvis right back at him. We stood there, singing to each other [*L.A. Times*, January 4, 1981].

Next up was "How Do You Think I Feel," initially attempted—then abandoned—a year earlier at Sun Studios. This time, with a drum pattern that closely mimicked the original work of Jimmie Lott, who some musicologists have erroneously blamed for the failure of the Sun attempt, Elvis and the band managed to complete an acceptable version of the rhumba-tinged workout in just seven tries. Then, after completing a studio master of "How's the World Treating You," a country weeper co-written by Chet Atkins and Boudleaux Bryant, they decided to call it a day.

When the musicians reconvened at 4:00 p.m. on September 2, they first completed work on "When My Blue Moon Turns to Gold Again," a country hit from 1941 that is unfortunately burdened by a laughably histrionic coda from the Jordanaires. From there, Elvis, at the insistence of Steve Sholes, who was always on the lookout for album filler, moved on to the first of three songs closely associated with Little Richard, "Long Tall Sally," which they wrapped up in just four takes. (The following day, Elvis and the group would complete studio masters of two more Penniman songs, "Ready Teddy" and "Rip It Up." While all three are certainly workmanlike, only "Rip It Up," thanks to a balls-to-the-wall solo from Scotty Moore, comes close to outshining the original.)

"Old Shep," an ode to a beloved canine that won Elvis fifth place in a Tupelo talent contest 11 years earlier, was next, and with Presley on piano, it took just one attempt to lay down a final version. From there, it was on to Otis Blackwell's "Paralyzed." Given the charm of the finished version, it's puzzling that Elvis and his group would have as much trouble as they did completing an acceptable version of this track. "Paralyzed" shares the same infectious groove as Blackwell's "Don't Be Cruel," but after just a single attempt, Elvis called a halt and decided to move on to the next track, "Too Much," a straight-up rocker that ended up as the B-side to "Playing for Keeps," a 1957 RCA single.

"Too Much" is something of an oddity; it lacks a bridge and is in A-flat, an unusual key for Elvis. "Too Much" also gave Scotty Moore fits; from the beginning, he struggled to keep pace with the song's tempo and then fought to complete his solo. Still, primarily due to the song's sledgehammer groove, the finished version works. As he listened to the playback and Moore's quirky solo, Elvis turned and grinned at the guitarist. "He knew I had gotten lost," Moore said later, "but he loved the way it turned out. When the song ended, he raised up and said, 'That's it,' and he did it for damned meanness. He knew I had gotten lost and he knew damned well I would have to live with it" (Moore and Dickerson, *That's Alright, Elvis*).

After completing studio masters of "Anyplace Is Paradise" and the heavily echoed ballad "First in Line," Elvis and the group returned to "Paralyzed," which, blessed with an effective walking bass line from Bill Black, sterling piano work from Gordon Stoker, and solid support from The Jordanaires, at last clicked. The studio master of "Paralyzed" is a splice of take 12 and a subsequent insert.

16

Rip It Up

On Sunday, September 9, Elvis, to a curious and amped-up public and a press corps ready to pounce, made his first appearance on the Ed Sullivan show, which at this stage was still known by its original title, *The Talk of the Town*. Because Sullivan was hospitalized recovering from an auto accident, the show was hosted by actor Charles Laughton. During his segment, Elvis sang "Don't Be Cruel," "Love Me Tender," "Ready Teddy," and a truncated version of "Hound Dog," prior to which, Presley, in a clearly scripted segment, sent his best wishes to the recovering Sullivan.

For anyone unsure of what all the noise was about during this period, a quick glimpse of Presley's performance this night provides ample evidence not only of his appeal, but of the outsized antics that outraged half the country. Decked out in a plaid sport coat with enough Pennzoil in his hair to lube a diesel, Elvis spewed sparks throughout. "Ready Teddy" was clearly a highlight, with an unbridled Presley working the stage as Scotty Moore unleashed a manic solo. In the years since, it's become common lore that, in order to shield tender American sensibilities from his lascivious gyrations, Elvis was photographed from the waist up only during this appearance. In fact, it was only for his final appearance on the Sullivan show the following January that he was partially shown. The ratings for his first appearance were extraordinary, with over 80 percent of American televisions tuned in for the performance. It's also interesting (and sobering) to note that for his three appearances on the Sullivan show, Elvis was paid $50,000. For each of the three nights, Scotty, Bill, and D.J. made $78.23.

On September 21, Elvis wrapped up the filming of *Love Me Tender*, then, two days later, using the alias of "Clint Reno," Elvis, along with his new friend actor Nick Adams, flew home to Memphis. Days later, Elvis was back in Tupelo for an appearance at the Mississippi/Alabama Fair and Dairy Show, where, before a sell-out crowd, he was filmed by Fox Movietone News for a featurette that would play in theaters nationwide in the weeks to come.

On October 11, Elvis launched a four-night mini-tour of Texas that hit Dallas, Waco, and Houston before concluding in San Antonio. At month's end, Elvis was back in New York for his second appearance on the Ed Sullivan show. In a tan sport coat, tie, and white bucks and with his hair now dyed black, Elvis performed "Don't Be Cruel," "Hound Dog," "Love Me Tender," and "Love Me," during which, in a moment that could easily have turned catastrophic, he forgot his next lyric, stammering "I—, I—, I—," then, as if summoning help, blurted out "Somebody!" before finally regrouping.

The following day, in an unusual event, Elvis was at a studio on east 69th Street in New York to film a revised ending for *Love Me Tender*. In the weeks since it became public knowledge that Clint Reno, Elvis's character in the film, was slated to die, fans around the country expressed their displeasure. In fact, picket lines had formed outside Paramount Studios in Hollywood with fans carrying signs that read "Don't Die Elvis Presley." Yielding to pressure, studio execs decided to have Elvis reappear as a ghostly apparition superimposed over the film's closing scenes, singing the title song.

In early November, Elvis, nervous over the looming release of *Love Me Tender*, departed for Las Vegas. At this point, Presley held the number-one and number-two spots on the *Billboard* charts with "Love Me Tender" and the two-sided hit of "Hound Dog" and "Don't Be Cruel," the first time in history that both positions were held by the same artist. As he had the previous spring, Elvis availed himself of all the pleasures that Vegas had to offer, including repeated trips to see Billy Ward and His Dominoes, where he became captivated by a member of the troupe (an unbilled Jackie Wilson), who performed a galvanizing version of "Don't Be Cruel." In fact, Elvis was so taken with Wilson that he would cite the singer as a musical and performing inspiration for the remainder of his life.

On November 15, *Love Me Tender* premiered at the Paramount Theatre in New York. For the first showing, the theater, which had mounted a 40-foot cutout of Elvis above its marquee, was besieged by more than 1,500 fans. Days later, it was released to 550 theaters nationwide, and *Variety* reported that, in its initial week, *Love Me Tender* grossed $540,000. Reviews for the film ran from the sarcastic ("Is it a sausage?" asked *Time* magazine regarding Elvis's performance) to the outright vitriolic, as this snippet from the *Pittsburgh Sun-Telegraph* makes clear:

> The professional actors of "Love Me Tender" seem to be making fun of the village idiot in the picture and Elvis Presley plays the role to perfection. In a part far out of proportion to his acting ability, our boy did what any other

Movie poster promoting Presley's first movie, *Love Me Tender*.

no-talent high school boy would do, but the badgers wouldn't let him alone. The screen actors had to use exceptional restraint to keep from laughing in his face [*Pittsburgh Sun-Telegraph*, November 24, 1956].

In December, Elvis, Scotty, Bill, and D.J. played their final Louisiana Hayride in Shreveport. In fact, Presley was contracted for additional appearances, but Tom Parker, sensing bigger paydays elsewhere, had worked out a deal back in April wherein he would buy Presley out of the remainder of his contract for $10,000 and agree to a Hayride charity show in December. Accompanying Elvis for this appearance was Hollywood director Hal Kanter, who was preparing to direct Presley in his second film, a project that currently had a working title of *Lonesome Cowboy* and was scheduled to start filming in January. For the young fans in attendance, the show was an unqualified success. To a reporter from the *Shreveport Journal*, it was something less:

> One thing is clear: the youth is a phenomena [sic]. Roll Crosby, Vallee, Sinatra and all the others into one and they still couldn't get the wild ovation that the 21-year-old Mississippian got. The odd part is that Crosby, Vallee and Sinatra had a definable talent. Presley has none according to accepted standards, but then he may be the prototype of a new form of entertainment. All one can do is hope, of course [*The Shreveport Journal*, December 17, 1956].

By year's end, Scotty Moore and Bill Black were feeling the squeeze. Two men who were critical to helping Presley reach music's pinnacle were still scraping by on $200 per week and paying their own expenses when Elvis was touring and half that when they weren't. And with Elvis now spending much of his time in Hollywood, there'd been just 14 days of work over the past four months. In truth, their dissatisfaction wasn't relegated only to money; there was also the issue of billing. In the early days, as either "Scotty and Bill" or "The Blue Moon Boys," they'd received separate credit on records and wherever Elvis appeared. No longer. And it hadn't gone unnoticed by the pair that their musical brethren, the Jordanaires, seemed to be faring much better, with separate billing on every Elvis album and no restriction in their freedom to perform with other artists, something that Scotty and Bill were contractually barred from doing. Of course, there was also the issue of Tom Parker. It was clear to Scotty and Bill that the Colonel viewed them with thinly veiled contempt, and both men were convinced that their once close relationship with Elvis was being undermined by a man they viewed as nothing more than a former carny huckster.

"We knew he didn't want us around," Scotty Moore says of the Colonel.

Elvis was being brainwashed. We'd be traveling together in the same car and Elvis would bring up something—"The Colonel said so and so"—I'd say "Elvis, you have to stand up and speak your mind. There's nothing wrong with your arguing about something." He'd say "Ah, well, I made a deal with him. I'd do the singing and he'd take care of the business." He'd mumble and grumble about it for a day or two and that'd be it. He'd go ahead and do whatever it was he didn't want to do [Moore and Dickerson, *That's Alright, Elvis*].

In fact, Parker's antipathy toward Moore and Black can be chalked up as either the inability of a musically ignorant man to grasp the essential role both men played in Presley's ascent or a desire to further extend his control over the singer. Likely both. Especially galling was Parker's overt rudeness; on numerous occasions, he'd enter the dressing room where all three were congregated and, without acknowledging them, speak to Elvis as if they weren't present.

To make matters even worse, Parker seemed to delight in shooting down any opportunity that Scotty or Bill might have at improving their situation. Twice during 1956 they'd been approached by companies eager to have both men endorse their products; one offered each a new Chrysler if they agreed to praise the car in print ads. Hearing of this, Parker immediately said no. And while Scotty Moore would spend succeeding decades absolving Elvis of any blame for the financial pickle that he and Black were in, Presley's unwillingness to do anything to help his bandmates can't be defended. As newspapers around the country trumpeted the news that Elvis Presley had attained millionaire status (at a time when a million dollars still denoted unimaginable wealth to the average person), Scotty and Bill were sharing a room on the road and paying for their own meals.

None of this is to suggest that either musician should stand on the same financial ground as Presley. Elvis clearly was the star; it was his voice on the hits and it was he who put butts in arena seats. But it's simply ludicrous to assert that Scotty and Bill were nothing more than adjuncts to Presley's success, when their contributions to his music— and it was music, after all, that started it all—were critical to his ascent, sentiments that are echoed by Gordon Stoker.

"You know, he didn't give D.J., Bill Black and Scotty cars or anything," Stoker recalls. "The Jordanaires either." (Throughout his life, Elvis passed out cars to friends and hangers-on like other people passed out chewing gum.)

And together, we made him what he was, on record, anyway. We encouraged him. He once told us, "If it hadn't been for the Jordanaires, there might not have been a me." We'd help him with his arrangements and everything he did because we loved him. We didn't help him for the money. We did it because he was a friend and we loved him. At the same time, he just lost track of reality. What I would have done had I been him was help Bill Black and Scotty Moore, regardless of the Colonel [Burke and Griffin, *The Blue Moon Boys*].

Whatever his role in all this, there's still no disputing that Elvis was on the spot. He had to implement Parker's dictates, that was a given, but maintaining a sense of *esprit de corps* within the band was equally critical. Finally, with their patience and their bank accounts exhausted, Scotty and Bill approached Elvis and, following some airing of grievances, a compromise was hammered out. Once Elvis had completed his recording work for the coming year, he promised to turn the recording studio over to Moore and Black so they could to record their own album. To goose up sales, the profits of which would go exclusively to Scotty and Bill, the tracks would be instrumental versions of Presley hits and Elvis himself would participate. It seemed the perfect solution. Speaking to a reporter in mid–December, Black waxed enthusiastic over the opportunity. "We don't even know how they will title us yet," he said. "Maybe as 'Elvis' Boys'" ("These Are the Cats Who Make Music for Elvis," *Memphis Press-Scimitar*, December 15, 1956).

17

Always the Last to Leave

"It wasn't a big deal at the time."—W.S. "Fluke" Holland (www. tampabay.com, January 4, 2012)

On the afternoon of Tuesday, December 4, Elvis, back home following his most recent tour, was tooling around Memphis in his new Cadillac Seville. Perched in the shotgun seat was Marilyn Evans, a raven-haired Las Vegas showgirl he'd met on his recent vacation, who listened attentively as Elvis pointed out local landmarks. As he made his way up Union Avenue, Elvis spotted a fleet of cars outside Sun Studios and, figuring that a session was in progress, quickly pulled over. After being warmly greeted by Marion Keisker, Presley made his way into the studio, where he encountered Sam, along with Carl Perkins and his two brothers, listening to a playback of a just-completed session. Also on hand was a new Sun recording artist, a flame-haired pianist who, hoping to pick up some extra cash, had been hired to work the session.

In the intervening years, the date of December 4, 1956, has taken on legendary status. Not only because of the impromptu jam session that took place that day involving Elvis, Perkins, Jerry Lee Lewis, and Johnny Cash, but also because the session shows Elvis, who made a life-long practice of never submitting to in-depth interviews, unguarded and speaking extemporaneously about music in a way never heard before. (For years, it's been surmised that Cash, whose voice is not prominent at any point during the session, wasn't in attendance, but the "Man in Black" contends otherwise:

> I was there. I was the first to arrive and the last to leave, contrary to what has been written. I was just there to watch Carl record, which he did until mid-afternoon, when Elvis came in with his girlfriend. So, again contrary to what some people have written, my voice is on the tape. It's not obvious, because I was farthest away from the mike and I was singing a lot higher than I usually did in order to stay in key with Elvis, but I guarantee you, I'm there [Cash, *The Autobiography*].

An article published the following day in the *Memphis Press-Scimitar*—in which the foursome is labeled for the first time as "The Million Dollar Quartet"—contributed to the session's reputation as one of early rock's seminal events. Recordings of the jam session wouldn't surface until Sun Records was sold in 1969 and its catalog licensed for reissue in Europe. In 1981, it was made available on record for the first time and has been re-mastered and re-released several times since, the most recent being for the 50th anniversary in 2006. In 2010, the jam session became the subject of a Tony-award winning Broadway musical that purported to reproduce, however inexactly, what songs were played and the interactions that took place that long-ago day between four men credited with playing key roles in the history of early rock 'n' roll. Today, the four musicians gathered that December day are heralded by many as comprising rock's first super group, but to those who were there, it was just four guys out to have fun.

"It's hard for people to understand, but there were no big stars there," says W.S. "Fluke" Holland, who was in attendance that day and who also played drums on Perkins's seminal "Blue Suede Shoes," the first million-selling country song to cross over to both the R&B and pop charts. "Elvis was getting pretty popular, but really we were all just guys in a band. Everybody was equal. It wasn't a big deal at the time" (W.S. "Fluke" Holland, www.tampabay.com, January 4, 2012).

Also present that day was Knox Phillips, Sam's 10-year-old son. Spotting Knox, who, with his Brylcreemed hair and loud clothes, wasn't easy to miss, Elvis gestured to the boy. "Stay with me son, stay with me," he said, pulling the boy close. "And," Knox added years later in an interview with *Rolling Stone*, "he meant it. I think he saw me coming up as an embodiment of the Southern rebel thing and the other things he represented" (*Rolling Stone*, September 22, 1977).

Because the impromptu jam session involved musicians best known for playing rock 'n' roll, it might surprise anyone unfamiliar with this event to learn that gospel and country, and not rock, were the musical focus that day. To be sure, rock is acknowledged, with rough, but spirited versions of Presley, Chuck Berry, and Little Richard songs served up, but the session, replete with such standards as "When the Saints Go Marching In," "I Shall Not Be Moved," and "Don't Forbid Me," skewed heavily toward the down home and the spiritual.

After listening to a playback of what Perkins recorded that day (possibly including "Matchbox," one of his best-known tracks and one that would become a standard in years to come), someone passed Elvis a guitar. Sensing that something interesting, if not momentous, was about to take place, Sam Phillips hit the record button on the tape machine in the

Sun Studios control room. And just like that, the jam session was under-way. Throughout the afternoon, the sound of people could be heard drifting in and out, of doors slamming, random comments from Elvis's girlfriend, and regular asides from session musician Smokey Joe Baugh, who, in a scratchy voice, contributed comments and vocal harmonies.

The session kicked off with a blues jam, before the group segued to an instrumental version of "Love Me Tender," then, in keeping with the season, into "Jingle Bells" and "White Christmas." Following that, Elvis launched into a story of his recent trip to Vegas and his exposure to Billy Ward and His Dominoes. "There was guy out there that was doing a take-off on me," Elvis told everyone gathered in the studio that day, not real-izing that he was talking about the soon-to-be-celebrated Jackie Wilson and the version of "Don't Be Cruel" he sang that night. "He tried so hard till he got much better boy, much better than that record of mine." At this point, Elvis started to strum his guitar and stopped, unable to remem-ber what key one of his most famous songs was in. "Carl," he said, turning to Perkins, "what key did I do 'Don't Be Cruel' in?" After being reminded, Elvis then kicked into his impersonation of Jackie Wilson, doing an impression of him. When he was finished, he turned to another one of his own songs, "Paralyzed" (to which he also forgot the key), before returning again to "Don't Be Cruel" and additional impressions of Jackie Wilson.

From there the session took on a gospel feel as Elvis switched from guitar to piano and back again, before finally surrendering the key-board to Lewis. "The wrong man's been sitting here at this piano," Elvis remarked, taking note of Jerry Lee's chops. "Well," Lewis responded, "I been wanting to tell you that all along. Scoot over!"

An absolute highlight of the session was the repeated attempts the group made at remembering the lyrics to Chuck Berry's "Brown-eyed Handsome Man," clearly a favorite of everyone present. Bit by bit, the lyrics were summoned, and the group did three truncated versions of the song, each culminating in shared laughter.

As a sidebar, it's interesting to note that Elvis, perhaps not wanting to spoil the session's high spirits, said nothing regarding news he'd just received from the Memphis draft board. He'd been ordered to report, in less than a month, for his pre-induction physical.

For Presley fans, "The Million Dollar Quartet" is a fascinating, fly-on-the-wall listening experience and serves as perhaps that only time in Elvis's career where he can be heard discussing his music in a conversational and completely unselfconscious fashion. When the ses-sion finally broke up, Elvis remarked casually as he got ready to leave, "That's why I hate to get started in these jam sessions. I'm always the last one to leave" (RCA-Song BMG, *The Million Dollar Quartet*, 2006).

18

Slowly but Surely

On January 4, 1957, Elvis Presley, the country's most famous personality, became America's most famous potential draftee when he reported for his army physical. During this period, newspapers around the country carried breathless stories on Presley's possible induction, with a generational divide when it came to perspectives on the matter. On the one hand, there were the teenage girls, who, if polls were to be believed, viewed the possibility as nothing short of tragic. But there was also a wide-swath of Middle America who wanted nothing more than to shut this glorified misfit up, and if putting him in fatigues would do the trick, that was fine.

For Elvis, the physical was make or break. If he somehow failed the examination (other seemingly healthy young men recently had—baseball superstar Mickey Mantle, for example), he would be permanently removed from draft consideration. If, however, he passed, he'd be eligible for immediate induction, though recent practice indicated that draft notices generally followed six to eight months after the exam. The physical was conducted in secrecy, with Elvis as the only potential inductee present, but nonetheless, a fleet of photographers was on hand, as the following report from the *Miami News* indicates: "He emerged from his white Cadillac in black slacks and a black shirt and a crimson windbreaker," the paper reported.

> He was immediately surrounded by photographers, cameramen, reporters and fans. Remaining seated in the car while he underwent his physical was a girl he recently met in Las Vegas, Dotty Harmony. He invited the press inside and told the gathered reporters that he was thankful for what the country had given him and "Now I'm ready to return it a little. It's the only adult way to look at it" [*Miami News*, May 15, 1957].

Once the physical was behind him, Elvis, along with Scotty, Bill, and D.J., hopped a train for New York for his third appearance on Ed Sullivan's *Talk of the Town*. For this appearance, Sullivan would give Elvis something akin to free rein, allowing him to perform seven songs

Once word broke that Elvis was draft bait, newspapers around the country weighed in on the likelihood of Presley donning fatigues. This image is typical of editorial cartoons that appeared in newspapers around the country during 1956 and 1957 (*Memphis Press-Scimitar*).

spread out over three segments, while at the same time instructing his camera crew to photograph Elvis only above the waist. Resplendent in a gold lamé vest, Elvis sings "Don't Be Cruel" (during which he briefly mimics Jackie Wilson's pronunciation of "telephone"), "Too Much," and "When My Blue Moon Turns to Gold Again." Following a typically tongue-tied intro by Sullivan, Elvis, in the final segment, sings the gospel standard "Peace in the Valley," an earnest yet heartfelt (so heartfelt, in fact, that, in less than one week, Elvis would be in the recording studio to begin work on an extended play gospel record) attempt to soften his image with American viewers. At the song's conclusion, Sullivan moved to Presley's side, signaled for quiet, and then declared Elvis to be a "real, decent, fine boy." The gesture would pay dividends, for in the following days, Elvis, for just the second time in his short career, would be the subject of largely sympathetic reviews.

The glow resulting from Sullivan's approbation, however, would be short lived. Just days following the show, the Selective Service announced the results of his physical. Elvis was graded as an "A-profile," the highest army rating, making his induction a virtual certainty. From this day forth, the press would badger Presley with questions about his looming induction, and each time Elvis would serve up the same reply: he had no interest in preferential treatment, and, if called, he would do his duty and report.

Behind the scenes, however, things weren't so cut and dried. In the past, the army had given famous individuals special treatment, something that both Elvis and the Colonel were aware of. For example, during World War II, former heavyweight champion Joe Louis was granted "Special Services" status, sparing him from combat so long as he agreed to engage in boxing exhibitions to bolster troop morale. Elvis couldn't box, but certainly he could sing, and having him serve as a goodwill ambassador would, in the eyes of army brass, aid mightily in recruitment. Whether the Colonel or Elvis ever seriously considered this option is unclear, but if they had, a firestorm of protest would likely have resulted. Reporters around the country were already planting seeds in their columns that the fix was in, suggesting that the Colonel was pulling strings to get Presley special treatment or worse, have him avoid service altogether. To these guardians of public morality, it was bad enough that Elvis was fomenting juvenile delinquency, but now this upstart from Tennessee was trying to shirk his duty.

While all this was transpiring, the Colonel, after weighing all available options, was hatching a plan. To his mind, this rock 'n' roll thing would probably fade, but that didn't mean his boy had to. Maybe by casting Elvis as dutiful and patriotic, no better than anyone else and willing to serve his country, they might succeed at winning over average Americans, many of whom to this point viewed Presley as a threat to the moral order. Then, once two years had passed, Elvis could emerge from the service rehabilitated in the public eye and ready to resume his career.

Clearly, none of this pleased Elvis. After all, it was his life that would be put on hold for two years, not Parker's. But whenever he expressed his concerns, the Colonel did his best to reassure him. Besides, he reminded Elvis, in the wake of the Korean armistice, induction quotas were way down, which meant he might not be drafted at all. Whatever the outcome, Parker made clear, Elvis had no choice but to put it out of his mind, continue with his career, and hope for the best.

On January 11, Elvis arrived in Hollywood by train to prepare for his second film, now with a new working title of *Running Wild*. In the coming days, the film would undergo yet another title change, this time to *Loving You* in an effort to capitalize on a new Elvis recording that everyone saw as a certain hit.

The Music—January 12–13, 1957—
Radio Recorders, Hollywood

Just days before he was scheduled to step foot on the Paramount Studios lot to begin filming, Elvis was back at Radio Recorders to lay down tracks for a new single and a long-delayed extended play gospel release. In the days leading up to this session, Scotty Moore swapped his Gibson L5 for a blonde Gibson S 400, a guitar that he would forever be associated with. Of his playing during this period, Scotty would say later: "We couldn't get the highs or bend the strings as far as many players do now, because we didn't use light gauge. We just had to work harder. The Gretsch Chet Atkins strings were the only ones that would hold up on the particular guitar. On a couple of earlier guitars, I'd used different ones, though. By today's standards, they're like rope, they're so big" (Green, "Perhaps the First Rock & Roll Guitarist," *Guitar Player*, 1974).

The first track recorded on January 12 was "I Believe," a gospel song originally done by one of Elvis's personal favorites, Roy Hamilton. After completing a finished version in nine attempts, Elvis went to work on "Tell Me Why," a song written by Titus Turner, a composer for one of Elvis's favorite R&B groups, The Clovers. However, just when they were on the verge of completing the recording, someone realized that tune was strikingly similar to the gospel standard "Just a Closer Walk with Thee," and the song was shelved over concerns of plagiarism.

From there, it was on to tracks slated for Elvis's upcoming film.

Kicking off with lightning bolt energy, "Got a Lot o' Livin' to Do" served as something of a leitmotif for his new movie, as Elvis sang the tune numerous times throughout *Loving You*. Present in the studio that day was Ben Weisman, the song's composer, who relates an interesting story of his first meeting with Elvis.

"During a break in the session," Weisman recalls, "I noticed Elvis sitting alone in the corner of this big studio with nobody around him, adlibbing some blues on the guitar."

> I wandered over to the piano next to him, sat down and joined in. He didn't look up, kept on playing and even changed keys on me, but I followed along. Then he looked up with that smile he was famous for, and asked who I was and what I was doing in the studio? I told him I was invited to the session and that I composed one of the songs he was about to record called "Got a Lot o' Livin' to Do." He immediately called out to his musicians, "Guys, get out here" and on the spot they all got together again, and I was there watching, and I went back in the control room and they did the tune [Adams, "Interview with Ben Weisman," elvis.com.au, July 2020].

For the final song on January 12, Elvis turned again to the songbook of Otis Blackwell, composer of "Don't Be Cruel" and "Paralyzed." Leisurely and seductive, "All Shook Up" is blessed with note-perfect contributions from Bill Black, Gordon Stoker on piano, and Elvis, as he had on "Don't Be Cruel," supplying the song's percussion with slaps to the backside of his guitar case. A minimalist's dream, "All Shook Up" sounds as fresh and innovative today as the day it was recorded and denotes a clear high-water mark in the musical canon of Elvis Presley.

At noon the following day, everyone was back at Radio Recorders for a session that would run for seven hours. First up was "Mean Woman Blues," a track with an epic groove that contains one of Presley's finest vocal performances. Early versions show Scotty, perhaps forgetting Sam Phillips's admonitions to "keep it simple," riffing almost constantly through the song's verses and overly prominent piano licks from Gordon Stoker, approaches that would be jettisoned by take 14, which was designated the studio master. Interestingly, "Mean Woman Blues" would survive in altered form in years to come. A year after Presley's version was released on the *Loving You* soundtrack album, Jerry Lee Lewis would include a revamped version on his debut Sun Records album, and in 1963 Roy Orbison would score a top-10 hit with yet another version.

Next up was "I Beg of You," a song that everyone viewed as a potential hit single. But after 12 abortive attempts to nail down an acceptable version, Elvis, frustrated, decided to move on to "(There'll be) Peace in the Valley," a gospel tune slated for an upcoming extended play release that they completed in nine takes. Shortly before breaking for dinner,

Elvis and the group started work on "That's When Your Heartaches Begin," a song originally done by the Ink Spots that Elvis had remarked upon so pointedly during his Sun Studios jam session a month earlier. The completed master of "That's When Your Heartaches Begin" is a tape splice combination of takes 7 and 14. Finally, at 8:00 p.m., Elvis and the group started work on "Take My Hand, Precious Lord," yet another track for the upcoming gospel EP, which they completed after 14 attempts. With that, the session was over, but in just two days, everyone would reconvene, this time on a Paramount soundstage, to continue with soundtrack recording.

On January 14, Presley reported to Paramount to begin principal shooting of *Loving You*. For Elvis, who was still nurturing dreams of becoming a serious actor, the movie represented a serious step in the wrong direction. For his previous film, Elvis was required to sing just four songs and nearly an hour elapsed before he sang a note. In *Loving You*, Elvis starts crooning within the first six minutes, then proceeds to sing four songs in the film's first half-hour. While *Loving You* is infinitely more pleasurable than his first movie and includes a number of exciting musical numbers. It established a template that would endure for the remainder of Presley's movie career: cast Elvis as a societal misfit *cum* musical nova, who roams the countryside showering locals with song. When the songs are good, as most of the *Loving You* tracks are, the whole thing works, but when they aren't, and in most post–army Presley vehicles they weren't, incessant bludgeoning of audiences with sub-par material could only backfire.

For *Loving You*, Elvis kept his word to Scotty, Bill, and D.J., and the trio would be featured in the movie's musical scenes. Initially excited at performing in a Hollywood film, their enthusiasm quickly flagged when they learned they were considered "extras" and not "actors" and would be paid no more than $100 per day. As an added insult, they'd be needed no more than once or twice per week (this for a film with a five-week shooting schedule). For Scotty, Bill, and D.J., this meant days of sitting around doing—and making—nothing. And though they were separated by just two floors at the Hollywood Knickerbocker hotel, they rarely saw Elvis, a fact disconcerting to all three. After a couple weeks of this, they became fed up and told Hal Wallis they were going home. They had the producer over a barrel, and they knew it. Numerous scenes involving the three had already been completed, which meant that replacing them would necessitate extensive reshooting. Acknowledging reality, Wallis relented and mandated that all three would henceforth be paid actor's scale for their appearances. They were still sitting around with little to do, but at least they were being better paid for it.

Movie poster promoting Presley's second film, *Loving You*.

The Music—January 15–18, 21–22—Paramount Sound Stage, Hollywood; February 14, 1957—Radio Recorders, Hollywood

At 10:00 a.m. on January 15, Elvis was on a Paramount sound stage to continue work on the soundtrack for his new movie. Presley, who began his career in a recording studio that measured just 20 by 35 feet, was immediately discomforted by the cavernous setting. To make matters worse, studio employees, ranging from movie technicians to office workers, eager for a look at him, were free to come and go as they pleased. In response to his objections, Paramount engineers in the ensuing days would erect partitions at strategic points in the huge room in an effort to generate a feeling of intimacy.

The sessions would grind on six days, yet despite his dissatisfaction with the surroundings, Elvis and his group managed to complete final versions of soundtrack recordings "(Let's Have A) Party," "Lonesome Cowboy," a truncated version of "Got a Lot o' Livin' to Do" that appears in the film's opening moments, two versions of "Loving You," the radio-friendly "Teddy Bear," and "Hot Dog." During these sessions, Elvis and his band also tinkered with Fats Domino's current hit, "Blueberry Hill," a track they'd revisit on January 19 at Radio Recorders where they'd also complete studio masters of three additional songs: "It Is No Secret (What God Can Do)," which was targeted for an upcoming gospel EP, "Have I Told You Lately That I Love You," and "Is It So Strange."

Looking on as the Paramount sessions progressed was producer Hal Wallis. "I was fascinated by the way Elvis recorded," he recalled, "never bothering with arrangements. He and his boys noodled, improved, ad-libbed, and worked out numbers for hours. Finally, he would rehearse a number straight through. Night after long night I watched and listened, fascinated. I never said a word, just observed" (Wallis and Higham, *Starmaker, The Autobiography of Hal Wallis*).

January 18 is notable for Elvis's first pass at "One Night (Of Sin)," Smiley Lewis's 1956 ode to debauchery that contains the lyrics "One night of sin, is what I'm now paying for" and "The things I did and I saw, would make the Earth stand still." Elvis's enthusiasm for the track was not shared by Tom Parker and RCA, who viewed the song's message as far too incendiary for general release. Nonetheless, Presley didn't give up and in a little over a month's time would record a subsequent version with slightly scrubbed lyrics that he hoped would pass muster with the Colonel and RCA.

By mid–February, Elvis's discontent with the Paramount facilities reached such a point that producer Hal Wallis agreed to a switch in recording venues, and on February 14 the remaining soundtrack recordings were completed at Radio Recorders. "We went to California and they were trying to do it the Hollywood way. They'd put us on a soundstage like a football field, and we were supposed to play," D.J. Fontana recalls.

> We tried that one day at Paramount or MGM. They put baffles and everything up, so we finally had a room about this size, but it still wasn't comfortable. They finally started doing it at Radio Recorders, which was just about the size we needed. We did most of the soundtracks there. Elvis wouldn't even go on a soundstage. It was just too big, because he wanted the vocal group right on top of him and the band right next to him. It just wasn't comfortable working half a mile away. Of course, they wanted separation, but with us together, there wasn't a lot they could do about it. They had what they had, and that was it. But that's the way Elvis recorded, and they weren't going to change him. So he'd say he was sick that day and go home. We knew something was wrong. When they would suggest going to Radio Recorders, he'd say, "Yeah, that's a good idea," but he'd get sick [*Modern Drummer*, May 1985].

In *Loving You*, Elvis is cast as "Deke Rivers," a truck-driving hick with a penchant for breaking into song at the drop of a hat. While it certainly wouldn't end up on any critic's year-end list of favorites, the film hums in places and boasts a couple of exciting musical numbers, the best being the juke joint segment where Elvis is confronted by a local punk. With a sneer and fuck-you coolness, Elvis proceeds to sing and dance for the crowd before separating his antagonist from his senses in a post-song punch-out. In the years since the film's release, Presley's co-stars, when prompted for their memories of working with him, are virtually unanimous in their praise. "He was quite a gentleman, with a quality of simplicity, humor, and shyness about him," co-star Dolores Hart recalls. "It was very much his persona at that time" (interview with Dolores Hart, elvisau.com).

While these comments are typical from people who encountered Elvis at this point, there's also evidence that by 1957—a period when he was being hounded by the press, seen as a symbol of youthful insurrection (in St. Louis, he was burned in effigy by Catholic schoolgirls), and pursued relentlessly by fans—Presley was clearly feeling the pressure. During a break in soundtrack recording, Jordanaires leader Gordon Stoker accepted an invitation to sing on "Young Love," a ballad by movie heartthrob Tab Hunter. Despite the fact that neither Stoker nor the Jordanaires were contractually prohibited from performing with other artists, Presley, learning of this, blew up at Gordon. The following day, Elvis, sensing he was wrong, apologized repeatedly. When Gordon told him that contrition was unnecessary, Elvis doubled down, telling Stoker that he wouldn't forget what he'd done until the day he died. Then, gesturing toward a stagehand sweeping the floor nearby (the conversation took place on a Paramount soundstage), Elvis mentioned that if he ever offended the man, he'd be unable to rest until he apologized. He then concluded by telling Stoker, "I guess I'm just a weird guy" (elvis.com.au, October 2018).

The Music—February 23–24, 1957—
Radio Recorders, Hollywood

In a session that began at 10:00 a.m. on February 23, Elvis was back at Radio Recorders for a (mostly) non-soundtrack recording session. The first song attempted was "Don't Leave Me Now," a mid-tempo ballad that, according to studio logs, required 29 attempts before they arrived at a completed master. The task was no less arduous for the next song, "I Beg of You," which Elvis, after numerous tries, had given up on back in mid–January. This version, which deviated from the guitar-centric approach of the previous month, featured a more prominent rhythm section and background support from the Jordanaires. Also contributing to the song's subtler feel was Elvis, who was once again keeping time on the backside of his guitar case.

For the session's third song, Elvis returned to "One Night," lyrics scrubbed so references to "one night of sin" became "one night with you." Despite the bowdlerized content, "One Night" stands to the current day as an unparalleled Presley triumph, a track on which he not only delivered one of his most impressive vocals, but on which he also played lead guitar. In the days following this session, Elvis, clearly enamored of the track, played it repeatedly for friends, while never failing to note, "That's me playing guitar."

Before wrapping up the session at 2:00 p.m., Elvis, with an eye on completing the *Loving You* soundtrack, polished off a version of Cole Porter's "True Love" and an "Ivory" Joe Hunter composition, "I Need You So." The following afternoon, he completed in just four tries the version of "Loving You" that would become the RCA single. Then, to wrap things up, Elvis knocked off "When It Rains, It Really Pours," the track he'd attempted and ultimately abandoned in his final Sun recording session, after eight attempts.

Midway through the filming of *Loving You*, Elvis was joined by his parents, who were making their first visit to Hollywood. For Vernon and especially for Gladys, the trip was a welcome diversion. Back home in Memphis, things had taken a dark turn. Initially delighted by their new home on Audubon Drive, they quickly found out that their new neighbors didn't share their joy. At first they complained about the fans who lingered out front at all hours, making noise and leaving trash behind. From there, the neighbors groused about other aspects of the Presley lifestyle they found grating, including Gladys's habit of hanging their laundry outside to dry. Any hope of finding common ground was permanently dashed when a petition was circulated to have them ousted. For Gladys, it was simply too much. The fans she could deal with; after all, they were there because they loved Elvis. But complaints from neighbors regarding their lifestyle raised her ire, and, to her mind, the entire affair was an invasion of family privacy.

None of this is surprising. People react to lifestyle changes in a myriad of ways, and their ability to adjust depends on numerous factors, including upbringing, personal resilience, and age. For Elvis, the upheavals of the prior year were the culmination of a dream he'd harbored since he was a boy. For Gladys, who wanted nothing more than a settled existence, the seismic upheaval of the past months had left her feeling as if she'd been airdropped onto alien turf. Troubled by a sudden onset of physical problems and what they viewed as symptoms of depression, Vernon and Elvis urged her to seek help, and Gladys reluctantly admitted herself to Memphis's Bryant Hospital for tests. While nothing serious was detected, a "general malaise" was diagnosed, likely due to stress. "From my due diligence of Elvis, and my similar background of growing up very poor in that area, it really strikes me now that Elvis' mom Gladys was almost literally in shock," notes Tupelo resident and WTUP radio engineer Ron Brandon. "She simply could not mentally make the tremendous leap in lifestyle change that had taken place for them in the past year. Her preference would have been, as with most women it seems, to enjoy the security of their newfound monetary situation, but otherwise to go back to their life of closeness, privacy, family, which, of course, would not be possible" (elvisinfonet.com, 2011).

Gladys may have struggled as Elvis's career skyrocketed, but for Vernon, the experience was altogether different. While certainly not immune to the changes overtaking his life, a certain smugness—a sense of "we showed 'em"—seemed to be taking hold as he found acceptance in a world that in former years had condemned him to life's lowest rung. But as Ron Brandon confirms, even acceptance has its limits. While many Southerners took pride in one of their own making it to the top, there was one sector that remained distinctly nonchalant. "I met many of the people in East Tupelo that had known the Presleys when they lived there," Brandon states, "and for the most part, they were happy for them, but pretty much unimpressed. They attributed Elvis' success at the time more to pure happenstance or luck than anything else. They were a hard crowd and were not impressed easily. But they were nice people, as the Presleys were. It was just a tough time and place to grow up" (elvisinfonet.com, 2011).

On March 10, Elvis attended a wrap-party for *Loving You*'s cast and crew, then headed back to Memphis on March 18 with a goal of finding more accommodating living conditions for Gladys and Vernon. During his stay, he viewed a two-story mansion on 14 acres in the outskirts of Memphis dubbed "Graceland." Immediately impressed, he quickly signed an agreement to purchase the property and, days later, plunked down $100,000 to complete the sale. "We will have a lot more privacy and a lot more room to put some of the things we have accumulated over the last few years," Gladys, seemingly relieved, told the press shortly afterward. For his part, Vernon, forever in search of the rusty lining, complained: "We just had the old place fixed up like we wanted it. Now we have to start all over again" (Moore and Dickerson, *Scotty and Elvis: Aboard the Mystery Train*).

While in Memphis, Elvis would occasionally drop in on an old friend, Sam Phillips. "Elvis would call at three in the morning," Knox Phillips recalls, "and my mother would get up and cook eggs for him and the twenty or so people he brought with him. It would always be Memphis people and maybe a Hollywood starlet. They would stay up all night shooting pool and listening to records" (*Rolling Stone*, September 22, 1977).

On March 28, Elvis kicked off a nine-day tour of the Midwest and Canada, with stops in Chicago, Fort Wayne, St. Louis, Detroit, Buffalo, Toronto, Ottawa, and Philadelphia. For this tour, Elvis, seemingly finding inspiration from a meeting with Liberace in Vegas the year before, would be clad in a $2,500 full-length, gold-leaf suit that was custom made for him by Colonel Parker. It was this outfit that Elvis appeared in on the cover of his second greatest hits album, *50,000,000 Elvis Fans Can't Be Wrong: Elvis' Gold Records, Volume 2*, issued by RCA in November of 1959. For Presley, the suit proved to be more of a headache than anything else; whenever he performed in it, the stage was littered with pieces of gold spangles that flaked off whenever he dropped to his knees.

If 1956 was remembered as a year of nearly non-stop touring and breakthrough television appearances, then for Elvis, 1957 would be characterized as the year of the Hollywood movie. To illustrate, by late April of '56, Elvis had completed in excess of 60 U.S. concert appearances, excluding a two-week engagement in Las Vegas. By the same time in 1957, he had made just nine. So it was fitting that on April 27, with yet another movie looming, Elvis once again found himself on a train, bound for Hollywood.

Blues Poetry

"I like the blues. I'll write with you."—Mike Stoller

With those words, Jerry Leiber and Mike Stoller forged one of the greatest songwriting duos in the history of American popular music. Which is not to suggest that it clicked from the very start. Stoller, a freshman at Los Angeles City College with a taste for be-bop and dreams of composing jazz for a living, was anything but enthusiastic when his phone rang one day in 1950. On the line was 17-year-old Jerome Leiber, a student at LA's Fairfax High School with a penchant for putting words to music.

"Can you write notes on paper?" Leiber asked Stoller after introducing himself.

"Yes," Stoller replied.

"Can you read music?"

"Yes."

"Do you think you'd like to write songs?"

"No" (Bluerailroad.com, November 2011).

Stoller wasn't trying to be rude, it's just that, as a classically trained pianist, with tastes that ran to Charlie Parker, Miles Davis, Dizzy Gillespie, and Art Blakey, Mike wondered what this young lyricist could offer him.

Still, Leiber was persuasive enough to induce Stoller to agree to a meeting a few days hence. At the agreed upon time, Jerry, with a notebook of his lyrics tucked under his arm, knocked on Mike's front door. Thrown by the boy's odd eye coloring—one was blue, the other brown—it took Mike a minute to invite Jerry in. Once inside, the two exchanged some small talk, then at some point Stoller took Jerry's lyric book and moved to the piano. With his eyes fixed on Leiber's scribbled lyrics, Stoller began laying down some elemental chords. "Hey," he said, turning back to glance at Jerry. "They're not the kind of songs I dislike. These are blues, aren't they?" After getting a nod in response, Stoller spent the next five minutes delving further into Leiber's work. When he was done, he closed the notebook, turned to Leiber, and, with an expression of delight, mouthed the words "blues poetry." Then, with a quick handshake, a partnership was forged; Jerry Leiber and Mike Stoller, both still in their teens, were now a songwriting tandem. In later years, Stoller, would speak with humor of the early days of their partnership. "Honestly, when Jerry and I started to write together, we were writing to amuse ourselves" (*Rolling Stone*, August 22, 2011). Amuse themselves they did, while simultaneously generating a body of work that, in years to come, would establish them as the poet laureates of early rock 'n' roll.

The songwriting duo's first breakthrough came when blues singer Jimmy Witherspoon crooned one of their compositions at a performance at Los Angeles's Shrine Auditorium. The track, "Real Ugly Woman," was such a crowd pleaser that Witherspoon recorded and released it as a single in 1951, providing Mike and Jerry with their first royalty checks. Their first national hit, "Kansas City" by Little Willie Littlefield in 1952, was a blues shuffle extolling the plentitude of feminine pulchritude in Missouri. (A 1959 version by Wilbert Harrison would go on to even greater success.) From there came "Hound Dog," written, according to Leiber, in just 12 minutes on a piano in bluesman Johnny Otis's front room. Released by "Big Mama" Thornton in 1953, "Hound Dog" would sell more than 500,000 copies and spend 14 weeks on the R&B charts.

By the mid–1950s, Leiber and Stoller, thanks to "Hound Dog," found themselves on the radar screen of Presley's primary source for new music, the Hill and Range publishers. Both men, incidentally, hated Elvis's version of the tune, though the financial remunerations were certainly welcome. "The first time I received a sizeable royalty check was in 1956," Stoller recalled. "It was for $5,000. I never thought I'd see that much money at one time again. $5,000 was a lot of money in the fifties. Jerry told me 'Mike, we have a smash hit!' 'You're kidding, which one?' And he said 'Hound Dog!' 'Big Mama Thornton's record?' I asked. He said, 'No, some white kid named Elvis Presley'" (Sharp, *Writing for the King*).

With the outsize success of "Hound Dog" on their minds, representatives from Hill and Range contacted Mike and Jerry. Did they have other material that might suit Elvis? When the answer came back "yes," a deal was negotiated. However, before it went into force, Mike and Jerry were informed of a critical caveat: henceforth, anything the duo submitted for Elvis first had to go the "appropriate channels," which, in this case, meant Hill and Range representative Fred Bienstock, who worked for and was related to Hill and Range owners the Aberbachs. This labyrinthine approach was set up by Parker and was solely designed to prevent anyone from approaching Elvis directly without first obtaining his sanction. Despite finding this odd, Mike and Jerry submitted "Love Me" for consideration, a tune the two had originally intended for friends in a San Francisco gospel group.

The duo's next connection to Presley took place in the run-up to the filming of Elvis's second movie, when they submitted "Hot Dog" and what would become the title track, "Loving You." Now, with planning underway for a subsequent film and Leiber and Stoller's cachet at an all-time high, Hill and Range co-owner Jean Aberbach approached Jerry and Mike for more material. Agreeing to write at least four songs for the movie, Leiber and Stoller, in the month before shooting was to begin and armed with a copy of the film's script, checked themselves into a New York hotel to start work. Still, despite the agreement with Hill and Range, the duo was anything but enthused over the idea of producing more material for someone—Elvis—they deemed a musical upstart:

> Jerry and I came to New York for about three weeks in March of '57. We were seriously considering the possibility of moving there. We took a suite at the Gorham Hotel on 55th Street and had a rented upright piano put in the living room, where I spent next to no time at all. One day Jean Aberbach gave us an assignment to write the score for the forthcoming Presley movie. We were so excited at being in Manhattan with all the Broadway shows and jazz clubs that we kept putting off the job [Sharp, *Writing for the King*].

When Aberbach turned up one day at Leiber and Stoller's hotel suite to see how things were going, he was stunned to find the film's script tossed in the corner with a stack of magazines and nothing done on the movie's score. Aghast, Aberbach began to pace the room and lecture the duo on the importance of meeting commitments. Then, demanding that they get down to work, Aberbach shoved a couch against the hotel room door, stretched out on the sofa, and said, "Boys, I'm gonna stay here until you give me the score" (Sharp, *Writing for the King*). With a shrug, Mike and Jerry went to work and, in roughly three hours' time, cranked out four songs, including the title track, "Jailhouse Rock."

The first meeting between Elvis and the songwriting duo came at a recording session on April 30, 1957, when, after a few moments of awkwardness, the three suddenly clicked. Mike and Jerry were later to say they were impressed with Presley's work ethic ("He could sing take after take and never get tired, he was unreal") and lack of any diva-like behavior (Sharp, *Writing for the King*).

In truth, no one, including the principals themselves, could've foreseen the tight bond forming between Elvis and the two songwriters. Just two years older than Presley, Mike and Jerry shared Elvis's fascination with and love of black culture and were amazed to learn that Presley's knowledge of R&B extended to Eddie "Cleanhead" Vinson and other obscure bluesmen. While they undoubtedly inhabited different musical worlds—Elvis leaned toward country and gospel, while Jerry and Mike worked almost exclusively with blues and humor—the combination worked, a fact immediately recognized by Steve Sholes, who, with Elvis's approval, approached Leiber and Stoller with a proposition. He didn't really understand this rock 'n' roll stuff, he told them. Would they be willing to take over? After a quick conference between themselves, then a powwow with Elvis, Mike and Jerry agreed to serve as producers for *Jailhouse Rock*'s soundtrack sessions, although they would receive neither credit nor remuneration for their efforts. (Years later, Jerry Leiber would say that the duo began working as producers purely out of self defense, finding that, unless they were present, their songs were likely to end up unrecognizable).

As the coming days would show, the trio's unlikely but ultimately

Elvis poses with the songwriting team of Leiber and Stoller in this publicity shot promoting *Jailhouse Rock*. Left to right: Mike Stoller, Elvis Presley, Jerry Leiber (Alamy.com).

fruitful partnership would pay dividends, with Elvis completely won over by Jerry and Mike's infectious enthusiasm and they by his perfectionist yet oddly relaxed method of recording. The three grew so close that by the time the soundtrack to *Jailhouse Rock* wrapped up, Elvis viewed both as something akin to talismans. "Elvis asked for us to be there," Stoller says. "He was a very good-looking young man, very energetic. I mean, he kept going and going in the studio. He'd say 'Let's do another one!' And it would go on and on until he felt he had it" (Kubernik, *Turn Up the Radio!*).

The Music—April 30, May 3, 1957—Radio Recorders, Hollywood; May 9, 1957— MGM Soundstage, Hollywood

In a session that began at 10:00 a.m. on April 30, Elvis, with Leiber and Stoller acting as producers, first went to work on "Jailhouse Rock," a track, that even at this early date, was slated as the movie's title. With a half-step, sledge-hammer opening devised by Scotty and Bill and Elvis at his larynx-shredding best, "Jailhouse Rock" is a prime example of the best of Presley's 1950s work. Nailing down a completed take, however, would prove arduous. After four failed tries at perfecting the song, Elvis, feeling the strain of repeated takes on his throat, said to everyone in the room, "We gotta get this thing, because I can't keep this up."

Take 5 kicked off promisingly, but ultimately broke down when Scotty hit a bum note during his solo. Prior to take 6, either Jerry or Mike suggested to Elvis that he should extend the song's coda. "Make it too long," he was told. "We can always cut it." "In other words," Elvis replied, "just keep going?" By the next attempt, they'd got it nailed, and take 6 was marked as the studio master.

Contributing to the appeal of "Jailhouse Rock" is a subtle, easily overlooked contribution of Bill Black, who slyly dropped out for one measure of the song's closing refrain before re-joining, fueling the song's irresistible groove. Interestingly, a second version of "Jailhouse Rock" was recorded this day to be used during the film's production number; it is simply take 6 overdubbed with vocal chicanery. Also completed were three versions of the ballad "Young and Beautiful," which were used to signify the artistic evolution of Vince Everett, the character Elvis portrays in the movie.

The next session, scheduled for Wednesday, May 1, ended up being cancelled due to a contretemps that flared up between Elvis and a representative from MGM studios. The rep, tasked with watching the clock and cutting down on waste, had looked on with annoyance as Elvis, typically indifferent to schedules, spent copious time harmonizing on gospel tunes with the Jordanaires at the previous session before finally getting down to work.

"We were sitting there," D.J. Fontana recalls, "and the guys, the higher ups, the big wheels, they'd come up and say, 'You know, tomorrow when Elvis comes in, guys, we're wasting a lot of time and money, don't sing with him, don't play with him, don't do anything.'"

> So we'd say, "OK." So he'd come in, sit down and start playing, and nobody moved, didn't play, the voices didn't sing. He said, "What's the matter, guys, are you mad at me or something?" And we told him, the higher ups didn't want us to play and sing. He said, "OK, so I got a sore throat, I'm going home." So he went home. Once he had a sore throat or something wrong, they couldn't say anything to him, see. So they didn't say another word after that. "Do what you want to do" [Melin, interview with D.J. Fontana, April 2006].

Friday's session was productive, with master recordings of Leiber and Stoller's "Treat Me Nice" and "I Want to Be Free" completed with a minimum of takes. (Elvis, seeing it as a potential single, subsequently grew dissatisfied with the version of "Treat Me Nice" recorded this day and re-recorded it at a subsequent session.)

The *Jailhouse Rock* sessions are notable for a stark improvement in Presley's recorded sound, primarily due to Bill Black forsaking his acoustic bass for a Fender Precision electric. First produced by Leo Fender in October of 1951, the early Precisions featured a non-contoured body, a blonde finish, a 20-fret maple neck, and a single pickup. In 1954, in an effort to make it easier to play, the Precision was revamped to emulate the contours of the Fender Stratocaster guitar. Further revisions were made to the bass in 1957 when a split-coil pickup was added, as well as bridge-mounted strings. By the mid–50s, the Fender Precision found increasing favor with musicians who were not only seeking a more portable instrument, but also needed it to sonically compete as rock 'n' roll took hold and groups—and audiences—became louder.

All of which brings us to the next track to be recorded on May 3, one of Elvis's most vibrant early rockers, "(You're So Square) Baby I Don't Care." From the outset, the track's prominent bass line seemed to plague Bill Black, and repeated attempts at executing it only left him frustrated. Finally, after another blown take, he'd had enough. Spitting out a curse, Black unstrapped his new bass, slid it across the room toward Elvis and stomped out of the studio.

From there, Gordon Stoker picks up the story: "Most artists would have said 'You pick that bass up and play it, buster, that's your job,' but not Elvis," Stoker recalls. "You know what he did? Elvis thought it was funny. He picked it up and played it himself. He just picked up that bass, put his foot up on a chair, and played that song all the way through" (bassmusicianmagazine.com, April 6, 2020).

Naturally, this made a vocal overdub necessary, which Elvis did on May 8 on an MGM soundstage. In years to come Elvis would develop an ongoing affection for the electric bass. "On the nights we stayed at the Perugia [Beverly Hills] house," friend Jerry Schilling says, recalling the 1960s, "we spent a lot of time around the pool table in the big round den with the open fireplace, and even more time hanging out in that little den. Elvis had become infatuated with playing a Fender electric bass guitar and a lot of nights he'd plug in, sit in front of a TV with the sound turned down, and play along at extremely high volume with a stack of records" (Schilling, *Me and a Guy Named Elvis*). It's also a fact that when Elvis met the Beatles during their 1965 tour of the U.S., their first image was of him seated in the living room, riffing on a Fender Precision bass.

The last song to be worked on on May 3 was "Don't Leave Me Now," which Elvis had tried and failed to complete back in February. Still, it would be another six days, at the final *Jailhouse Rock* soundtrack session, before Elvis would complete a satisfactory version of the tune.

For Presley, the *Jailhouse Rock* sessions were enormously satisfying and among the most productive of his career. Much of the credit, at least in Elvis's eyes, belonged to Leiber and Stoller, who, in working closely with him from the studio floor, provided a torrent of ideas and musical insights, the likes of which he hadn't experienced since the days of Sun and Sam Phillips. "Elvis got to a point where he became very superstitious and would not set foot in a recording studio without us," Jerry Leiber recalls. "Of course, we were very flattered" (Sharp, *Writing for the King*).

On Monday, May 13, Elvis reported to the studio for costume fittings, and his arrival at the MGM lot caused quite a stir, with office workers and film crews pouring out of their offices and soundstages for a gander. After being assigned Clark Gable's former dressing room, Elvis met with his co-stars, a group that included character actor Mickey Shaughnessy and brunette Judy Tyler, who broke into show business as the original Princess Summerfall Winterspring on the *Howdy Doody* children's program.

Performers and stagehands who interacted with Elvis during this period speak of his easy-going manner. "He interacted with everybody," recalls actor Bob Relyea.

One of the first days we were shooting a scene and we were held up—and one of the crew just said, "Well, we should have a song." So he got his guitar out and played a song. It wasn't any, "No, no, I don't do that, uh, don't embarrass me." He just said "Give me my guitar!" He had all these qualities that you knew he could succeed at whatever he wanted to do. He probably would have been good as a schoolteacher, he would have been a good mechanic. He was so dedicated and focused, he knew what it was about, he knew what tomorrow's work was going to be [Lichter, *Elvis in Hollywood*].

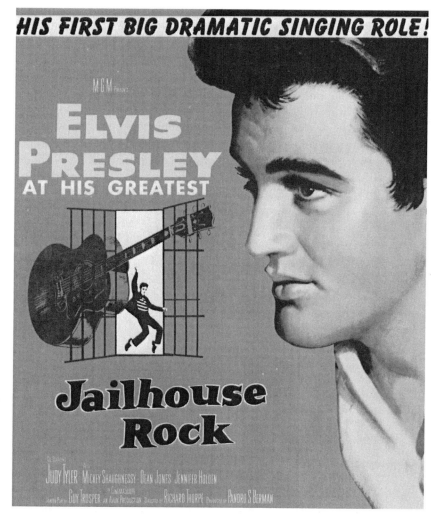

For his third Hollywood movie, Elvis portrays Vince Everett, an ex-con who sings and snarls his way to the top of the musical world.

While Elvis was in Hollywood, the retinue of cousins, lay-a-bouts, and ass-lickers that trailed him from Memphis, and who in future years would become known as the Memphis Mafia, assumed, for the first time, a somewhat formal role, when they were put on the Presley payroll. This was done at the urging of Parker, who told Elvis it was necessary for tax reasons. Now, instead of glutting up Elvis's dressing room, prowling the MGM lot ogling stars like Kim Novak and Anne Francis, and engaging in sophomoric hijinks for nothing, they'd be paid $50 per week to do so.

It was during the early days of filming *Jailhouse Rock* that an event took place that would have a profound and deleterious impact on Elvis's future career. Killing time between movie scenes, Presley was in his dressing room chatting with Mike Stoller when he casually asked Mike if he and his partner could write him a ballad. Sometime later, Stoller met with Leiber and, within a couple of days, they came up with "Don't," a charming tune that both men saw as a perfect vehicle for Elvis.

"I thought he was the best ballad singer since Bing Crosby," recalls Jerry Leiber. "I loved to hear him really do a ballad, 'cause there weren't too many people who could do our ballads to our satisfaction. We didn't have people like Tony Bennett or Frank Sinatra, because we were writing rhythm and blues—torch ballads—and they didn't do those things, you see. But Presley was the ultimate in the ballad" (Kubernik, *Turn Up the Radio!*).

Mike Stoller echoes Leiber's sentiments, while also commenting on Presley's choice of material. "Sometimes his intuition wasn't 100 percent," Mike Stoller recalls, "but it didn't matter much because he was a true performer. He was an artist" (*Musician*, October 1992).

When asked if Elvis understood his appeal, Stoller hesitates:

> I don't know. That's a hard question. And if he did, let's put it this way, in the early days, he was extremely confident in the studio. He was very confident, and if you read that as knowing how good he was, I suppose he did. On the other hand, when he went on the movie set, he was very insecure. I remember one incident in particular where a couple of actors were sitting around talking. They were talking about their wives or their cars, just family stuff, and they were laughing, and Elvis walked in and wheeled around and said, "You think you're so hot?" He thought they were laughing at him [interview with Mike Stoller, *Goldmine*, May 2002].

After Stoller demo'd "Don't" on the piano, Elvis was immediately won over and vowed to record it at his next session. However, when news of this reached Colonel Parker, he flew into a rage because the songwriter duo hadn't first funneled the track through Hill and Range. Parker's thinking was two-fold: First, routing everything through H&R

ensured that the song's author had previously agreed to surrender a share of songwriting royalties in exchange for Elvis recording the tune. And, equally important, it eliminated the possibility of any loose cannons infiltrating Elvis's inner-circle and undermining Parker's total control. To Leiber and Stoller, Parker's anger served as a wake-up call; it was suddenly clear to both that instead of being part of a creative team, they were nothing more than cogs in Parker's machinery, expected to march in lockstep to his dictates. The dustup over "Don't" would soon fade, but Parker's dictatorial impulses would resurface again, this time laying waste to arguably the most productive and creative partnership of Elvis's career.

Interestingly, *Jailhouse Rock* would provide a member of the Leiber/Stoller songwriting team with a new role, as an onscreen member of Elvis's musical group. At some point, director Richard Thorpe decided that a scene early in the movie needed a piano player, and, to Thorpe, Jerry Leiber looked the part. With no desire to do anything but compose music, Leiber begged off, conjuring up the excuse that he had an urgent dental appointment. Thorpe then turned to Mike Stoller, who reluctantly agreed, but on the condition that he be allowed to keep his beard. "Nope," came Thorpe's reply; Stoller's beard might be fashionable among the hipsters he and Jerry consorted with, but it wouldn't work in a Presley film. After a bit of convincing, Stoller relented, shaved off his goatee, and, looking chastened and ill at ease, filmed the scene.

For some inexplicable reason, the filming of *Jailhouse Rock* seemed rife with events that would roil Elvis's life, including one that would trigger a nearly permanent rift between Elvis and Dewey Phillips. It took place while Dewey was in Hollywood to spend a few days with Elvis. Enthusiastic over what was planned as his next single, Presley played Phillips a dub of "Teddy Bear," a song so engaging that Phillips immediately asked Elvis to play it again. Packing his bags later that day for a return trip home, Phillips, without telling Elvis, stuffed the acetate into his suitcase. Once back home, he wasted no time playing it for his radio audience. Later that same day, the telephone in Steve Sholes's office rang. On the line was a friend in Memphis, telling him he'd just heard "Teddy Bear" on the radio. Alarmed, Sholes quickly notified Elvis and Tom Parker.

In truth, it wouldn't be the first time that the bond between Elvis and Dewey would be tested. During his Hollywood visit, Elvis had sometimes been embarrassed at his friend's behavior. On one occasion, Phillips, upon being introduced to film star Yul Brynner, said to the actor, "You're a short little mother, aren't you?" To Presley, it was "just Dewey being Dewey." But stealing the acetate and playing it without approval was a clear betrayal in Elvis's eyes, and he immediately cut off all contact with the man who'd played a crucial role in kickstarting his career. That summer, a headline in the *Memphis Press-Scimitar* carried news of the breakup. "These reports are true," the headline stated. "Elvis and Dewey Had a Falling Out" (*Memphis Press-Scimitar*, July 1957).

20

Trouble

With work finally wrapped on *Jailhouse Rock*, Elvis, who during this period of his life flatly refused to fly, hopped a train for home, only to arrive in Memphis to find renovation work on Graceland still ongoing. While happy to be home, Elvis, in addition to worries over his draft status, was distressed by changes taking place with his mother, who, morose and seemingly depressed, rarely left her room.

In early July, Elvis was stunned to learn that Judy Tyler, his *Jailhouse Rock* co-star, had been killed in an auto accident. According to news reports, once filming ended Judy and her husband had set out for New York City, where she was due to appear on the CBS-TV program *Pantomime Quiz*. In the early evening of July 3, Judy, with her husband behind the wheel, was in their 1957 Chevrolet on U.S. Highway 30, three miles north of Rock River, Wyoming, when a car pulled onto the highway. Judy's husband swerved, sending their car skidding into the oncoming lane where they were broadsided by a northbound vehicle. Judy was killed instantly; her husband died the next day in a Laramie hospital from chest and back injuries. Also dead at the scene was a passenger in the other car. According to Presley confidant George Klein, Elvis was devastated upon hearing the news. Saying that "nothing has hurt me so bad," Presley, initially determined to attend the funeral, ultimately decided against it, concerned over turning it into a media event.

In August, Elvis, prompted by stories in two national publications, was forced to publicly deny that he was racially prejudiced. His supposed statement—"The only thing negroes can do for me is shine my shoes and buy my records"—had also been circulating for months among black communities throughout the South. Elvis issued a statement categorically denying both that he ever said it and that he was racist. In the years since his death, family members and friends have sketched a mixed portrait of Elvis and his perspective on race. While one states that he heard Elvis use the word *nigger* "maybe once or twice," another speaks of Presley's disgust at meeting a football coach who used the same term in his presence, saying of him subsequently, "That no good prejudiced bastard." Nonetheless, they all state that they'd never heard Elvis say anything as explicitly racist as the statement he was accused of saying. "It wasn't like him to make racist remarks like that," said one close friend (Nash, *Elvis Aaron Presley: Revelations from the Memphis Mafia*).

Myrna Smith, an African American member of the Sweet Inspirations vocal group who performed with Presley for years, flatly denies that Elvis was prejudiced. "As far as he treated me, there was not [a] racial bone in his body. I mean in the early days he even sneaked into those black gospel churches in Memphis which would have taken a lot of nerve. White boys just wouldn't go there, it was a brave thing to do but he was just determined" (interview with Myrna Smith, elvisinfonet. com, 2003). Nonetheless, concerned that rumors of racial prejudice would spread unless confronted head on, Elvis submitted to an interview with *Jet* magazine in 1957, in which he stated: "I never said anything like that and people who know me know I wouldn't have said it" (*Jet*, August 1957).

In early September, Elvis, at the express wish of Tom Parker, was back at Radio Recorders in Hollywood for his last recording session of 1957.

The Music—September 5–7, 1957— Radio Recorders, Hollywood

For months, RCA and Colonel Parker had been pressing Elvis to record an album of Christmas songs to be released in time for the winter holidays. Presley, perhaps sensing that his brand of blues-based rock 'n' roll might not be transferable to holiday music, was hesitant, but finally agreed. But there was a catch: he'd do the Christmas album, but first he was determined to revisit "Treat Me Nice," the track he tried and failed to perfect on May 3 but which he continued to view as a possible single.

On September 5, with a revamped arrangement from Leiber and Stoller that featured a new keyboard opening and galloping percussion from Elvis keeping time on his guitar case, "Treat Me Nice" was wrapped up after 15 tries and was slated as Presley's next single.

From there, Elvis, Scotty, Bill, and D.J. started work on the first of the scheduled holiday songs, "Blue Christmas." The song had previously been recorded by numerous artists, most prominently Ernest Tubb, who carried it to country music top 10 in 1950. For his version, Elvis, with prominent backing from the Jordanaires and the support of soprano

Millie Kirkland, successfully conjured up visions of a deep December day. Of all the numerous holiday-themed tracks that Elvis would record during his career, "Blue Christmas" would remain a personal favorite, and it would feature prominently in his comeback special 12 years later.

When everyone reconvened at noon the following day, they started work on "Ivory Joe" Hunter's "My Wish Came True," an exercise in aural excess that had somehow found Elvis's favor. However, after 28 attempts, the song failed to jell and Elvis ultimately decided to move on, though he would return to the song early in the new year.

From there, everyone went to work on a version of Irving Berlin's yuletide standard, "White Christmas," which they completed in just nine attempts. Clearly modeled on the 1954 Drifters version, Presley's take began with a tasteful piano opening by Dudley Brooks and strong vocal support by the Jordanaires. Then, channeling his inner Clyde McPhatter, Elvis kicked off the song's third verse using the same vocal stylings as the Drifters' lead vocalist. Appending a snippet of "Joy to the World" to the song's coda was an inspired choice; the addition greatly contributes to the tune's appeal.

After knocking off perfunctory versions of "Here Comes Santa Claus" and "Silent Night," Elvis switched gears and went to work on a song he found truly inspiring, "Don't," the ballad that fomented such strife between Leiber and Stoller and Tom Parker. Blessed with subtle vocal and instrumental support, a lovely melody, and convincing delivery by Elvis, "Don't" worked on practically every level. The track would ultimately be released as the A-side of an RCA single in January of 1958 and, by the time it completed its run, would rank as the third most popular song of the year.

On Saturday, everyone was back at Radio Records to finish off Elvis's holiday album. After completing a studio master of "O Little Town of Bethlehem" in just four takes and an Aaron Schroeder/Claude DeMetrius yuletide rocker called "Santa Bring My Baby Back (to Me)" in nine, somebody pointed out that they were one song short of what was needed to complete a full album.

"Elvis was back at Radio Recorders finishing a Christmas album," Jerry Leiber recalls. "They were shy one song. Colonel Parker entered the control booth and said, 'Hey boys, can you write me one more tune?' I said, 'When do you need it?' He said, 'Now.' We went into the men's room and wrote 'Santa Claus Is Back in Town' in about five minutes. Mike walked out of the men's room first. As he opened the door to the control booth, I heard Parker say, 'What took you so long?'" (Sharp, *Writing for the King*).

"Santa Claus Is Back in Town" begins with a deceptively mellifluous opening by the Jordanaires, but any suggestion of yuletide serenity is quickly ripped aside by rimshots, a stripper beat from D.J. Fontana, and lyrics not to found in any church hymnal. In the years to follow, Mike Stoller would comment on the song's suggestive lines. "It's a little risqué," he said. "Obviously RCA Victor didn't catch on to the fact that 'Santa Claus is coming down your chimney tonight' didn't really refer to a chimney" (interview with Mike Stoller, *Goldmine*, May 2002).

With "Santa Claus Is Back in Town" in the can, Elvis and his group knocked off "I'll Be Home for Christmas," a faithful reworking of the Bing Crosby hit from 1943, in 15 tries. Fleshed out with four previously recorded gospel tracks, "Elvis' Christmas Album" was released on October 15 and spent four weeks atop the *Billboard* album chart.

With the completion of the holiday album, the moment that Scotty Moore and Bill Black had so anxiously awaited had finally arrived. The previous December, Elvis assured them that once his recording work for 1957 was complete, the studio would be turned over to them to lay down tracks for their own album. But just as they were preparing to start work, Tom Diskin marched into the studio and said, "That's it, the session's over." Stunned, but figuring there was some mistake, Scotty and Bill protested that they had an agreement to record their own album. Diskin shook his head. The Colonel, he told them, had heard of the arrangement and ordered it shut down. Turning to Elvis for support, Moore and Black watched in disbelief as he wordlessly withdrew to the comfort of his entourage. Earnest attempts to reason with Diskin failed. The session was over, he told them. Furious and swearing audibly, Bill Black slammed his guitar into its case and stormed from the studio. Scotty, seemingly more dispirited than angry, said nothing.

In hindsight, this entire matter, to even the most dispassionate observer, establishes two unassailable truths. First, by not putting the agreement to cut their own album in writing, Scotty and Bill erred grievously. Secondly, it also makes clear that Presley's earlier promise that they'd share in his success—"My word is my bond" being his exact words, per Gordon Stoker—was nothing more than lip service and that, whenever the two musicians ran afoul of Parker, Elvis would invariably side with his manager (Burke and Griffin, *The Blue Moon Boys*).

Back at their hotel, Scotty and Bill shared resentments over drinks. Justifiably proud of what they'd contributed to Elvis's rise, both men had long resented the Colonel's dismissive treatment of them. As Scotty Moore would later describe it, Parker's attitude to them could be summed up as "Get them as cheap as you can and never give them the credit that they deserve" (*Guitarist*, November 1992). Nonetheless, Scotty and Bill could take small comfort in one reality: they weren't alone. *Nobody* liked the Colonel, with "cold-hearted" and "con man" serving as just two examples of what people would say of Parker once he was out of earshot. None of which, however, softened their feelings at Elvis's behavior. To both men, Presley's refusal to back them up in an agreement that all three had forged was an abject betrayal. As the night wore on and the drinks and the grievances flowed, a decision was made. Reaching for a piece of hotel stationery, Scotty, with Bill looking on, laid it all out. They'd been there from the start, and the sound they'd crafted was making cash registers ring from coast to coast. They'd been promised a share of Elvis's success, but he was making millions while they struggled to feed their families. To make matters worse, any attempt they might make at improving their financial state had been shut down by Parker. Given these realities, Scotty wrote, they had no alternative but to resign.

After affixing their signatures, Scotty and Bill, sensing a united front could only strengthen their case, approached D.J. Fontana and asked him to sign. But after perusing the letter, he shook his head. He'd been hired strictly on a salaried basis, he told Scotty and Bill, and simply didn't experience the sense of betrayal felt by his bandmates. Years later, Fontana would speak of his relationship with Presley during this phase.

"You wouldn't say anything to him because you were afraid to," D.J. recalls.

> He had too much power. He didn't push that power, but he had it. If something was wrong, he'd let you casually know about it with a couple of sly remarks, or he'd get sick. He was a nice man, though. A lot of times we'd go out to California to record and he'd say, "Are you guys making any money?" We'd say, "No, Elvis, the session is going too fast." And he'd say, "Don't worry about it. We'll take a lunch break in a minute." And he'd be gone for two or three hours. He'd come back and ask, "You guys make any money yet?" I'd say, "Yeah, we got two or three hundred made," and he'd say, "We might as well get started. What do you think?" [*Modern Drummer*, May 1985].

Dismayed by D.J.'s refusal to join them, but nonetheless determined, Scotty dispatched the letter to Elvis at the Beverly Wilshire Hotel, where, according to those present, he reacted with unbridled rage upon reading it. He'd been betrayed, he vented to everyone in the room, including his then girlfriend, Anita Wood. How could they do this to him? If they'd come to him and explained their situation, things could've been worked out. But not now, not after this. Now they could just go fuck themselves.

However, by the time he returned to Memphis on September 11,

Elvis's mood had softened and on Thursday he rang Scotty and offered both men a $50-per-week raise. Moore, perhaps sensing that he now had the upper hand, said that wasn't enough. He was in debt and needed a one-time payment of $10,000 to get back on his feet. After stating he wanted some time to think that over, Elvis called the Colonel. Hearing of this, Parker flipped, and, per Presley associate Lamar Fike, his attitude toward Moore and Black and their demands was "Fuck you, you're not going to get it. That's the way it is boys, cut and dried" (Nash, *Elvis Aaron Presley: Revelations from the Memphis Mafia*).

Days later, Scotty and Bill, in an effort to ramp up pressure on Elvis, took their case to the media. In a September 13 article that appeared in the *Memphis Press-Scimitar*, Scotty said, "[Elvis] promised us that the more he made the more we would make. But it hasn't worked out that way." That same day, a similar article appeared on the front page of the *Memphis Commercial Appeal*, in which Bill Black stated, "I don't believe Scotty and I could raise more than fifty bucks between us. I'm still living day-to-day" (*Memphis Press-Scimitar*, *Memphis Commercial Appeal*, September 13, 1957).

Embarrassed and indignant that the dispute had reached the public, Elvis issued his own statement to the press the following day, stating that if Scotty and Bill had come to him and not gone public with their financial concerns, things could've been worked out (clearly ignoring the fact that they had). He then added that there were certain people close to him who had recently tried to convince him to drop Scotty and Bill. He would not name those "certain people," but said he'd refused for sentimental reasons and "because they were good musicians." "We started out together and I didn't want to cut anyone out of anything," he said. But now, by taking their demands to the press, they'd made him look bad. All he could do, he stated finally, was to wish them both good luck (*Memphis Press-Scimitar*, September 13, 1957).

For Tom Parker, a musical illiterate who viewed Scotty and Bill as nothing more than annoying adjuncts to Presley's success, the sooner Elvis cut ties with both men, the better. Steve Sholes had his own reasons for welcoming the split. A dedicated clock-watcher, Sholes, under pressure from corporate bean counters at RCA headquarters to reduce the length of Presley sessions, had repeatedly lobbied the Colonel to dump Scotty and Bill and rely on the efficiency (and, yes, the accompanying bland professionalism) that came with studio musicians. "From a practical standpoint, as far as recordings are concerned," Sholes said in an October 2 memo to Parker, "I hope Elvis doesn't take Scotty and Bill back" (memo from Steve Sholes to Tom Parker, October 2, 1957).

Having the support of his manager and producer may have

bolstered Presley's spirits, but with gigs looming, first for an upcoming benefit at the Tupelo fairgrounds for a planned "Elvis Presley Youth Center" and a tour of California's west coast in early October, Elvis was under pressure to find a new guitarist and bass player. On September 27, before a huge banner promoting *Jailhouse Rock*, Elvis took the stage at the Tupelo Fair, backed by Hank Garland on guitar and a friend of D.J.s, Chuck Wiginton, on bass. The response from the audience was typically electric, but still, there were calls from the crowd asking where Scotty and Bill were. Just how much Elvis missed Scotty and Bill depends on whom you listen to. Presley hanger-on Lamar Fike contends that Elvis, after hearing his band complete their first song, turned to him with a grin and said, "Shit, I didn't need Scotty and Bill anyway, did I?" (Nash, *Elvis Aaron Presley: Revelations from the Memphis Mafia*). Other accounts, including that of D.J. Fontana, suggest that Elvis's reaction was altogether different and that he spoke of feeling disoriented and ill at ease without Scotty and Bill backing him.

When the truth, it's nonetheless a fact that, a week following the Tupelo performance, Tom Diskin, at Elvis's insistence, reached out to Moore and Black asking them to rejoin Elvis for his upcoming four-day tour of California. The pay would be on a per-diem basis of $250 per show, plus paid travel expenses, and both men accepted.

"We never did go back on the payroll after that," Scotty Moore said later. "We went back to do one tour" (*Guitarist*, November 1992).

When the duo arrived in San Francisco in preparation for a performance there on October 26, hellos were exchanged, but nothing was said regarding the events of the past three weeks. "We went onstage and it was just like nobody said a word," Scotty Moore remembered. "Like we'd never been anywhere, said anything" (Burke and Griffin, *The Blue Moon Boys*).

21

Blue Moon

After playing to sold-out crowds in three Bay Area shows, Elvis and his troupe headed south for a performance at Los Angeles's Pan Pacific Auditorium on October 28. After touching down in LA, someone handed Elvis a newspaper with a feature article on rock 'n' roll with comments from Frank Sinatra, who, it seems, was out to prove that he owned a dictionary: "Rock and roll smells phony and false," the singer said. "It is sung, played and written for the most part by cretinous goons and by means of its almost imbecilic reiteration and sly, lewd, in plain fact, dirty lyrics, it manages to be the martial music of every side-burned delinquent on the face of the earth. It is the most brutal, ugly, desperate, vicious form of expression it has been my misfortune to hear" (Martin and Seagrave, *Anti-Rock, The Opposition to Rock 'n' Roll*).

If the press was hoping that the article would ignite a war of words between the two singers, they were disappointed. "I admire the man," Elvis stated graciously. "He has a right to say what he wants to say. He is a great success and a fine actor, but I think he shouldn't have said it. He's mistaken about this. I consider it the greatest in music. It is very noteworthy," he continued, before concluding with "because it's the only thing I can do" (press conference, October 28, 1957).

The audience response to Presley's performance at the Pan Pacific Auditorium that night toggled between chaos and euphoria with many in the crowd at levels of near-hysteria. Taking it all in from his vantage point in the bleacher section was a young Malcom Leo, who, in subsequent years, would make his name as a director of Hollywood films. "I performed my chores to get my mother to let me go to see Elvis at the Pan Pacific Auditorium," Leo remembers.

> He had the gold suit on and he rolled on the floor with Nipper, the RCA Victor dog. I sat off to the side, like on county fair seats. The moment he came onstage, my heart skipped a beat and I lost my breath. Okay, the guy could sing. But there was an aura about him that was so commanding. I was staring at him and locked in. It was almost overwhelming for me because

you know, you see this guy and you see his movies, but when you see him onstage live ... it just brought me to my knees [Kubernik, *Turn Up the Radio!*].

The national press on hand to cover the performance viewed it less charitably. "Elvis Presley Will Have to Clean Up His Show or Go to Jail" stated a headline in the *New York Journal-American* ("L.A. Outraged

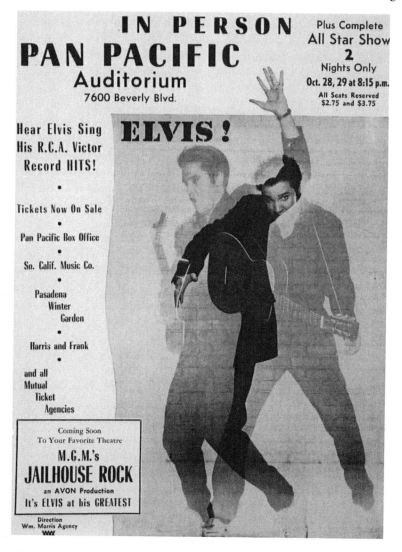

On October 28, 1957, Elvis appears at Los Angeles's Pan Pacific Auditorium, where he's filmed by the Los Angeles Police Department's vice squad, who threaten Presley with jail unless he cleans up his act.

at Presley," *New York Journa- American*, November 8, 1957). Equally offended was the *Los Angeles Mirror-News*, which opined of the performance: "If any further proof were needed that what Elvis offers is not basically music but a sex show, it was provided last night" (*Los Angeles Mirror-News*, October 29, 1957). As if to underscore just how offensive some found this performance, Colonel Parker was approached by representatives of the Los Angeles Police Department's vice squad following the first show. "Your boy," Parker was told in no uncertain terms, "better clean up his act"; otherwise, he risked arrest.

When informed of this, Elvis's initial response was to shrug it off. It was only when he hit the stage and spotted a pair of camera-toting cops positioned just feet away that he realized the seriousness of the situation. He attempted to joke about it ("I wonder if they're going to release this in theatres?"), but it was clear he had to tone things down. Watching the show from backstage were Ricky Nelson and members of his band, guitarist James Burton and legendary slap bassist James Kirkland, along with country singer Bob Luman. In a 2018 interview I conducted with Kirkland, he told me that at points during the show when Presley would typically be at his most physical, Elvis, with a sly grin, would lift both hands above his head to form a halo.

Following the show, Elvis hosted guests in his hotel suite, including the 17-year-old Nelson. Spotting him as he entered, Elvis quickly made his way across the room and bear-hugged the young TV star, telling him he never missed an episode of the family TV show *The Adventures of Ozzie and Harriet*. When he learned that Nelson was about to embark on his first tour, Elvis pulled him into a huddle, imparting tips and insights that he hoped would help Ricky with his upcoming shows.

"You'll never know how much tonight has meant to me," Nelson told a friend later that night. "Imagine Elvis Presley watching our show. He repeated episodes I'd even forgotten about. He remembered them word for word. And he gave me some great tips about things to do on my tour" (Bashe, *Teenage Idol*).

On November 5, Elvis sailed for Hawaii, where, over a period of two days, he would play three shows for both the general public and service personnel stationed at Honolulu's Schofield Barracks. No one realized it at the time, but these would be Presley's last public performances for over three years.

Given the likelihood of his possible army induction, Elvis's first Christmas at Graceland would prove to be a somewhat joyless affair. On the surface, nothing had changed. Elvis shopped for presents at local stores, he and his buddies partied at night, and donations still flowed to local charities. But the overall feel was aimless and arbitrary, as if ceaseless activity could somehow forestall what everyone knew was coming. Finally, Milton Bowers, chairman of the Memphis draft board, ended the suspense on December 19, when he sent Elvis the following message: "You are hereby ordered for induction into the Armed Forces of the United States and to report to Room 215, 198 South Main St., Memphis, Tennessee, at 7:45 a.m., on the 20th of January, 1958, for forwarding to an armed forces induction station" (telegram to Elvis Presley December 19, 1957).

Later that evening, Elvis was cornered by a reporter from the *Press-Scimitar* as he was returning home from a night out. What was his response to his draft notice? After Elvis expressed gratitude for what the country had given him, the reporter asked him if he wanted to go into Special Services.

"I want to go where I can do the best job."
"What about your movie contracts?"
"Don't know—just don't know."
"How about a look at your draft notice?"
Elvis grinned sheepishly. "Man, I don't know what I did with it."
The search was on.
"Maybe in the kitchen," someone suggested. It wasn't.
"Last time I saw it, it was right here," said Elvis and pointed to a place in the front hall. No notice.
Finally: "Here's the envelope—the notice must be in my parents' bedroom."
One thing sure: This is a notice for Elvis and "I'll do what I have to—like any American boy" [*Memphis Press-Scimitar*, December 21, 1957].

The following day, Elvis was driving around Memphis, when, on a whim, he decided to stop by Sun Studios where, in a tone that bordered on flippancy, he announced, "I'm going in." But back home at Graceland, it was clear to everyone that he was devastated at the news. Friends made repeated attempts at cheering him, saying he was too big or too important to be drafted and that, at some point, his fans would rise up and the draft board would yield to public pressure. He listened, grasping for straws of hope, but nothing could mitigate his misery.

For weeks, he'd listened as the Colonel filled his head with pie-in-the-sky plans for post–army success. Do your time, he was told, keep your nose clean, and once it was over, he would emerge transformed as a patriot, someone who viewed himself as no better than anyone else, who'd been willing to sacrifice everything to do his duty. All the hatred and abuse that had been shoveled his way over the past two years would be replaced with the glowing approbation of a grateful and forgiving public. Elvis listened, trying to believe. But all that stuff, all the goodies the Colonel promised, was two years off. For a man of 22, it might just as well have been 200. It was easy for the Colonel to be upbeat—he wasn't going anywhere. But for him, it promised to be hellish, an experience from which he had nothing to gain and everything—fame, money, freedom—to lose.

22

Way Down

"I'm the most miserable young man you've ever seen. I have got more money than I could ever spend. I have thousands of fans out there and I have lots of people who call themselves my friends, but I am miserable."—Elvis Presley, 1957 (Burk, *Early Elvis: The Humes Years*)

Concerns over his looming induction were just one source of a troubling malaise that had settled over Elvis Presley by December of 1957. Despite a level of success that any performer would envy (three number-one singles, a top-grossing film, sold out tours, and the purchase of a grand estate that would remain his home until he died), an ennui, accompanied by a growing agitation, had crept into his life during the waning months of the year. He'd always been easily bored, but lately his discomfort with routine had manifested itself in angry outbursts that concerned his friends. To be sure, there was the issue of Dewey Phillips. He'd been there from the start, but Elvis felt acutely betrayed when Phillips played a pre-release version of "Teddy Bear" on his Memphis radio show. Then there was the matter of Scotty and Bill, who, feeling underpaid and unappreciated, had quit. Of course, they both returned after being offered modest raises, but the unity that once characterized the trio was gone.

Old friends were changing too. Marion Keisker, so key to his success at Sun, had, in a moment of pique with Sam Phillips, left Memphis to join the military. And while he did his best to ignore it, there was always the issue of his spiritual backsliding. The same boy who'd just recently told the press that "whatever I am, whatever I will become, is what God has chosen for me" (*God Is My Refuge*, Photoplay July 1957) was now openly dating showgirls and strippers. ("I'm as horny as a billy goat in a pepper patch," he'd said to Vegas stripper Tempest Storm, professionally known as "The $50,000 Treasure Chest," in October. "I'll race you to the bedroom" (Storm, *The Lady Is a Vamp,* Peachtree Publications, 1987).) And hanging over all of this was the gnawing concern over his future; a career that for the past 24 months had sustained a breathless momentum, now appeared, if not over, to at least be on ice for the next two years, an eternity for any popular singer.

In a muted gathering at Graceland on January 8, Elvis celebrated his 23rd birthday. Nothing seemed to cheer him, not even the delay the Memphis draft board had granted to allow completion of a new movie. Two days later, along with friends Alan Fortas, Gene Smith, Cliff Gleaves, and Bitsy Mott, he boarded a train for Hollywood to begin work on his next film, which was based on the book *A Stone for Danny Fisher* by Harold Robbins, who, at his peak, was known as the "Rembrandt of trashy novels." In Robbins's work, Danny Fisher is a New York prizefighter hell-bent on kicking enough ass to ascend to boxing's top rung. In the film, Fisher, as played by Elvis, is an alienated New Orleans youth with (wait for it...) a talent for singing. His co-stars for this, his fourth movie, would include Carolyn Jones, Dean Jagger, his *Loving You* co-star Dolores Hart, and Walter Matthau as crime boss Maxie Fields.

News of Elvis's looming induction seemed to infuse his fans with a manic desire for one final look, and, as the train carrying Elvis and his pals whistle-stopped its way west, adoring crowds gathered. "Every town we passed through, no matter what time of morning or night, the whole station was jam-packed," Alan Fortas recalls. "These people knew as soon as Elvis finished this movie, he was going in the Army, so most of them considered it the last time to see him. As soon as he got on the train here in Memphis, it hit the wire, it got in the papers and on radio. People knew and they were lined up along the track all the way across America" (Hopkins, *Elvis, the Biography*).

The film, which would ultimately be titled *King Creole*, presented Presley with the rare opportunity of working with a truly outstanding Hollywood director, in this case 69-year-old Michael Curtiz. The Hungarian Curtiz, who was responsible for such legendary films as *The Adventures of Robin Hood, Mildred Pierce,* and *Casablanca,* was a no-nonsense taskmaster, a rep that was quickly born out when, prior to production, he instructed a startled Elvis (whom he referred to in his thick accent as "Elvy") to "lose fifteen pounds and shave off those sideburns." Elvis did both.

Before principal photography on *King Creole* could begin, there was first the matter of the film's soundtrack. So, on Wednesday, January 15, Elvis, along with Scotty, Bill, and D.J., entered Radio Recorders studio in Hollywood to start work. Once again on hand to assist Elvis were

Jerry Leiber and Mike Stoller, the songwriting duo who would serve as de facto session producers. "We were told numerous times after *Jailhouse Rock* that he considered us his good luck charms" Mike Stoller recalls. "He always wanted us in the studio. He respected us. We came to know what a great talent he was very quickly after starting to work with him" (*Goldmine*, May 2002).

The affection that each felt for Elvis didn't extend to Tom Parker, who in the eyes of both had a Svengali-like hold over his singer. Evidence of this was manifested following a party that Jerry Leiber attended one night in New York. Recognizing the songwriter, a well-known agent and producer approached Leiber with a tantalizing offer to participate in a film based on the critically acclaimed novel *A Walk on the Wild Side*. The movie would be directed by highly respected Edward Dmytryk, and the screenplay would be handled by Bud Schulberg. "I want you and your partner to write the songs and Elvis Presley to play the lead," the producer told Leiber. Ecstatic over the offer, Leiber immediately headed for a phone booth. "I called Mike," Jerry recalled, "and he was thrilled."

> We thought the news was going to blow the minds of Elvis and the Colonel. We went up to the Hill & Range office 'cause Elvis Presley's music was co-owned by Elvis and the Aberbachs. Jean was there, and Julian came in. The Colonel was somewhere else. The whole thing was laid out for them. They said, "We will have to speak to the Colonel. Can you wait outside?" So we waited outside and we figured the Colonel would be over the moon about this. We waited a long time, and we were summoned in by Jean and he said [adopts Viennese accent], "The Colonel says if you ever dare try and interfere in the career of Elvis Presley again you will never work in New York, Hollywood, London or anywhere else in the world." That was it [Sharp, *Writing for the King*].

Whether Elvis, who harbored dreams of becoming a serious actor at this point, was ever informed of this offer is anybody's guess. And one can only speculate as to what impact a lead role in such a prestigious film, which ended up as one of 1962's highest grossing films and would garner three Academy Award nominations, would have on making that dream a reality. What is clear, however, is that, with just one edict, Parker not only sabotaged a golden opportunity for Elvis to fulfill a lifelong ambition but, in the process, also drove a wedge between Presley and pop music's most accomplished songwriting duo, who, in years to come, might well have steered Elvis away from the treadmill of musical mediocrity that comprised the bulk of his post–army career.

The Music—King Creole Soundtrack Sessions—January 15–16, 23, 1958— Radio Recorders, Hollywood; February 11, 1958—Paramount Studios, Hollywood

On January 15, Elvis, Scotty, Bill and D.J. were back in Radio Recorders in Hollywood to fashion a soundtrack for *King Creole*. Also present were a fleet of session men, who, with their application of clarinets, trumpets, and saxophones, were charged with lending a Bourbon Street vibe to the film's score.

First up was Claude DeMetrius's "Hard Headed Woman." Initially earmarked for a prominent spot in the movie, this rocker was ultimately reduced to serving as a transition from a street scene to the interior of the King Creole nightclub. Elvis's enthusiasm for this track—honed to a beefy, horn-driven sheen after 10 takes—is apparent from the count-in, with Presley spitting out the lyrics with venom and applying guttural whoops to the instrumental break. In an effort to sustain career momentum, "Hard Headed Woman" would be released as the A-side of Elvis's next single on July 26, by which point he would be in the middle of 10 weeks of advanced tank training at Fort Hood, Texas. In interviews subsequent to the release of this track, both Paul McCartney and John Lennon would describe their initial enthusiasm upon hearing the title of this track and expecting a compelling rocker, only to be disappointed at the brass-heavy arrangement. Point taken. Still, horns or not, "Hard Headed Woman" jumps from the speaker with a machine-gun blast and stands as one of Presley's most compelling late fifties tracks.

The second song to be attempted was Leiber and Stoller's "Trouble," a talking-blues workout that would be employed in the film to establish Danny Fisher's bona fides as a hardass. Interestingly, it would be re-employed for exactly the same purpose 10 years later when Presley used it to kick off his December 1968 comeback special. In each case, the song achieved its intended goal, first enabling Danny Fisher to confront Walter Matthau's crime boss in *King Creole* and then helping Presley shed his image as a hapless Hollywood joke after nearly a decade of cranking out forgettable travelogues. For Elvis fans of the late fifties, listening to "Trouble" would prove electric. A second exposure in 1968, in the context of an artist attempting to reestablish himself, could be viewed as bracing. But by Presley's mid–1970s "Superfly" phase, when his oft-stated goal was to be seen as "the most baddass man alive," listening to "Trouble" would prove impossible (for this writer, at least) without acute embarrassment. Foremost among fans of this track was

Mike Stoller. "I especially liked 'Trouble,'" Stoller recalls, "and I loved the way he did it in the comeback special. We had written songs like that before—'Riot in Cell Block' number, framed, kind of 'talking blues' things—and we knew Elvis could do that kind of stuff. That track captured less of the happy-go-lucky Elvis. It carried a menacing undercurrent of sexuality and danger. It was braggadocio, like John Henry, Paul Bunyan—one of those bigger-than-life folk heroes" (*Goldmine*, May 2002).

After four attempts at an acceptable version of "Trouble," take 5 was marked as the studio master. Elvis and his band next went to work on the blues shuffle "New Orleans," a place where, at least according to songwriters Sid Tepper and Roy Bennett, the "livin's lazy and the lovin's fine." This track showcases the vocal work of the Jordanaires, who, on screen during the performance of this song, are shown as horn-wielding members of Elvis's band, while Scotty Moore stands in the background, strumming a banjo. Take 5 was deemed the best and was marked as the final master.

The fourth song to be attempted on January 15 was another Leiber and Stoller composition, "King Creole," which spins a tale of a guitar man "with a great big soul" who lays down a beat "like a ton of coal." At the time of this session, the working title of the movie was *A Stone for Danny Fisher*, but no one expected that to last. In hopes of snagging the movie's title song, songwriters Ben Weisman and Fred Wise came up with "Danny," a tune that both composers (but apparently few others) viewed positively. Leiber and Stoller had other ideas, suggesting that their own "King Creole" was better suited for the film's title track. But changing the name of a major Hollywood picture involved more than the opinion of four songwriters, and during January memos flew and production meetings were held for nearly a month. By early March, one thing was clear: "Danny" was out, and though both Parker and Steve Sholes expressed doubts about it, "King Creole" would ultimately be tabbed as the film's title song.

As strong as Leiber and Stoller's "King Creole" was, the song's unique double time structure presented a challenge to at least one of the musicians at the January 15 session. In recent years, some musicologists have suggested that the song's structure taxed the ability of Scotty Moore, but early takes indicate otherwise. Initial efforts show Scotty effortlessly nailing down the single-string run that bolsters the song's verses, even as he continued to work out the extraordinary solo that would ultimately grace the studio master. The same takes, however, do show drummer D.J. Fontana struggling to maintain the song's locomotive pace.

Work at obtaining an acceptable master version of "King Creole" ground on (during which time the galloping feel of the earlier version was replaced with an R&B-centric approach that was wisely discarded), before, after 18 arduous attempts, Elvis finally gave up. As a palpable frustration settled over the studio, Elvis asked for takes 3 and 18 (the two he found to be most promising) to be transferred to a master reel that he would take with him and analyze in the ensuing days.

The final song attempted on January 15 was "Crawfish," another Wise and Weisman composition. Unlike the uninspired "Danny," "Crawfish" hits the mark. (Over the next two decades, Weisman, working with a variety of co-workers, would contribute an amazing 57 songs to the Presley songbook before he was through.) The track, which graces the film's opening scenes during which Elvis responds to a street vendor's cries, represents a dramatic change of pace for Presley. Enhanced by a stunning vocal contribution from Kitty White and a spare yet hypnotic musical backing that taps just enough into the Calypso craze that had recently swept America, "Crawfish," which Presley nailed down in just seven tries, stands as one of Elvis's most unusual yet beguiling 1950s recordings.

When sessions resumed the following day, Elvis and the group immediately started work on "Dixieland Rock," an energetic track featuring a hefty dose of Bourbon Street brass, playful lyrics, and a typically impressive Presley vocal that they wrapped up after 14 tries. Also completed on this day were master recordings of the soundtrack ballads, "Don't Ask Me Why," "Steadfast Loyal and True," and "As Long as I Have You."

By the time everyone regrouped at Radio Recorders on January 23, eight days had elapsed since they labored to perfect "King Creole." During that time, Elvis, after playing and replaying the master tape he'd taken home, had concluded that the song was fine; it was the percussion work of D.J. Fontana that lacked snap. So when the musicians arrived on the 23rd, they found a second drum set in the studio, and perched behind the traps was Hollywood session whiz Bernie Mattinson, who had just one assignment: punch up the percussion on "King Creole." In a three-hour session that began at 8:00 p.m., Mattinson did just that, supplying a drive and energy that fueled the song's groove in a way D.J. had not. The final version also showcases one of Scotty Moore's most fluid and disarming solos. With "King Creole" finally in the can, Elvis went to work on another soundtrack ballad, "Young Dreams," which they wrapped up after just eight tries.

The session was successful, but Elvis was nonetheless troubled by the absence of Leiber and Stoller. Presley, increasingly reliant on Jerry and Mike's songwriting and arranging talents, told Tom Diskin in no uncertain terms that he wanted them present at the final *King Creole* recording session, scheduled for February 11. In a telegram dated January 24, Diskin informed Steve Sholes of Elvis's wishes, stating that Presley "is able to work out ideas with them" (telegram from Tom Diskin to Steve Sholes, January 24, 1958). When he received a noncommittal reply, Diskin fired off a subsequent message five days later. "I had Elvis read your letter," he stated, "as he specifically was interested in having Leiber and Stoller here. If both of them aren't available, he can work with Jerry Leiber, as the boys were very helpful to Elvis on a couple of the songs during the recording session for the picture. If for some reason they will not be available for this coming Saturday, he thought we might postpone the session until such time as either Jerry or both might be available" (telegram from Tom Diskin to Steve Sholes, January 29, 1958).

Sholes, now aware of Elvis's seriousness, immediately called Mike Stoller in New York. Stoller, sensing the urgency in Sholes's voice, told Steve that he would contact his partner. But, unbeknownst to Mike, Jerry Leiber was in a bed in the emergency ward of a Harlem hospital fighting pneumonia. When he was finally released days later and learned of efforts to reach him, he dialed Tom Parker. When asked how he was doing, Leiber responded, "'I'm OK. I had a real close call there. I had walking pneumonia and I just got out of the hospital." "Fine," Parker responded, before stating that Elvis needed him back in the studio. At that point, Leiber demurred, saying it would be a day or two before he felt well enough to travel. Shifting direction, Parker asked Leiber if he'd received the contract he'd sent days earlier procuring the services of the writing team for the *King Creole* sessions. After taking a minute to rifle through some scattered mail, Leiber located the document. But upon opening it, he was taken aback. With the exception of two lines at the bottom where signatures were to be added, the contract was completely blank. Telling Parker there must be some mistake, the Colonel replied, "There's no mistake—just sign it. We'll fill it in later." The next sound Leiber heard was the click of Parker hanging up.

Ticked off by Parker's arrogance, Leiber immediately dialed his partner. Mike Stoller, a man viewed by virtually everyone as imperturbable, was equally annoyed by Parker's hubris; his anger cresting, he suggested that Leiber call Parker back and suggest that he perform an impossible sex act. "So I called Colonel Parker back," Leiber recalls, "and said, 'Tom, I thought about what you told me.' He said, 'Good! What time are you gonna get here?' I said, 'Tom, I spoke to Mike about the contract, and he told me to tell you to go fuck yourself.' I hung up, and I never spoke to him again" (Vellenga and Farrin, *Elvis and the Colonel*).

For the Colonel, the entire affair proved, at least to his mind, instructive. Following the debacle, Parker, in no uncertain terms, instructed his brother-in-law Bitsy Mott to never again let "those type of people" (in essence, anyone that Parker could not control) near Elvis, a decision that, in subsequent years, would exact a devastating toll on his creative legacy. And while Presley's career would suffer grievously from the absence of Leiber and Stoller, the same cannot be said for the songwriting team. In the years ahead, they would compose such classics as "Stand by Me" and "Spanish Harlem" for Ben E. King, "There Goes My Baby" and "On Broadway" for the Drifters, and numerous hits for the comic doo-wop aggregation the Coasters.

On January 20, principal filming was scheduled to begin on *King Creole*. This usually signaled an opportunity for members of the press to conduct interviews with the film's stars, a practice that not only benefited the actors but also helped drum up publicity for their movies. But instead of being welcomed, the numerous columnists who were expecting to interview Elvis during breaks in shooting encountered obstacles. "They've put the lid on Elvis," Hollywood entertainment reporter Bob Thomas complained in his February 5 column. "Hal Wallis has banned all interviews and set visitors while Presley is making *King Creole*. The producer wants nothing to interfere with the film schedule, since Elvis has a deadline to meet with Uncle Sam" (Bob Thomas, *Associated Press*, February 5, 1958).

Despite the blackout, James Bacon, a Hollywood columnist of long standing, pulled a few strings and managed to snag an interview with Elvis on February 12, reporting in his column that "Presley is sporting a normal haircut for his current movie and it makes him look quite handsome" (James Bacon, February 13, 1958).

Another columnist who managed to get through was Sheilah Graham, who flagged Elvis down as he peddled a bike on the Paramount lot. After remarking on how thin he appeared, Graham also opined that Presley "sounded like the boy next door." Speaking of his looming army induction, Elvis told her, "I'm glad I'm going into the Army this year and not last year. A year ago, they were saying I couldn't last. I've proved to myself that I can" (Sheilah Graham, *Hollywood Today*, February 1958).

When prompted for his impressions of Elvis, *King Creole* director Michael Curtiz told the press that Presley was extremely professional and was always the first one on the set each morning with his lines memorized. Columnist Mike Connolly reported that Elvis entertained himself between takes by playing Cole Porter tunes on a baby grand piano in his dressing room and teaching co-star Carolyn Jones how, in Connolly's words, to "bump and grind."

With another soundtrack session looming on February 1, Steve Sholes was feeling the heat. Not only had he failed, with a large assist from Tom Parker, at securing the services of Leiber and Stoller, but with Presley's induction date approaching and Elvis consumed with soundtrack work on *King Creole*, he saw little hope of obtaining any additional recordings from Elvis before he left for his army basic training. Presley's RCA contract stipulated four single releases per year, but all Sholes had in supply was 1957's unreleased "One Night." Any hope of sustaining Elvis's popularity, Sholes knew, was to time-release a series of singles while he was away to create the illusion that nothing had changed. It was imperative that he get Elvis back in the studio to record the additional tracks he needed. But with Presley's induction date closing in, that seemed impossible.

The Music—RCA Studio Session—February 1, 1958—Radio Recorders, Hollywood

From the beginning, the session of February 1, 1958, at Radio Recorders in Hollywood, seemed jinxed. Elvis, learning of the rift between Parker and Leiber and Stoller, and realizing the songwriters wouldn't be present, wanted to cancel, but when forcibly reminded of his contract obligations and what little time remained before his induction, reluctantly agreed to proceed. However, from the moment he arrived, Presley appeared downcast and with his mood infecting the gathered musicians, it would take a full nine hours to come up with just four acceptable tracks.

First up was "My Wish Came True," a song that came to Elvis's attention in late 1957 when composer and performer "Ivory" Joe Hunter visited Presley at Graceland. Elvis was a fan of Hunter's 1950 hit "I Almost Lost My Mind" (retooled just six years later by Hunter as "Since I Met You Baby," an even bigger success), and during their visit asked Hunter, "You got a song for me?" To which Hunter replied, "Yeah baby" (RCA Records, *Elvis, The King of Rock 'N' Roll, The Complete 50's Masters*, 1992). If only he hadn't. "My Wish Came True" represents the nadir of Presley's pre–army recording work. Overwrought and histrionic, this leaden track is burdened by a comically melodramatic arrangement and over-the-top, revival-tent backing by the Jordanaires and an uncredited Millie Kirkham. "My Wish Came True" supplies an early glimpse at Presley's unfortunate inclination toward pomposity, something that would metastasize in the coming years and burden much of his 1970s work.

From there, things improved only marginally as Elvis and the group tried and failed to produce an acceptable cover of Hank Williams's "Your Cheatin' Heart." Presley's version, intended as an homage to the country legend, instead comes off as obligatory and lifeless, a judgment apparently shared by RCA. It would be a full seven years before "Your Cheatin' Heart" appeared on a Presley LP, finally showing up as part of 1965's *Elvis for Everyone*.

Thankfully, things improved from there as Elvis went to work on what would comprise the A- and B-sides of his next single, "Wear My Ring Around Your Neck" and "Doncha' Think It's Time." "Ring" is a sizzling rocker that showcases a rousing percussive assault by D.J. Fontana and aggressive fretwork by Scotty Moore. After 22 takes, everyone appeared satisfied, but Elvis wasn't sure, and it wouldn't be until February 26, in a hastily arranged session where he bolstered the song's percussion with a series of guitar case slaps, that he was satisfied.

The undisputed highlight of this session is "Doncha' Think It's Time," a track composed by Clyde Otis and, possibly, Brook Benton. Critics in recent years have unfairly maligned this track, terming it desultory and suggesting that Elvis's repeated attempts at perfecting a studio master—no fewer than 48 takes—are somehow indicative of a lack of faith in the song, when in fact it signals exactly the opposite. It simply strains credulity to suggest that any artist would invest 48 attempts at perfecting a track for which he lacked enthusiasm. Moreover, session logs throughout Presley's career provide ample evidence that whenever Elvis lacked interest in a song, he dispatched it hastily. Pre-army Presley was an acknowledged perfectionist in the studio, and whatever issues he had with this track likely were focused on its arrangement or its instrumentation, not with the song itself.

Graced with a meditative air, delicate and effective contributions from the Jordanaires and Scotty Moore, and an elegant rendering from Presley, "Doncha' Think It's Time" stands as one of Presley's most sublime fifties ballads. The final version of the song is spliced from takes 40, 47, and 48. For reasons unknown, the complete version of take 40 appears on *50,000,000 Elvis Fans Can't Be Wrong, Elvis Gold Records, Volume 2*, released in November of 1959.

On March 1, Elvis boarded a train for New Orleans for 10 days of filming in the French Quarter and on Bourbon Street. Just prior to his departure, he received a call from former schoolmate Red West, who was on a two-week leave from the Marines and who'd stopped by Graceland to say hello to Gladys Presley.

"I was home on leave," West said later.

Elvis was making *King Creole* and I went by Graceland to see [Gladys] and Vernon and they called Elvis. They said Elvis wants you to fly out and then ride the train back to New Orleans. Elvis wouldn't fly in those days and they were finishing up in Hollywood and then we got a ride in the train to New Orleans. The last thing his mother said to me was, "You take care of Elvis," and I took that seriously for the rest of my life [Dunleavy, *Elvis: What Happened?*].

Upon his arrival in New Orleans, Elvis and his posse checked into a hotel just off the French Quarter. Any chance of keeping the crowds in check while shooting progressed evaporated when New Orleans's mayor proclaimed his arrival as "Elvis Presley Day" in the city. "The kids just absolutely turned us into an island," Dolores Hart would recall, "and in some situations we literally had to go to the top of the hotels because we couldn't go from street to street. They had to put planks from rooftop to rooftop; the kids just wouldn't allow us to move. They wanted to touch Elvis" (Edelman, *Matthau: A Life*).

To further complicate things, two days of filming were lost when it rained the first weekend. When co-star Jan Shepard encountered Elvis in the makeup room the day after, she asked him what he'd done during the dismal weather. Other than long conversations on the phone with his mother, he told her, he'd done nothing.

When location shooting finally wrapped, Elvis returned to Hollywood, where, on February 11, he briefly returned to the recording studio, where he recorded a version of "Danny," the Wise/Weisman track that had been under consideration as the film's title track. It was also during this session that Elvis put final touches on the Leiber and Stoller ballad "Steadfast, Loyal and True."

In mid–March, Elvis attended a wrap party thrown by producer Hal Wallis for the cast and crew of *King Creole*. Among the attendees was *New York World-Telegram* columnist Vernon Scott, who pestered Elvis for his thoughts on his looming induction into the army. "I've worked in factories, drove a truck, cut grass for a living and did a hitch in a defense plant," Presley told Scott, while in the background, the Colonel passed out giant balloons with *King Creole* printed on them. "I'll do whatever they tell me and I won't be asking for no special favors" (*New York World-Telegram*, March 15, 1958).

On Friday, March 14, Elvis arrived home in Memphis, where he was greeted by a newspaper reporter who inquired about his mother's reaction to his being drafted. "Well," he stated, "my mother is not different from millions of other mothers who hated to see their sons go in." What about his career? Would his popularity survive the two years he'd spend in the army? After a long pause, Elvis shook his head. "I wish I knew," was his uncertain reply (*Memphis Commercial Appeal*, March 15, 1958).

In an effort to take his mind off his looming induction, Elvis surrounded himself with friends and, in his waning days of freedom, skated at the local rink and shopped for records at a downtown music store, where he purchased "Looking Back" by Nat King Cole, "Maybe" by the Chantels, "Return to Me" by Dean Martin, "Too Soon to Know" by Pat Boone, "I Can't Stop Loving You" by Don Gibson, and "Sweet Little Darling" by Jo Stafford. Then, as if to get a jump on the army, he popped into Jim's Barber Shop in downtown Memphis for a haircut.

On the evening before his induction, Elvis, too wired to sleep, pulled an all-nighter, first going to a drive-in movie with girlfriend Anita Wood. They saw *Sing, Boy, Sing*, a film starring Tommy Sands that was originally written with Elvis in mind and then spent the rest of the night skating. At 6:30 the following morning, Elvis, somber and silent and dressed in black trousers, a blue shirt, a gray jacket, and black boots, reported to the draft board.

While Presley's induction certainly upended a celebrated life, there's no reason to view it as any more or less burdensome on him than it was on other young men his age. But when you stop and think about *how* he was inducted, you might find room for sympathy. The young men surrounding Presley, likely away from home for the first time, were able to perform all the duties required of new draftees in a merciful anonymity. For Elvis, now in his new role as pawn in Tom Parker's cynical plan to transform him into America's favorite reformed rebel, it was decidedly different. Every act—from being sworn in, to stripping down to his underwear for a physical, to having his head shaved, ad nauseum—was performed in the white-hot glare of newsreel cameras whose output would, in less than a week, be featured in theaters nationwide. For a congenitally insecure young man, who over the past year had attempted to insulate himself from the outside world by surrounding himself with a cadre of supplicants and barricading himself behind the gates of his new Memphis mansion, the entire experience had to be brutal.

Once he was sworn in, Elvis, along with 12 other recruits, boarded a bus for the Kennedy Veterans Hospital, where he was assigned serial number 53 310 761. After being put in charge of the new inductees, Elvis then boarded an army bus to Fort Chaffee, Arkansas. Then, following a three-day orientation, he was dispatched to Texas to start his basic training.

Elvis the man may have been gone, but Elvis the commodity rolled on. To create the impression that nothing had really changed, RCA released "Wear My Ring Around Your Neck" and "Doncha' Think It's Time" as Elvis's latest single on April 7. It would peak at number three on the *Billboard* charts.

Last Stop on the Mystery Train

The recording session of February 1, 1958, Presley's last full session before entering the U.S. Army, represents something far greater and far more poignant than just the completion of four Elvis Presley tracks. It's also the final time that Elvis, Scotty Moore, and Bill Black—three men who stood shoulder to shoulder as they revolutionized American popular music—would play together. "His attitude," Moore recalls of Elvis's mood at the time, "was like, 'So long, see you when I get out'" (Moore and Dickerson, *Scotty and Elvis: Aboard the Mystery Train*).

While it's certainly inarguable that in the years following the breakup all three would achieve varying degrees of success—Presley would accrue riches flowing copiously through the twin spigots labeled "uninspired movies" and "bland music"; Black would, before his untimely death, find success with his own Bill Black Combo; and Moore would make good as a record producer and musician—it's equally evident that none would ever again approach the creative heights they'd scaled as a unit. Certainly Elvis, due to his loftier position, had farther to fall, and it's indisputable that in the years following the split, he would remain mired in a creative backwater and, with the exception of a brief renaissance in the late sixties, never again break new musical ground.

Equally indisputable is the fact that throughout his post–army touring years, Presley would trade heavily on music created by himself, Scotty Moore, and Bill Black to keep showrooms filled and audiences entertained. In his highly regarded essay *Elvis Presliad*, Griel Marcus states that in the years following his split from Scotty and Bill, Presley "disappeared into an oblivion of respect and security, lost in interchangeable movies and dull music" (Marcus, *Mystery Train*).

As the years passed and their accomplishments assumed historical significance, prominent musical figures would weigh in on the demise of rock 'n' roll's first true band, with the comments of musician, producer, and Presley accompanist David Briggs (who also cites the contributions of D.J. Fontana) among the most cogent. "I mean, they should've been like the Beatles. There should have been four of them" (*Musician*, October 1992).

To which, I can only add: Amen.

23

The Men as Musicians

It's undoubtedly a truism to state that fans who attended an Elvis Presley show in the 1950s likely gave minimal thought to the three men laying down chops on the stage behind him. A charismatic figure snarling out hits and prowling the stage like a panther has a way of drawing attention to himself. It would be like going to a Hollywood blockbuster and trying to focus on the supporting cast. Yet Scotty Moore, Bill Black, and D.J. Fontana were far more than just bit players in Elvis Presley's sonic saga, and for anyone with an operative pair of cochleae, it's clear that their extraordinary contributions played a critical role in Elvis's rise to the music world's highest summit. Before splitting up on February 1, 1958, Presley, Moore, Black, and Fontana would launch a frontal assault on the cinched-up world of 1950s formula pop and leave rubble where mainstream crooners once held sway.

As a trio with one foot in delta mud and the other in a country hoedown, Elvis, Scotty, and Bill ignited the musical genre known as rockabilly in 1954. Their sound was organic and based on economy and feel rather than flash and technique. In 1955, at the urging of Scotty and Bill, D.J. Fontana was added on drums. Now, as a quartet, they would establish a configuration blueprint for a generation of rock bands to come: that of two guitars, bass, and drums. It was a musical collective that, in the years that followed, would be acknowledged as nothing less than the world's first true rock 'n' roll band. In the end, it would all come to cross purposes ... most things do, and following their split, they all would move on: Scotty to producing and session work; Bill, prior to his untimely death, to his own successful combo; D.J. to session work; and, of course, Presley to a level of success that in the end would reduce his bandmates to near anonymity, a fate staggering in its unfairness.

Did Presley's otherworldly success and the descent of Scotty, Bill, and D.J. to relative afterthoughts in the minds of most fuel a sense of bitterness toward Elvis? Numerous interviews conducted in the years following the breakup suggest not, with both Moore and Fontana displaying a surprising equanimity until the day each died. Still, there were those who were close enough to both men who suspect that resentments, whether expressed or not, certainly lingered.

"Scotty won't admit what he did, what everybody knows he did," musician and producer David Briggs said in 1992. "He was literally the musical producer, the manager, he worked with him, he rehearsed with him, he was the band's leader. And I'm sure he's very bitter about it" (*Musician*, October 1992).

Bitter or otherwise, there nonetheless remained something to which they could forever cling: in the brief time they shared the stage as equals, Moore, Black, Fontana, and Presley—four men whose lifeblood was music—would successfully span the great divide that had separated rhythm and blues from white America, and, in so doing, change music forever.

In the sections that follow, I've compiled a sampling of comments, perspectives, and insights from noted figures from the musical world on how they viewed Scotty, Bill, D.J., and Elvis as musicians, including a sprinkling of comments from the men themselves on how they viewed their bandmates. You'll note that it's not all rainbows and unicorns; in the interest of balance, I've thrown in remarks from the occasional naysayer.

Scotty Moore

If you were a kid in the 1950s who wanted nothing more than to play loud guitar and get laid, you started with either Chuck Berry or Scotty Moore. A full decade before the romantic notion of the guitar hero surfaced, the notes that Scotty coaxed out of his Gibson ES-25 would lend grace and force to the best of Presley's early work and, in so doing, would establish once and for all the role of the lead guitarist in a rock 'n' roll band.

Arguably the most influential guitarist of all time, Scotty played with an uncommon originality, seemingly determined to never repeat the same lick twice. From his fearsome fretting on such tracks as "Mystery Train" and "Baby Let's Play House" to his savage assault in "Hound Dog," whatever Scotty had to say was always essential. Never one to play it safe, Moore would sometimes carry himself to a cliff's edge, only to fret his way back home, as his unhinged work in 1957's "Too Much" illustrates (a portion of which was lifted a decade later by Deep Purple to serve as the opening bars to their "Why Didn't Rosemary?"). For the generation of aspiring guitarists in the decade to come, the work of Scotty Moore would give them the shove they needed. And if you're inclined to lend credence to such things, *Rolling Stone* magazine in 2015 ranked Scotty Moore as number 29 in its ranking of the 100 greatest guitarists of all time (*Rolling Stone*, December 8, 2015).

Scotty Moore through the eyes of others:

"I had been playing guitar, but not knowing what to play ... without any direction. When I heard 'Heartbreak Hotel,' I knew that was what I wanted to do in life. It was as plain as day. I no longer wanted to be a train driver or a Van Gogh or a rocket scientist. All I wanted to do in the world was to be able to play and sound like that. Those early records were incredible. Everyone else wanted to be Elvis. I wanted to be Scotty."—Keith Richards (Moore and Dickerson, *That's Alright, Elvis*)

"Scotty Moore had such an unusual style. You could walk into a building somewhere and not ever know he was there and tell it was him. He had his own style. He played with all his fingers. Us two-string guitar pickers who played with a pick would sit around and watch him make chords. He'd make these big ol' crab chords and we'd say 'What's he doing?' He had a sound that just knocked you out."—Paul Burlison, lead guitarist for Johnny Burnette. (Burke and Griffin, *The Blue Moon Boys*)

"Scotty Moore was always such an underrated guitar player. He plays around everything on the track and just fills the holes. And then when he solos, it's from Mars."—Tom Petty (*Rolling Stone*, October 27, 2011)

"Scotty Moore plays one of the first really amazing riffs in rock history on 'Heartbreak Hotel' with Elvis Presley. It was dangerous. It scared everybody's parents, which was part of the attraction."—Roger McGuinn (hillmanweb.com, 1992)

"What Scotty did was what I try to do, to create a new sound. When he first recorded with Elvis, he didn't have a road map. He just did it. Of course, he had influences, but what he did was start rock and roll. He's my favorite, overall guitar player."—Brian Setzer (longislandweekly, November 16, 2017)

"Elvis wouldn't have been the same without Scotty Moore. Scotty's playing on those early songs was the inspiration for thousands of youngsters to start out on guitar."—Mark Knopfler (markknopfler.com, June 30, 2016)

"In my mind, Scotty Moore was the first deeply musical guitarist to blend alternate-genre guitar into the budding beginnings of high-energy rock-and-roll. He used jazz chords, Merle Travis–type fingerpicking, altered chord substitutions, fast, jazzy runs and pre-surf rock-guitar lines. He was way ahead of his time. It's always thrilling to hear recordings of him playing. He was also a superb accompanist. A timeless inspiration and a true testament to the voice of guitar to make fine music."—Eric Johnson (*Vintage Guitar*, October 2016)

"I was taught by a bloke, a guitar player in Liverpool, all those old songs like from the '20s and the '30s and a lot of those had what I call the naughty chord, which is the diminished chord. But if you listen to Elvis, that chord turns up in the most unexpected places, like the solo to 'Milk Cow Blues.' Scotty used it in quite a few places as a passing chord. The original guitar players that knocked me out were James Burton, who played on, in those days, the old Rick Nelson records; Scotty Moore for his Elvis Presley sessions."—George Harrison (georgeharrison.com, April, 1999)

D.J. Fontana

For a man who provided the raging backbeat to some of the greatest early rock ever made, D.J. Fontana was surprisingly modest. "I just tried to stay out of their way," he replied, when asked what it was like to play with Elvis, Scotty Moore, and Bill Black.

But there was nothing humble about the way D.J. Fontana played the drums. Without question, one of the most influential skinsmen in rock history, D.J.'s rolling beat fueled Presley's music with a swagger and authority. Chops and flash weren't D.J.'s, thing, but originality and power were, and night after night he effortlessly straddled the line between song-serving subtlety and ass-kicking aggression.

Fontana was there when Elvis got out of the army, ready to apply his distinct trap work to Presley's session and soundtrack work, and before he was done he would lend his unique feel and swing to an array of rock and country legends, including Ringo Starr, Paul McCartney, Charley Pride, Jerry Lee Lewis, Waylon Jennings, Dolly Parton, and Roy Orbison. In 1997, Fontana reunited with old bandmate Scotty Moore for an all-star record titled *All the King's Men*, on which he collaborated with Keith Richards, Levon Helm, Steve Earle, Cheap Trick, Ron Wood, and Jeff Beck. In 2016, *Rolling Stone* ranked D.J. as Number 13 in its ranking of "100 Greatest Drummers of All Time" (*Rolling Stone*, March 31, 2016).

D.J. Fontana through the eyes of others:

"This was about the best band I'd heard up to that time. D.J. Fontana planted those drums down and started stacking verses against one another with his fills, building up to the solo, riding the solos in and riding them out again. He had incredible technique and fast hands, so he could employ those Buddy Rich press rolls whenever he wanted to. He played like a big-band drummer—full throttle. Now Elvis had a real foundation, some architecture and he made the most of it. D.J. set Elvis free. Elvis and Scotty and Bill were making good music, but it wasn't rock & roll until D.J. put the backbeat into it."—Levon Helm (Helm and Davis, *This Wheel's on Fire: Levon Helm and the Story of the Band*)

"I always used to call D.J. the 'blap-blap king' because like on Jailhouse Rock ... most drummers would play it 'dum dum, bonk bonk,' but when D.J. played, he did like a 64th pickup. He added a little clip to it."—Ray Walker (author interview, September 24, 2020)

"When you hear D.J. Fontana playing his drums, you are hearing a kid from Shreveport, LA tell you what he thinks music should sound like. Rock 'n' roll had a clean slate. There were no drum parts written for him on those Elvis records. He dictated the groove and made you feel it. There is no one on this earth that can make music move the way he did. He set the standard."—Stan Lynch, Tom Petty and the Heartbreakers (*Los Angeles Times*, June 15, 2018)

"D.J. Fontana was the drummer I saw who made me want to be a drummer. Before Ringo. He was on *The Milton Berle Show*. It wasn't just Elvis, it wasn't just the singer, it was four guys playing. As a five year old, D.J.'s drumroll in 'Hound Dog' was an explosion for me. That drum roll, that triple roll, was shocking. D.J. Fontana was my hero. I don't think that it's an understatement to say that he created and made famous, rock 'n' roll drumming. What Elvis was to rock 'n' roll music, D.J. was the first guy. The archetypal rock 'n' roll drummer. He was an original. D.J. had chops, he had power, he had taste. When he played the drums, no matter what he played on, it sounded like an Elvis Presley tune. And this is really crucial, a lot of people may not realize: they were a *band*. It was Elvis, sure, but it wasn't like Elvis was 'Elvis Presley' yet. On a daily basis, it was the four of them in a car, driving 400 or 500 miles, with only each other to count on. Taking turns driving, playing all these little honky-tonks and small places—those guys were dependent on each other."—Max Weinberg (*Max Weinberg*, as told to Christopher Phillips, June 22, 2018).

Bill Black

Today, some 60-plus years later, it remains astonishing that just one man was responsible for anchoring Presley's early musical universe and supplying the sonic foundation that made Elvis's Sun sides so compelling. It's also key to acknowledge reality: Bill Black wasn't artful. Bill Black didn't pluck and Bill Black didn't strum. What Bill Black did, as anyone who was there can attest, was joyfully and exuberantly beat the shit out of his bass. And in so doing, he infused early classics like "Mystery Train" and "Milkcow Blues Boogie" with the sound and feel of a full rhythm section despite a total absence of drums. Paul McCartney, no slouch on the instrument himself, was so obsessed with Black's playing on "Heartbreak Hotel" that, years later, his wife Linda tracked down Black's original double bass from that session and presented it to him as a gift. In 2020, *Rolling Stone* magazine rated Bill Black as number 40 in its ranking of "The 50 Greatest Bassists of All Time" (*Rolling Stone*, July 1, 2020).

Bill Black through the eyes of others:

> "Bill was one of the worst bass players in the world, but, man, could he slap that thing! The best slap bass player in the city."— Sam Phillips (*Rolling Stone*, February 13, 1986)

> "Bill jumped up and grabbed his bass and started slapping it, singing 'Blue Moon of Kentucky' in a high falsetto voice. It was Bill doing what Bill did best. The song was recorded as a ballad, but Bill sang it up-tempo, his bass lines thumping at a feverish pace. Elvis loved it."—Scotty Moore (*Rolling Stone*, July 1, 2020)

> "If it hadn't been for Bill, we would have bombed so many times in the early days. What you don't realize is that some of the crowds had not seen Elvis. They'd heard the records, but they had not seen him. They're sitting there like, 'What is he?' And Bill would start riding the bass and clowning, and get the crowd loosened up. Once he'd done that, then Elvis would have them in the palm of his hand. He was winding them up for us."—Scotty Moore (elvis.au.com, February 2020)

> "I want you to give Bill Black the credit. I want to emphasize the fact that Bill Black was such a big part of Elvis' making it. Bill Black, the way he hit his bass fiddle, he sounded like a band all by himself. He could hit the bass like nobody in the world. Like I hit a downbeat or slap beat on the bass like a drum, well, he could hit a double-lick on that bass fiddle. He did that on 'That's All Right Mama' and 'Blue Moon of Kentucky.' Elvis sang the way Bill Black played bass. That helped Elvis start jumping around."—Tillman Franks (Louisiana Hayride, 2006)

Elvis Presley

To even the most casual observer, it's clear that few human beings have viewed themselves with a level of self-importance that matched

Elvis Presley. Whether it was assuming the stage to the "He is among us!" strains of *Thus Spoke Zarathustra*, his studied stage poses, or his sartorial excesses, Presley, over the course of his career, clearly engaged in a degree of self-mythologizing that might shame Narcissus. All of which makes his strenuous efforts at *demythologizing* at least one area of his life so curious. Because from his earliest days in the public eye to his final concert decades later, Elvis Presley—the man who single-handedly created the romantic image of the guitar-wielding rebel—never once passed up an opportunity to debunk his skill with the instrument.

The examples are plentiful. First this from 1956: "There's been another rumor of sorts that's kind of amusing," Elvis said.

> I read in one magazine that I can't play a note on the guitar, and in another, the same week, that I'm the greatest guitar player in the world. Well, both of those stories are wrong. I've never had any music lessons like I told you. But I've always enjoyed music of any kind and musical instruments. My daddy bought me a department store guitar when I was pretty young. I learned to pick out a couple of chords on it, but I didn't try to get fancy or anything like that. I can plunk on it pretty good and follow a tune if I'm really pressed to do it. But I've never won any prizes and I never will. Then when I went out on stage in my first personal appearance, I just naturally took my guitar along with me, to sort of keep me company. I used it as a prop or whatever you want to call it. To me, in that first appearance, it was the best friend I ever had because it kept me company and I knew I wasn't alone out there making a fool of myself. I've just kept on taking it out there with me and I've got a new one now, a gift to me, that even has my name carved on it. There's always another fellow in the band who does most of the playing, and if you'll watch me real close in a performance sometime, you'll see how it works [interview, August 28, 1956].

Another example from a conversation with his father Vernon, circa 1957: "I never was much of a guitar player was I daddy?" Then we have this from 1965:

> People seem to think I'm married to the guitar but the truth is, I'm not very good at it. I usually get credited with beating up a storm on it, but usually I have another and much better guitar player backing me up when I play it. For me the guitar has just been something to do with my hands and beat time with. What I'm really studying to play is the drums [interview, 1965].

Lastly, we have this tidbit from one of his last concerts in Rapid City, North Dakota, in 1977: "I'm going to play the guitar. I know three chords, believe it or not. But I faked 'em all for a long time."

I find this all to be quite quizzical, especially coming from a man whose ego reached such towering heights that by the early 1970s he boasted of an ability to alter weather patterns. Why? Because even a guitar player of the most limited ability (a category to which I belong) can quickly label Presley's 1977 confessional that he knew "three chords" as pure bullshit. Even the most cursory examination of Presley's playing in the 1950s makes it clear that he not only mastered his major chords, but also his minor and his seventh chords as well. When you do the math, it's evident that Elvis held sway, at a minimum, over no fewer than 21 chords.

So how to explain the false modesty? Well, I have an idea, and it's all based around my theory that guitar players, who often cultivate an aura of snobbishness, are in reality among the most insecure people on the planet. And that's because every ax man, from the most rudimentary (Elvis Presley) to the most proficient (say, Eric Clapton), knows that on any given day, it's possible to walk into a local music store and, musically speaking, have your lunch eaten by a 16-year-old. Faced with this grim reality, humility, for even the best players, is seen as the preferred option. For those less skilled—and for someone as inextricably linked to the instrument as Presley was and who spent his career surrounded by extraordinary fret-men—it's essential, lest he pretend otherwise and risk humiliation.

In truth, critical comments on Presley's guitar playing weren't all self-generated. Much of the criticism of his fretwork arose in the late 1960s, when the role of the guitar hero first took on currency. Whether it was Jimmy Page using a violin bow to coax otherworldly strains from his Gibson Les Paul or Jimi Hendrix cranking out licks on his Strat with his bicuspids, suddenly, the notion of someone laying down a tight, rhythmic, and, yeah, unglamorous foundation on an acoustic six-string lacked street cred. And for all his efforts as self-debunking, Presley did himself no favors by posing with a double-necked guitar on the poster for 1966's *Spinout*, an image that suggested his ax skills were simply too awesome to be contained by just a single guitar. By the end of the decade, Presley seemed to finally grasp that he was being seen as hopelessly unhip by most musicians. Evidence of that fact is apparent during the jam session segment of his 1968 comeback special when he appropriates Scotty Moore's Gibson 400 CES for his own use, as if determined to demonstrate that he, too, knew his way (sort of) around an electric guitar.

In truth, all of this was unnecessary. Because for anyone who'd ever lent an attentive ear to "Mystery Train" or "Baby Let's Play House" or "Milkcow Blues Boogie," it's more than evident that, while no virtuoso, Elvis Presley was a solid rhythm guitarist whose churning lines were an indispensable component of the Sun Studios sound.

So, on to the testimonials (and the occasional brickbat, as well):

"The thing I really noticed was his guitar playing. Elvis was a fabulous rhythm player. He'd start into 'That's All Right, Mama' with his own guitar alone and you didn't want to hear anything else. I didn't anyway. I was disappointed when Scotty Moore and Bill Black jumped in and covered him up. Not that Scotty and Bill weren't perfect for him—the way he sounded with them that night was what I think of as seminal Presley, the sound I missed through all the years after he became so popular and made records full of orchestration and overproduction. I loved that clean, simple combination of Scotty, Bill, and Elvis with his acoustic guitar. You know, I've never heard or read anyone else praising Elvis as a rhythm guitar player."—Johnny Cash (Cash, *The Autobiography*)

"A lot of people used to put Elvis down, say he held his guitar like a prop. But he could make his way through all right and he could play a bit of piano too."—Steve Cropper (*Rolling Stone*, September, 22, 1977)

"In 1956, I was playing with the western-swing band and we were the house band for a band that was playing at the Northside Coliseum in Fort Worth. One Saturday night, I had my girlfriend with me, and they told us this young guy named Elvis Presley was coming that night. And sure enough, in comes Elvis with Scotty and Bill, no drums. Elvis looked his typical way as he did in '56, and I didn't like him for two reasons: One, my girlfriend went crazy (laughs). Two, he borrowed our guitar player's beautiful old Martin D-18 classic guitar after he'd already destroyed all the strings on his, and he just trashed it, marked up all the wood on it, you know. So we thought: 'Ah, this guy is just...' I told him that story later on when I met him. But I was never really a big fan of his until 1969, and I met him. Once you meet him and you understand the charisma that the man had, you just can't help but love what he does. We immediately had a great rapport."—Ronnie Tutt, drummer, TCB band (elvisnews.dk)

"Well, I didn't have much respect for his musicianship, as a person that played an instrument, but as a singer I had a lot of respect for him."—Ronnie Tutt, drummer, TCB band (elvisnews.dk)

"He wasn't a great guitar player, but he had such a sense of rhythm. His tempos were almost perfect every time he would start a song off."—James Burton, guitarist, TCB band (*Musician*, October 1992)

"I don't know if he had perfect pitch, but he had absolute relative pitch; he could keep in mind the key of the last song and then start singing another song in another key relating to that. He could do that perfectly."—Jerry Scheff, bassist, TCB Band (*Musician*, October 1992)

"He only played rhythm guitar, what I call self-accompaniment. He played a little piano, too. But he didn't consider himself a guitar player as such, but his playing did add to the group, because he played rhythm and more or less tied things together from the rhythm standpoint."—Scotty Moore (Green, "Perhaps the First Rock & Roll Guitarist," *Guitar Player,* 1974)

"He had a good sense of timing and rhythm. He didn't know a whole lotta chords, but those he knew, he really could use 'em. And he'd play a little bass, a little drums. He had rhythm in his voice, he just had a natural thing about that. He could hear a song, and he knew what he could do with that song. And nobody else could do it. They're still imitating him today but they just can't do it. They just don't have whatever it is that Elvis had."—Scotty Moore (interview, Arjan Deelan March 1998)

"Although he played fairly good piano and good rhythm, he wasn't an accomplished musician by any means. But he had a real uncanny sense of rhythm, and I think that's what made him such a great singer. That rhythm just seemed to come out of him, especially on up-tempo things."—Scotty Moore (Woods, *Vintage Guitar,* November, 1992)

"Actually, he wasn't a bad piano player. The Jordanaires said Elvis used to come in in the middle of the night and they'd play all night long—he'd play piano and they'd all sing gospel songs."—Scotty Moore (Knight, *Guitar UK,* 2004)

"I know he did play a little bit. I thought he was about the worst piano player I ever heard!"—Glen D. Hardin, pianist, TCB band (Deelan, elvis.au.com, January 2016)

"He knew what he wanted in his own mind, and he played just enough piano, just enough guitar, just enough bass, and just enough drums where he could tell you and show you what he wanted if he had to."—D.J. Fontana (moderndrummer.com, May 1985)

"He loved to sing and always wanted to play guitar real good. Of course, he never did learn to play guitar that good. And he wanted to play piano like Jerry Lee Lewis."—Sam Phillips (Dawson, *Country Music,* December 1977)

"I had seen some TV clips when he was on the Louisiana Hayride and he had a Martin D-18 guitar. And to have a Martin guitar is to have the ultimate in acoustic guitars. So I saw this kid up on stage and he was just beating on this guitar. All of us kids who played would have killed to have had a guitar like that. We certainly wouldn't have beat on it. It kinda' hurt my feelings to beat a guitar like that. I made a decision that one day I was gonna meet this hillbilly cat and tell him 'You can't play guitar worth a damn.' I was 11 years old—or 10, one or the other—and he was second-billed to a country singer called Hank Snow. They were coming to Springfield (in 1956) for a concert downtown. I thought, 'Here's my chance.' That weekend—Elvis was performing on a Saturday—my parents decided to take the day and go down to the lake. On the radio, it said Elvis was coming to town and they were doing a soundcheck in the afternoon.

"So with Mom and Dad gone, I got on my bicycle and went to where he was playing. I went up the back stairs and I started looking for Elvis. I went down the hallway looking right and left. Nobody. I could hear music from the stage, it was Hank Snow doing his soundcheck. Then, in the very last room on the left, I looked in there, and there he was. He had his feet up on the table sitting back in a chair. Had a bag of burgers on one side, and a six-pack of Cokes or Pepsi's on the other. I knocked on the door. He looked up and I said, 'You're Elvis Presley,' and he said, 'I know.' I thought, 'Oh God. I'm 10, he's 20 or whatever and he's a smartass.' This wasn't what I wanted to confront. But he invited me in, stood up, shook my hand. He got me a chair and we talked, it must have been the better part of an hour. He asked about my family, where I went to school, all sorts of stuff. And then my chance arrived. I said, 'Elvis, there's a reason I come looking for you.' And I said, 'I have to tell you, you can't play guitar worth a damn.' He looked at me with a grin and said, 'You think you can play better than me?' and I said, 'I know I can.' There was an old beat-up Gibson J-45 leaning up against the wall and I asked to borrow it. I took out a pick which I carried with me and I played him some music. I did a little of 'Foggy Mountain Breakdown' bluegrass banjo picking on that guitar. And then I sang a couple of old folk songs. When I finished, he said, 'You're pretty good,' and I said, 'I know.' And we both laughed. I got even.

"Then I heard what sounded like a herd of elephants running down the hall, and it turned out to be two of his bodyguards, and to this day I don't know who they were. They came in, looked at me and said, 'Hey kid, who are you, you don't belong here.' Elvis looked straight at them and said, 'Fellas, now just a minute. This is a friend of mine, his name is John Wilkinson and he just gave me a guitar lesson.' They said I had to leave anyway. As I headed for the door, Elvis called me back and gave me a big hug, and said, 'Johnny, I know that one day we're gonna meet again.'"—John Wilkinson, rhythm guitarist, TCB band (Jenkins, interview with John Wilkinson, June 2006)

24

The Secret Recording Session

"Ready on the right, ready on the left, ready on the firing line!"

With those words, Elvis Presley, just back from his U.S. Army basic training and still in his uniform, set the tone for the strangest and, arguably, most productive recording session of his entire career.

The Music—June 10, 1958—RCA Studio B, Nashville

Steve Sholes had gotten his wish. Bitterly disappointed that the session of February 1 had produced just two satisfactory tracks and desperate for additional material to parcel out while Elvis was away, he'd approached Tom Parker back in March with an idea. Elvis, Sholes reminded Parker, would be home for a two-week furlough in June before he shipped out for Germany to complete his army stretch. Would the Colonel okay a recording session while Elvis was stateside? "One night," he told the Colonel, "is all I need." After a thoughtful moment, Parker agreed, but on the condition that the session be done at RCA's Nashville studio and not Hollywood.

With the session a "go," RCA's Nashville manager, Chet Atkins, with just a single night to lay down the five new tracks Sholes demanded and little time for re-takes, turned to an elite group of session musicians. With a reputation for precision and productivity rivaled only by Hollywood's famous Wrecking Crew, Nashville's "A Team" consisted of Hank Garland on guitar, Bob Moore on bass, Floyd Cramer on piano, and Buddy Harman on drums. The lone holdover from Presley's original instrumental group was D.J. Fontana, who would share percussion duties. And, as they had for the past two years, the Jordanaires would be on hand to lend vocal support.

With the stakes so high and the possibility of failure so acute, RCA bigwigs were determined to keep news of the session from leaking to the press. The blackout was so pervasive it extended even to the musicians involved. As a result, many of those who showed up for work at RCA's Studio B that early June night had no idea with whom they'd be working.

"The call came from one of the girls at RCA," bassist Bob Moore recalled. "They would always tell you who the artist was when they booked you, but when I went to put the date in my book she said, 'Well I can't tell you on this one.' Of course right then I knew it was Elvis. I'd be at RCA just about every day doing something or other, so we soon worked out who it would be. They didn't want us broadcasting it around for security reasons" (artofslapbass.com, April 6, 2020).

For Jordanaire Ray Walker, who'd recently joined the group as its bass singer and was participating in his first Presley session, the memory of Elvis's arrival is still fresh:

> We were standing in RCA B, close to the door that goes back into the control room and I was standing at about a 45-degree angle and Gordon [Jordanaires leader Gordon Stoker] whispered to me "Here comes Elvis." So I turned around and instead of coming in through the control room, he came in through the loading door and I turned around and he was right on me. He stuck his hand out and said "I'm Elvis Presley." I said, "I know who you are, I'm Ray Walker." And he said "I know who you are." That rascal had checked me out!

After greeting the rest of the musicians, someone in the room, noticing that Elvis was wearing his army uniform, asked him why. "Simple," Elvis replied. "I'm kinda proud of it" (author interview with Ray Walker, September 24, 2020).

With little time to waste, Elvis, forgoing his usual habit of warming up with a few gospel tunes before recording, got straight to work. First on the agenda was "I Need Your Love Tonight," a driving expression of youthful lust written by Sid Wayne and Bix Reichner. Just before starting, Elvis, perusing the lyrics and sounding playful, trumpeted the song's message by announcing "I'll tell you what I need." However, take 1 broke down after the first instrumental break. By take 4, the Jordanaires, looking for openings, had added some vocal doo-wops in the bridge that Elvis, after consideration, ultimately nixed. By take 8, Ray Walker had added a swooping bass vocal following each verse, a sonic layer that Elvis immediately okayed. However, that take, which started promisingly, ultimately broke down at the song's bridge.

By take 9, something interesting had happened. Elvis, perhaps feeling the song lacked urgency, instructed Buddy Harman and D.J. Fontana to add additional percussion to the song's bridge. The presence of two drummers at this session is a curiosity, only the second time that

Presley utilized such a configuration. "The situation was a bit of a nightmare for the engineers to get a balance," Bob Moore recalls, "what with the separation and all that, and in fact only on the odd occasion did both drummers play their full kit at the same time, even though they'd each be sitting behind their respective drum sets."

> More often than not, one of them would be playing a hi-hat whilst the other one would be taking care of the beat, although I remember we did one song where Elvis went into that slowed-down "stripper" routine on an ending and both sets of drums went all to hell for about two minutes. One of them hit a bass drum and slammed it off when the other one would and Elvis laughed and hollered out that it sounded like two elephants falling down a set of stairs! [artofslapbass.com, April 6, 2020].

"Right, we had two drummers on that session," recalls Ray Walker. "Here's how it worked. If Elvis came to a song where he wanted D.J.'s feel, the other drummer [Harman] wouldn't play. I always used to call D.J. the 'blap-blap king' because like on 'Jailhouse Rock' ... most drummers would play it 'dum dum, bonk bonk,' but when D.J. played, he did like a '64th pickup.' He added a little clip to it" (author interview with Ray Walker, September 24, 2020).

Take 9 began promisingly, but a percussion flub following the song's bridge ultimately doomed it. Nonetheless, it was close, and Elvis's enthusiasm for the song's feel was evident as he shouted during the instrumental breaks. Starting with the next take, Ray Walker's bass vocals were more prominent, but the track broke down almost immediately, with Elvis shouting "Hold it fellas, hold it!" By take 15, the band was racing toward the light; this version was infused by the low growl of Garland's guitar and Elvis snapping his fingers. However, an audio drop-out during the guitar solo ultimately doomed it. The final master of "I Need Your Love Tonight," however, roars and snarls. Spattered with exemplary work from Bob Moore and thunderous percussion from Harman and Fontana, the song's explosive energy threatens to swallow the listener up.

The next song to be attempted was one of Elvis's most driving rockers, "A Big Hunk of Love," from the pen of Aaron Schroeder and Sid Wyche. Perhaps more than any other track recorded this day, "Big Hunk" drips with the confidence of an artist whose musical palette has swung away from the Tennessee truckstop rockabilly that initially had hot-wired Presley into the national psyche to a harder, more powerful sound. Take 1 had something of a laidback vibe as Elvis and the band felt their way through the tune. With take 2, the difference was stunning, emerging as a nearly perfect track. Elvis, his voice infused with a grit that he tried (and failed) to replicate following his release from the army, spat out the lyrics with abandon. Propelled by a driving piano from Floyd Cramer that would rival anything done by Jerry Lee Lewis, a throbbing bass line from Bob Moore, and swaggering guitar work from Hank Garland, Elvis's joy as the track came together was palpable, as he scatted and hiccupped his way through the song's instrumental breaks.

Key to the song's savage power are the driving vocals of the Jordanaires. "Elvis came over," Ray Walker recalls, "and said, 'This song needs something. Can you go 'No, no, no, no no?' I said, 'Not to you I can't!' and Elvis fell out. I then asked, 'When do I start?' and he said 'When the band does.' So when they counted off, we did 'No, no, no, no, no, no,' and that was it" (author interview with Ray Walker, September 24, 2020).

Walker further elaborates on Presley's approach on recording with the Jordanaires:

> He always stood back about five feet from his microphone, and we were never more than six or seven feet from him to his left. And the engineer would always say, "Elvis, would you move in a bit closer, because we're getting the Jordanaires in your mic" ... so he'd move in about an inch and they'd say it again "Elvis can you move in a little bit more ... we're getting an awful lot of feed from the other guys." So he moved in another inch. The third time they asked him, he said, "You just handle the knobs, I'll handle the mic," because he wanted us to leak in. That way you included everything in the mix. We wouldn't stay on the mic with him, we had our own mic not far from him. But if he held out his arm and I held out mine, we usually could touch. That's how close we were [author interview with Ray Walker, September 24, 2020].

Scotty Moore echoes Walker's perspective on the studio configuration used when working with Presley:

> The normal setup would be Elvis against the wall facing us, with the Jordanaires at his side, and we'd be facing back toward him. That was about the best they could do back then, separation-wise. Everything I ever did with him, feel was the most important. If he missed something he might stop, but if somebody else hit a little clinker and the thing felt good to him, he'd leave it. He'd let everybody work out how they wanted to play and then he might make a suggestion like "Can you do this?" If they would say no, he'd say, "Well, just do what you can" [Courthousenews.com, June 29, 2016].

The final master of "Big Hunk" combines takes 3 and 4, the third showcasing fiery licks from Garland and the fourth included to feature a particularly tasty piano solo from Floyd Cramer. "Big Hunk of Love" stands to this day as one of Elvis's most subliminal works. His affection for the tune endured, standing alone as perhaps the only lesser-remembered Presley song from the 50s that he retained in his

Vegas stage act, albeit served up in a rushed and perfunctory manner. Those dismissive of Presley's role as a rock innovator, their memories perhaps tainted by a later period when Presley's limits had been exhausted, would be well advised to pay heed to the energy that pours from every second of this track.

With a final master of "A Big Hunk of Love" in the can, Elvis next turned to "Ain't That Lovin' You Baby," a bluesy tune originally recorded in 1952 by a man with the wickedly appropriate musical sobriquet of "Eddie Riff." Presley, undecided on the best tempo for the tune, performed two different versions of the song during this session, a shuffle version somewhat similar to Riff's interpretation and another as a straight-up rock raver.

Early attempts by Elvis at a slower version of the song failed to jell. Take 2 broke down as Presley flubbed a lyric, while a percussion mistake doomed take 3. Just before the next take, Elvis, demonstrating the high spirits that characterized this session, made a joke to friend Red West, who was on hand along with other members of Presley's entourage. Take 4, which featured a great vocal by Presley and tidy fills by Garland, would become the RCA master.

Next on the agenda was an up-tempo version of "Ain't That Lovin' You Baby." After early attempts failed, take 8, which kicked off at warp speed and was propelled by sledgehammer percussion, ultimately broke down (with Elvis laughing heartily) when Moore's bass line crept through Presley's final verse. At this point, in an attempt to infuse the track with more energy, Elvis decided that keyboard flourishes from Floyd Cramer and handclaps from the Jordanaires should be made more prominent. The results were impressive, but the track broke down at 31 seconds in, when Elvis flubbed the song's second verse.

The next take featured a scorching solo from Hank Garland and nearly flawless work by the rhythm section. For this version, Elvis changed the song's final verse from "putting on my Sunday suit and going downtown" to "I'm putting on my coat," perhaps to better fit the song's lyrics to its tempo. Because no master exists, the final version is a compilation of takes 1, 8, 10, and 11. For reasons that remain unclear, RCA did not release the slower version as a single until the mid-sixties, by which time Presley's recording career was in freefall. The song, far superior to anything Elvis was cranking out (mostly tepid movie soundtracks) during this period, failed to dent the top 10. Even more puzzling, the sizzling, up-tempo version wouldn't be released by RCA for another two decades, when it finally showed up on an album of compilations. More's the pity, as both versions represent a performer at the top of his game.

With the session approaching its halfway point, Elvis next turned to "(Now and Then There's) A Fool Such as I," a song written by Bill Trader that had originally been a hit for Hank Snow. Such was the song's popularity that it was subsequently recorded by a number of other artists, with middling results, keeping it on the charts with varying degrees of success throughout the early to mid-fifties. "Elvis waited a long time to record that song," remembers Ray Walker. "He would never do a song while it was in the charts for another artist" (author interview with Ray Walker, September 24, 2020).

Dispensing with the mournful strain of Snow's version, Elvis infused the song with a dense, bluesy edge, grounded by Bob Moore's walking bass line, Hank Garland's two-string flourishes, and strong backing vocals from the Jordanaires. Elvis, determined to leaven the track with a prominent bass vocal, waved Ray Walker over to his mic. "As we were recording it," Walker recalls, "Elvis said, 'Come on over here, on my mic.'"

> He said to me, "Can you sing this verse down an octave, you know, sing it low?" I did it, he heard it, he liked it. And while we were recording "A Fool Such as I," that rascal, he'd put his little finger on my lips, in my ear, run his fingers up and down my spine and pull the hair on the back of my neck to break me up! It was a wonder I got through it all because this was my first session with Elvis. He wanted me on his mic because he didn't like the way they mixed his records in New York [author interview with Ray Walker, September 24, 2020].

In subsequent years, Scotty Moore would repeatedly speak of Elvis's frustration with how his music was mastered in New York, complaining that, in Presley's words, they "EQ'd the shit out of it." Elvis's dissatisfaction finally reached such a point that RCA yielded and agreed to have the mastering done in Nashville.

Soundboard recordings of this session, especially during "A Fool Such as I," reveal a loose and seemingly carefree Presley, remarkable given his predicament: his career had been stopped dead in its tracks by Uncle Sam, and he was just days away from an 18-month exile in Germany. Throughout the session, Elvis is heard making joking comments to members of his entourage and engaging in hijinks to keep the musicians loose.

"I'd stand across from him," Gordon Stoker later recalled, "and sing into the same mic. Back then you couldn't overdub or double track and all that. But it was funny to look him straight in the face because he'd wink at you, punch you in the jaw, stick his finger in your mouth, anything to break you up. And of course many times he did break me up and we'd have to start over. Elvis was never concerned with the clock" (elvisinfo.net, May 11, 2004).

Watching the pranks from the control room, perhaps with dismay, was Elvis's manager, Colonel Tom Parker. When asked about Parker, Walker shakes his head:

> We didn't really have any communication with him. He just knew that Elvis wanted us on his records and he was proud to have us there. We had no particular arrangement with him, except this: Gordon Stoker and the Colonel agreed that we wouldn't put the Jordanaires' name on anybody else's label, except Presley's. Gordon and the Colonel agreed to that before I joined the Jordanaires. We never got credit with anybody, other than Elvis. Elvis was the very first person to give everybody credit on a session in the liner notes of an album. He said, "I want everybody on this session mentioned" [author interview with Ray Walker, September 24, 2020].

Initial attempts at "A Fool Such as I" broke down almost immediately. Before attempting a third take, Elvis, apparently unhappy with his vocals, said to Steve Sholes, who was listed as the session's producer, "Can you put me on a little more echo, Steve?" The musicians who backed Presley had their own thoughts as to who was really in charge. "You know how on those records it says 'Produced by so—and—so'?" D.J. Fontana recalls. "Nobody but Elvis produced those records. Absolutely" (Rodman, *Elvis After Elvis*). Ray Walker seconds D.J.'s comments. "Presley did all his own producing. Even Chet Atkins, who was there, didn't produce it. Nobody produced those sessions but Presley" (author interview with Ray Walker, September 24, 2020).

Just prior to take 6 of "A Fool Such as I," Elvis shushed the musicians with yet another army reference: "At ease!" However, this version, along with take 7, quickly broke down. It'd be two more attempts before Elvis was satisfied, with take 9 becoming the RCA master. On the only occasion that Elvis performed "A Fool Such as I" on stage (on March 25, 1961, in Honolulu, his last concert appearance for eight years), he would change the line "You taught me how to love and now" to "You taught me how to milk a cow."

The session, which had begun at 7:00 p.m., was now creeping into late night, and with fatigue setting in, the musicians took an extended dinner break at 10:30. At some time past midnight, they resumed their places to tackle the session's final song, "I Got Stung," a boogie-woogie-tinged raver written by Aaron Schroeder and David Hill. Takes 1 through 8 show Elvis and the group trying, but failing to find the song's feel. Initially, Hank Garland struggled with his part, alternating between runs on his bass strings and answering Elvis's vocals with guitar flourishes. By take 15, he'd nailed it; doubling Moore's bass line with a dazzling run, Garland, along with stabbing offbeat piano licks from Cramer and thunderous drumming, transformed the song. But the take ultimately broke down at 50 seconds in, with Elvis laughing. Obviously liking what he was hearing from Garland, Elvis brought Hank's guitar to the forefront for the next take. The result was powerful and nearly perfect, but Elvis, clearly enamored of the song, decided to press on in an attempt to improve what they'd done.

Just prior to take 17, Gordon Stoker of the Jordanaires was having trouble picking up Elvis's vocals and said to him, "We can't hear what you're saying," suggesting that perhaps Presley could angle himself so the vocal group could see what he was singing. Elvis replied, "Okay," then, in a joking aside, added, "Well, here's where we goof up!"

As the band prepared to launch into take 18, Elvis suddenly halted the proceedings, yelling to Sholes in the control room, "Hold it up just a minute, Steve." After taking a minute to familiarize himself with the song's opening line, Presley announced, "I'm ready for anything." And he was. For its first two minutes, take 18 was letter perfect, with Garland and the rhythm section firmly in the pocket. Responding to the band's energy, Presley grunted a "yeah" following the first verse. But at 2:12, Elvis blew a line and, in frustration, spat out "shit!" then "fuck!" in succession. Three takes later, following a percussion error, Steve Sholes announced from the control booth, "Slight goof there. We'll try it again." As attempts to get a master take ground on, Elvis, sounding weary and eyeing a studio clock that read 4:00 a.m., said, "My brain is getting weaker by the minute!" It took another three attempts before, finally, at shortly before 5:00 a.m., he was convinced: take 24 couldn't be improved upon and would be the version released as a single. It had been an exhausting and arduous experience, but now, with the sun starting to rise, there were nods all around among the exhausted musicians. They'd done it: In less than eight hours, Elvis and his elite cast of musicians had completed the five new tracks insisted upon by RCA.

On June 14, Elvis returned to Fort Hood to complete 10 weeks of advance tank training. Two weeks later, *King Creole* was released to theaters where, at its peak, it reached number five in *Variety*'s National Box Office survey. In the days following its release, the critics weighed in and, for the first time, Elvis was extended grudging praise for his acting.

Hal Wallis has attempted to take the curse off Elvis Presley, for those still resistant to his charms, by giving him an extraordinary backing in *King Creole*, a solid melodrama with plenty of action and color. The Paramount presentation shows the young singer this time as a better-than-fair actor. In all fairness, Presley does show himself to be a surprisingly sympathetic and believable actor on occasion [*Variety*, May 26, 1958].

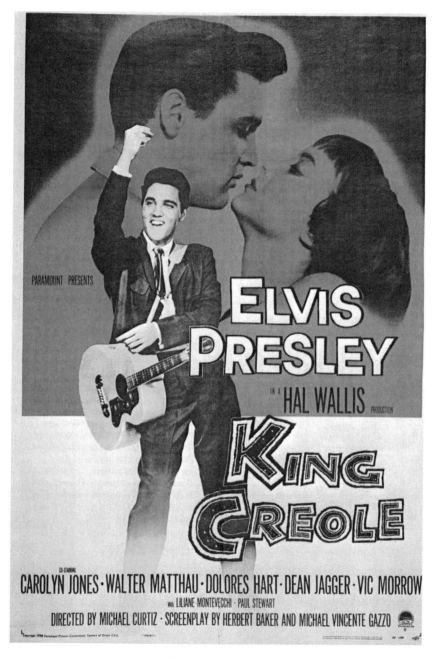

Elvis receives the best reviews of his career for *King Creole,* with even the *New York Times* praising his work.

Even the normally curmudgeonly *New York Times* seemed impressed: "As the lad himself might say, cut my legs off and call me Shorty! Elvis Presley can act" (*New York Times*, May 26, 1958).

And make what you will of the following schizoid take from *The Spectator* magazine, which seemed to signal approval while still managing to bloody Elvis in the process.

> As the most extreme example of a contemporary idol, Mr. Presley is pretty fascinating, and though you may be put off at first by his pale, puffy, bruised looking babyish face, by the weary cherubic decadence you might imagine in Nero, and the excessive greasiness of his excessively long, spiky locks, his films, however bad (and *King Creole* is pretty low on his list), are well worth taking a look at [*The Spectator*, May 1958].

25

"Everything I have is gone"

On Saturday, June 14, Elvis returned to his rented home in Fort Hood, Texas, where he was immediately confronted with health issues related to his mother. For much of the summer, Gladys had complained of feeling run-down and of wanting to do nothing but sleep. By August, Elvis was so alarmed by her deteriorating condition that he insisted she return to Memphis to consult with her personal physician. Following a series of tests, it was revealed that Gladys was suffering from not only jaundice, but also a severely damaged liver, likely trigged by a decades-long abuse of barbiturates she'd consumed to control her weight. On Saturday, August 9, she took a sudden turn for the worse and was rushed by ambulance to Memphis Methodist Hospital, where her condition was described as grave. Three days later, Elvis, granted an emergency seven-day leave, immediately flew from Fort Worth to Memphis to be at her bedside. At the hospital, Elvis and Vernon maintained a round-the-clock vigil, but on August 14, Gladys Presley died of a heart attack. She was just 46 years old.

In the years since her death, volumes have been written on the impact of Gladys's death on Elvis. If press reports are to be believed, Elvis, in the days following her passing, was a man bordering on a complete mental and physical collapse. On the day after her death, reporters arrived at Graceland to find Elvis and Vernon, seemingly oblivious to their presence, sobbing uncontrollably on Graceland's front steps. That afternoon, as hundreds of fans gathered out front, Gladys's body was moved to Graceland for viewing. Throughout the day, Elvis, sobbing uncontrollably, remained by the coffin, rising only to greet friends and family. The scene, in the words of one of those present, was "abject grief." As night fell, Sam Phillips arrived and managed to pull Elvis away from the coffin long enough to extend condolences and counsel acceptance. Minutes later, Dewey Phillips, hammered on pills and booze, also showed up. Days earlier, Phillips had been fired from WHBQ, ostensibly due to the station's switch to a more restricted top-40 format, but his boozing and drug habit certainly contributed to the decision. His dismissal would ignite a seemingly endless downward spiral, and, in the years between 1958 and his death 10 years later at age 42, Phillips would bounce from one small-market radio station to another, quickly wearing out his welcome at each.

For the remainder of the night, the wake continued, with one attendee describing Colonel Parker as schmoozing with the press and doing his best to make an "extravaganza out of it." On the day of the funeral, the Associated Press described Elvis as "nearly hysterical" during the services, where he was overheard saying, "Oh God, everything I have is gone. I lived my life for you. I loved you so much." When the ceremony finally concluded, Elvis had to be supported by friends as he made his way back to the limousine that carried him back to Graceland. The impact of his mother's death was clearly traumatic and would linger until the day he died.

In the years subsequent to her death, much has been written and said regarding what some see as Elvis's outsized response to Gladys's passing and the deleterious impact it would have on the rest of his life, but there's simply no denying the impact the loss of a beloved parent can inflict on a child. And while generalizations are always perilous, there's sufficient evidence to indicate that for Southern males, the death of a mother is particularly profound. In the year's since Presley's death in 1977, much has been chronicled regarding his deep emotional connection to Gladys, with Vernon's second wife, Dee, going so far as to advance a controversial theory to the *National Enquirer* in 1977 that Elvis and Gladys engaged in a "special relationship," which, in essence, is Southern code for an incestuous bond. In fact, any suggestion of an illicit relationship between the two is likely predicated on the fact that Elvis and Gladys shared a bed when Vernon was in prison for check forging. By the time of her death at 88 in 2013, Dee Presley had transformed herself into a one-woman rumor mill and Presley profiteer, even suggesting at one point that Elvis had committed suicide to avoid facing an agonizing death from bone cancer. Because the Presley name was attached to these theories, they naturally drew attention.

To those closest to them, the accusation of an incestuous relationship between Elvis and his mother is beyond the pale. "This stuff that Dee Presley told the *National Enquirer* about Elvis and Gladys being lovers is just totally nuts," Lamar Fike said. "I don't care what Vernon supposedly said. I knew Gladys very well and that never happened" (Nash, *Elvis Aaron Presley: Revelations from the Memphis Mafia*). And insofar as Dee Presley's suicide angle goes, does anyone credibly believe that Elvis truly intended to shuffle off this mortal coil while perched on the toilet with his pajamas bunched around his ankles?

While sensationalistic suggestions such as these are easily shot down, there's still no question of the profound impact that Gladys's death would have on Elvis's future life and emotional health. Studies show that as male children grow and mature, it's crucial for guidelines to be established and for a measured distance to be erected between child and mother. If not, dependency issues may arise resulting in crippling psychological issues in later life, including depression, anxiety, and a dependence on prescription medications. Because she died while he was still in his early 20s, Elvis was never able to transform his relationship with Gladys from one of acute dependency to a more mature mother-son relationship.

Whether this is an accurate characterization of Elvis's bond to Gladys or merely psycho-babble, it's nonetheless clear that, to the end of his life, Elvis would with every significant romantic partner regress into a childlike state in which he would speak in the coded baby talk that he'd honed and practiced with his mother. It's equally evident that from the moment of her passing to his own death 19 years later, Presley would engage in an endless search for someone who could fill the emptiness engendered by her loss. It would be a void that would not only remain unfilled, but one that would alter him profoundly. "He changed completely," a close relative said of the Presley who emerged following the death of Gladys. "He didn't seem like Elvis ever again" (*Remembering Elvis*, Life, 2007).

26

Any Way You Want Me

apostasy
apos·ta·sy | \ ə-ˈpä-stə-sē
noun
definition: abandonment of a previous loyalty

It was April of 1959 and, for the previous 15 months, things had pretty much gone according to plan for Army Specialist Fourth Class Elvis Presley. Every morning he awakened at 5:00 a.m., then made his way to his army base at Friedberg, Germany, where he served as a jeep driver for the First Medium Tank Battalion, 32nd Armor. Meanwhile, back in the States, the press was issuing breathless reports on just how the country's most famous draftee was faring, including this from the *Louisville Courier*:

> Pfc, Elvis Presley is under virtual house arrest. This alarming situation has nothing to do with the fine military record that the drafted rock n' roll star has amassed in slightly more than a year of wearing army greens. It is the price of fame. It is the only drawback to the Army's ultra-fair policy of treating Presley "just like anyone else." Presley cannot leave his three-story home here at night because he is Elvis Presley and Elvis Presley would get mobbed, even on the streets of the dignified German spa of Bad Nauheim. "I stay at home with my dad and my grandma," Elvis says. "Only time I leave, just about, is to go to work" [*The Louisville Courier-Journal*, April 19, 1959].

The skeptics who'd so vocally and publicly doubted Presley's ability to adapt to army life had, it seemed, been proven wrong. For more than a year, Elvis had kept his head down, done what he was told, and never asked for special treatment. "He's never angled himself into anything easy," an army senior commander said, obviously impressed. "Elvis has made it popular to be a good soldier. He fooled us all" (Levy, *Operation Elvis*).

In truth, "fooled" might be the right word, because by June of 1959, Elvis Presley's meticulously honed image as a humble rock 'n' roller

222

willing to serve his country was starting to show signs of wear. "Too many people come here and make a nuisance of themselves," he told a reporter in June of 1959. "I wish they'd leave me alone." When asked if he'd been dating local girls, he shot back, "I'd rather not talk about any of these girls, and for that matter, it's none of your business. My private life is my own and anything I do outside of show business should be regarded by the public as my business and not theirs. I can't even go into a night club without some snooping photographer pushing a camera into my face."

Perhaps seeking a more favorable topic, the reporter asked Elvis what he thought of performers he'd inspired to follow in his footsteps. "They were only trying to climb on my bandwagon. Why don't they try and make a go of it themselves?" When prompted for his musical influences, Presley tartly replied, "No one influenced me at all." When asked if he had advice for someone just starting in the business, he replied, "I have no advice for anyone. They will have to learn for themselves the same way I did. Let them find it without my help." Finally, he was asked if he had anything to say to his fans back in the States. "I have no message for my fans," he replied. "What could I say to them?" ("Time Brought Many Changes to Rock and Roll King Elvis Presley," *Ottawa Citizen*, June 13, 1959).

Comments such as these make it clear that the carefully constructed image of the selfless soldier had given way to a thinly veiled resentment of the entire charade. No doubt contributing to Presley's dissatisfaction was the constant issue of *The Question*. He'd been increasingly hectored by reporters seeking his response to just one query: What would he do if he arrived back in the States and found that his fans had forgotten him? An article in Nashville's *The Tennessean* is typical of the coverage that Elvis was habitually confronted with during this period.

> How long can it last? That's the question that must haunt him through many long nights. Because the day he plays to a less than full house or releases a record that sells less than a million copies, or can walk down the street as safely as you or I, on that day, Elvis Presley will begin to die [*The Tennessean*, April 24, 1960].

To make matters worse, back in the States, the word was out, and as far as Elvis was concerned, it wasn't good: rock 'n' roll, it seemed, was now *passé*. A May 1960 article in the Charleston, West Virginia *Gazette Mail* titled "Rock and Roll: An Obituary?" serves as just one example of reports now appearing regularly in U.S. newspapers signaling the demise of rock music. The drumbeat had gained such force that even crooner Bing Crosby was asked to weigh in on Elvis's future.

"I believe that he'll make a grave mistake if he doesn't change," Crosby stated publicly. "He'll soon find it compulsory to do so" (*Atlanta Constitution*, May 9, 1960).

Half a world away, Elvis couldn't help but hear speculation that the musical revolution he'd helped ignite was flaming out. While harboring his own doubts, he nonetheless strived to maintain a brave front. Rock 'n' roll had been pronounced dead many times before, he reminded reporters, only to bounce back stronger than ever. Still, the uncertainty lingered, and, in his private time, he would spend hours on the phone with friends back in the States, speaking of how homesick he was and openly expressing fears over his career prospects.

None of this is to suggest, of course, that being Elvis Presley, career worries or not, didn't come with certain advantages. An early summer trip to Paris where he spent the better part of a 15-day furlough in the company of showgirls and strippers provided a necessary diversion.

"The ten days I spent in Paris," Elvis told the press, "it was just wonderful. I had a great time. If you want to have fun, you've got to see Paris. I went there to recuperate from a bout of tonsilitis, but I wound up in worse shape than when I got there. I didn't have much sleep. I hope to come back to Europe as an entertainer. Then I'll have a chance to go places. But most of all, I would like to get back to Paris" (*Akron Beacon Journal*, October 11, 1959).

Then there was the matter of Margit Buergin, the 16-year-old Brigitte Bardot look-alike who captured his fancy ("grind city" he replied when a friend asked him to characterize the relationship) then lost it when she bragged to the press that she was "Elvis' girlfriend" and began posing for racy pictures.

Still, despite the diversions, uncertainty over his future lingered, and the more he tried to push thoughts of them out of his head, the more entrenched they became. When asked late in 1959 what his plans were once he was freed from the military, Elvis couldn't hide his doubts. "What the future holds for me," he replied evenly, "I have no idea" (*Akron Beacon Journal*, October 11, 1959).

Ideas were one thing that Tom Parker didn't lack. In the weeks and months before Elvis shipped off to Germany, Parker had hatched a plan to keep the money spigots flowing after Presley's hitch was up, and it all revolved around creating a version of Elvis more palatable to Middle America. Presley's willingness to submit to army service had won over some naysayers, but Parker knew that pockets of Presley haters still lingered, as recent comments on rock 'n' roll and Elvis from famed cellist Pablo Casals made clear:

You want to know what I think of that abomination? Well, I think it's a disgrace. When I hear it, I feel very sad not only for music, but for the people who are addicted to it. I am also very sorry for America, that such a great country should have nothing better to pour into the expectant ear of mankind that this raucous distillation of the ugliness of our time, performed by juveniles for juveniles [*The Spokesman-Review*, May 17, 1959].

When asked about Elvis, Casals stated, "I have seen Elvis Presley on television, and I consider him an evil influence."

In truth, comments like these were nothing new to Tom Parker; they'd rained down steadily for over two years. They'd once troubled him, but no longer, because now he had a plan. It might not win over the Pablo Casals of the world, but typical Americans, he felt sure, would go for it, hook, line, and sinker. And the key to it all was sidelining the rock 'n' roll that angered so much of the country and transforming Elvis into a full-time movie star. And by "movie," Parker wasn't talking about the type of thought-provoking cinema that came from Bergman or Kurosawa, but the sort of frothy fare that Americans had flocked to since time immemorial. Downplaying the music and shifting the focus to movies might be a brazen example of the "tail wagging the dog," but to Parker that didn't matter. As a master "snower," the Colonel could already discern the tantalizing sound of cash registers ringing from coast to coast.

Naturally, Parker was acutely aware that Elvis's great unfulfilled dream was to become a serious actor, but he also knew that the real bucks would be in cheaply made movies that showcased Elvis as someone fast with his fists and irresistible to women. Of course, there'd always be those malcontents who'd view his goal of transforming one of popular music's fiercest innovators into a purveyor of schlock cynical and distasteful, but he didn't care. Anyway, the boy always did what he was told.

As any decent magician will tell you, every great trick requires a setup. And with Elvis about to receive his discharge, Parker's "setup" meant getting him in front of the public as quickly as possible to capitalize on the excitement of his homecoming. Negotiations had been tough, particularly over Parker's demand of $125,000 for a single appearance, but after some haggling, everyone came to terms. On March 26, Elvis would appear on a nationwide Frank Sinatra television special to be called *Welcome Home Elvis*. If Sinatra, who'd once denounced rock 'n' roll as being "sung, played and written for the most part by cretinous goons," could be won over, could Middle America be far behind? Elvis would come out in his army uniform—nothing wrong with reminding everyone of his selfless patriotism—croon a couple of inoffensive numbers, schmooze with Ol' Blue Eyes, then walk away with a cool $125K. In Parker's eyes, the whole thing was a masterstroke.

On March 5, 1960, an army transport with Elvis on board landed at Fort Dix in New Jersey, where, insulated from screaming fans by six military cops, Elvis picked up his final check for $109.54 and sat down for a full-scale press conference. One of the first questions posed was about Priscilla Beaulieu, the young girl he was seen bidding goodbye just before leaving Germany. For months, Elvis had tried, and failed, to keep details of his relationship with Priscilla from reaching the public, as the following March 1 report in a Texas newspaper makes clear.

"Elvis Presley flies home Wednesday to get his Army discharge and return to show business. The rock and roll singer leaves behind a 16-year-old [sic] American high school girl he has been dating often, but quietly, for several months" (*Abilene Reporter News*, March 1, 1960).

Mindful of the 1957 Jerry Lee Lewis scandal, where it was revealed that the pianist was married to his 13-year-old third cousin, Presley was terrified that word would leak out that he was dating such a young girl. The previous fall he'd had a close call when a would-be doctor (it later turned out that he lacked medical credentials) Elvis was seeing for skin treatments threatened to expose Elvis's "illicit relationship with a teen-age girl." Before the story could leak out, the man was paid off to disappear.

"I am fond of Priscilla," Elvis said to the gathered press when questioned about her, "but I have no plans to call or write her. I don't just date sixteen-year-olds" (*Elvis Remembered*, Life, 2007). (This was a factually true statement; Priscilla was actually 14.)

Following the press conference and a brief stop in Washington, Elvis boarded a railway car that would carry him to Memphis. The trip would be an event; Parker had alerted the press to Elvis's itinerary, and, as a result, fans gathered by the hundreds at every town through which the train passed.

"Every little whistle-stop where trains no longer stopped, there was mobs of people," Charlie Hodge recalls. "Every little whistle-stop. And they'd be waving when the train went by, because they knew Elvis was on there. But at every whistle stop in every town, all the way out there" (interview with Charlie Hodge, elvisinfonet.com, April 2005).

In the midst of a heavy snowfall, Elvis finally arrived at Graceland on March 7, where, that afternoon, he again met with the press. For the next hour, he was questioned about Priscilla ("It was no great romance," he insisted); then, when prompted for his future plans, he indicated that his first priority was to record some new songs.

The Music—March 20, 1960—
RCA Studio B, Nashville

On March 20, Elvis arrived at RCA's Nashville studio to lay down tracks for a new single and album, where, for the first time, he would record using a three-track machine. Recording would be interrupted by Presley's upcoming appearance on the Sinatra TV special, but once that was done, everyone would meet up once again on April 3 to complete work on the album.

This session, Presley's first in almost two years, would establish a template for the remainder of his life. "They would begin setting up around 8 p.m.," Chet Atkins recalls, "and Elvis would come in after nine."

> He would do karate, swap stories. I remember at the early sessions he would come in with pockets full of press clippings and show them to his friends and laugh. Anyway, they would start cutting around 11 or 12 and then they'd send out for a hundred Krystal burgers or some other kind of fast food. They'd eat and around two or three a.m., they'd take a little siesta. Then it would be back to work [*Rolling Stone*, September 22, 1977].

What Atkins failed to mention is that, before actually recording anything, Elvis would first sift through a stack of Hill and Range demos for the better part of an hour in search of songs he wanted to record.

First up was "Make Me Know It" from Otis Blackwell, whose "Don't' Be Cruel" and "Paralyzed" were among Presley's most appealing pre–army recordings. Take 1 emerged as nearly complete and deviated from the release version only in its repeated closing verses. Take 2 broke down when Elvis blew the final verse, laughed, and then told everyone to "Hold it!" Takes 5 through 7 also broke down, with Elvis whistling as he forgot to come in on time. From there, things ground on until takes 12 and 14 broke down when Elvis blew a verse and, in frustration, muttered "Shit!" Despite subsequent versions that barely differ from the initial take, Elvis decided to press on until, following 19 attempts, he was finally satisfied.

Obviously targeted at the young girls whose pulses quickened at the sight of Presley in his dress blues, the next song to be worked on was "Soldier Boy," a song from the Brooklyn doo-wop group the Four Fellows that reached the top 10 of *Billboard*'s R&B chart in 1955. Elvis and his group had a nearly complete version with take 1, but Elvis blew the song's final line. Laughing at his mistake, Elvis asked Steve Sholes in the control room, "Why don't you get a straight singer?" During a subsequent take, Sholes cautioned Elvis, "We've got a mic pop on boy," suggesting that he soften his delivery of that word.

Next up was "Stuck on You," which was scheduled to be Presley's first post–army single. Unlike the multiple takes required to get finished versions of "Make Me Know It" and "Soldier Boy," Elvis and the group completed a master recording of "Stuck on You" in just three tries.

"Fame and Fortune," slated to be the B-side to "Stuck on You," was next and represents the type of ballad that would characterize much of Elvis's post–army work. It also illustrates the changes that had taken place in Presley's voice in the two years he was away. Smoother, more flexible, with a control over his vibrato that was absent in his pre–army work, "Fame and Fortune" was designed to demonstrate Elvis's command over this type of material and clearly succeeds. Early takes included Scotty Moore's tasteful two-string guitar flourishes during the song's bridges, but in takes 5 through 8 they're omitted, only to reappear again in take 9. The studio master is a splice of takes 14 and 15.

After a 30-minute break, Elvis started work on Doc Pomus and Mort Shuman's "A Mess of Blues." Graced with an infectious groove and one of Presley's grittiest post–army vocals, "A Mess of Blues" provides solid evidence that Elvis could still out-rock his competitors with ease when so inclined. Presley's affection for the song is apparent from the first count-in as he enthusiastically snaps his fingers to the beat and employs the same slurred delivery he'd used so effectively in his best 1950s work. Take 2, which started out promisingly, broke down when Elvis suddenly erupted in laughter mid-way through. Take 4 fared no better when Elvis blew a lyric and blurted out, "Aw hell!" in frustration. Take 5 proceeded flawlessly and was designated as the studio master.

Before calling it quits for the night, Elvis took on Fred Wise and Ben Weisman's blues workout "It Feels So Right." Take 1 was nearly perfect, but Elvis decided to press on, apparently feeling he could improve his vocal. After four more attempts, he was satisfied, and take 5 was marked as the studio master.

With five songs in the can, Elvis and members of his growing entourage boarded a train the following day for Miami to prepare for his appearance on the Frank Sinatra TV special. At one point in the nearly all-night train ride, Elvis passed some Dexedrine tablets to Scotty and D.J., telling them the pills would keep them awake. In later years, Scotty would characterize this moment as momentous; it was the first time he would see Elvis openly consuming drugs. It may have been a first for Moore, but if Presley hanger-on Lamar Fike is to be believed, Elvis's use of drugs actually began three years earlier.

"It started around 1957," Fike states. "He got them from his mother. You got such a high from them you wanted more. At the time Gladys couldn't work out why she was taking so many pills. It was actually Elvis swiping them. I tried them and boy I wanted to stay on that elevator for a while!" (elvisinfonet.com, 2005).

Once in Miami, Elvis spent the next 48 hours in rehearsals. In the days leading up to the show's taping on March 26, Sinatra was peppered with questions from members of the press. Did having Elvis on his TV show mean he'd changed his mind about Presley and rock 'n' roll? And what would he do if Presley behaved lasciviously on his show?

"I still don't like it," Sinatra responded when prompted about rock. "But after all, the kid's been away for two years and I get the feeling that he really believes in what he's doing. I think he really loves it and that's the secret to his success. Other guys go through all the motions just for the dough, that's the difference." When asked if Elvis would control himself on the show, the singer replied, "We'll have some kind of an understanding on that matter" (*Kingsport Times-News*, October 18, 1959).

Throughout the days of rehearsal, the co-mingling of Elvis and Sinatra was treated with the frenzied press coverage usually associated with summit meetings between heads of state. Newspapers and magazines splashed images of both singers on their covers, and entertainment reporters filed breathless behind-the-scenes accounts of what actually transpired when the two most celebrated singers of twentieth century came face-to-face.

While taking pains to present a cordial relationship, Elvis, at least according to some members of the press, seemed uneasy with Sinatra and members of his entourage. In one article, a reporter focused on Elvis's insecurity, suggesting that he was ill at ease during rehearsals for the TV special and intimidated by the hipster slang tossed around by Sinatra, Sammy Davis, Jr., and Joey Bishop. "When you talk to Elvis for a few minutes," concluded reporter Joan Ketchum, "you can see despite money, fame and beautiful girls, he is anything but sophisticated." According to Ketchum, Elvis was also troubled by Sinatra's well-known refusal to take rehearsals seriously (*The Angus-Leader*, February 12, 1961).

In the end, the Sinatra special, hyped as momentous, if not historic, supplied little in the way of memorable entertainment. After performing both sides of his new single, Elvis, with his hair piled so high it's likely he needed a ladder to comb it, engaged in a duet of sorts with Ol' Blue Eyes, rendering his version of "Love Me Tender" while Elvis did what he could with Sinatra's "Witchcraft."

The following day, overnight ratings showed that the program was a clear hit, with over 67 percent of American TVs tuned in. Unfortunately for Elvis, also watching with interest were America's entertainment critics, and, if the following comments are any indication, they found the whole affair lacking. First, there was this dollop of cyanide from *The New York Times*: "The recent liberation from the Army of Elvis Presley may have been one of the most irritating events since the invention of itching powder. There was nothing morally reprehensible about his performance; it was merely awful" (*The New York Times*, May 13, 1960). For their part, the recording industry bible, *Billboard* magazine, also found Elvis lacking, while nonetheless managing to praise Joey Bishop:

> Frank Sinatra and Elvis Presley had their long-awaited TV get-together this week. The expected dynamite was, to put it politely, a bit overrated. The impression lingers that Presley has much to learn before he can work in the same league with pros like Sinatra, Joey Bishop and especially Sammy Davis Jr., who just about broke up the show with his chanting and impressions. Presley had a disturbing tendency to swing his arms back and forth, a distracting habit which gives the impression he's never at ease. Let nobody touch his singing. That's fine as is. What he needs is a lot of coaching on how to stand and how to talk [*Billboard*, March 13, 1960].

Today, from a vantage point of over half a century, it's arguably unfair to cast judgment on a television program produced so long ago. And while an audience of 1960 might certainly have been genuinely excited by the first-time pairing of Sinatra and Presley, it's simply difficult to view the program today without cringing at its failings. If Elvis was embarrassed by his Steve Allen appearance four years earlier, then his bullshit alarm had to be flashing deep red when, tricked out in his army dress blues, he came on stage to be greeted by the girlish gushing of Nancy Sinatra and the oily adoration of Joey Bishop and Sammy Davis, Jr. As he reached center stage and joined Sinatra, Presley's obvious chagrin at having to participate in the entire sad spectacle was clear.

"Elvis was so embarrassed when he did that show with Frank Sinatra after he got out the Army," friend Red West said later. "He was singing one of Frank Sinatra's songs and Frank Sinatra was singing one of his. That was the most horrific, embarrassed he ever became, because that was not his type of song" (interview with Red West, elvisinfonetwork.com, 2010).

Presley's embarrassment over his role in the Sinatra debacle is unfortunate, but predictable. It's what happens when a man finds himself at the intersection of art and commerce and takes the wrong path. As to why Presley would subject himself to such an ordeal, one can only wonder. Did thoughts of the $125,000 that was now padding his bank account make it tolerable? Certainly possible. Or was Presley, knowing he was about to embark on a movie career that, before it was done, would find him singing to a chimp and crooning dreck like "Yoga Is as Yoga Does," perhaps steeling himself for even greater humiliations to come? One can only surmise.

The Music—April 3, 1960—RCA Studio B, Nashville

In early April, with a goal of wrapping up enough material to fill Presley's first post–army LP, Elvis and his band gathered again in RCA's Nashville recording studio. Joining Elvis for the first time in nearly two years was Hank Garland, who, henceforth, would take over lead guitar duties from Scotty Moore.

"Hank came in and did a lot of recordings, which I was glad of because it gave me some relief," Scotty Moore said later. "And I was a great fan of Hank's. He was a great player" (*Guitarist*, November 1992).

Since its release two years earlier, Elvis had been a devoted fan of Peggy Lee's version of Little Willie John's "Fever," and throughout his army hitch he spoke often of recording his own version. The song, which would show up as the second track on *Elvis Is Back*, features an arrangement virtually identical to Lee's 1958 version, with Elvis's finger-snaps and Buddy Harman's congas establishing the beat. Prior to take 1, Elvis said to the gathered musicians, "I'll hit a few bad notes here, coz' I can't get my bearings right," to which someone replied, "You sound great." Take 2 faltered when Elvis missed a note and whistled in response. It took just two more attempts before they hit the mark, and take 4 was designated as the master.

Next up was "Like a Baby," Presley's version of an R&B song that reached the charts for Vikki Nelson in 1957. Featuring a prominent rhythm guitar from Elvis and efficient sax support from Boots Randolph, take 1 kicked off promisingly after a false start until Elvis called out, "Whoa, yeah, I can't make it," as he strained to reach the bridge's falsetto notes. For take 2, Elvis added a guitar opening from Hank Garland, who contributed some improvised blues licks that trailed each verse. Early takes broke down for a variety of reasons before everything came together on take 6, which will be marked as the studio master. Interestingly, "Like a Baby" would find favor with other artists in the years ahead; James Brown would take the track to the top 20 of the *Billboard* R&B charts in 1964.

Next up was the familiar "It's Now or Never," a song based on the turn-of-the-century Italian ballad "O Sole Mio" ("My Sunshine"). In its long history, the song has been covered by literally hundreds of artists, including Mario Lanza, one of Elvis's favorites singers. Presley first became aware of the tune while he was in the army, when someone played him the 1949 version by Tony Martin. Inspired by its grandiosity and sense of drama, Elvis vowed to record it as soon as he was discharged. "It's Now or Never" borrows its chord structure and melody from "O Sole Mio" but includes updated lyrics by songwriters Aaron Schroeder and Wally Gold. With its operatic overtones and pretensions toward art, "It's Now or Never" is nothing less than the sonic personification of Colonel Parker's cynical plan to transform The King of Rock 'n' Roll into a purveyor of aural dreck. Not that the song didn't meet with success—it did, spending five weeks atop *Billboard*'s Hot 100 chart and, in the process, completely overshadowing the single's B-side, the vastly superior "A Mess of Blues."

Takes 1 and 2 of "It's Now or Never" omitted the piano flourishes that trail each verse in the bridge of the release version. Take 2 also featured a wood block percussion not found in the final version, likely done by D.J. Fontana, and a false ending that's clearly a mistake. The studio master of "It's Now or Never" is a splice of takes 2 and 4, with claves and additional piano figures from Floyd Cramer overdubbed later.

Following a 45-minute dinner break, the session resumed at 12:45 a.m. with "The Girl of My Best Friend," a mid-tempo ballad that, to some, sounded like a potential hit single. After some arrangement tinkering, Elvis wrapped up a completed version in 10 takes. In fact, "The Girl of My Best Friend," which would never be released by Presley as a single, did indeed have hit potential. Shortly following the release of *Elvis Is Back*, singer Ral Donner, sensing an opportunity, would cover the song, adding a Calypso beat and crooning in a voice so similar to Elvis that many listeners were convinced it was indeed Presley. In 1961, Donner would take "The Girl of My Best Friend" to the American top 20. Interestingly, "The Girl of My Best Friend" wouldn't be Ral Donner's final link to Elvis. Twenty years later, he would supply the voice of Presley to the 1981 theatrical film *This Is Elvis*.

Despite the ill will that still lingered between Jerry Leiber and Mike Stoller and Tom Parker, the songwriting team's "Dirty, Dirty Feeling" was next up. Originally slated for *King Creole*, "Dirty, Dirty Feeling" was never recorded, likely due to the enmity that had sprung up between the songwriting team and the Colonel during filming. Perhaps more than any other track on *Elvis Is Back*, "Dirty, Dirty Feeling" illustrates how much was sacrificed when Parker's controlling ways drove Leiber and Stoller from Presley's musical circle. Gritty, tough and direct, "Dirty, Dirty Feeling," as written, touches all the bases and should've resulted in vibrant rock 'n' roll; yet despite Hank Garland's stirring solo, the track comes off as strangely lifeless, prompting one to wonder what might have resulted if Jerry and Mike had been on hand to toughen the arrangement. The completed version of "Dirty, Dirty Feeling" is a splice of take 4 with Garland's solo lifted from take 1.

From there, Elvis went to work on "Thrill of Your Love," a Stan Kesler ballad that, when coupled with the backing of the Jordanaires, took on a quasi-religious air. In the three attempts he made to complete this track, Elvis delivered a fervent vocal performance that nonetheless failed to elevate this song above the pedestrian.

With the clock now reading 3:00 a.m., Elvis went to work on "I Gotta Know," a slice of pop fluff that Parker and Steve Sholes nonetheless viewed as a strong candidate for an upcoming single release. Take 1 quickly broke down with Elvis signaling everyone to "Hold it!" Take 2 was completed without issues and was marked as the studio master. "I Gotta Know" would ultimately be slated as the B-side to "Are You Lonesome Tonight?" and was designed, in the words of an RCA publicist, to be "the kind of mild rock beat that today's kids like." All that depends, of course, if RCA's "today's kids" were fans of Presley's ferocious 1950s work. If so, they would have been hard pressed to view "I Gotta Know" as anything but capitulation set to music.

At 4:00 a.m., Elvis started work on "Such a Night," a track originally recorded by the Drifters that climbed to the top 10 in the U.S. R&B charts in 1953. It was later redone by histrionic ballad singer Johnny Ray, who topped the English charts with it in 1954. Work on "Such a Night" proceeded smoothly, and after less than an hour's work, take 5 was marked as the completed master. It's interesting to note that four years after this session, RCA, unable to lure Elvis to the studio to record anything other than movie soundtracks, released "Such a Night" as a single in 1964. With the British invasion dominating the U.S. record charts at the time, the song barely scraped its way into the *Billboard* top 20.

"Are You Lonesome Tonight?"—a song pressed on Elvis by Colonel Parker (it was a favorite of his wife)—was next. Featuring just a single acoustic guitar, likely played by Presley, and characterized by a melodramatic soliloquy that, in future years, Elvis would mock when performing it live, the group managed, with the benefit of a splice using a snippet of take 2, to complete a master recording in five tries.

"Girl Next Door Went A-Walking," a track written by Thomas Wayne (who was affiliated with Fernwood Records, a company established by Scotty Moore during Presley's army hitch), was next up. Take 1 broke down right away, with Elvis instructing the band to follow Scotty's lead in setting the rhythm. Subsequent takes also failed, with

Elvis laughing each time and saying "We lost a little bit of tempo" after one aborted attempt to nail down the song's feel. Elvis was satisfied with the next attempt, and take 4 was labeled as the completed version.

With dawn about to break, Elvis made short work (just four takes) of a charming ballad called "I Will Be Home Again," a track that features a duet between Elvis, on rhythm guitar, and army buddy Charlie Hodge. "I came up from my home in Decatur, Alabama, after visiting my parents, to see Elvis because he wanted me to record a song with him on his first album. And that was the first singing we ever did together on record which was the *Elvis Is Back* album," Hodge said later. "We did a duet called 'I Will Be Home Again,' which was from an old Golden Gate spiritual album. And we started singing that in Germany" (interview with Charlie Hodge, elvisinfonet.com, April 2005).

At 7:00 a.m., everyone attacked the session's final track (and one of its best), a straight-up 12-bar blues called "Reconsider Baby." A favorite of Presley's since hearing the original version by Lowell Fulson in 1954, "Reconsider Baby" showcases the first saxophone solo by Boots Randolph on a Presley recording and something akin to an unusual free-form jam during the track's instrumental break. "Reconsider Baby" also provides unmistakable evidence of the dramatic change that had taken place in Presley's voice in just the two short years he was away from recording. Throughout the track, Elvis can be heard striving to replicate the grit and timbre he'd applied so easily to such pre–army classics as "Jailhouse Rock" and "One Night," and coming up short each time. His voice was still an effective instrument, but the vocal currents that had infused so much of his fifties work with fire and mettle were gone and weren't coming back.

In the years since its release, opinion seems to have coalesced around the perspective that *Elvis Is Back* is a good, perhaps great, album, one that reflects, in the words of various critics, Elvis's "newfound maturity" and his "expanding musical vision"; it not only represents a "triumph on every level," but is nothing less than "an artistic watershed," making it clear that "Elvis was really back!" This, of course, is poppycock. It's not that it's a bad album. Skillfully produced by Presley and diligently performed by the most able sidemen in the music business, *Elvis Is Back* hints at promise but ultimately devolves into a dreary landscape of formula pop. In truth, things go wrong from the very start; kicking off an album as eagerly anticipated as *Elvis Is Back* with a track as tepid and uninspired as "Make Me Know It" is truly puzzling, suggesting that Presley's previously inerrant musical sense must've have been left on a training hill back in Germany, something assistant engineer Bones Howe noticed the first day Elvis arrived for work: "I was flabbergasted," Howe recalls. "He looked great, he had everything he could want ... but it just wasn't the same. It was like 'Wait a minute, how did I do this? What was it I did?' Maybe through being away all that time he'd had too much of a chance to think about what he'd been doing and tried to figure out what it was. But something was gone" (Guralnick, *Careless Love: The Unmaking of Elvis Presley*).

Howe's observation that Presley had "too much of a chance to think," is borne out by Elvis himself, in comments he would make to the press during this phase. "The Army has changed me," he told a reporter. "I've had a lot of time to think, something you don't have time for in show business. I've had time to sorta take stock of myself" (*Ottawa Citizen*, October 17, 1959).

When asked if this meant there was a "new Elvis," he replied, "I'm older. The Army helped me mature and sometimes maybe I did get carried away. But all I ever tried to do was please people" (*Sydney Morning Herald*, November 6, 1960).

To be fair, some tracks on *Elvis Is Back* threaten to ignite, but are ultimately sabotaged by lackluster arrangements and instrumentation. "Dirty, Dirty Feeling" should have been great, but when compared with the vibrancy and power of Presley's earlier collaborations with Leiber and Stoller, it comes off as flaccid. And as commendable as loyalty undoubtedly is, including a song as mediocre as "The Girl Next Door Went A-Walking" on his first album in two years as a favor to Scotty Moore was simply carrying friendship too far.

Elvis once stated with boldness "that you can't please everybody. It took me a long time to learn it, but I know it now" (*Salt Lake Tribune*, June 19, 1960). But *Elvis Is Back* gives lie to that statement. In the final analysis, Presley's first post–army album is a deeply disappointing work from a once great artist apparently still reeling from an army hitch that he was congenitally unsuited for and paralyzed by fear that the musical form that made him famous had run its course. "It was amazing to see how scared Elvis was," someone observed of Presley during this period. "He thinks he's all washed up" (*The Angus-Leader*, February 12, 1961). In the final analysis, *Elvis Is Back* stands as a calculated and cynical attempt to please everyone that, in the end, would inspire no one.

27

Too Much Monkey Business

Between the years of 1960 and 1969, millions of otherwise sensible Americans flocked to movie theaters where they would spend upwards of two hours watching an otherwise talented human being engage in a desperate and soul-deadening pursuit of middle-class approbation. For the architect of this depressing spectacle, it would be the ultimate snow job. For the man charged with carrying it out, it would become a nightmare that would nearly destroy his career.

With an album and a heralded TV special now in the rear-view mirror, Tom Parker was ready to move on to phase two of his grand plan to transform a man once viewed as a corrosive influence on America's teenagers into someone incapable of offending anyone. In truth, the inflection point came in the fall of 1958 when Parker, with his eyes fixed firmly on the future, negotiated a three-picture, post–army deal with Hal Wallis and Twentieth Century–Fox. The upshot? With Elvis freed from the service and bogged down with movie commitments, the Colonel knew Elvis would be forced to sideline music and focus on his new career: playing aimless itinerants, racecar drivers, cycle bums, or navy frogmen in cheaply made travelogues tailored toward undiscerning audiences. Parker's plan, such as it was, comprised a pantheon of mediocrity, in which, the Colonel felt sure, his boy would willingly take up residence. As for Elvis's oft-expressed desire to become a serious actor? Well, if this 1962 interview is any indication, that too had been sacrificed to "the plan," with Elvis expressing satisfaction with making frothy films: "A certain type of audience likes me," he told *Parade* magazine.

> I entertain them with what I'm doing. I'd be a fool to tamper with that kind of success. It's ridiculous to take it on my own and say I'm going to appeal to a different type of audience, because I might not. Then if I goof, I'm all washed up, because they don't give you many chances in this business. If you're doing all right, you better keep at it until time itself changes things [Shearer, *Parade*, September 16, 1962].

For devoted fans of Presley's best 1950s work, the whole idea of turning Elvis into the centerpiece of junky films stunk to the heavens, but to the Colonel, a man singularly unencumbered by any notions of artistic integrity, that meant bupkis. "They'll never win any Academy Awards," Parker often said regarding Presley's movies. "All they're good for is to make money" (*New York Journal-American*, June 13, 1960).

So, with the ground rules laid out, Presley went to work, churning out two or three pictures per year, none of which ever found favor with a film critic—or lost a dime. Still, a plan so singularly dedicated to wasting talent over such a prolonged period comes at a cost, so to ease the grind, Elvis turned to whatever diversions might be available, be it constant womanizing, karate lessons, engaging in New Age mysticism, or frequent Vegas vacations. In fact, if one were to lump the years of 1960 through 1968 into a PowerPoint presentation, the life of Elvis Presley could be synopsized as follows:

- Elvis makes two or three movies.
- Elvis romances and (likely) beds his female co-stars.
- Elvis uses karate to break a few boards.
- Elvis finds deep meaning in inspirational tracts like *The Autobiography of a Yogi.*
- Elvis makes frequent trips to Las Vegas.
- Lather, rinse, repeat.

And if a steady diet of martial arts, Vegas vacations, and female conquests ever started to pale, Elvis could always turn to his cadre of court jesters, the omnipresent group of lackeys who'd bray at his jokes and gulp his pep pills and for whom he trod the middle ground between pal and deity. (According to one of his followers, Elvis's "aw shucks" country-boy persona had become a shtick by the early sixties. "It was no longer natural," he said. "It became his line. Once he discovered how easy it was for him to get girls, we were routing them through his bedrooms two and sometimes three a day" (*Remembering Elvis*, Life, 2007).) If the following quote is accurate, they'd even follow him to the sets of his movies: "None of us slept more than a few hours at a time," Joe Esposito said later. "We lived on amphetamines. We woke at five o'clock each morning to report to the set, then spent the rest of our time screwing around" (Guralnick, *Careless Love: The Unmaking of Elvis Presley*).

Nice work if you can get it.

Bolstered by a complete refusal to be embarrassed, Parker's plan to ingratiate Presley to Middle America via vapid movies and uninspired soundtracks paid extraordinary dividends. In the early years of the

For *Blue Hawaii*, Elvis swaps his guitar for a ukulele and croons a total of 14 songs. Tom Parker's plan to transform Elvis into a likeable everyman is well underway.

1960s, Presley movies regularly showed up in year-end rankings of most profitable pictures, while early soundtrack albums, nothing more than pale-shadows of Presley's best pre–army work, reached the top of the *Billboard* album charts, results that certainly put smiles on the faces of Hollywood producers and record company executives.

"We look upon him as a sort of latter-day Valentino, appealing to all age groups," a top RCA official told the press in 1960. "His singing is much better now and he conducted himself so well in the service that he won the respect of a lot of older people, particularly the women who felt inclined to mother him" (*Rochester Democrat and Chronicle*, May 8, 1960).

So it was, that by the early sixties, Parker's audacious plan to overhaul Presley's persona and reap millions while doing so was, by any yardstick, a clear success. Somehow, dead wrong had been transformed into perfectly all right.

Still, any plan, no matter how successful, requires occasional tweaking, if for no other reason than to stay abreast of changes in tastes and attitudes, an approach pooh-poohed by Parker. But over time, things began to shift, and by the middle of the decade, Parker's plan of having Presley crank out a steady stream of awful but hopefully profitable movies, had been strip-mined down to ground water. While Elvis busied himself with filmmaking, board-breaking, and chick-making, a generation of teenagers, with little or any awareness of Presley's norm-busting fifties work, were turning to new sounds emanating from the British invasion. Cringe-worthy soundtrack songs from Presley like "Do the Clam" and "Petunia, The Gardener's Daughter," anemic enough to start with, seemed all the more laughable when compared to the tough strains of "Satisfaction," "House of the Rising Sun," and "Ticket to Ride," coming from the Rolling Stones, the Animals, and the Beatles. "Some of the first movies were pretty good music-wise, but after we started getting to *Harem Scarum* and *Kissing Cousins*, everything started sounding the same," Scotty Moore recalls.

> We'd get to the studio at around four or five in the afternoon and Elvis would show up at eight or nine. He'd already heard the material and he was just dreading it. He knew they were bad songs. He hated all of it, just about. There might be one song in each picture that he really liked, mostly he'd say, "Come on guys, let's do this piece of shit and get it over with" [*Musician*, October 1992].

Not that this had any impact on the gaggle of sycophants who surrounded Elvis day and night and spoon-fed him a bouillabaisse of bullshit over everything he did, as record producer Norman Putnam recalls. "After a pretty good take, the control room would explode, all the guys that worked for him, the yes-men, guys leaping in the air, 'Gas Elvis! Smash, Elvis, yeah King, King, King,'" Putnam recalls. "And the rhythm section has only played this thing twice, maybe not even twice. David [Briggs] and I used to talk about how embarrassing it was to have played on the absolute worst records Elvis ever made. You can't make classic records in one take. But Elvis was no longer interested by 1965" (*Musician*, October 1992).

And while Presley was crooning his way through his newest cinematic embarrassment, 1964's *Tickle Me* for bargain-basement studio Allied Artists, the Beatles were starring in *A Hard Day's Night*, a film that opened to critical raves and about which New York's influential *Village Voice* exclaimed, "It's the *Citizen Kane* of jukebox movies."

For Tom Parker, the clue phone was ringing. Yet, despite overwhelming evidence that it was time to shift directions, the Colonel, incredibly, signed agreements in 1965 for five new Presley movies, an agreement that would leave Elvis tied up for the next three years. The contracts were similar to previous Presley deals, with one critical exception. Elvis's films, while still marginally profitable, weren't the sure box-office hits they once were. And with Parker still demanding a fee of upwards of $200,000 for Elvis for each picture, the studios were in a bind. Finally, a compromise was reached. Movies that would take six or so weeks to shoot, such as *Blue Hawaii*, were, henceforth, out. Going forward, economy and efficiency would rule, and Presley films would be cranked out in as little as three weeks, slashing production costs while enabling the studio to meet Elvis's salary demands. Which explains why Presley films, never Oscar contenders to begin with, would become increasingly burdened with recycled plots, cheap production values, and a cannonading of songs so godawful moviegoers could be heard groaning audibly whenever Elvis launched into another.

By the mid-sixties, Presley's cinematic stock had reached such a low ebb that one effort (*Harum Scarum*) opened as the second half of a double bill with *Ghidrah, The Three-Headed Monster*. Still, the movies tumbled forth, two, sometimes three, per year. By the time of 1968's *Clambake* and *Live a Little, Love a Little*, cinematic embarrassments that barely broke even, it was obvious to everyone, even the monumentally obtuse Parker, that his elaborately, breathlessly balanced house of cards was on the verge of collapse. Clearly, something had to be done, and fast.

28

Don't Leave Me Now

Having fully participated in the dismantling of his legacy and cognizant of the damage he'd inflicted to his career, Elvis reentered RCA's Nashville studios in September of 1967 to work on a (mostly) non-movie soundtrack recording session, his first in over two years. Serving as producer would be Felton Jarvis, whose first encounter with Presley came as a fan at a 1955 Norfolk, Virginia show. (Soon after, he would kick off a musical career as an Elvis impersonator.)

The Music—September 10–11, 1967— RCA Studio B, Nashville

While in Los Angeles over the summer, Elvis had heard an up-tempo slice of bayou funk by Jerry Reed called "Guitar Man" and vowed to record it at his first opportunity. Initial attempts at crafting an acceptable version of the song would fail on September 10, until somebody realized that without Reed himself, they'd never be able to duplicate the distinctive guitar sound of the original track. After a bit of scrambling, Reed, who had been fishing in the backwoods outside of Nashville, was finally reached and showed up for the recording session unshaved and looking for all the world like he'd been adrift at sea. After taking a few minutes to hone his chops ("Phew," he told the musicians, "I haven't played all weekend"), Reed joined in on guitar, and a completed master was achieved in 12 takes (Jorgensen, *Elvis Presley, A Life in Music*). In addition to four recordings targeted to Presley's upcoming *Clambake* and *Spinout* movies, five additional masters were recorded, including another Reed composition ("Big Boss Man"), "High Heel Sneakers," and three additional tracks that would serve as B-sides to upcoming Presley singles.

The following January, Elvis was back in RCA's Nashville studio, this time to complete soundtrack recordings for *Stay Away Joe*, a

1968 comedy-western for MGM. In addition to a pair of soundtrack recordings, one of which was Chuck Berry's "Too Much Monkey Business," Elvis completed a studio master of yet another Jerry Reed track, "U.S. Male."

In recent years, the praise that fans and critics have awarded both "Guitar Man" and "U.S. Male" as somehow indicative of a creative rebirth for Presley is understandable. While doubtlessly an improvement over his soundtrack work—a low bar if ever there was one—neither track has aged well. "U.S. Male"—with its cringeworthy sixties sloganeering of "sock it to me" and "tell it like it is," phrases that had already reached cliché status well before the song was recorded—is particularly egregious and reveals Elvis as an artist cast adrift in a musical world he no longer ruled or understood.

Singer Presents Elvis

Anemic box-office receipts and slumping record sales were alarming enough, but the real wake-up call for Tom Parker came in the summer of 1968 when his scheme to produce and sell a half-hour Elvis Christmas special to radio stations nationwide drew yawns from media chieftains. "The aim was always the money," one radio executive said of Parker's asking price of $850,000 for the half-hour show. "The pictures weren't making any money and nobody was willing to come up with the type of money the Colonel thought he should have" (Guralnick, *Careless Love: The Unmaking of Elvis Presley*). Now genuinely concerned, Parker approached NBC-TV executives with another wrinkle: what about a prime-time Christmas show in which Elvis, after crooning an hour of holiday tunes, would bid his audience "happy holidays" and say good night. Would they go for that? Hearing of this, Presley, who heretofore had blank-checked everything the Colonel had pitched, actually rebelled and was relieved to learn that, while NBC had green-lighted the show, the holiday theme was out. The program, to be underwritten with a $400,000 sponsorship by the Singer Sewing Machine Company, would be titled *Singer Presents Elvis*.

With the show scheduled to start taping in early June, producer Bob Finkel and director Steve Binder, who'd cut his directorial teeth on the *T.A.M.I. Show* concert film and TV's *Hullabaloo*, reached out to Elvis. Was there a specific direction he wanted it to take it? Presley, it turns out, was sure of only one thing: under no conditions could the special resemble the movies he'd been making. Other than that, he was open to suggestions.

Using that as a starting point, Finkel and Binder went to work, telling Elvis that, by the time he returned from a planned Hawaiian vacation, they'd have a framework for the show ready for his consideration. Over the next two weeks, Finkel and Binder sketched out a plan for the special based on *The Blue Bird*, an early 1900s play about a driven man who travels the globe in search of happiness only to find that it was in his own backyard the entire time. And serving as the program's leitmotif would be Presley's recently recorded "Guitar Man."

On June 3, Elvis reported to Binder's offices on Sunset Boulevard for the start of rehearsals. Days later, Senator Robert Kennedy was assassinated in Los Angeles, a development that disrupted work on the show and left Elvis anguished. Presley's emotional response to Kennedy's assassination provided director Steve Binder with what he felt was a penetrating insight into Presley's character. "I just felt a real sense of compassion on his part," Binder recalled. "I wanted to let the world know that here was a guy who was not prejudiced, who was raised in the heart of prejudice, but who was really above all that. I wanted to bring to the show ... that this was somebody to look up to and admire" (Guralnick, *Careless Love: The Unmaking of Elvis Presley*). Fueled by this insight, Binder wondered if he might find a way to convey the qualities he'd glimpsed in Elvis to the TV's show's viewing audience.

During rehearsals, Billy Goldenberg, the show's musical arranger, experienced a special moment with Presley. Walking into the studio, he found Elvis sitting alone at the piano, playing Beethoven's "Moonlight Sonata." When he reached a section he was unfamiliar with, Elvis asked Goldenberg if he knew it. Nodding, Billy sat down, and, for the succeeding hour, the two men sat side by side playing the first movement of Beethoven's piece. Goldenberg then witnessed something curious. The moment that members of Presley's entourage entered the studio, Elvis immediately jerked his hands away from the keyboard as one of his guys yelled, "What the fuck is that?" Embarrassed, Elvis quickly got up and joined his buddies. The special moment, Goldenberg realized, was over.

On June 22, Scotty Moore and D.J. Fontana arrived from Nashville to start work with Elvis on a program segment that would reunite Presley with members of his original band in what was intended to be an informal jam session. Inspiration for this came from Binder, who looked on with interest as Presley, relaxing following rehearsals each day, jammed with members of his entourage in his dressing room. "They would unwind after rehearsal and start improvising all of these blues songs and just rock & roll," Binder recalls. "It was just a way of unwinding and that's when I really got the idea. Wouldn't it be great if I had a camera in here and they didn't know I was here?" (Jorgensen, *Elvis Presley, A Life in Music*). When the concept of actually filming in the dressing room proved cinematically problematic, the idea was, of course, to film Elvis onstage playing with members of his old group.

"We did this in-the-round jam session," Scotty Moore recalled. "It was great, because he was as much like he was in the early days as I'd ever seen him" (Cronin, "The Sun King," *Country Guitar*, 1994).

Effective as the reunion segment was, there was one area in which it fell flat. For some reason, director Steve Binder decided it would be a good idea to have Elvis expound on rock 'n' roll and its formative roots and name-check some current groups he admired. A really bad idea, as it turned out, given that Presley was congenitally incapable of speaking effectively on stage without the aid of cue cards. It's evident in the footage that his heart wasn't in it—"I'm not sure this is a good idea," he told Binder at one rehearsal—and, as a result, he comes across as feigned and insincere, particularly when mentioning groups he supposedly likes, "the Beatles and the Beards and whoever." Still, despite the constant sycophantic braying of Charlie Hodge (who was on stage to harmonize with Elvis), the segment was clearly one of the program's high points. Equally effective was the boxing ring segment, in which Elvis, surrounded by audience members, ran through a series of his hits, including "Heartbreak Hotel," "Jailhouse Rock," and "All Shook Up." With his energy at fever pitch, and obviously out to re-establish himself, Elvis paced the stage in a leather black suit, seemingly enjoying himself for the first time in years.

"That show was a lot of fun, but Elvis was very nervous at the beginning," Scotty Moore recalls. "He hadn't been in front of a crowd for so long ... well, since he came out of the Army. I'm sure half of America was watching the show that night. I wasn't nervous, because to me, it was just another crowd" (Wingate, "The Guitar Man," *Music Mart*, 2005).

Throughout the program's preparation, Colonel Parker, who'd grudgingly surrendered his original vision of the show being an hour-long Christmas card, nonetheless clung to a demand that Elvis close the special with a holiday tune. To Steve Binder, who'd labored from the start to re-establish Presley's image as a vital and contemporary artist, the entire notion of Elvis crooning "I'll Be Home for Christmas" and then saying good night would undermine everything he'd set out to accomplish. Which is where the show's vocal arranger, Earl Brown came in.

Binder was willing to push back against the Colonel's demand, but knew he'd need ammunition before he did. And with the last day of formal recording approaching, time was of the essence. With that in mind, Binder had approached Brown and asked him to compose something that might convey the compassion and concern he'd witnessed in Presley's response to Robert Kennedy's assassination. With his assignment laid out, Brown returned home, worked through the night, and, at 7:00 a.m. the following morning, rang Binder. "I've got it," he told the director.

Later that day, with Brown at the piano, Elvis heard "If I Can Dream" for the first time. When it concluded, he asked to hear it again, then another four times. Cognizant of Parker's demand that the program conclude with a holiday song, Elvis was clearly in a spot. In the years that he'd been managed by Parker, he'd rarely rebelled against the Colonel's wishes. But the song was good, and he knew it. Besides, he liked the show's director, and, for all he knew, Binder's vision of what was good for Elvis Presley might be better than Parker's or even his own. After listening to "If I Can Dream" once more, he was sold. Eyeing Binder and Brown, he uttered the words they wanted to hear. "We're doing it," he said.

Outfitted in an all-white suit, with the days of rehearsals imbuing his voice with an edge that only enhanced the song's social overtones, Elvis closed the program with Brown's new song. "If I Can Dream" remains a revelation, a performance in which Elvis summons a passion and commitment to equality previously unsuspected, as if they'd been lying in wait for use only in case of emergency. And "emergency" might not be too strong a term. Presley's most recent soundtrack album, *Speedway*, topped out at a humiliating number 82 on the *Billboard* album chart, suggesting that, without a radical shift in direction, his recording career was likely finished.

A stunning untethering from anything he'd previously done, "If I Can Dream," when coupled with 1969's "In the Ghetto," suggested that Presley was not only unthreatened by a new generation of socially-conscious musicians but also now ready to join their ranks. However, instead of serving as a foundation for an entirely new career path, "In the Ghetto" and "If I Can Dream" would end up as nothing more than curios in the career of Elvis Presley, songs that hinted at promise and renewal, but sadly, were symbolic of nothing more. Presley would perform "In the Ghetto" intermittently during his earliest Vegas engagements, but then dropped it from his setlist entirely. He would never perform "If I Can Dream" on stage. And though Elvis would create new and vibrant music in the months to come, any hopes that he might build on the promise of "In the Ghetto" and "If I Can Dream" were dashed, and he would quickly retreat to proven strategies. It was easier just to roll.

Released as a single on November 5, "If I Can Dream" peaked at number 12 on *Billboard*'s Hot 100, the first time a Presley tune had reached the top 20 in three years. When broadcast on December 3, *Singer Presents Elvis* was watched by more than 43 million Americans, making it the most viewed program of the year. Critical response was mostly positive, with one comment from Jon Landau, music producer and future manager of Bruce Springsteen, standing out: "There is something magical," Landau said, "in watching a man who has lost himself finding his way home again" (*Eye*, December 1968).

At the show's conclusion, Elvis, infused with an exuberance he hadn't experienced in years, approached Scotty and D.J.

"He called D.J. and me aside then and asked us if we'd be interested in doing a European tour," Moore recalls. "We told him we sure would, and he said, 'Well, I really want to do one.' Of course, it never happened, but he definitely wanted to do it" (*Guitarist*, November 1992).

The Music—January 13–16, 20–23, 1969— American Studios, Memphis

After fulfilling commitments for two films that consumed the remainder of 1968, Elvis, hoping to capitalize on the success of his TV special and at the urging of friend Marty Lackner, agreed to record at American Studios, a Memphis facility where Lackner was employed. Tiny, shabby, and in need of a thorough cleaning, American and its producer, Chips Moman, were nonetheless *au courant* in 1969, having run up an impressive record of recent hits spanning a number of musical genres. Despite having cut his musical teeth in the city, 13 years had elapsed since Presley last sang a note in a Memphis studio. As he entered the front door of American Studios, Elvis took in the surroundings, then turned to a member of his entourage. "What a funky studio," he declared (*Great Minds*, Anthem Publishing, 2016).

"He'd gone to Hollywood and recorded in different places, big studios," recalls songwriter Mark James, who would be responsible for writing two of Presley's biggest late-career hits. "So he was probably a little uneasy about coming back to Memphis, wondering 'Should I do this or not?' But a lot of his friends talked him into it and of course, there was a lot of great music coming out of Memphis at that time. So he came down and booked the studio for two weeks and did forty songs" (*Great Minds*, Anthem Publishing, 2016).

A musician who once backed early rocker Gene Vincent and a founder of Stax Records, Chips Moman had formed one of the music world's most impressive collections of session musicians, a unit that included guitarist Reggie Young, keyboardists Bobby Wood and Bobby Emmons, and drummer Gene Chrisman. All were Southerners, roughly the same age as Elvis and somewhat nonchalant regarding his fame. Working with Presley was a "thrill," one member said later, but it "wasn't like working with Neil Diamond." Essentially a studio-for-hire, American had attained a reputation as something of a hit factory in recent years, turning out chart-toppers for artists as diverse as Diamond, Dionne Warwick, Dusty Springfield, and the Box Tops.

Subdued and fighting a cold, Elvis spent the early minutes of the first session getting acquainted with Chips and his musicians. Glenn Spreen, an American Studios staff writer and arranger, saw Elvis pull out a small black cigar, then watched with amazement as members of his entourage battled to see who could be the first to light it. Spreen wondered why they felt compelled to do that and was equally amazed at Presley's seeming need for such sycophancy.

In many ways, Elvis's experience at American Studios would leave him feeling like a stranger in a strange land. Moman, like most producers, insisted that all vocal tracks be recorded separately to avoid leakage coming from other instruments, an approach directly in contrast to Presley's habit of having everyone play together. If Elvis wanted to sing with his group, that was fine, but it would only be a "scratch" vocal, Chips informed him, with the actual vocal done separately. Additionally, Moman, to the amazement of Presley's hangers-on, freely criticized Elvis, admonishing him when he was off-key or asking for retakes when he felt Presley could do better.

Between January 13 and February 22, Elvis completed the songs that would comprise his 1969 album *From Elvis in Memphis*. Of the 12 songs on the album, the emphasis from the start was on Moman's "Memphis sound," in essence a gumbo of country and soul with a smattering of gospel stirred in for seasoning. Throughout the sessions, Moman played a key role in song selection, doing what he could to limit the input of Elvis's friend Lamar Fike, who was there to push Hill and Range tunes as forcefully as he could. "There was a lot of them old Hill & Range songs that some of the people around him wanted him to cut real bad," Moman recalled, "and they kept pushing for them. I don't even want to tell you what I thought of some of those songs" (*Great Minds*, Anthem Publishing, 2016).

The album's opener, "Wearin' That Loved on Look" is probably as close to straight-up funk as Elvis would ever come, with Reggie Young's guitar and Tommy Cogbill's establishing the groove throughout. Among the other tracks recorded were "Long Black Limousine," which is among Presley's better work from this period; "It Keeps Right on A-Hurtin'," a traditional country ballad; and the dobro-drenched, gospel-cum-backwoods workout "I'm Movin' On." "Power of My Love" brings a sledgehammer vibe and effectively straddles Moman's thin line between blues and soul, while "Gentle on My Mind" is an early example—and one that would grow exponentially in the coming years—of Presley's unfortunate 1970s habit of recording songs that were recent hits for other artists. There's nothing wrong with Elvis's version of the song—composed by John Hartford and a million-seller for Glen Campbell just a year earlier—but he brings nothing new to it, prompting questions about why he felt compelled to record it at all.

Of course, the album's truly outstanding track is "In the Ghetto," written by Mac Davis. A compelling story of a star-crossed young boy, the track is blessed with a subtle acoustic guitar opening and a minimal arrangement that leaves Presley ample room to convey his message. Powerful and evocative, it stands as one of Elvis's most iconic recordings and raised hopes, ultimately dashed, that more songs of this quality would be forthcoming. Upon its release, "In the Ghetto" would climb to number three on *Billboard*'s Hot 100, Presley's first top-10 hit in three years.

At 12:30 a.m. on January 22, Elvis sank his teeth into "Suspicious Minds," a track composed by Mark James, who had had recent chart success with "The Eyes of a New York Woman" and "Hooked on a Feeling," both sung by B.J. Thomas. Written and recorded by James a year earlier, "Suspicious Minds" failed to chart and disappeared without a trace. Members of Presley's entourage loved the song and encouraged him to record it, but Elvis needed little convincing. To his mind, "Suspicious Minds" had all the earmarks of a certain hit. A studio master of the track was completed after eight attempts, with the final version a composite of three different vocal takes. Upon its release, "Suspicious Minds" made a steady climb to the top of the *Billboard* charts, giving Elvis his first number-one hit in seven years.

Shortly following the recording session, Elvis, his buddies, and Tom Parker arrived in Las Vegas for a planned vacation. Once in their limo for the drive to the hotel, Parker, with the glow of recent successes still fresh in his mind, turned to Elvis. "You know," he said, "you can do the show that you did for the Singer special here in Vegas." Listening, Elvis said nothing. But when they pulled up at their hotel, Elvis stepped out of the car, then turned to one of his buddies. "Looks like I'm getting ready to do Vegas," he said (Nash, *Elvis Aaron Presley: Revelations from the Memphis Mafia*).

29

Flaming Star

"You're going where? To do what?!"

It's the summer of 1969, and those words belong to Jim, the singer in my late-sixties rock group, who, a moment ago, was fiddling with the volume knob on our P.A. system, but has now turned toward me with a look of disbelief.

"I'm going to Las Vegas. To see Elvis Presley."

"You're kidding. Why?"

I started to speak, but my reply was cut off by a chorus of laughter. It came from Joe and Denis, keyboardist and bassist for Touch, our San Bernardino, California, rock band whose sole claim to fame was once sharing the stage with the one-hit wonders Strawberry Alarm Clock.

As their laughter crested, another voice came from my left. "Hey Parker, just think, maybe he'll sing 'Do the Clam!'" That *bon mot* came compliments of our drummer, Gary, and prompted a renewed chorus of hilarity.

It wasn't easy being an Elvis Presley fan in 1969.

But a fan I was, which explains why, on the afternoon of August 23, 1969, I'm sitting in the Bun Boy restaurant in Baker, California, staring out at what is advertised as the "World's Tallest Thermometer." Paris had its Eiffel Tower, Venice its canals, Pisa its leaning tower. Baker, which promoted itself as "the gateway to Death Valley," had the world's tallest thermometer. You go with your strengths.

If there's one truism regarding travel, it's this: No one rides the bus unless they have to. But with my current chariot, a 13-year-old Mercury sedan with teardrop vent handles that my friends, with great hilarity, referred to as "donkey dicks," out of commission, it was the bus or bust. And with Elvis Presley assuming a concert stage for the first time in nine years, this is a journey that, despite ridicule from friends and family, I must undertake.

As I wait for our Greyhound driver to signal it's time to resume our journey, my mind flashes back to that long-ago night when I saw

Elvis Presley for the first time. It's Sunday, September 9, 1956, and I, along with my family, are staring in stunned disbelief at the images flashing from our black and white Admiral TV. It's Elvis, on Ed Sullivan's *Toast of the Town*, kicking hard against ... well, I really wasn't sure. In successive years, pundits of all stripes have weighed in on Presley's early television appearances and what they signified. Some contend that Elvis was rebelling against America's cinched-up notions of morality, while others have gone so far as to suggest that Presley, intuitively of course, was pushing back against notions of mindless conformity being pounded into the pliant minds of the baby boomer generation. As a six-year-old kid, with nothing deeper on my mind than what would be in my *Rocky Jones, Space Ranger* lunch pail the following day, I neither knew, nor cared. But of one thing, I was sure: I'd never seen anything like it.

At the time, I had no idea that Elvis had recently ignited a nationwide furor over his appearance on *The Milton Berle Show*. Nor was I aware that, in the wake of that performance, Ed Sullivan, America's self-styled guardian of public morals, stated categorically that Elvis would never darken the set of his Sunday night variety show, an edict to which potential huge ratings would lay waste.

Given the passage of time and the vagaries of memory, it's probably not surprising that my memories of that long-ago night are somewhat selective. For example, I have no recollection of who else aside from Elvis appeared that night. (Research shows it was hosted by actor Charles Laughton, substituting for a hospitalized Sullivan. Also appearing were singers Dorothy Sarnoff and Amru Sani and The Vagabonds, a vaudeville act). I also have no specific memory of what Elvis sang ("Don't Be Cruel," "Hound Dog," "Love Me Tender," and "Reddy Teddy"). One thing, however, remains crystal clear: the thunder roll of Elvis's music and the seismic impact it had on my six-year-old sensibilities. Looking back, I now view the night of September 9, 1956, as nothing less than transfigurative: the precise moment when the seeds of a lifelong love of music were first planted.

As the months passed, my interest in music—and in my first ambassador to its pleasures, Elvis Presley—only deepened. Extended play 45s—gifts from my Presley-obsessed older cousins hell-bent on improving my current musical leanings toward "Fess Parker sings The Ballad of Davy Crockett"—soon found their way into my hands. The first was "Jailhouse Rock," a five-track EP containing the title song and four others. That was followed by a Christmas EP some months later, then finally a "King Creole" on my eighth birthday, a day I spent viewing Presley's final pre–army film at a local theater, where I was surrounded by teenaged girls who screamed at ear-splitting levels whenever Elvis appeared on screen.

Some months later, my cousins, sensing a heightened musical maturity, gifted me my first long-playing record. By the time RCA released "A Date with Elvis" in July of 1959, Presley was serving time on a German army base, which, I guess, explains why the album cover shows him outfitted in his dress blues, perched behind the wheel of a convertible. Lining the bottom were three pictures of Elvis in his pre–army prime, with two showcasing his uncanny ability to somehow smile and sneer simultaneously. There was something else: on the album cover, somebody had pasted a large red sticker with the words "Never Before on LP" in bold letters, which, I later learned, was "RCA-speak" for "Hey, we're vault-scraping until Elvis gets back." I knew that one song, "We're Gonna Move," was from *Love Me Tender* and three, "Young and Beautiful," "(You're So Square) Baby I Don't Care," and "I Want to Be Free," had been plucked from the *Jailhouse Rock* EP. Another, "Is It So Strange," was from 1957's *Just for You* EP, and "I Forgot to Remember to Forget" was Presley's final Sun Studios release from 1955. That left four with which I was unfamiliar.

At the time, I had no way of knowing that "Blue Moon of Kentucky," "Milkcow Blues Boogie," "Baby Let's Play House," and "Good Rockin' Tonight" all predated Presley's RCA work. Nor that each had been crafted a half-decade earlier by three musicians and a musical visionary holed up in a tiny Memphis studio, wood-shopping their way to a sound that would sweep the country. What I did realize was that these songs were vital, raw, and infused with magical properties. I played the entire album a few times, but soon focused almost exclusively on the four tracks that I later learned had come from Sun Studios. And each, I felt sure, was indicative of the great music that would surely follow once Elvis exchanged his fatigues for civvies and reentered the recording studio in 1960.

At the time, I had no way of knowing that Presley's first post–army release, *Elvis Is Back*, was Tom Parker's opening salvo in his campaign to transform Elvis into an inoffensive, family-friendly entertainer. Not that that mattered, because all it took was one spin on my record player for me to realize that something had changed. With the exception of "A Mess of Blues" and one or two near misses, *Elvis Is Back*, when placed in relief to the vibrant music that preceded it, seemed flaccid. Which explains, I suppose, why, after playing it a handful of times, I passed it to my older brother, who, it turns out, didn't care for it either.

And for anyone hoping that *Elvis Is Back* might prove to be nothing more than a forgivable misstep and anticipating more vibrant music ahead, a series of low-energy singles would give lie to that notion. Tracks like "Stuck on You," "It's Now or Never," and "Are You Lonesome Tonight" may have raised goosebumps in Tom Parker's targeted demographic of Middle America, but for anyone who'd thrilled at Presley's cogent fifties work, the drop-off was dispiriting. Still, as pedestrian as those songs may have been, they would sound epic when compared to movie soundtracks that followed in their wake, burdened with such sonic embarrassments as "Ito Eats," "We're Comin' in Loaded," and "Fort Lauderdale Chamber of Commerce." By the time of execrable aural exercises like 1964's "No Room to Rhumba in a Sports Car," I'd had enough. Enough tilting at windmills. It was time to permanently shift my allegiances to Presley progeny like the Beatles, the Animals, and the Rolling Stones, who were generating the kind of tough, authentic music in the mid-sixties that Elvis had clearly forsaken.

But then, in the fall of 1968, word filtered out that Presley, apparently rebelling against the creative backwater in which he'd been moored, was itching for a change. According to reports, he was filming a one-hour TV special for the Singer Sewing Machine Company during which he'd appear before a live audience for the first time in almost a decade. To paraphrase recording industry mucky-muck Jon Landau, there's something truly righteous about watching a lost man get found again. It's not that *Singer Presents Elvis*, also known as the "Comeback Special," was without flaw. I still find the production numbers to be a garish and tasteless mess; similarly, the program's storyline of a boy setting out in search of happiness only to find he possessed it all along seems clumsily fleshed out. Still, the show provided something unseen in nearly a decade: a Presley stripped down for fighting, rediscovering, however belatedly, the power and possibilities of the musical form that gave birth to his career 14 years earlier. And not, incidentally, a renewal of my interest in Elvis.

I had no way of knowing, of course, that the best was still to come. A few months later, I was tooling around town in my Mercury sedan (the one with the "donkey dick" vent handles) when something caught my ear. Announced as Presley's new single, "In the Ghetto" was stark, spare, and honest, precisely the kind of socially aware music that Elvis had spent years dodging. Coming on the heels of "If I Can Dream," which had closed out his TV special, the message seemed clear: Elvis was serious about reestablishing himself. Henceforth, music this tough would be the rule, the single suggested, not the exception. So when word came down that Presley was planning a return to the concert stage, I, heartened by recent events, vowed to be in attendance. I confess to being disappointed upon learning that Las Vegas would host his return to performing. To the musically obsessed members of my generation, Vegas was a forlorn outpost where entertainers who'd lurched past their sell-by date retreated to milk rubes of their hard-earned wampum. But given the potency of Presley's recent work, it was a concession I was willing to make, even if it meant a four-hour bus ride from my home in San Bernardino, California.

All of which brings us back to the afternoon of August 23, 1969, and me, with my buns nestled on a Greyhound bus, hell-bent for Las Vegas. As the miles passed and barren desert scrub gradually yielded to billboards that lined the highway, I noticed that most of them contained the same message: "Elvis! Elvis! Elvis! In Person at the International Hotel!" Arriving at the hotel that night, the sensory overload only increased. Bordering the hotel were concession booths pedaling all manner of Presley bric-a-brac, including pins, calendars, 8×10 photos, record albums, and teddy bears. Inside, the bombardment continued unabated, with seemingly every square inch of wall space plastered with Presley: Elvis smiling, Elvis not smiling. Elvis in a scarf, Elvis without a scarf. Some may have reveled in the ballyhoo, but I found the whole thing tasteless, and as I queued up to enter the showroom, I felt my mood darkening.

After being shown to my table, a waiter approached to take my order. After scanning the souvenir menu (Seafood cocktail supreme–$1.50, Lobster tail or steak–$15.00, Chopped chicken livers a bargain at just $1.00), I opted for the lobster. Midway through my meal, a heavily toupéed "comedian" named Sammy Shore bolted on stage, to, in Vegas parlance, "warm up the crowd." (Sample joke: "Youth is wasted on the young. Give us what the kids got and you know what you'd have? A lot of old people with pimples.") Shore's tired act may have wowed them in Peoria, or whatever stereotypical locale was used by marketeers of the time to gauge Middle American acceptance, but it left me feeling nostalgic for a recent root canal I'd had. At that moment, the jibes of my bandmates came flooding back. Maybe they were right. Maybe this was a bad idea.

But then, an orchestral flourish gave way to the pounding strains of drums and guitar. In later years, Presley's arrival on stage would be treated with all the grandiosity accorded The Second Coming. That night Elvis emerged unannounced, clad head to toe in midnight blue and looking smaller than I expected. After briefly acknowledging the crowd, he seized his Gibson acoustic—the one with "Elvis Presley" running down its fretboard—and, without a word, tore into a fiery take of "Blue Suede Shoes." Behind him, Ronnie Tutt and Jerry Scheff laid down

Marquee advertising Elvis's return to performing, August 1969 (author's photograph).

a blistering fusillade of searing rock, while James Burton chugged out beefy support on his trademark Fender Telecaster. From there, Elvis stormed into "I Got a Woman" and "All Shook Up" without letup, both delivered at a fiery momentum. The impact was nothing short of electric, and suddenly, all grievances—the over-the-top ballyhoo, Sammy Shore, the cheesiness of Vegas itself—seemed a million miles away. On the heels of a wasted decade, Presley had reentered a space where it was *music that mattered* and, in so doing, had redeemed himself.

As time has passed and memory faded, a few things still stand out from that magical night of so many summers ago. First of all, I was shocked to realize that Presley simply couldn't talk. Devoid of the scripts that had bolstered the illusion of articulateness in past years, his few attempts to address the crowd would result in rambling, dissociative spiels that underscored just how tongue-tied he really was. One attempt at communication, however, did yield an insightful nugget. "I went into a record company one day," he told the crowd, recounting the early days of his career, "and made a record and when the record came out, you could hear folks around town saying 'Is he, Is he?'" Here, Presley was clearly referring to the belief of those who, upon first hearing "That's All Right," assumed he was black.

And while it may seem frivolous, I remember noticing his hair, which at some point during his performance evolved from the swept-back look of his youth into a Beatle-esque fringe that framed his eyebrows. In subsequent years, his wife, Priscilla, would relate tales of Presley, weighing a return to live performances, expressing concerns that he would appear out of fashion unless he adopted a more current hairstyle. To address this, Elvis had decided that at the mid-way point of his show, he would simply turn his back to the audience and brush his hair forward.

After an incendiary version of "Mystery Train," which he coupled with Rufus Thomas's "Tiger Man," Elvis did renditions of two Beatles songs, "Yesterday" and "Hey Jude" ("Did you see the telegram they sent me?" he asked of a reporter before his first show, pointing to the congratulatory message from the Beatles tacked to his dressing room wall, [*London Evening Standard*, August 2, 1969]), before launching into a seven-minute take of a track that would not be released for another week. Delivered at a bonfire clip, "Suspicious Minds" would be Presley's first chart-topper since 1962's "Good Luck Charm" and the last number one of his career. By the time he left the stage, I knew I'd witnessed something extraordinary, a towering and redemptive performance from a man that I, like so many, had written off. And, as I would later learn, by viewing Presley's return to live performances as significant, I was in good company: "Two days after Elvis's Vegas shows, I was back in New York and went into Albert Grossman's office because I was trying to see Bob Dylan and he managed him," British rock journalist Ray Connelly recalls.

He said that he was in Woodstock. For some reason he suddenly put me on the phone with Dylan and I didn't know what to say to him because I hadn't planned to interview him. I told him I'd just been to see Elvis. From that moment, instead of me being a Bob Dylan fan, we were both Elvis fans. Dylan asked me precisely, "What did he do? Did he do the Sun stuff? Did he do 'That's All Right, Mama'? Did he do 'Mystery Train'? Who's in the band?" Dylan read the New York Times review but he wanted to know what I thought of it. All these questions. Then, two days later I'm back in England and I'm on the phone with John Lennon and I get exactly the same questions from him about Elvis. Lennon asked, "How was the show? Did he do any of the Sun numbers? Did he play 'Mystery Train'?" [interview with Ann Moses and Ray Connelly, elvisinfonet.com, 2010].

In an impromptu press conference that had followed his initial Vegas performance, Elvis spoke of his return to the concert stage and its importance to him.

"I've always wanted to perform on the stage again for the last nine years," he said, "and it's been building inside of me since 1965 until the strain became intolerable." When prompted for thoughts on his movie career, he was surprisingly blunt.

"I wouldn't be being honest with you if I said I wasn't ashamed of some of the movies and the songs I've had to sing in them," he replied. "I would like to say they were good, but I can't. I've been extremely unhappy with that side of my career for some time. But how can you find twelve good songs for every film when you're making three films a year? I knew a lot of them were bad songs and they used to bother the heck out of me. But I had to do them."

A reporter then asked his opinion of the Beatles. "They're so interesting and so experimental," he replied. Then, strumming an imaginary guitar, he said, "But I liked them particularly when they used to sing 'She was just seventeen. You know what I mean'" (*London Evening Standard*, August 2, 1969).

Today, over a half-century later, it's clear that Presley's return to the concert stage represents a high-water mark in the career of an artist so many had viewed as creatively spent, demonstrating that a man out to prove something can sometimes work wonders. The ferocity of Presley's performances that long-ago summer stand as forceful evidence of his determination to reassert his artistic relevance in the fading months of a decade in which he'd been so adrift. Sadly, this triumph would prove fleeting. In the years ahead, as the Vegas stints piled up and the audiences continued to swoon, the boredom would set in.

"He was ready to fly around the room," his bassist Jerry Scheff recalls, referring to Elvis as he prepared for his first appearance at the International Hotel. "His leg was going a million miles an hour, and his hands drumming on things. He was nervous about how people were going to receive him after all those years. When we ended our first song, the place went crazy and I could see the look change on his face, like, 'Oh God, they still love me!' From then on it was too easy for him" (*Goldmine*, November 25, 2019).

In a sobering harbinger of what lay ahead, Presley was back at the International Hotel a mere five months later, kicking off what in years to come would be an endless and ennui-inducing series of Vegas stints.

By the time of his final shows in 1976, he'd performed in Sin City a mind-numbing 641 times. It was also during his January 1970 engagement that Elvis, inexplicably, began to devote much of his set to recent hits by other artists, such as "Proud Mary," "Sweet Caroline," and "Polk Salad Annie." To anyone in attendance a mere five months earlier, watching Presley suddenly transform himself into a Vegas balladeer crooning cover versions of other performers' hits had to be disconcerting. "Yeah, I think that was one of the sad parts of the whole thing," Scheff observes.

> Elvis didn't want to be a rock 'n' roll singer. He just didn't want to. I've seen this happen to other artists. They've done that, you know, you get older and want to go on to something else, but people won't let you. That was part of the tragedy of this whole thing, because Elvis felt trapped. He had a great voice, and wanted to be known for that voice. He wanted to sing songs that showed off the virtuosity of his voice. Rock 'n' roll songs didn't do that, and he didn't want to do them. Anytime anybody does a medley of some songs, you know that they don't want to do these songs [Deelan, elvis.com.au, January 2016].

Which explains why, starting in January of 1970, Presley's disinterest in playing the hits that had made him famous first became evident.

"I think he did them because people expected those songs," said drummer Ronnie Tutt, speaking of Presley's approach to performing hits like "Jailhouse Rock" and "Don't Be Cruel." "You could tell he just wanted to rush through them. He wasn't necessarily thrilled with who he was in the fifties. Because he had become a different man" (time.com, 2019).

Elvis, in the words of Ronnie Tutt, "may have become a different man," but one thing hadn't changed. In the weeks following his TV special the previous summer, Presley, clearly energized by a new career direction, summoned Scotty Moore and D.J. Fontana to his home and shared his plans to at last fulfill a life-long dream.

"We went for dinner out to his house in Belair," Scotty Moore recalls, "and when we were done eating, he called D.J. and I into another room and said, 'How would you guys like to do a European tour?' I said, 'Great, fantastic.' Elvis said, 'Ever since I was over there in the Army, I've really wanted to do one.' Then he turned to me and said, 'You still got your studio? Do you think it would be possible for us to go in and just lock up for about a week and see what we come up with?' I said, 'Sure'" (Cronin, "The Sun King," *Country Guitar*, 1994).

Alas, it was not to be.

Comebacks are the stuff of show biz lore. Frank Sinatra, virtually forgotten, wins an Oscar for his supporting role in 1953's *From Here to Eternity* and revives his moribund singing career. Judy Garland, shunned by virtually every major Hollywood studio, resuscitates her career with a galvanizing performance at New York's Carnegie Hall in 1961. Then, of course, there's Tina Turner and her resurgence with *Private Dancer*. Just three examples, among many, of performers, seemingly down for the count, pursuing redemption and finding it. And so it was with Elvis Presley. Disdained by moviegoers who'd tired of his mindless travelogues and viewed by a new generation of music fans as irrelevant, Presley reached down and summoned the bravura that had transformed him into a symbol of generational change just over a decade earlier. And, for one brief shining moment in the summer of 1969, the resurrection was real.

30

Pinning Presley Down

In 2006, the respected author Neal Gabler produced what is generally acknowledged as the definitive biography of the groundbreaking animator and Hollywood producer Walt Disney. By the time I completed it, I had the distinct and very peculiar sensation of having read a book about two very different men. One was the early Disney, the creative, benevolent, and beloved figure who ran his animation studio as equal parts workshop and playground until the early years of World War II. The other was a resentful and suspicious man, who, from 1941 until his death in 1966, prevailed over his studio with a militant and unrelenting austerity. By the time I was done, I was left with a question I simply couldn't answer: Which was the true Disney?

And so it is, at least for me, with Elvis Presley. As I noted in the introduction, I've devoted over a year to researching and writing the book you hold in your hand. I've also spent hundreds, if not thousands, of hours over the course of many years listening to Presley's music, digesting books and documentaries on his life, interviewing individuals who knew and worked with the man, and even watching his (mostly) execrable movies, all in search of an answer to one question: Who was Elvis Presley?

With that said, let me clarify. I acknowledge that the details of Presley's life have been chronicled exhaustively and are known to millions: Born in Tupelo in 1935 to impoverished parents, Presley is drawn to music from an early age, a fascination that flowers into a compulsion by the time his family relocates to Memphis in 1948. As a loner and an indifferent student, Elvis is seemingly destined for a career as an electrician until Dame Fortune, in the guise of Sam Phillips, singles him out. Now, as a rebel and a record-maker, troubadour and troublemaker, Presley enthralls half the country and enrages the other half, before using a two-year army stretch to disarm his critics. Following his discharge, he drapes himself in a cloak of respectability and spends the better part of a decade cranking out treadmill travelogues and by-the-numbers soundtracks, before staging a brief comeback that he quickly sabotages with drug abuse, possibly fueled by a depressive personality and unresolved issues related to the death of his mother. He dies obese and in ill health in August 1977, at age 42.

All true, all irrefutable. But, nonetheless, insufficient to explain how Presley—like the elephant that is only partially conceptualized by the blind men of fable who first encounter it—could be viewed so differently, by so many, for so long. To wit: in the years since his death, innumerable books on Presley have been published documenting a multitude of Elvises, Presleys so vast in number that even those who knew the man personally have weighed in on the phenomenon.

"I've heard it said," Johnny Cash once said, "that we all have our own Elvis, and I can appreciate that idea, even though my Elvis was my friend, flesh and blood in real life" (Cash, *The Autobiography*). Cash's notion of an "Elvis for everyone" was amplified by Dave Nicholson of the *Washington Post* in 1997, who observed, "There are a multiplicity of Elvises. ... Elvises enough for every taste and circumstance, a catholicity of Elvises that allows each of us to find one that appeals" (Nicholson, *Washington Post*, August 17, 1997).

For some, there may be, as Nicholson suggests, a "multiplicity of Elvises," but for me, there are just two, and therein lies the rub. For I've discovered a pair of Elvises so contradictory, so antithetical, so in opposition to each other—so Disney-like, if you will—that the thousands of hours I've spent researching Presley's life have proven insufficient to resolve their contradictions. The first is the seemingly fearless Presley of the 1950s, the 19-year-old who instinctively melded country and R&B into a musical form that upended the music world, while simultaneously harboring a great dream to become a serious actor. The second is the cowed and cautious figure who emerged from the army seemingly stripped of his musical moorings, who quickly surrendered his goal of becoming a respected actor and then spent nearly a decade blithely throwing away his talent walking through a series of frothy films.

Yet, despite the countless hours I've spent delving and digging into Presley's life, I can state with certainty that I'm no closer to resolving the mystery of these disparate Presleys than when I started. In fact, I've come to see my pursuit of the "true Elvis" in terms of a parable, that of the man who peels layer after layer from an onion seeking its core, only to find more layers, until finally, nothing remains.

If I couldn't resolve the mystery of the dueling Presleys, was there someone who might? At that point, I returned to the words of Marion Keisker, the woman who played such a critical, yet unheralded, role in Presley's rise. "He was like a mirror in a way," she stated in the years following her days at Sun Studios. "Whatever you were looking for, you were going to find in him. He had all the intricacy of the very simple" (Guralnick, *Last Train to Memphis*).

Interesting, to be sure, perhaps even insightful, but, in truth, of little help in explaining Presley's clearly contradictory personas. Unsure of where to look next, I turned to the calendar. A bit of digging made it clear that the bifurcation of Presley's personality took place somewhere between the date of his army induction of March 24, 1958, and the day he was freed from active duty, March 5, 1960. With that as a starting point, I began digging through newspaper archives in search of statements Presley made to the press during that period that might explain his puzzling and obvious transfiguration. Following a thorough investigation, I found this quote from October of 1959:

"The Army has changed me," Presley said. "I've had a lot of time to think, something you don't have time for in show business. I've had time to sorta take stock of myself" (*Ottawa Citizen*, October 17, 1959).

When it came to draftees, "change," as I would soon learn, was nothing less than the U.S. Army's *raison d'etre*, at least according to Josh Jackson, assistant professor of psychology at Washington University in St. Louis: "One of the goals of the military is to break down the mentality you had in the outside world," says Jackson. "If you're going to find some life experience leading to changes in personality traits, it seems like one of the best environments for that to happen would be the military experience" (psmag.com, June 14, 2017).

If the army's goal to was to "break down" Presley's mentality and alter his "personality traits," as Professor Jackson avers, there's certainly evidence that they succeeded. To bolster this perspective, let's return to the words of producer Bones Howe, who, upon reuniting with Presley following his release from the army, could scarcely believe it was the same man he'd known just two years earlier. "It was like, 'Who am I?' He'd had that great edge to him and you could see the toughness was gone" (Guralnick, *Careless Love: The Unmaking of Elvis Presley*).

If Presley's toughness and edge were gone, as Howe contends, might that also explain how Elvis, between the years of 1956 and 1958, could forcefully and repeatedly state that his greatest dream was to become a serious actor "like Brando, Dean, Richard Widmark and Rod Steiger," then, in a startling about-face, state the following in 1962:

I've had intellectuals tell me that I've got to progress as an actor, explore new horizons, take on new challenges, all that routine. I'd like to progress. But I'm smart enough to realize that you can't bite off more than you can chew in this racket. You can't go beyond your limitations. They want me to try an artistic picture. That's fine. Maybe I can pull it off some day. But not now. I've done eleven pictures, and they've all made money [Shearer, *Parade*, September 16, 1962].

Which, perhaps parenthetically, brings us to Presley's view of money and his definition of success in the years following his army stint. While he certainly wasn't the first, I simply can't think of any public figure who so publicly and with such bravura failed to grasp the difference between excellence and success. Excellence is a state that arises from a singular, self-determined pursuit of transcendence in one's work, something that is lasting and wholly within the individual to control. Success is another animal entirely, bestowed from without and it seems in Presley's case, defined purely in terms of money and possessions.

It's been the credo of crowned heads and the aristocracy for eons: money means nothing once you have enough. But like many born into poverty and who later attain wealth, there could never be enough. It's a tragic commentary on Presley's life that he would become so besotted by "success," so entranced by loot, and so primed for a future that only promised more that he junked what brought him to the dance to begin with, his music. Then, with the cynicism and money-grubbing cranked up to 11, Elvis, in the years between 1960 and 1968, would churn out every possible permutation of bland, because "bland," at least for a while, filled the coffers.

Which, of course, brings us back to the music. It's a sad reality that in contrast to the deeply felt and compelling music that Presley produced in his early years, Elvis would devote nearly a decade to cranking out toothless soundtrack albums. Dreck like "The Bullfighter was a Lady" and "El Toro," both from 1964's *Fun in Acapulco*, are the sound of Elvis hitting a wall and free-falling, and by the mid-sixties, even the most starry-eyed devotee had to acknowledge that Presley was shadow-boxing with a previous incarnation of himself and getting his ass kicked.

All of this, of course, was a by-product of Presley's unflinching embrace of Tom Parker's cynical campaign to transform his boy into an "Elvis for Everyone" (not uncoincidentally, the title of a mid-sixties album). While there was certainly nothing wrong with attempting to broaden Elvis's appeal, few could match Parker's proclivity for hatching an idea, then mopping the floor with it. It was egregious enough that the Colonel had summarily banished Jerry Leiber and Mike Stoller from Elvis's inner circle, thereby hobbling any notion of post–army musical relevance, but shoehorning Presley into a role for which he was spectacularly ill-suited—that of the star of lame Hollywood musicals—is just one example of terrible advice in a career pockmarked with horrible edicts.

Assuming that it was ever actually considered, it's abundantly clear that for Parker and, yes, for Presley, any tug-of-war between art and commerce had long since been settled by 1965. This is most clearly illustrated by Parker's epiphany that there was no need to invest hundreds of thousands in making a Presley film when you could spend a fraction of that and still fill theaters, a discovery that rivaled in credibility the first sighting of aliens in Area 57.

Still, despite a level of cynicism that would make Machiavelli blush, the ploy worked. Until it didn't. By the late sixties, a public writ large that had been happy for the better part of a decade to trundle off to movie theaters and embrace Presley's shtick had finally had enough.

Can all this be blamed on Parker's cynical plan and Presley's seeming need for ever-greater riches? Clearly, no. The seeds of Elvis's slavish devotion to Colonel Parker were planted long before he strapped on his fatigues and chowed down on his first MRE. Still, regardless of when it took root, it was nonetheless clear to Ray Walker, bass singer for the Jordanaires, that, by the mid-sixties, Presley was courting disaster.

"I said to him one time," Walker recalls, "If you're not careful, this thing is going to eat you up.' And he said, 'I think it's already started.'" Ray points to a May 1966 session with the singer as particularly significant. "Elvis was sitting at the piano, and he'd already recorded one song. And he was messing with the keys and notes and carrying on. And he said, 'Guys, I'm going to record a religious album. Do you have any suggestions?' I said, 'Elvis, you should really record 'How Great Thou Art.'"

"We started recording," Walker continues, "and I think we did three takes. A few minutes later, he came over to me and said, 'Have you got another?' I suggested 'Where No One Stands Alone' [a track that Elvis would ultimately record at a May 25, 1966 session]. He said he didn't know it. The Jordanaires started singing it and I did the verses and I could see in my peripheral vision his expressions. Then I sang the lyrics...":

> Like a king, I may live in a palace so tall,
> With great riches to call my own...
> But I don't know a thing in this whole wide world that's worse....
> Than being alone [Lillenas Publishing, 1955].

"As soon as he heard those words," Walker recalls, "Elvis turned blood red, then white as a sheet. He sat down to learn that song, but he didn't regain his normal color for several minutes. I knew right then, the boy was in trouble" (author interview with Ray Walker, 2020).

"Elvis suffered a lot," agrees bassist Bob Moore, "and I've had tears in my eyes for him. He once said to me, 'Boy, I'd give anything in the world to go over and get a hamburger with you guys. I never had any idea it was going to get like this.' I think he realized toward the end of his life that there weren't a lot of people that cared about him in the right ways" (artofslapbass.com, April 6, 2020).

By "people," I'm guessing Moore was referring to Tom Parker and to evidence that came to light in the years following Presley's death, detailed in an Appendix of this book, of how Parker cheated Presley out of millions. It's also possible he was also referring to the Memphis Mafia, the tiresome troupe of taint lickers who surrounded Presley and who, in clear acts of self-hatred turned outward over their years-long supplication, would sell Presley out in the years following his death.

"Music was his most interesting side; the rest was just a bunch of guys hanging out in a room telling jokes," Bones Howe says, looking back. "I mean, how smart were those guys? What could have gone on in the room except boredom? I think Elvis Presley died of boredom" (*Musician*, October 1992).

For a similar perspective, we have this from legendary session drummer Hal Blaine: "Once in a while he [Presley] would say something like, 'I'm a little bit thirsty.' And God, fifteen guys would run at him with Coke bottles in those days to see who could knock down the other guy. It was really disturbing" (*Rolling Stone*, March 12, 2019).

For a performer who'd spent the sixties resembling someone fumbling for a light switch he couldn't find, it's a testimony to Presley's cultural standing that his career was capable of resurrection. Cogent singles like "If I Can Dream," "In the Ghetto," and "Suspicious Minds" tumbled forth at the close of the decade, suggesting the arrival of a rejuvenated performer, one ready to throw off the tiresome persona of being "just an entertainer" and eager to resume a march toward renewed musical relevancy.

American poet William Carlos Williams once observed that "the pure products of America go crazy." For Elvis Presley, as pure a product of America as has ever been brought forth, there's evidence that's true. Following his brief creative renaissance, Presley, instead of insisting on quality songs and demanding that Parker allow him to tour Europe, lapsed into a seemingly endless series of Vegas appearances, engagements that would drain his energy and creative drive. The corrosive impact of all this would exact its toll, and soon the carefully constructed public mask of humility would slip as Presley began to genuflect before an altar of excess. The day that Elvis starting wearing capes and bejeweled jumpsuits and taking the stage to the strains of *Thus Spoke Zarathustra*, the game was up. Then, with the leash of self-discipline severed, his concerts devolved into Seconal-drenched spectacles, where Presley, like a drunk on a tightrope, would keep his audience on the edge of their seats. Will he make it through? For the blindly devout, just seeing Presley in person might have been enough, but for the rest of us, it was hell to watch.

With abdication or withdrawal seemingly not possible, Presley's descent from grandeur to dilapidation was nearly complete by 1975. Now, with the cluttered, unkempt corners of his nature fueled by an ever-increasing intake of pharmaceuticals, Elvis was free to nourish his substance-fueled notions of magnificence and engage in a headlong dive into reasons for his very "Elvis-ness." Fame of such degree and adoration of such magnitude, his thinking went, simply had to be the work of a higher power.

To those who inhabit a reality-based world, the ascension of Presley to the entertainment world's highest pinnacle is no more the handiwork of a supreme being than the stray gangland bullet that finds its way into the brain of a bystander. For Presley to believe otherwise supplies irrefutable testimony that he woefully missed the point of *Autobiography of a Yogi*, *The Impersonal Life*, and other spiritual tracts he immersed himself in during much of his later years, which counsel sublimation of the ego, not providential nourishment of it. As Ecclesiastes made clear centuries ago: "The race is not to the swift, nor the battle to the strong, nor favor to men of skill, but time and chance happeneth to them all." And so it was with Presley. Or as Scotty Moore so succinctly put it, "It was a fluke."

Of these sad later years, when a constant diet of uppers and downers magnified the fault lines in Presley's personality, Ray Walker says, "Well, that was still part of him. Somebody said to me one time, 'Well if Elvis was as good as you say...' and I interrupted him and said, 'I didn't say he was good, I said he was sensitive to other people and he let them get into his life and hurt him.' In many ways, Elvis didn't understand life" (author interview with Ray Walker, 2020).

Lest you think that I'm being too severe with Presley, a quick review of what I've written of his pre–army years should lay to rest any notion of animus. As someone who attained an unprecedented level of fame at such a young age—in essence, the world's first rock 'n' roll star–Elvis, as someone forced to make it up as he went along, deserves our forbearance and our admiration, as musician and life-long Presley devotee Tom Petty makes clear.

"We all owe him for going first into battle," Petty says. "He had no road map, and he forged a path of what to do, and what not to do. We shouldn't make the mistake of writing off a great artist by all the clatter that came later. We should dwell on what he did that was so beautiful and everlasting, which was that great, great music" (*Los Angeles Times*, April 13, 2018).

As a country boy barely out of his teens, tossed into the grinder of public notoriety, one can certainly argue, as Petty does, that Presley did the best he could. It's also critical to remember that, despite the gaggle of hangers-on and the multitudes that strained to reach him, no one aside from Elvis himself experienced what he did. "We [the Beatles] used to feel sorry for Elvis," George Harrison said once. "We had the four of us, but he was all alone" (Beatles Anthology, 1995). These sentiments are amplified by a reporter covering Presley for a Tennessee newspaper in 1960: "Even the musicians who work closest to him, despite their affection for him, don't feel that they know him," the reporter observed. "'You can't forget he's Elvis Presley,' one said. 'He's all alone'" (*The Tennessean*, April 24, 1960).

Generational leaders of the sixties such as the Beatles, who eyed Presley's fervent embrace of grandiosity and his eagerness to fly ever closer to the sun, would absorb the lessons of Elvis's reign and steer clear of his excesses. There's a reason, after all, that Paul McCartney takes the stage bereft of fanfare and with Abe Laboriel's drumhead laughably festooned with "PM" fashioned from electrician's tape. McCartney, like so many of Presley's progeny, has witnessed firsthand the hazards of an ever increasing need for greater glory and, in essence, said "fuck that, lesson learned."

All of which, I suppose, brings me back to where I began, an attempt to unravel the mystery of the dueling Presleys. During many idle moments, I've found myself ruminating over what might have been. If not for the deleterious impact of his army service, I've wondered, would the Elvis who entered the sixties have maintained the fiery musical momentum of the historic secret recording session of June 1958? Or, perhaps yielding to the ministrations of Tom Parker, would he have assumed the guise with which we're so familiar, that of a wary and tentative performer cut adrift from his musical instincts, in headlong pursuit of more and more approbation? Sadly, we'll never know. And maybe it doesn't matter. Because, in the end, Presley may not have done it his way, but it certainly can be argued that he fought the good fight against a determined opposition.

When it's all said and sifted, Presley's deft manipulation of his multiple obsessions—country, rhythm and blues, and gospel—into a swirlingly innovative mixture of hair-raising rock 'n' roll and balladry remains one of the music world's true miracles. "'One day,' J.D. Sumner, his musical collaborator stated in 1977, 'there won't be any more pop or country or rhythm and blues. It'll just be named American music and Elvis Presley did as much to make it that as anyone who ever lived'" (*Rolling Stone*, September 22, 1977).

For Elvis Presley, stardom was the promise and he made the trip, but at an extraordinarily high cost. And in the end, he may have had no choice but to watch helplessly as his formidable talent, diluted by a toxic cocktail of fame, pressure, and drugs, finally collapsed back in on himself like a black hole. It had been a losing battle, but, in truth, the victory had already been won. Because if artists, as I fervently believe, are to be judged by their best work, Elvis Presley stands tall as a musical innovator of the first order, a man who not only changed musical history, but, as the record clearly shows, history itself.

31

The Sublimes

If you've made it this far, you've undoubtedly gleaned that my preference in Elvis Presley music skews heavily to his pre–army work, a period when two distinctly American musical forms, country and blues, would be twined together by Presley, Scotty Moore, and Bill Black to form what would come to be known as rockabilly. Between the years of 1954 and when he entered the army four years later, the sheer volume of great music generated by Elvis Presley makes culling a select few from the list a formidable challenge. Nonetheless, I've decided to give it a shot.

To be sure, any purported list of an artist's greatest songs is, by definition, subjective rather than definitive. So, with that in mind, here they are: 16 of what I deem to be Elvis Presley's most essential works. Your musical mileage, of course, may vary.

That's All Right

Recorded July 5–6, 1954—Sun Studios, Memphis.

One of those songs that, quite simply, changed everything. Kicked to life in the sweltering summer hotbox of Sun Studios by a 19-year-old kid with nothing left to lose, this is the nascent sound of Sam Phillips, Presley, Scotty Moore, and Bill Black laying waste to the boundary line that segregated blues and country. A strummed acoustic opening from Elvis, tasty fills from Scotty, and a vibrant slapped bass attack from Bill all contribute to the song's fresh currency. From its opening notes, you can feel the energy of these guys, outsiders all, launching a frontal assault on the cinched-up, buttoned-down 1950s. And they were just getting started.

Blue Moon of Kentucky

Recorded July 5–6, 1954—Sun Studios, Memphis.

If "That's All Right" represents, as many contend, the big bang of rock 'n' roll, then "Blue Moon of Kentucky" is the sound of the world's

268

first rock 'n' roll band finding their footing. Faced with the seemingly impossible task of following up "That's All Right," Elvis, Scotty, and Bill come up with this hot take on Bill Monroe's original and end up with something as different from Monroe's dirge-like version as swans are from ducks or caviar is from sardines. Infused with rolling rhythms that sound as fresh today as the day it was recorded, "Blue Moon of Kentucky" is a vivid early example of the musical form that was soon to be dubbed rockabilly.

Blue Moon

Recorded August 19, 1954—Sun Studios, Memphis

Hypnotic and soulful, this version of the Rodgers and Hart standard conjures up a sense of angst so thick you can slice it with a knife. Scotty Moore's muted single string tapping and Sam Phillips's slapback echo, when set in relief against Presley's spectral crooning, shape this track into something truly offbeat. Bleak and atmospheric ... and not to be missed.

Good Rockin' Tonight

Recorded September 1954—Sun Studios, Memphis

A follow-up to "That's All Right," this track captures Elvis and the newly christened Blue Moon Boys in high, bright flight. An exploration into what it would sound like if you mixed country and race music, "Good Rockin' Tonight" showcases an arrangement that's honed to a beefy sheen, while still providing ample room for Scotty Moore to spew sparks with his twin solos. As rich and consequential as any song recorded in rock history, "Good Rockin' Tonight"' is one of those tracks seemingly crafted for one reason: to show all of us what we'd been missing. He would get bigger, but Presley would never sound fresher or more alive than he does here.

Milkcow Blues Boogie

Recorded November/December 1954—Sun Studios, Memphis

Definitive Presley: A spicy stew of fatback twang and country swing, graced with taut, galloping solos from Scotty Moore, dynamic slap bass lines from Bill Black, and Elvis's spoken admonition of "Hold it fellas. That don't move me! Let's get real, real gone for a change" serve as irrefutable testimony to the potent musical assemblage of Presley, Moore, and Black. And if anyone ever tries to tell you that Elvis Presley wasn't a first-rate rhythm guitarist, let "Milkcow Blues Boogie" serve as Exhibit A to their errancy.

Baby Let's Play House

Recorded February 1955—Sun Studios, Memphis

From its hiccupped opening to its first echo-drenched notes, "Baby Let's Play House," in addition to an epic groove, serves up a hefty dose of libidinal menace that surely gave radio programmers pause when it was released early in 1955. Supposedly inspired by Eddy Arnold's 1951 "I Wanna Play House with You" (which contains the line "You play the mama and I'll play the papa, 'coz I wanna play house with you"), "Baby Let's Play House" was originally written and recorded by Arthur Gunter for Leonard Chess's Excello Records in 1954. Burdened by an uninspired arrangement and Gunter's square phrasing, the song still managed to scrape its way into the top 20 of the U.S. R&B charts late in 1954, its marginal success likely due to its suggestive lyrical content. ("Playing house" was generally viewed in the 1940s and '50s as a metaphor for getting horizontal with a member of the opposite sex.) Elvis himself evidenced concern over the song's suggestiveness, revising the recorded version's "I'd rather see you dead little girl, than to be with another man" to "wed another man" when he performed the song live. In the mid–60s, John Lennon, in a move he later regretted, lifted that same line and used it as the opening for the Beatles song "Run for Your Life."

"Baby Let's Play House" shows Presley squarely connecting the dots between country and R&B and, in the process, creating a cross-cultural musical hybrid that would soon be called rockabilly. Showcasing a band stripped down and serious, "Baby Let's Play House" features a swaggering vocal performance by Elvis (one that he struggles to sustain at the song's conclusion), a fiery bass performance from Bill Black, and a pair of skin-peeling solos from Scotty Moore. Without question, one of Presley's finest moments and a track rightfully regarded as one of rock's foundational pillars.

Trying to Get to You

Recorded February, July 1955—Sun Studios, Memphis

This song supplies clear evidence of the magic at work at 706 Union Avenue in the mid-fifties. Following a failed attempt to complete a releasable version of "Trying to Get to You" in February of 1955, Elvis took another shot at it in July and this time nailed it. A country shuffle marked by steady riffing from Scotty Moore and time-keeping from Memphis drummer Johnny Bernero, in only the second time a percussionist would appear on a Presley side, "Trying to Get to You" detours into a pair of bluesy bridges during which Presley's heavily echoed voice spins a tale of travail and loss that only the intervention of Providence can redeem. Elvis's affection for this track would persist, and he memorably resurrected it for the jam session segment of his 1968 comeback special, during which he delivers it with a fiery intensity.

Mystery Train

Recorded July 11, 1955—Sun Studios, Memphis

This track, in which Presley overlays the lyrics from Junior Parker and the Flames original 1953 hit atop the rhythmic groove of Parker's "Love My Baby," "Mystery Train" endures as one of early rock's most powerful and influential works. Today, from a vantage point of over 60 years, it's no less astounding to realize that this swampy, smoky classic is the product of just three men and demonstrates the extraordinary musical gestalt of Presley, Moore, and Black. From the day this track was recorded to the end of his life, Sam Phillips would forcefully state that "Mystery Train" was the best thing Sun Studios ever produced. Time has proven him right.

Heartbreak Hotel

Recorded January 10–11, 1956—RCA Studios, New York

A product of Presley's initial RCA session, this is the song that turned the music world upside down. Inspired by a newspaper article about a man who, before jumping to his death, left a note stating "I walk the lonely street," it was co-written by Mae Axton, the mother of songwriter-guitarist Hoyt Axton, who urged Elvis to make it his first RCA single release. Her hunch turned out to be prescient. Released on January 27, "Heartbreak Hotel" made a steady climb to the top of the *Billboard* charts, where it spent a total of seven weeks as the country's number-one record. Nobody's idea of a mood lifter, "Heartbreak Hotel," thanks to the work of Elvis, Scotty, Bill, D.J., and pianist Floyd Cramer, in the first of many significant contributions he'd make to Presley records in the years to come, conjures a mood of desolation and despair. The track's dense echo was Steve Sholes's attempt at replicating Sun Studios' trademark slapback by rigging a microphone at the end of one hallway and a speaker at the other, then routing the sound back to the studio. Against all odds, it worked. Unquestionably, one of the most influential songs of all time, with Presley progeny—ranging from John Lennon and Paul McCartney to Tom Petty and Bruce Springsteen—citing it as a major influence.

My Baby Left Me

Recorded January 30–31, 1956—RCA Studios, New York

Ignited by a series of rimshots from D.J. Fontana, this track kicks off with the momentum of a runaway locomotive. "That was mine," D.J. Fontana said later. "I wanted to cut up that day. Elvis wanted something on the front of it, so I just started playing that thing" (*Modern Drummer*, October 1985). Recorded during Elvis's second RCA recording session, "My Baby Left Me" showcases one of Presley's most searing vocal performances, and his deliciously slurred invocation to "Play the blues boys" propels Scotty and Bill into a blistering break, with D.J. hammering out offbeats on his ride toms and Moore and Black firmly in the pocket. "My Baby Left Me" represents Presley's first no-holds-barred stab at roadhouse rock, and, unless my ears deceive me, it sounds like the precise moment when country, R&B, and its offspring—rockabilly—are finally and completely transformed into pure rock 'n' roll.

Hound Dog

Recorded July 2, 1956—RCA Studios, New York

This was the big troublemaker, nothing less than a clarion call for a generation. Just hours before the start of this session, Elvis, outfitted in evening wear, had crooned "Hound Dog" to a basset hound before a nationwide audience on *The Steve Allen Show*. Now he was back in RCA's New York studios to craft his own take on Jerry Leiber and Mike Stoller's ode to busted love.

By the time of this session, RCA producer Steve Sholes's patience was wearing thin with Scotty Moore and Bill Black. Under pressure from RCA bigwigs to cut down on the length of Presley sessions, Sholes, frustrated at the numerous retakes that Scotty and Bill seemed to need, was convinced that Elvis could work more efficiently with studio musicians and was already lobbying Tom Parker to influence Elvis to make a switch.

If one were to seek out and pinpoint the day when Sholes's frustration with Scotty and Bill likely boiled over, the recording session of July 2, 1956, might well be it. In an hours-long session that likely induced Steve Sholes to yank out what little hair he had left, studio logs show that no fewer than 31 attempts were needed to generate a studio master of what everyone felt convinced would be Presley's next hit single. In the years since, numerous chroniclers have pointed to Elvis's supposed "perfectionism" with his own performance and not missteps by Scotty or Bill as the reason so many attempts were needed to perfect "Hound Dog." While concern with his own singing might well have contributed to the session's length, let's go ahead and assume that Moore and Black, talented musicians, but hardly honed studio professionals, hit the occasional bum note, necessitating additional takes that undoubtedly frustrated the clock-watching Sholes.

To which I reply: So what? As the old saying goes, "It's not how many times you're wrong, but how often you're right." Because it's clear that the success of "Hound Dog" doesn't lie solely with Presley's fiery delivery, but also in the jackhammer drumming of D.J. Fontana, the percussive *ass* of Bill Black's bass, and certainly in the clawing snarl of Scotty Moore's untethered riffing ... licks, I venture to say, that no session man, no matter how honed, seasoned or, time-conscious, could have matched. In fact, Keith Richards once described Scotty's second solo on "Hound Dog" as sounding as if Scotty "just took off his guitar and dropped it on the floor," somehow generating the perfect moment. "To me, it was an angry song," Moore said later. "People used to ask me if I was mad at someone. I'd say 'Yeah, I was.' It was a rough, grunting song and that's what I tried to portray" (Moore and Dickerson, *That's Alright, Elvis*). From its opening blast to Elvis's muttered coda, "Hound Dog" would, for a generation of teenagers, define the sound and spirit of 1950s America and signal that the transition from rock 'n' roll to rock was fully—and irreversibly—underway.

Mean Woman Blues

Recorded January 12–13, 1957—Radio Recorders, Hollywood

Arguably the most overlooked of Presley's many fifties classics, this bluesy workout, part of the *Loving You* soundtrack, shows Elvis at his fighting best. Blessed with an unshakeable groove, the brawn of this song's juke-joint attack comes via a hot plate of tasty riffing from Scotty Moore and Bill Black and solid vocal support from the Jordanaires. The track would remain a favorite of Tom Petty's to the end of his life. "'She kissed so hard she bruised my lips/Hurts so good my heart just flips.' That was pretty heavy stuff for a little kid like me to hear," Petty recalls. "He brought in backup singers the Jordanaires, and used them as a rhythm instrument, which was usually done in old gospel music. That added a whole other dimension" (*Rolling Stone*, October 27, 2011).

Under attack from multiple quarters at this point of his career,

"Mean Woman Blues" is the sound of Presley against the world. And for the time being at least, he would win.

One Night

Recorded February 23–24, 1957—Radio Recorders, Hollywood

Blues without polish, grit without compromise, this track provides forceful evidence of Presley's ability to deliver balls-out R&B with a fiery authenticity. This song, in which "one night of sin" from Smiley Lewis's 1956 original version is scrubbed to "one night with you," was originally slated to be part of the *Loving You* soundtrack, but by the time he's done recording it, Elvis views it as a potential hit and it's shelved for future release. Presley, whose affection for this song endured to the end of his life, took particular pride in the fact that he played lead guitar on "One Night." "It starts as a standard blues," Tom Petty says, "but then he takes things even higher with the bridge, which leaps out of the song. You're not expecting that, and it's heavenly" (*Rolling Stone*, October 27, 2011).

With his voice infused with a raw edge that he would strain and fail to replicate in his post–army years, Presley taps into something primal and soars on this track. I defy you not to go with him.

Jailhouse Rock

Recorded April 30, 1957—MGM Soundstage, Hollywood

The soundtrack recordings for Elvis's third movie would signal the beginning of what is arguably the most productive and creative collaboration of Presley's career. Neither Jerry Leiber nor Mike Stoller were particularly excited about providing songs for *Jailhouse Rock* (it took being held hostage by Hill and Range rep Jean Aberbach to force them to knuckle down), and they were even less enthused at the notion of working with Presley, whom both viewed as a backwoods flash in the pan. But when coming face to face with the country's most famous figure, they found themselves charmed by Elvis's politeness and his encyclopedic knowledge of rhythm and blues. In the coming days, an extraordinary relationship would spring to life, one in which the songwriters would work nose to nose with Elvis in the studio crafting songs and arrangements. "Jailhouse Rock" is rife with the clever lyrical wordplay so common to Leiber and Stoller's compositions and, interestingly, many of colorful figures mentioned in the song were not conjured up, but based on actual people. ("Shifty Henry" was a Los Angeles–based musician who'd worked with Leiber and Stoller, and the "Purple Gang," also known as the "Sugar House Gang," were bootleggers and hijackers whose exploits were chronicled in newspapers of the early twentieth century.)

"Jailhouse Rock" is ablaze with potent contributions from Scotty Moore and Bill Black, who devised the track's sledgehammer, half-step opening, an idea based on the 1940s swing track "The Anvil Chorus." "There was a scene where convicts were breaking rocks and they had to have the sound to match," D.J. Fontana said. "So Scotty and I were piddling around and just lucked out on that lick. When you do pictures, you don't have to worry about commercial records so much; you have to worry about how it's going to look. So they would suggest something to us, and then we'd come up with something from working together. We lucked out a lot of times" (*Modern Drummer*, May 1985).

Doncha' Think It's Time

Recorded February 1, 1958—Radio Recorders, Hollywood

Composed by Clyde Otis and Brook Benton (or Clyde Otis and Willie Dixon or, as some sources suggest, by Clyde Otis with Brook Benton calling himself "Willie Dixon" ... if you can figure out who the hell wrote this song, you're doing better that I), "Doncha' Think It's Time" was released as the B-side to 1958's "Wear My Ring Around Your Neck." In recent years, some Presley chroniclers have unfairly maligned this track, contending that the numerous attempts Elvis made at perfecting it, 48, are somehow proof of either a lack of enthusiasm or a commentary on the quality of the song itself. Nah.

A wistful, minimalist masterpiece, this track is graced with subdued aural pleasures, ranging from the subtle counterpoint contributions of Scotty Moore and pianist Dudley Brooks, to the smooth, melodic currents of the Jordanaires, and, of course, Elvis himself, keeping time on the back of his guitar case. Interestingly, the completed version of "Doncha' Think It's Time" utilizes portions of takes 40, 47, and 48 to complete a studio master. For reasons unknown, the complete version of take 40 appears on *50,000,000 Elvis Fans Can't Be Wrong, Elvis Gold Records, Volume 2* released in November of 1959. Graced with the smoky blue feel of a descending melancholy, "Doncha' Think It's Time," if you're not familiar with it, is worth your time.

A Big Hunk of Love

Recorded June 10, 1958—RCA Studio B, Nashville

A Presley catharsis, cranked out in a secret all-night Nashville session in June of 1958 while he was on leave from his service hitch,

"A Big Hunk of Love" is the sound of Elvis blowing off steam accrued from weeks of army basic training. Obviously invigorated by the presence of Nashville's "A Team" and jacked up by the fiery support of guitarist Hank Garland, Presley unleashes an impassioned and blistering assault on this Aaron Schroeder/Sid Wyche composition, suggesting, perhaps, that balls-to-the-wall rock might beat back the darkness of his upcoming Germany deployment. An unintentional swan song—he would never sing with this fierceness and intensity again—"A Big Hunk of Love" stands as Elvis Presley's most uncompromising descent into pure rock.

32

Diamonds Amidst the Dross

Today, recording logs show clearly that between 1960 and 1969, when he filmed his final Hollywood musical, the majority of Elvis Presley's recording work was devoted to movie soundtracks. It would be an understatement to say that history has not been kind to Presley's movie recordings; the songs were cranked out with little thought to quality and showed up in his movies at such a clip that, by the mid–60s, audiences would often make a run for the concession stand rather that suffer through another. "I feel like a goddam idiot," Elvis once told his wife, "breaking into a song when I'm talking to a chick on a train" (*Remembering Elvis*, Life, 2007).

On occasion, a stray gem might sneak though, but that was the exception; overall, the material was pedestrian at best, with cringe-inducers like "Britches," "We're Coming in Loaded," "Queenie Wahinie's Papaya," and "There's No Room to Rumba in a Sports Car" representing the nadir.

"When Elvis hit the movies and he started getting these chicken-shit songs, for the most part, I just kinda lost interest," recalls Scotty Moore.

> The songs had no meat to them, and they had to be songs that fitted the movies. I was still leader on the sessions for quite a while, and I'd play on some of the songs—the ones I liked—but it just wasn't my thing anymore. I never fell out with Elvis over this. He'd always wanted to be in the movies, and they never did get to really use his talent as an actor, as far as I'm concerned, mainly because of all of the music he had to do. He could've had good songs in those movies, but they were mostly just bull crap, teenybopper songs [Wingate, "The Guitar Man," *Music Mart*, 2005].

The material was terrible and Presley knew it, once remarking during a recording session, "What am I supposed to do with this piece of shit?" (*Musician*, October 1992). Despite the poor quality of the music he was saddled with, there nonetheless remained evidence, at least through the early sixties, that Elvis hadn't given up on producing something worthwhile. (During a soundtrack recording for 1962's *Kid Galahad*,

Elvis, in an attempt to muster some enthusiasm for a lackluster track, can be heard prompting the gathered musicians with these words: "We gotta' blast the hell outta the bridge!")

With the bar set so low, it's no surprise that Presley's post–army, non-movie recordings have been viewed somewhat more favorably. Still, while they were skillfully produced and performed, many of the tracks brought forth in the years between 1960 and 1968 nonetheless represent a musical backwater for a recording artist whose music, just years earlier, had transformed American popular culture. It's simply the price you pay for trying to please everyone and neglecting to please yourself.

Still, on the few occasions that Presley entered a recording studio during this period to cut non-soundtrack material, he managed to produce some truly outstanding music. So with that in mind, I offer up some "diamonds amidst the dross," a listing of what I perceive as the finest of Presley's post–army studio, and yes, soundtrack work, songs that stand the test of time. No "Britches" or "We're Coming in Loaded" to be found here.

A Mess of Blues

Recorded March 20, 1960—RCA Studio B, Nashville

This track, a product of Presley's first post–army recording session, was written by the Brill Building songwriting team of Doc Pomus and Mort Shuman, who, over the next five years would compose, as a team or as individuals, at total of 10 songs for Elvis. Kicked off with a venomous flourish by Floyd Cramer and a heavily echoed vocal by Elvis, this track makes it apparent that while the army may have tamed him, Presley was still capable of spewing sparks when the right song came along.

Following a pair of false starts, take 1 emerged as a nearly complete track with the Jordanaires "boo-hoos" already part of the arrangement and Elvis snapping his fingers between song verses. Ultimately this version was ruined when Elvis was unable to suppress a laugh during the third verse, though he and the band went on to complete the song. Take 2 was similarly marred by laughter at the start. Take 3 kicked off impressively, with Elvis snapping his fingers and Buddy Harman supplying more aggressive drum work, but ultimately broke down when Elvis blew a verse. As with the previous attempt, Buddy Harman's drums were again prominent on take 4 and Elvis kept time by snapping his fingers on the offbeat. The track was completed, but Elvis, apparently dissatisfied with Harman's trap work, instructed him to eliminate the fills, and take 5 ended up as the studio master and the flip side to Presley's worldwide hit "It's Now or Never." In 2011, Tom Petty cited this track as a key influence on his own music. "It was one of his first sessions when he came back from the Army, recorded with this great band from Nashville—one of the best ones of that era. The lyrics are sad, but he sounds triumphant" (*Rolling Stone*, October 27, 2011).

Reconsider Baby

Recorded April 3, 1960—RCA Studio B, Nashville

This session, Elvis's second since returning from the army, didn't start until 7:30 Sunday evening on April 3, and would run for nearly 12 hours before the exhausted musicians finally wrapped things up. After concluding master takes of "It's Now or Never," "I Gotta Know," "Are You Lonesome Tonight," and a ballad titled "I Will Be Home Again" that featured a prominent harmony vocal from army buddy Charlie Hodge, it was nearly 7:00 a.m. when Elvis reached for his Gibson Super 400 and absent-mindedly began to strum the chords to "Reconsider Baby," an R&B track that dated to 1954. In short order, the rest of the group joined in, and it soon became clear to Elvis that what had initially kicked off as nothing more than a jam now had the potential to be an album-closer for his first post–army LP, *Elvis Is Back*. A potent blues-based rocker, "Reconsider Baby" is characterized by Elvis's prominent guitar and an extended sax solo by Kentucky-born "Boots" Randolph, who, apparently taking Presley's admonition "To play the blues boy" to heart, launched into a gritty 24-bar saxophone solo that ignites the track. Elvis's affection for the song remained potent: it was part of the setlist for his 1961 Hawaiian concert and intermittently showed up in concerts to the end of his life. The power of this song, though indisputable, is nonetheless somewhat undermined by Presley's repeated and failed attempts to duplicate the guttural quality that made 1957's "Jailhouse Rock" and 1958's "One Night" so powerful. It's simply a fact that Elvis's voice matured in the two years he was away in Germany, leaving him arguably a better ballad singer at the time of this recording than the gritty blues shouter he once was.

I Feel So Bad

Recorded March 12, 1961—RCA Studio B, Nashville

With a grit and drive not common to Presley's early-sixties work, this track storms out of the gate as nearly perfect from the first attempt. A rousing take on Chuck Willis's 1954 original, "I Feel So Bad" recaptures the energy and feel of the best of Elvis's pre–army work. Take 1 featured stabbing offbeat piano stylings from Floyd Cramer and aggressive trap work from Fontana and Buddy Harman. By take 2, which became the studio master, Cramer had taken his keyboard flourishes up an octave and Boots Randolph had fine-tuned his sax solo. Elvis, clearly energized by Randolph's riffing, shouted joyfully during his eight-bar solo, juicing the song's energy. In his book *Elvis Presley, A Life in Music*, Ernst Jorgenson points out that during Randolph's solo, Presley, who moves from his mic to in front of Randolph during the solo, causes the solo to suddenly shift from the left channel onto Elvis's center channel on the master, a development that went unnoticed for years on both takes of this song.

(Marie's the Name of) His Latest Flame

Recorded June 25, 1961—RCA Studio B, Nashville

This track could serve as exhibits A through Z for anyone taking a class on musical arranging. At approximately 2:00 a.m. on June 25, 1960, Elvis and his gathered musicians started work on Doc Pomus and Mort Shuman's "(Marie's the Name of) His Latest Flame." Over the next three hours, they laid down version after version of this extraordinary song, only to repeatedly scrap everything, sensing that transcendence awaited if only they stayed with it. "It's a good song, I like it," Elvis proclaimed at one point, "even if it takes us thirty-two hours." Early takes show the musicians feeling the tune out, with acoustic guitars and bongos marking the spare arrangement.

Subsequent takes show prominent work by Scotty Moore and an organ figure by Floyd Cramer that was ultimately ditched. By take 4, the stripped-down arrangement was beefed up when bongos were replaced by an aggressive drum pattern, likely played by Buddy Harman, and stabbing piano and guitar figures during the song's bridges. By the next take, the electric guitar that opened the track had been replaced with an acoustic guitar, that, while slightly reducing the song's edge, brought a robustness to the track. Finally, at the conclusion of take 12, everyone agreed they'd nailed it. "(Marie's the Name of) His Latest Flame" stands to the present day as a shimmering example of the best of Presley's early sixties work. "An acoustic guitar and a snare drum played with brushes carry the rhythm," Tom Petty states, "but when the six-string bass comes in and the piano goes up to the high register, the whole thing jumps out of the speaker. I used to have a tape of alternate takes. It was kind of a mess when they started, and it turned into this beautiful arrangement" (*Rolling Stone*, October 27, 2011).

As rich and consequential as anything Presley ever recorded, "His Latest Flame" is a powerful aural artifact that can stand shoulder to shoulder with any of his best '50s work and prompts one to wonder about what further marvels Elvis might have blessed us with if he'd spent more time producing tracks like this and less time astride the treadmill of mediocrity that comprised his movie soundtracks.

Little Sister
Recorded June 25, 1961—RCA Studio B, Nashville

Before rolling tape on this track, recording engineer Bill Porter shouted, "It's got a classic in there." As it turns out, Porter was right. Released as the B-side of "His Latest Flame," a one-two punch that would go unequaled until Capitol Records issued "I Want to Hold Your Hand" and "I Saw Her Standing There" on the same single three years later, "Little Sister" kicks off at warp speed with the sneering twang of Hank Garland's guitar, Bob Moore's tic-toc bass line, and D.J. Fontana's drums. Early takes show Hank Garland wrestling with his opening licks; by take 5 he'd got it, but a missed drumbeat sabotaged his efforts. Take 6 emerged as nearly perfect, but Elvis still wasn't satisfied. The next attempt skipped along nicely, but Scotty Moore mistimed his entry and the song quickly broke down. Throughout this session, Elvis's well-chronicled unflappability was on display: he simply responded "Okay" whenever there was a miscue by a member of his group.

The next take featured some erratic trap work from Harman, but Elvis, perhaps happy with the song's feel, persisted. For this track, Hank Garland, who was contracted to Gibson guitars, swapped the Gibson ES-45 he usually played in the studio for a borrowed Fender Jazz Master, sensing that the Fender better suited the track's energy. In the days after the completion of this track, composer Mort Shuman said that he and Elvis had visualized the song in very different ways. "I played it a totally different way," Shuman said. "Elvis cut the tempo in half and slowed it down" (Jorgensen, *Elvis Presley, A Life in Music*). In subsequent years, "Little Sister" would live on and would be covered by artists as disparate as Pearl Jam, Dierks Bentley, Dwight Yokum, and Ry Cooder.

King of the Whole Wide World
Recorded October 26–27, 1961—
Radio Recorders, Hollywood, California

As evidence that not every Presley movie soundtrack tune lacks verve, I offer up this rousing workout from 1962's *Kid Galahad*. At this stage, film soundtracks were the coin of the realm for Elvis, who, due to the sheer number of pictures he was making, needed upwards of 48 new songs per year. For a songwriter desirous of having a song included in a Presley film, the process generally went as follows: Three to four weeks prior to the beginning of filming, an overview of the movie storyline and a description of specific scenes that required music would be distributed. From there, a songwriter would compose music and lyrics to fit the scene, then cut a demo to be submitted for consideration in the weeks before filming began.

This track, by Ruth Batchelor and Bob Roberts of the Hill and Range publishing group, was seen as hit-record material by Elvis, who was so smitten by it that he recorded 31 takes of the track on October 26 before returning the following day to perfect the version that would become the studio master. This session, just Presley's second without the presence of Hank Garland, featured Scotty Moore on lead guitar. (A month earlier, Hank Garland sustained major injuries in a car crash that nearly killed him and left him disabled for the remainder of his life).

Early takes on October 26 kicked off without the driving saxophone featured on the release version and lacked the revival-tent vocal shadings so evident on later tracks. Elvis, perhaps responding to the length of take 1, jokingly said, "You guys don't get paid any more if you go overtime, so let's hurry." Take 2 kicked off in double-time and featured added accompaniment by the Jordanaires, but broke down with Elvis laughing at a keyboard mistake by Dudley Brooks. From there, efforts at completing a studio master ground on. By take 22, Scotty Moore had added some tasty guitar fills between verses, but the track broke down when Elvis blew a lyric. From there, the work continued for another five takes before Elvis decided to call it a day.

On October 27, attempts at a studio master continued, and the renewed energy of the rest of the musicians was immediately discernable. Take 1 started off promisingly propelled by an extraordinary bass line from Bob Moore, some tasty triplets from Dudley Brooks on piano, and prominent guitar licks from Scotty, but ultimately failed when the band stopped abruptly. "What the hell happened?" asked Elvis. He was told that somebody dropped something. Take 2 started off just as promisingly, but Elvis flubbed the second verse and told the group, "I did something wrong!" Take 3 was nearly letter perfect, with Elvis throwing himself into the verses, Boots Randolph delivering an impassioned and extended coda, and the band firmly locked in behind him. This take would ultimately be designated the studio master, with Boots Randolph's closing solo deleted to reduce the song's running length.

She's Not You

Recorded March 18–19, 1962—RCA Studio B, Nashville

This track is a unique collaboration between songwriters Doc Pomus, Jerry Leiber, and Mike Stoller. "Doc Pomus called us up one day," Stoller recalls. "We were all in the Brill Building. Doc was an old friend, and we had produced lots of Doc and Morty's [Shuman] songs with The Drifters. Doc called us and said, 'Come on up. Let's write a song for Elvis.' So we wrote with him, the three of us. That was written for Elvis at Doc's request" (interview with Mike Stoller, *Goldmine*, 2002).

Early takes of "She's Not You" jelled almost immediately. Featuring a delicate walking bass line from Bob Moore and solid backing from the Jordanaires, "She's Not You" also showcases an ethereal vocal contribution from Millie Kirkham that sounds double-tracked. Take 1, which ran just 1:28, dispensed with the final verse found on the released version. Take 2 faltered soon after, starting with Elvis, finding something humorous, breaking out in laughter. After Elvis shushed the room with "Cool it," take 3 reinstated the added verse and wrapped up nearly flawlessly, but Elvis was unhappy with Ray Walker's bass vocal, and, before the next attempt began, he turned to Walker and said, "Hey Ray, more oooooh's," suggesting that Walker add emphasis to his vocal part. Take 4 was completed without error and was marked as the studio master. Without question, one of Presley's most affecting ballads, with Elvis at his honey-throated best in one of his most elegant post–army performances.

"Elvis did a really good job on it," Jerry Leiber said later. "He never did a bad job on any song. 'She's Not You' is based on the style and sentiment of 'I Really Don't Want to Know,' one of the greatest country songs ever written" (Sharp, *Writing for the King*).

It Hurts Me

Recorded January 12, 1964—RCA Studio B, Nashville

This track was composed by Joy Byers and Charles E. Daniels (better known as Charley Daniels, flag-waving country fiddler). In his book, *A Life in Music*, author Ernst Jorgenson states that "It Hurts Me" features a vocal performance from Elvis that "must rank among the absolute best of Elvis' pre–1968 efforts," and it's hard to dispute that evaluation (Jorgensen, *Elvis Presley, A Life in Music*). Devoid of Presley's self-conscious attempts at demonstrating his vocal prowess, which marred tracks like "It's Now or Never" and "Surrender," "It Hurts Me" shows Elvis effortlessly demonstrating his range without one-upping the track's delicate melody. By the time "It Hurts Me" was recorded, Presley's recording career was in free fall, and songs of this quality were largely overlooked by radio programmers and the record-buying public. In truth, Presley must accept responsibility for this situation. Had he asserted himself and insisted on more songs of this quality, his reputation would have fared much better during this period.

Take 1 of "It Hurts Me" emerged as a nearly perfect rendition, but Elvis, feeling it could be improved, decided to push on. Takes 2 and 3 broke down almost immediately when Elvis blew his opening line. For take 4, Elvis experimented with his phrasing for two verses before signaling to stop tape. Take 5 emerged flawlessly and was marked as the studio master.

Down in the Alley

Recorded May 25–28, 1966—RCA Studio B, Nashville

This session marks the first time that Elvis worked with producer Felton Jarvis, who often traced his love of rock 'n' roll to seeing a virtually unknown Elvis perform at Norfolk, Virginia, in 1955. After securing a promotion position at ABC Records in the 1960s, he worked his way up to a producer position and first came to prominence as the producer of Tommy Roe's "Sheila," a top-10 hit from 1962. Despite widespread rumors of Felton's womanizing and eccentricities, he was lured to RCA to produce Presley by Chet Atkins, who'd grown weary of Presley's ritual of all-night recording. As it worked out, Felton and Presley immediately hit it off, and Jarvis would continue as Presley's producer until the end of Elvis's life.

A full-bore R&B workout, "Down in the Alley" is something of a revelation, coming during a particularly fallow period when Presley appeared simply incapable of producing anything worthwhile in a rock or R&B vein. The sessions that yielded "Down in the Alley" stretched over a three-day period and had two goals: to produce enough material for a new gospel album by Presley and to record a number of secular tunes that would be used to flesh out a forthcoming soundtrack album for his latest movie, *Spinout*.

After spending six hours on May 25 recording a series of gospel tunes, it was 4:00 a.m. before Elvis and his musicians started work on "Down in the Alley," a track originally done by the Clovers, one of Elvis's a favorite groups. The contrast is startling; in the earlier hours of this session, Elvis devoted himself to such gospel standards as "How Great Thou Art" and "Where No One Stands Alone." Then, with "Down in the Alley" (announced from the control booth by Felton as "Funksville, take one"), he sang:

Janie, Janie, Janie, Janie, Jane Jane
Down in the alley, just you and me
We're going ballin' till half past three

Take 1 emerged as nearly complete, but Elvis, dissatisfied, wanted to try it again. Take 2 broke down quickly, followed by Elvis muttering the track's opening lines to himself, as if he'd forget them otherwise. Take 3 appeared to break down midway due to a technical glitch, resulting in uncontrolled laughter from Elvis and the group. The laughter, which Elvis was obviously trying but failing to contain, carried over to take 4. As the band readied themselves for take 5, Elvis erupted in giggles again, finally yelling out, "Hey wait a minute, man," as he again attempted to stifle his laughter. Finally, after a couple of successive attempts, take 9 was marked as the master.

In the Ghetto

Recorded January 20, 1969—American Studios, Memphis

Seeking absolution and renewed relevance, Presley deep-sixed his long-held resistance to social commentary and reestablished his artistic credibility with this graceful track. A stark meditation on race and poverty, "In the Ghetto" hinted at an entirely new career path for Elvis—one predicated upon promise and renewal—but in the end would prove, along with the equally cogent "If I Can Dream," to be nothing more than a career curio. After performing "In the Ghetto" intermittently during 1971, Elvis dropped it from his setlist and never sang it again. One detour too many into relevance, it would seem.

Suspicious Minds

Recorded January 22, 1969—American Studios, Memphis

The song, a high-water mark in the career of Elvis Presley, was one of the last tracks recorded during Elvis's marathon sessions at Chips Moman's American Studios in January of 1969. Unveiled weeks prior to its official release during his Las Vegas engagement of that summer, "Suspicious Minds" not only reaffirmed Presley's relevancy, but, through its bracing assault, gave long-time Presley naysayers pause ... maybe there was something to this guy after all. With an arrangement that borders on regality and ablaze with sterling contributions from Chips Moman's crack group of session musicians, "Suspicious Minds" represents the last chart topper of Presley's career.

Appendix A

The Strange Case of Andreas Cornelis van Kuijk

Following Elvis's death in August of 1977, and as stipulated in his will, Vernon Presley was named executor and trustee of Presley's estate, with Minnie Mae Presley (Elvis's grandmother), Vernon, and Elvis's daughter, Lisa Marie, named as beneficiaries. In the days following Elvis's passing, Tom Parker warned Vernon that unless he, Parker, was granted control over Presley estate finances, unauthorized Presley-related merchandise would flood the market, meaning that millions of dollars would end up in the hands of fast-buck artists and not the Presley family. Sufficiently alarmed, Vernon quickly signed a letter granting Parker total empowerment over the Presley estate's financial affairs.

With the agreement in hand, the Colonel immediately went to work nailing down agreements with vendors to meet the ravenous public appetite for Presleyana that had exploded upon Elvis's death. (Deals, incidentally, from which Parker would pocket a cool 50 percent, with less than a quarter going to Elvis's estate). He also hammered out an arrangement with RCA to have the record company run all of its pressing plants at full capacity in the immediate aftermath of Elvis's demise, knowing that the demand for Presley records would skyrocket in the coming weeks. "It's still Elvis and the Colonel, but now it's Elvis and Vernon Presley and the Colonel," Parker told the press. "Elvis didn't die, the body did" (Hopkins, *Elvis, the Biography*).

On June 26, 1979, representatives for Lisa Marie Presley filed allegations in the Shelby County Probate Court charging Parker with mismanaging the financial affairs of the Presley estate. In response, the court appointed Priscilla Presley, her accountant, and Elvis's bank as executors and trustees for Lisa. Additionally, attorney Blanchard Tual was tasked with looking into accusations of fiduciary mismanagement and investigating Parker's financial dealings.

When Tual issued his report in 1980, facts emerged that both stunned and outraged the Presley family. According to Tual, Elvis, who'd made millions over the course of his career, had an estate valued at no more than $500,000 at the time of his death, and, with the IRS demanding almost $15 million in back taxes, the estate was facing bankruptcy. Additionally, Tual, turning his focus to Parker, charged that the Colonel had kept Elvis on a treadmill of Vegas engagements solely to pay off his gambling debts. (At the time of Presley's death, it's estimated that Parker was in hoc to the Las Vegas Hilton for upwards of $30 million in unpaid gambling debts). Tual also accused Parker of mismanaging a 1973 deal with RCA related to royalties from Presley's music catalog, an agreement in which Parker pocketed $1.5 million more than Elvis did. Lastly, Tual characterized Parker's managerial contract with Elvis—an agreement from which Parker took one-half of everything Presley made, at a time when the industry average was between 15 and 20 percent—as extortionate. "These actions against the most popular American folk hero of this century are outrageous," Tual told the court, "and call out for a full accounting from those responsible" (RCA vs. Hanks, 1982).

On August 14, 1981, the presiding judge ordered Elvis Presley Enterprises to sue Parker for mismanagement. In response, Parker countersued. In 1983 Parker and the Presley estate settled out of court, with RCA and the Presley estate paying Parker $2 million. In return, Parker agreed to turn over any and all Presley audio recordings or visual images that he owned and to cease any future claims to the Presley estate.

Obese and riddled with gout and diabetes, Parker suffered a stroke and died on January 21, 1997. Speaking at his funeral, Priscilla Presley concluded her remarks with the following: "And now I need to locate my wallet, because I noticed there was no ticket booth on the way in here, but I'm sure that the Colonel must have arranged for some toll on the way out" (Nash, *The Colonel: The Extraordinary Story of Colonel Tom Parker and Elvis Presley*).

Appendix B

Hank Garland

Elvis Presley's June 1958 recording session stands as a compelling showcase for the talents of Hank Garland, one of music's unheralded innovators, yet also one of its enduring tragedies. Before his career was cut short in 1961, the million candlepower brilliance of Garland's fretwork graced the recordings of not just Elvis, but Patsy Cline, the Everly Brothers, Jerry Lee Lewis, and many other luminaries.

Walter Louis Garland was born in Cowpens, South Carolina, in 1930. He was first exposed to country music as a child, and his parents, recognizing his musical potential, bought him his first guitar at age six. Of his formative years, Garland was later to say: "There was a man living down at the end of River Street in Cowpens who knew how to play so I went down to his house and said 'Tune this thing up for me and show me how to play it.' He tuned it up and started giving me lessons on the thing. I went on to play whatever I could think of or hear. What I heard on the radio, I tried to copy" (*Guitar Player*, January 1981). Drawing inspiration from the countrified sounds that were emanating from WSBA radio in nearby Spartanburg, he attempted to electrify his guitar by attaching an electrical cord to its strings and plugging it into the wall, a Rube Goldberg approach that virtually destroyed the instrument.

By the time he was a teenager, his skill at his guitar was evident to all, most fortuitously to a man named Paul Howard, who'd encountered Garland at Alexander's Music Store in downtown Cowpens. After learning that Hank played the guitar, Howard, a member of the Georgia Cotton Pickers, a western-swing outfit who'd appeared regularly on the Grand Ole Opry, asked Hank to play for him. Immediately impressed, Howard offered the 15-year-old a job and told him to be in Nashville in two weeks to play at the Grand Ole Opry. But apparently Howard had a short memory, because when Hank showed up, he didn't recall the encounter at the music store. Crushed and desperate

289

for an opportunity to show his stuff, Garland told Howard that he had quit school and traveled all the way from South Carolina based on the bandleader's promises. Relenting, Howard agreed to allow Garland to perform that night with the Pickers, where he played with such skill that he received a standing ovation. Impressed, Howard quickly issued an invitation for Hank to join the Cotton Pickers full-time, but after six weeks he was forced to return home when he ran afoul of child labor laws (he was just 15). When he finally celebrated his next birthday, he returned to Nashville and joined the Cotton Pickers full-time at last.

It was during this period that Hank first encountered Nashville guitar legend Chet Atkins, who at the time was supporting Red Foley. "He was a little old, fat, red-faced punk," Atkins recalled of Hank years later, "and he hadn't gotten all of his height yet. He was playing choruses that he heard on Bob Wills' records. And he rushed an awful lot; he'd pick up tempo" (Salas, *Guitar Players*).

At about this same time, Garland became acquainted with Nashville session musician Billy Byrd, who, in addition to serving as Ernest Tubb's lead guitarist, was also a fine jazz picker. Garland and Byrd became fast friends, and in time Garland took a room in Byrd's home. Billy, recognizing Hank's talent, began schooling the young man in the rudiments of jazz, a passion that quickly consumed the guitarist. Byrd, more seasoned than Hank, also advised him on how to improve his technique. "Billy showed me how to use my little finger," Garland said later, "He'd say, 'Use the damn thing; stick it up on the string there and use it!" (Salas, *Guitar Players*).

Jazz may have fueled Hank's imagination during this period, but it didn't pay the bills, so in 1947, he signed on as primary guitarist for country singer Cowboy Copas, with whom he would tour and record for the next three years. Whether he was playing country or jazz, Garland labored constantly to improve his technique. One of the tricks he adopted during this phase was to play his chords using a wound-G as his first string, simply because he liked the way it sounded. Legendary Nashville bassist Bob Moore witnessed firsthand Hank's relentless pursuit of excellence. "Hank used to show me how he was developing the muscle in his right thumb," Moore recalls. "He'd take a pick and hold it in all these different positions between the forefinger and thumb and just work it as fast as he could without a guitar. He'd do that to develop strength. With his left hand he'd do all these finger exercises from one end of the guitar to the other, and he would play on the low E string as high as he could and learn any jazz run. He would sit and play it from one fret to the next, learning it in every position." Asked to rank

Garland as a guitar player, Moore doesn't hesitate. "I can't recall anyone any better" (*Guitar Player,* January 1981).

Garland's newly honed jazz licks were first showcased on Autry Inman's 1948 recording of "You Better Leave Them Guys Alone" and quickly drew comparisons to the work of such greats Les Paul and Django Reinhardt. "I started listening to Django," Hank said at the time, "after Chet told me he was the greatest guitar player in the world. And he was right" (*Guitar Player,* January 1981).

By 1949, Garland, after departing Copas, began freelancing around Nashville and soon struck up a friendship with producer Paul Cohen. Cohen, impressed with a song called "Sugarfoot Rag" Hank had written as a fingering exercise, decided to record an instrumental version played by Garland. At some point, lyrics were added, and the tune, paired with a recording by Red Foley, was released as a single early in 1950. In a move rare for a producer, Cohen gave the 19-year-old Garland label credit, and the tune hit number five on the *Cash Box* country charts. For the remainder of his life, Garland carried the nickname "Sugarfoot."

Upon assuming his rightful place among Nashville's musical elites, Garland quickly found himself in demand by such hitmakers as Patsy Cline, Eddy Arnold, and Jim Reeves. By the mid-fifties, Hank was making his mark, not just on records but in guitar design. In 1955, Garland, collaborating with Billy Byrd, designed Gibson's Byrdland (an amalgam of the men's last names) guitar, and Hank began using it on session work. Forever in search of a new horizon, Garland began tinkering with electronics and soon developed an early echo device that he subsequently used on the opening licks of Patsy Cline's hit "I Fall to Pieces."

In 1955, with the nascent rumblings of rock 'n' roll beginning to shake the world of music, Hank, sensing the future, began to listen incessantly to Nashville's WLAC, which had recently switched its format from country to rhythm and blues. In September of the same year, Garland, in his first foray into rock 'n' roll, added his chops to Roy Hall's version of "Whole Lotta Shakin' Goin' On," a full two years before the song would launch the career of Jerry Lee Lewis.

In June of 1958, Elvis Presley was home for a brief furlough before being shipped off to Germany. While he was stateside, RCA and Steve Sholes had scheduled a Nashville recording session for Elvis, with the goal of generating enough material to keep Presley in the public eye for the next two years. With just one night to nail down the five tracks insisted on by RCA, Chet Atkins, acting as session director, summoned Nashville's "A Team," the epic assemblage of reliable session pros that included bassist Bob Moore, drummer Buddy Harman, pianist Floyd Cramer, and Hank Garland. By the time the sun rose on the morning of June 11, it was "mission accomplished." In the span of 10 hours, Elvis and his crackerjack cadre of musicians had completed master recordings of five powerful tracks, each fueled by the high-voltage assault of Hank Garland's guitar.

In 1960, Garland indulged his growing fascination with jazz, when, along with 17-year-old vibraphonist Gary Burton, bassist Joe Benjamin, and Dave Brubeck drummer Joe Morello, he collaborated on the classic Columbia release "Jazz Winds from a New Direction," the first jazz album to be recorded in Nashville. Garland, obviously feeling liberated from the limitations imposed by country and rock, revealed a talent only hinted at in his earlier work and, on tracks like "Move" and "Riot-Chorus," engaged in tandem riffing with Burton that's so infused with magical properties that it leaves the listener breathless.

"He's one of the most talented musicians I have encountered in my career," Gary Burton said later. "His obvious enthusiasm for whatever music he was playing was inspiring to everyone around him. I've always thought that was one of the reasons he was so popular in Nashville and why everyone wanted Hank to be on their sessions. His very presence seemed to create a buzz among the musicians, whether it was country, rock, or jazz" (Burton interview, elsewhere.co.nz).

Jordanaires bass vocalist Ray Walker speaks of Garland with affection.

> Hank Garland was a down-to-earth, good little guy. Always self-effacing. He'd pick on himself. Nobody else did. He wanted to do better every time he did something. I'll tell you this about Hank. There was a producer who came in from.... I think it was Chicago. And he had written arrangements, note-for-note arrangements. So he came out of the control room and he said, "Mr. Garland, would you please play it the way I wrote it?" So we did some more and he came back out and said "Mr. Garland, you're not playing your part the way I wrote it." So Hank kept playing. And the man came out again and said, "Mr. Garland, can you not play what I wrote?" And Grady Martin says "Oh boy." And Hank laid his guitar down and looked up and says, "Can you write what I play?" [interview with Ray Walker September 20, 2020].

When Elvis Presley finally mustered out of the service in 1960, one of his first acts was to secure the services of Garland as his lead guitarist. Between March of that year and the fall of 1961, Garland's chops graced some of Presley's most forceful post–army work, including "Little Sister," "Dirty, Dirty Feeling," and "His Latest Flame." When asked later in life of his impression of Elvis, he said, "He never got upset about anything. You hear a lot of people talk about him, saying 'Elvis did this' and 'Elvis did bad' in record sessions, but that's all junk! He never did.

He ran in and sang what he was supposed to sing, and afterwards he shook hands with everybody and said thanks" (takeoffguitarblogspot. com, November 2014).

By the time he appeared with Elvis at a charity show in Hawaii on May 25, 1961 (the singer's last concert appearance for over eight years, during which he introduced Hank as "one of the finest guitar players anywhere in the country today"), Hank Garland had rightfully assumed his place among America's musical elite.

All of which makes what happened that fall day in 1961 so shocking—that a career ablaze with such promise could unravel at such speed. On the morning of September 8, Garland quarreled bitterly with his wife. Upon returning home from a Presley soundtrack session that evening, he was stunned to find his wife and children gone. Guessing that she was returning to her native Wisconsin, Hank jumped into his Chevy Nomad and set out after her. At 5:00 p.m., Garland was speeding north on Route 41 north of Springfield, Tennessee, when his station wagon flipped, throwing Hank from the vehicle. Severely injured, Garland spent weeks in a coma. In the ensuing months, the gravity of his injuries, coupled with numerous electroshock therapy treatments administered by a Nashville hospital, left Garland permanently disabled. A hospital report following the shock treatments offered a grim prognosis: "He has no memory now. He's retarded."

As years passed, Billy Garland aggressively disputed the cause of the accident that nearly claimed his brother's life. "The story that they put out was that he was chasing his wife, down the road in a car and his tire blew out and he got brain damage," Garland says.

> That's not true at all. Hank fell out of the car and he didn't die. So they took him to the hospital and from there, they took him to a sanitarium and gave him shock treatments. They continued to shock his brain until he was a two-year-old and they let him go. When I saw him again, he had the mind of a two year old. I took care of him, kept him hid for ten years. No one knew where he was. Because I thought someone would end up killing him [*Guitar Player*, January 1981].

At various times over a number of years, Billy Garland would not only contend that Hank's accident wasn't an accident at all, but in fact the result of a criminal conspiracy. Displaying pictures of Hank's destroyed car, Billy pointed to what he believed were bullet holes, suggesting that someone had attempted to murder his brother. When asked why anyone would want Hank Garland dead, Billy posited that Hank had inside information regarding corruption in the Nashville music industry that would threaten powerful interests. In later years, Hank himself embraced this theory. "I have reason to believe somebody might have shot my tire because I knew too much," he said when asked (biz-journals.com, August 2001).

Hank also suggested that his love of jazz may have played a role in his injury. In the still segregated south of 1960, jazz was primarily identified with black artists, a group certainly not embraced by some fans of country music and its practitioners. Garland told stories of playing many middle-of-the-night recording sessions with jazz musicians because Nashville studio heads wouldn't allow African Americans to be seen entering or exiting their studios. "They'd ask me, 'Why do you play with all them guys around you?'" he was to say later. "I just said, 'That's the rest of the band. We're playing jazz'" (bizjournals.com, August 2001).

In the years following his accident, Garland struggled to relearn the most mundane of everyday activities, including walking and talking. Any attempts at remastering his guitar proved futile, undermined by a loss of dexterity and an inability to focus. At just 31 years of age, Hank Garland faced the end of his once-promising career. As financial problems bore down on the Garlands, his friends on Nashville's A-Team often signed his name on Musicians' Union cards to at least ensure that the family had something to live on.

Ultimately, Garland and his wife Evelyn relocated to Milwaukee, where, just four years following his accident, she perished in an auto crash. Feeling star-crossed, Hank relocated to Florida, where he was cared for by his brother. He spent his remaining years battling health problems and attempting to pry royalties from a recording industry that he felt had treated him unfairly. A particular sore point was the classic holiday tune "Jingle Bell Rock," which Hank insisted he'd co-written with singer Bobby Helms. Garland would point to a 1957 Decca recording session during which producer Owen Bradley approached him with a tune he called "Jingle Bell Hop." "I let it hop back to where it came from," Hank was to say later. "It wasn't any good" (bizjournals.com, August 2001). But fueled by the idea of conjuring up a perennial holiday classic, Garland, in collaboration with Helms, altered the tune by adding a bridge and additional verses and changing the lyrics. Once it was complete, they recorded it the same night. "Basically, it was a whole new song," Helms was to say later. But Decca, according to Garland, had other ideas, viewing Garland and Helms's version as derivative of the original tune and refusing to recognize their copyright interest. Shortly before his death, Garland filed a lawsuit in federal court over authorship of the tune, seeking royalties from the record. The suit was unsuccessful, and to the present day, both "Jingle Bell Hop" and "Jingle Bell Rock" are licensed by American Society of Composers, Authors and

Publishers (ASCAP) with Joseph Carleton Beal and James Ross Boothe listed as the sole writers.

In 1975, Hank made an emotional reappearance at a Grand Ole Opry old-timers show where, struggling to perform a song that once danced so effortlessly from his fingers, he completed a shaky version of "Sugarfoot Rag." In 2004, betrayed by fate, bedridden, and virtually forgotten by both the listening public and the music industry, Hank "Sugarfoot" Garland died of a staph infection in Orange Park, Florida, at age 74.

Unfair? You bet. But—thankfully—transitory, because in recent years the work of Hank Garland is being discovered and appreciated by a new generation of artists. In the years following his passing, country musician and songwriter Jerry Reed was one of the first to publicly trumpet the work of Hank Garland. In more recent years, country artist and guitarist extraordinaire Brad Paisley has seldom passed up an opportunity to praise him. "Hank Garland, who brought a lot of jazz to country music, was a major influence," Paisley states. "Hank was this great session player who did this great album called 'Jazz Winds from a New Direction,' which took a lot of people by storm" (startribune.com, January 14, 2010).

Also acknowledging Garland's influence is Grammy winning guitarist Steve Vai. "I've certainly been familiar with Hank Garland's music, but I didn't really know a lot about his story. What I discovered was what an important figure he was. He introduced jazz to the Nashville scene and he was one of the first guitarists to confront racial stereotypes by playing with black musicians, which rattled a lot of cages back then" (musicradar.com, June 30, 2010).

It's tributes such as these that have brought a renewed attention to Garland's work, and today, polls by music magazine and websites consistently rank him among country music's greatest guitarists. And perhaps because of testimonials like these, Hollywood took notice. After Jerry Reed made a number of unsuccessful attempts to secure funding for a Garland biopic, an independent film company released *Crazy* in 2007, a movie based on Garland's life, starring Waylon Payne as Hank. While the film success at the box office was minimal, *Crazy* was well received by critics and was awarded "Best in Fest" from the Real to Reel International Film Festival in 2008.

On a less favorable note, the thoroughly discredited institution that (laughably) calls itself "The Rock and Roll Hall of Fame" has completely ignored Hank Garland and refused to nominate, much less induct Hank into its "Award for Musical Excellence" category. Established in 2000, this category, originally devoted to and entitled "Sidemen," was

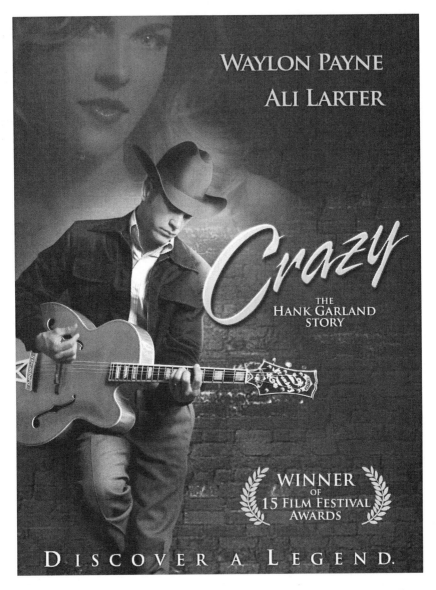

WAYLON PAYNE
ALI LARTER

Crazy

THE
HANK GARLAND
STORY

WINNER
OF
15 FILM FESTIVAL
AWARDS

DISCOVER A LEGEND.

Hollywood takes note of Hank Garland and the tragic events of his life, as this poster from 2007's *Crazy* illustrates.

established to "honor those musicians who have spent their careers out of the spotlight, performing as backup musicians for major artists on recording sessions and in concert" (a criteria for induction that sounds as if it were created with Hank Garland in mind). In 2010, the category was renamed "Award for Musical Excellence," and according to the institution's president, Joel Peresman, "This award gives us flexibility to dive into some things and recognize some people who might not ordinarily get recognized." Today, admirers of Hank Garland's extraordinary body of work wait for Peresman and his associates to dive into Hank Garland's legacy and recognize his contributions. Given the Hall's less-than-stellar recent inductees, I, for one, am not holding my breath.

If you ever visit Hank Garland's resting place in Jacksonville Memory Gardens, Orange Park, Florida, you'll find the following words etched into his tombstone:

Hank "Sugarfoot" Garland
The greatest guitar player that ever walked planet Earth.

That just might be right.

Appendix C
The Movies

Before he hung up his thespian togs in 1969, Elvis "acted" in a total of 31 movies (a total that includes two performance documentaries). As the four films that Presley made in his pre–army years have been covered, to some degree, in the pages of this book, I thought it might be fun to take a (hopefully) light-hearted look at the cinematic efforts Elvis engaged in between the years of 1961 and 1969.

I'm probably not going out on a limb to state that Presley's movie career is not viewed as particularly stellar by most folks and is seen even less charitably by those who frequent the critical ranks. A brief sampling of their perspectives on Presley's cinematic *oeuvre* follows:

Time magazine, commenting on Elvis's appearance in 1956's *Love Me Tender*, asked, "Is it a sausage?" (*Time*, November 1956).

Of Presley's second film, *Loving You*, *DownBeat* magazine said, "[Presley's acting has] all the emotion of a well-bred head of livestock" (*DownBeat*, August 1957).

Not to be overlooked, here's what the *Los Angeles Times* had to say regarding a pair of Presley films from the mid–1960s. First, *Kissin' Cousins*: "You get your money's worth before monotony sets in, as it does in nearly all the Presley pictures" (*Los Angeles Times*, July 1964).

A year later, they were even less enamored of *Tickle Me*: "Lousy color, cheap sets, hunks of stock footage, painted scenery" (*Los Angeles Times*, June 1965).

Lastly, we have the venerated *New York Times*, a paper known for hating everything, who served up this morsel of vitriol regarding 1965's *Harum Scarum*: "Elvis," the paper noted, "acts with all the animation of a man under deep sedation" (*New York Times*, June 1965).

I could go on, but you get the picture. First let me state that I don't necessarily disagree with the above sentiments. If you've made it this far, you've undoubtedly gleaned that I'm not a huge fan of Elvis's sixties work. I find most Presley films to be, at best, passable time-killers and, at worst, the cinematic equivalent of shaving your head with a cheese grater. I also find the oft-stated premise of Presley boosters everywhere that Ol' Elvis really could've become a great actor, had he only applied himself, to be borderline hilarious.

But none of this is to suggest that I find Presley movies to be completely undeserving of respect. Why? Simply because there exists an entire sub-genre of American cinema that has been unjustly ignored by respectable critics and is long overdue for re-evaluation: trashy movies aimed for the drive-in crowd. Just because a movie has cruddy production values, lousy acting, awful writing, and crummy songs doesn't mean it doesn't have something to offer to someone, somewhere. Heck, well-known directors like Roger Corman and celebrated actors like Keanu Reeves have spent entire careers cranking out cinematic dreck, and do they look unhappy to you?

Before we go any further, it helps to remember that Elvis wasn't the first singer to try to make it in the movies. In the twenties there was Al Jolson and Rudy Valle; in the thirties and forties, there was Bing Crosby; and then a decade later, Frank Sinatra. Each held his own, but when it comes to cranking cinematic cheese, there's simply no contest, Elvis and his 31 turkeys win hands down. If you take away nothing from this book, it's essential that you remember this: *Of all those singers turned movie star, nobody made more stinkers than Elvis.* And that's deserving of a measure of respect. Sort of.

So with that in mind, I, with tongue firmly in cheek, serve up an alternate perspective on Presley's cinematic *oeuvre*, one not based on the outmoded perspectives of humorless, hidebound critics, but one that unabashedly embraces the notion that really crummy movies can provide their own form of entertainment, one unburdened by bothersome notions of art and competence.

(Oops, almost forgot. Before you dive into my perspectives on Presley films, here's a tidbit to gnaw on: In 1956, Elvis stalked out of the musical *The King and I* because he found the notion of people bursting into song at the drop of a hat "ridiculous.")

G.I. Blues—Paramount, 1960. If you put your brain in neutral, you'll love this one. For his first post–army film, Elvis re-enlists just long enough to portray Tulsa McLean (with the film's producers apparently finding "Tupelo" or "Memphis" McLean insufficiently colorful). As Tulsa, Elvis spends most of his time singing and sniffing around Juliet Prowse. Presley himself once said, "The only thing worse than watching a bad movie, is being in one." Who would know better? (Connolly, *Being Elvis*). Four Stars.

Flaming Star—Twentieth Century–Fox, 1960. For this outing, one of Presley's "serious roles," he plays Pacer Burton, a young man of mixed heritage caught up in a war between Native Americans and white settlers. Elvis is so wooden in this one, someone should've sent out for varnish. Four Stars.

Wild in the Country—Twentieth Century–Fox, 1961. Elvis gets serious again in this melodrama, in which our boy plays Glen Tyler, a troubled yet appealing lad with a burning desire to (wait for it...) become a writer! Can anyone fail not to be moved? Four Stars.

Blue Hawaii—Paramount, 1961. In this, his most commercially successful movie, Elvis is Chad Gates, fresh from the service, tasked to squire a group of hormone-crazed teenagers around Oahu. Elvis swings for the fences here, crooning no fewer than 14 (!) timeless classics including "Ito Eats," "Slicin' Sand," and "Ku-u-i-po." Four Stars.

Follow That Dream—United Artist, 1962. Back on the mainland, Elvis is Toby, a guitar-plucking, tune-crooning, skirt-chasing hillbilly. This effort, not one of my favorites, made me wish that I'd cracked the latest issue of *Jugs* instead. Two Stars.

Kid Galahad—United Artists, 1962. Here, Elvis plays a young boxer, with Charles Bronson as his trainer. Wherever local muscle-heads cry out for their teeth to be kicked in or gorgeous girls require bedding, Elvis will be there. Allow me to engage in a bit of turd polishing: *Kid Galahad* is possibly Presley's best post–army film, but that's like saying that Wayne Newton is one dynamic entertainer. Four Stars.

Girls! Girls! Girls!—Paramount, 1962. In this one, our boy is Ross Carpenter, a man who boats by day and serves as catnip for women by night. This one's got "bitchin'" written all over it: bitchin' babes, bitchin' fights, bitchin' boats. Four stars.

It Happened at the World's Fair—MGM, 1963. Here, in a break from his normal screen romps, Elvis chases girls and sings songs. This one reminded me of *A River Runs Through It*, except there's no river and nothing runs through it. Not a particular favorite. Elvis certainly had better things to do than act in turkeys like this ... like maybe leaving piss-rings in front of the Pizza Hut. One Star.

Fun in Acapulco—Paramount, 1963. In this one, Elvis is Mike Windgren, a soul tortured by a psychic inability to jump off tall rocks in his underwear. *Fun in Acapulco* is a major cinematic departure for Elvis. In this one, he's a brooding loner with a penchant for kicking ass and breaking into song every five minutes ... oh, wait. Still, a classic. Four Stars.

Kissin' Cousins—MGM, 1964. While the Beatles were commandeering U.S. recording charts and moistening the panties of teenage girls everywhere, Elvis was playing the dual roles of Jody, an Air Force official, and a happenin' hillbilly named Josh, who has a salami for a brain. Trailer park kung fu? Doncha' dare miss it. Three Stars.

Viva Las Vegas—MGM, 1964. Lucky Jackson meets his musical and sexual alter ego in the form of Ann-Margaret. Racecars, romancing, falling off diving boards, waiting tables—what could be more fun? When confronted with an artistic statement of this caliber, all you can say is, 'Wow!' Four Stars.

Roustabout—Paramount, 1964. In this one, Presley plays a circus roughneck with unresolved anger issues. The movie starts out with Elvis kicking some teeth in and then hitting the road on his Honda 50 in search of more fun. Complex and thought provoking ... a portrait of an America when men settle their differences the way they should, by beating one another senseless. Works for me. Three Stars.

Girl Happy—MGM, 1965. Elvis is Rusty Wells, with his eye on Mary Ann Mobley and Shelley Fabares. *The Wizard of Oz* had "Over the Rainbow." *West Side Story* had "Maria" and "I Feel Pretty." *The Lion King* had "Circle of Life." *Girl Happy* has "Do the Clam." 'Nuff said. Four Stars.

Tickle Me—Allied Artists, 1965. Elvis has a "jones" for Jocelyn Lane. (Can you blame him?) In this one, Elvis, as Lonnie Beale, roams the Southwest, doing good deeds and kicking teeth in. Sort of like a pomaded Lone Ranger. Three Stars.

Harum Scarum—MGM, 1965. Elvis, a man in desperate need of a new life, but not sure where to find it, dons a turban and plays Johnnie Tyrone, a man who croons his way through the Middle East before being captured by a band of subversives. (That's one way to make him stop singing.) He spends the rest of the movie wailing the tar out of some slimebuckets. A must-see. Four Stars.

Frankie and Johnny—United Artists, 1966. In this effort, Elvis divides his time between battling a gambling addiction and trying to nail Elly May Clampett, who apparently has a family of five living in her giant hair. If you love monster truck rallies and think wrestling is real, this one's for you. Three Stars.

Paradise Hawaiian Style—Paramount, 1966. In this one, Elvis, forsakes a previous career of shaving dogs and cats for surgery to run a charter service. This flick has it all. Songs? Check. Chicks? Check. Ass kicking? Check. Elvis, who has so much lacquer in his hair you could bounce rocks off it, is starting to look a little pudgy here, like he'd eaten his weight in Paydays the day before shooting started. Three Stars.

Spinout—MGM 1966. A movie about Elvis, well, spinning out. He plays Big Mike McCoy, who races cars, kicks some ass, and gets hounded by women. Rainer Werner Fassbinder, the auteur behind such cinematic milestones as *Fear Eats the Soul, Despair,* and *Love is Colder Than Death,* cites *Spinout* as his favorite Presley film, with *Girls! Girls! Girls!* a close second. One of the greats. Four Stars.

Easy Come, Easy Go—Paramount, 1967. A modern American classic, spattered with dreams, hope, and desire. Elvis plays a demolition expert. Listings say this movie runs two hours. It seems longer. Come for the bimbos, stay for the fight scenes. Three Stars.

Double Trouble—MGM, 1967. Elvis heads across the pond to London (without leaving Culver City) to run a disco and punch out some jewel thieves. By this time this turkey hits the theaters, the songs are coming so fast and frequent, theater punks are smarting off before Elvis even opens his mouth. Not a particular fave. Those seeking a brief respite from the mortal coil would be advised to look elsewhere. Two Stars.

Clambake—United Artists, 1967. In this epic, Elvis is Scott Hayward, water-ski instructor. This film remains as cogent and compelling as the day it was made. By the time it's done, you'll be asking yourself a series of complex questions. Why did I waste two hours of my life on this? Why are there mountains in Florida? Where are all the black people? Why didn't Bill Bixby ever win an Emmy for *My Favorite Martian*? So killer. Four Stars.

Stay Away Joe—MGM, 1968. Elvis plays Navajo Indian Joe Lightcloud in this "satirical farce" in which he uses a Cadillac convertible to drive cattle. Contains so many head-busting fight scenes that stagehands spent hours sweeping up the eyeballs. Mordant, ironic, and thought provoking. Superior in every way to *Citizen Kane*. Four Stars.

Speedway—MGM, 1968. Elvis plays racecar driver Steve Grayson. Approaches Oscar-level quality, but falls just short. Three stars.

Live a Little, Love a Little—MGM, 1968. As Greg Nolan, newspaper photographer, Elvis seems to attract a lower class of bimbo in this one. Still, he stays busy, and before he's done, the fire marshal has to hose down his bedroom for overcrowding. Just so-so. This one makes those two-hour YouTube videos on clog dancing seem riveting by comparison. Two stars.

Charro—National General, 1969. Elvis as Jess Wade, in a role originally turned down by Clint Eastwood (good thinking). A sad but uplifting story of an outsider who finally accepts that love beats kicking someone's teeth in. Short on brains, but long on action. Three Stars.

The Trouble with Girls—MGM, 1969.

Elvis, as Wally Hale, is the manager of a traveling Chautauqua company. Not one of my favorites; made me nostalgic for that eight-hour bus trip I once took with 40 people and a chemical toilet. One Star.

Change of Habit—NBC Productions, 1969. Every now and then, a movie comes along that changes the world. This isn't one of them. Elvis, as Dr. John Carpenter, runs a medical clinic in a really shitty section of New York. Mary Tyler Moore (in a habit, get it?) can't decide who she digs more, God or Elvis (really). This film contains a powerful message that is beyond the feeble powers of my keyboard to convey. A must-see. Four Stars.

Bibliography

Newspapers and Periodicals

Abilene Reporter News, March 1, 1960.

Akron Beacon Journal, October 11, 1959.

The Angus-Leader, February 12, 1961.

Associated Press, February 5, 1958.

The Austin American, October 6, 1955.

Billboard, "Teenagers Going for Music with a Beat," April 22, 1954; August 18, 1954; November 20, 1955; March 14, 1956.

Cash Box, May 1955; March 1956.

Charlotte Observer, "Elvis Presley Is a Worried Man," June 27, 1956.

Corpus Christi Caller, April 18, 1956.

Country Guitar, 1994; 1977.

Country Music, December 1977.

Courthouse News, June 29, 2016.

Cowboy Songs, Number 41, June 1955.

Daily Telegraph, October 22, 2016.

DownBeat, August 1957.

Esquire, February 1968.

Goldmine, "The Guitar That Changed the World," August 23, 1991; May 2002; December 25, 2011.

Good Housekeeping, "Elvis by His Father Vernon Presley," January 1978.

Guitar Player, Green, "Perhaps the First Rock & Roll Guitarist," January 1974; January 1981.

Guitar UK, 2004.

Guitarist, November 1992.

Hollywood Today, February 1958.

Jet Magazine, August 1957.

Las Vegas Star, April 28, 1956.

The Leader-Post, Regina, Saskatchewan, November 17, 1956.

Lexington Dispatch, March 22, 1956.

Look Magazine, August 7, 1956.

Los Angeles Times, June 15, 1965; January 4, 1981; "Presley's Blue Moon: His Best Ballad?" August 18, 2011; April 13, 2018.

Melody Maker, October 10, 1956; 1957.

Memphis Commercial Appeal, April 1951; May 13, 1956; March 15, 1958.

Memphis Press-Scimitar, July 14, 1954; October 20, 1954; November 22, 1955; "These Are the Cats Who Make Music for Elvis," December 15, 1956; "Elvis and Dewey Had a Falling Out," July 22, 1957; September 13, 1957; December 21, 1957.

Miami Herald, August 4, 1956.

Miami News, August 4, 1956; May 15, 1957.

Modern Drummer, May 1985.

Morristown Gazette Mail, January 24, 1955.

Musician, October 1992.

New York Daily News, April 7, 1956.

New York Herald Tribune, April 9, 1956; August 18, 1956.

New York Journal-American, April 7, 1956; "Elvis Presley Will Have to Clean Up His Show or Go to Jail," November 8, 1957; June 13, 1960.

New York Times, July 2, 1956; May 26, 1958; May 13, 1960; June 12, 1965.

Newsweek, "Hillbilly on a Pedestal," May 14, 1956.

The Oklahoman, October 16, 1955.

Ottawa Citizen, "Time Brought Many Changes to Rock and Roll King Elvis Presley," June 13, 1959.

Parade, September 30, 1956.

Paris News, October 3, 1955.

Pittsburgh Sun-Telegraph, August 11, 1956; November 24, 1956.

Rochester Democrat and Chronicle, May 8, 1960.

Rocky Mountain News, "Rage Over Elvis

Presley Is a Bit Sickening," April 10, 1956.

Rolling Stone, September 22, 1977; February 13, 1986; April 1990; April 13, 1998; June 24, 2004; April 7, 2011; August 22, 2011; October 27, 2011; August 2015; March 31, 2016; July 1, 2020.

San Antonio Express, April 16, 1956.

Saturday Evening Post, August 1965.

The Shreveport Journal, December 17, 1956.

The Spectator, May 1958.

The Spokesman-Review, May 17, 1959.

Sydney Morning Herald, November 6, 1960.

The Tennessean, April 24, 1960.

Tiger, 1956.

Time, November 21, 1956.

TV and Movie Screen, April 1957.

Ultimate Guitar, June 1977.

U.S. Works Progress Administration Guide, 1938.

Variety, April 11, 1956; May 26, 1958.

Vintage Guitar, 1992, 1993, 2016.

Washington Post, August 17, 1997.

Winston-Salem Journal, February 1956.

Websites

amromusic.com, June 2014.

bloginroll.blogspot.com, 2016.

elvis.com.au, January 2016; March 2016; October 2018; February 2020; July 2020.

elviscommercialappeal.com, 2012.

Elvisinfonet.com, March 2005; April 2005; July 2007; July 2010.

georgeharrison.com, April 1999.

hillmanweb.com, 1992.

longislandweekly.com, November 16, 2017.

markknopfler.com, June 30, 2016.

memphismusicalhalloffame.com, 2009.

706unionavenue.nl, 1997.

tampabay.com, January 4, 2012.

Books

Arnold, Eddy. *It's a Long Way from Chester County*. New York: Hewitt House, 1969.

Bashe, Phillip. *Teenage Idol*. New York: Hyperion, May 1992.

Burk, Bill E. *Early Elvis: The Humes Years*. Memphis: Red Oak, 1990.

_____. *Early Elvis: The Tupelo Years*. Memphis: Propwash, 1994.

_____. *Elvis, a 30-Year Chronicle*. New York: Osborne Enterprises, 1986.

Burke, Ken, and Dan Griffin. *The Blue Moon Boys*. Chicago: Chicago Review Press, 2006.

Cash, Johnny. *The Autobiography*. New York: HarperOne, 2003.

Connolly, Ray. *Being Elvis*. New York: Liveright, 2016.

Cosby, James. *Devil's Music, Holy Rollers and Hillbillies*. Jefferson, NC: McFarland, 2016.

Crouch, Kevin. *Sun King*. London: Little, Brown UK, 2009.

Denisoff, Serge, and William Romanowski. *Risky Business: Rock in Film*. New Brunswick: Transaction, 1991.

Dobbs, Dale. *A Brief History of East Tupelo, Mississippi*. Compiled by members of the Heights Garden Club, Lee County, Mississippi.

Dundy, Elaine. *Elvis and Gladys*. New York: Dell, 1986.

Dunleavy, Steve. *Elvis: What Happened?* New York: Ballantine, July 1977.

Escott, Colin, and Martin Hawkins. *Good Rockin' Tonight*. New York: St. Martin's, 1998.

Escott, Colin, and Martin Hawkins. *Sun Records: The Brief History of the Legendary Label*. New York: Quick Fox, 1980.

Guralnick, Peter. *Careless Love: The Unmaking of Elvis Presley*. Boston: Little, Brown and Company, 1999.

_____. *The Last Train to Memphis*. Boston: Little, Brown and Company, 1994.

Guralnick, Peter, and Ernst Jorgensen. *Elvis Day by Day*. New York: Ballantine, 1999.

Helm, Levon, and Stephen Davis. *This Wheel's on Fire: Levon Helm and the Story of the Band*. Chicago: Chicago Review Press, 2013.

Hopkins, Jerry. *Elvis, the Biography*. London: Plexus, 2010.

_____. *The Life and Times of Colonel Tom Parker*. London: Plexus, 1977.

Johnson, Robert. *Elvis Presley Speaks*. New York: Rave, 1956.

Jorgensen, Ernst. *Elvis Presley, a Life in Music*. New York: St. Martin's, 1998.

Kubernik, Harvey. *Turn Up the Radio!* Santa Monica: Santa Monica Press, 2014.

Lee, Harper. *To Kill a Mockingbird.* New York: Harper, 2002.

Levinson, Peter. *Livin' in a Big Way.* London: Da Capo Press, 2006.

Levy, Alan. *Operation Elvis.* London: Consul Books, 1962.

Lichter, Paul. *Elvis in Hollywood.* London: Hale, *1975.*

Marcus, Griel. *Mystery Train—Images of America in Rock 'N' Roll Music.* New York: E.P. Dutton, 1976.

Martin, Linda, and Kerry Seagrave. *Anti-Rock, the Opposition to Rock 'N' Roll.* New York: Da Capo Press, 1957.

Moore, Scotty, and James Dickerson. *Scotty and Elvis: Aboard the Mystery Train,* University Press of Mississippi, 2013.

_____, and _____. *That's Alright, Elvis.* New York: Schirmer, 1997.

Nash, Alanna. *The Colonel: The Extraordinary Story of Colonel Tom Parker and Elvis Presley.* Aurum Press, 2002.

_____. *Elvis and the Memphis Mafia.* Aurum Press, 2005.

Nash, Alanna, Billy Smith, Marty Lacker, and Lamar Fike. *Elvis Aaron Presley: Revelations from the Memphis Mafia.* New York: Harper, 1995.

Norman, Phillip. *John Lennon—The Life.* London: Echo, 2009.

Peary, Danny. *Close Ups: The Movie Star Book.* New York: Workman Press, May 1983.

Remembering Elvis. Life, 2007.

Salas, Stevie. *Guitar Players.* Lincoln: University of Nebraska Press, 2006.

Schilling, Jerry. *Me and a Guy Named Elvis.* New York: Gotham, 2007.

Sharp, Ken. *Writing for the King.* FTD Books, 2006.

van Gestel, Jan and Ger Rijff. *Elvis Presley, Memphis Lonesome.* Memphis: Tutti Frutti, 1988.

Vellenga, Dick, and Mick Farrin. *Elvis and the Colonel.* London: Delacorte, July 1988.

Venhecke, Susan. *Race with the Devil.* London: St. Martins, 2000.

Wallis, Hal, and Charles Higham. *Starmaker, the Autobiography of Hal Wallis.* New York: Macmillan, 1980.

Wertheimer, Alfred. *Elvis '56: In the Beginning.* New York: Pimlico, 2007.

Williamson, Joel. *Elvis Presley: A Southern Life.* New York: Oxford University Press, 2014.

Zollo, Paul. *Conversations with Tom Petty.* London: Omnibus, 2020.

Music and DVDs

A Boy from Tupelo, RCA, 2014.
The Complete Sun Sessions, RCA, 1987.
Elvis '56, Lightyear, 1999.
The Elvis Is Back Sessions, RCA, 2009.
Elvis on Tour—Alternate Version, elvisdvdcollector.com, 2004.
Elvis on Tour—Complete Outtakes, elvisdvdcollector.com, 2004.
Elvis Presley, RCA-Song BMG, 2006.
Elvis '69 Comeback Special, RCA, BMG, 2004.
Elvis, the Beginning Years, 1954–1956, RCA, 1983.
Elvis—The Ed Sullivan Shows, Sofa, MMVI, 2006.
Follow That Dream, RCA, 2004.
Jailhouse Rock, the Alternative Album, Flashlight, 2012.
The Jungle Room Sessions, Flashlight, 2012.
The Kid Galahad Sessions, Flashlight, 2012.
The Million Dollar Quartet, 2006, RCA-Song BMG
Totally Stung, Madison, 2000.

TV and Radio Programs

Cradle of the Stars, PBS 1984.
The Elvis Presley Story, Watermark, Radio Documentary, 1971.
Elvis the Searcher, HBO, April 2018.
Interview with Linda Thompson, CNN, 2007.
Tales of Rock & Roll—Heartbreak Hotel, Arena Television, 1991.

Personal Interviews and Emails

Ray Walker, Conversation with Gary Parker. September 18, 2020.

Ray Walker, Emails to Gary Parker. October 7, 2019; September 13, 2020; September 14, 2020; September 15, 2020; September 20, 2020; September 23, 2020; September 24, 2020.

Index